RECOLLECTIONS
OF A LUCKY MAN

STANLEY TOLLMAN

RECOLLECTIONS
OF A LUCKY MAN

PATERNOSTER PUBLISHING

First published in Great Britain 2012

Copyright © Stanley Stephen Tollman 2012

The right of Stanley Stephen Tollman to be identified as the author
of this work has been asserted by him in accordance with the
Copyright, Designs & Patents Act, 1988.

A catalogue record for this book is available from the British Library

ISBN 978-0-9570309-0-9
Hardback

ISBN 978-0-9570309-1-6
Softback

Printed & Bound by Synergie

Published by Paternoster Publishing
Picquet House
St Peter Port
Guernsey GY1 1AF

TO BEA

… and to my children and grandchildren
… and to all those from future generations who may be curious to know
how it all came about

ALAS! THIS IS NOT
WHAT I THOUGHT LIFE WAS

Alas! This is not what I thought life was.
I knew that there were crimes and evil men,
Misery and hate; nor did I hope to pass
Untouched by suffering, through the rugged glen.
In mine own heart I saw as in a glass
The hearts of others. And when
I went among my kind, with triple brass
Of calm endurance my weak breast I armed,
To bear scorn, fear, and hate, a woful mass!

Fragment: Percy Bysshe Shelley

CONTENTS

Contents

PREFACE

In setting out an account of my life, I have tried to place on record the history of a man who accepts and admits his flaws and who is happy to draw the attention of others to his mistakes. My hope is that others may benefit by avoiding the mantraps which have cost me so dearly.

Please do not, however, imagine that my life has been bad, or that good things have never happened to me. In reality, life has been very good, but this is not one of those autobiographies. I have written less about my triumphs, and more about my disasters.

The truth is that much of my life in business has been successful – largely as a result of hard work and an incredible support system in the form of my family. I have also been lucky, as I would be the first to admit. But I have made some big mistakes, and my life and my career could so easily have run aground. I have, though, managed to survive, and in fact to prosper. I am indeed a 'Lucky Man'.

An old African proverb says that when an old man dies, a library closes down. I am no library, but I have met many people and done many things – far too much to cram into any book. I have, nevertheless, tried to represent my life in the round – a difficult challenge for an essentially private person.

I had little choice. At the age of 73, I found myself accused by the United States. Serious allegations were all over the press and, overnight, everything changed. I and my family found ourselves in the middle of a living nightmare. As you will read, we fought for our lives, and that dreadful episode is now behind us. Sadly, though, mud sticks. When my grandchildren, and their children, look back at these events, I want them to be able to read my own account of what happened. Then they can decide for themselves.

I was advised that it had to be written 'warts and all' and, throughout, this has been my aim. Surprisingly, that has not proved difficult. I only know one way to set the record straight, which is to start by being completely honest.

Here you have it, warts and all. Now you can be the judge.

Stanley Tollman
Antibes, France – July 2012

A WORD ABOUT SPELLING

As George Bernard Shaw once said, "England and America are two countries separated by a common language." Although this book is written in English – my mother tongue – I have also spent a good deal of my life on the other side of the Atlantic. It has been impossible to write this book and to stick throughout either to the English or to the American way of spelling. Some words simply do not look correct if spelled 'out of context'. In utilising both forms of spelling, as I have, I may merely have succeeded in offending everyone. If so, I apologise. Please do not take offense, or offence, whichever you would prefer.

ACKNOWLEDGEMENTS

This book was produced with assistance from a number of people, and I would like to thank those involved. These include Toby Baker, Howard Cooke, Deborah Collins, James Lewis, Ralph Melhuish, Colin Passmore, Neville Rolt, Michael Sissons, Nikki Sutherland, Christopher Tunnard, Les Wilson and Jim Webster. And I would like to say a particular thank-you to Alan Kilkenny, without whom this book could not have been written.

Most of all, though, I would like to thank Bea, who has been very much part of my story, and a very important element of this book. Bea is an example of what every man hopes for from his wife – someone who is not there simply for the good times. Everyone loves you when times are good, but when things aren't going well, that's when support really matters. When my life has been at its lowest, that's when Bea has been at her best. For well over 50 years, I have known that I can always rely on her to be right beside me. That's the mark of a great lady.

Finally, a word of thanks to Dr Paul Ettlinger, who has ensured that I am still around to write this.

Words delivered on the occasion of Stanley Tollman's 60th birthday
Paris, September 1990

"Stanley Tollman and I have known each other since we were eleven years old. We first met at school in 1942 – at Marist Brothers, Observatory, Johannesburg.

"The hardships Stanley endured at school were probably more cruel than the students in today's world could even begin to imagine. Remember that in those days Johannesburg was a raw and thrusting mining town. Fists counted. Stanley, like most of us, was at the receiving end of an oiled cane or a polished leather strap almost every single day.

"His strong and rebellious individuality could not be cowed. He refused to be one of their victims. The courage that was to be one of the hallmarks of his character was first forged in his defiance of mindless authoritarianism. Stanley managed to enjoy what he was supposed only to endure. He is a born survivor."

Raymond J Eskapa

GETTING OUR LIVES BACK
PART I

A cold and wind-swept piazza in a global financial district is a strange place to begin any life story, especially so for a man who rarely wore shoes until he was eight years old. Nevertheless, strange as it may sound, Ropemaker Street, London EC1 is where I shall begin my tale.

It is a cold and grey November day, one with little to commend it. The architecture surrounding the piazza is cheerless, and the desultory planting appears to be no happier than I am to be here. I know that I am going to hate what is about to happen, but I also know that I have no choice. Redemption lies just the other side of this. But, like open-heart surgery, knowing this to be the case makes it no less uncomfortable to contemplate.

The curved glass canopy of City Point was no doubt intended by its architect to provide a protective and softening welcome to an otherwise brutal office building. But I am not in the mood to appreciate such niceties. I take the elevator to the second floor, announce myself and take a seat in the reception area of Simmons & Simmons. Even the bizarre contemporary artwork around fails to divert my thoughts from the matter in hand. It is only when I am greeted by the man of whom I have seen far too much in the past six years that I am able to disengage from my own thoughts.

I have grown both to like and to respect Colin Passmore, but his continued presence in my life in 2008 is no less unwelcome. On this momentous morning, he deploys his usual combination of professionalism and good humour, ushering me along the seemingly endless corridors, and to the door of the room where it is all about to happen. This is just another door, like the dozens of others we have already passed. But this door is different. Unlike the other doors, which merely provide entry to yet another nondescript meeting room, this door enables me to step over its threshold and, almost like magic, enter courtroom 12A of the Daniel Patrick Moynihan United States

Courthouse in Foley Square, New York. I can do this just as easily as if I were to walk up the steps of the grey stone building alongside the Courthouse and, even though they are three thousand miles away, pass between its massive Corinthian columns. The anonymous meeting room is about to be transformed through the wonders of video conferencing into part of the United States Courthouse itself.

The Southern District of New York is the busiest and largest federal court in the United States. The Southern District was carved out of the District of New York in 1814, reflecting New York City's growing population and role as a key harbour and commercial hub. Over the next hundred years, the Southern District established its reputation in the field of maritime and admiralty law, dealing with issues such as collisions, customs, seamen's wages, marine insurance, engagement in slave trade, naval seizures of enemy property, and other armed conflict issues arising from the War of 1812 and the Civil War. Today, it is the single most important Federal District in America. This is where it all happens.

Loretta A. Preska is today the Chief Judge of the United States District Court for the Southern District of New York. Courtroom 12A has for many years been very much her personal domain and fiefdom. Within weeks, she would reportedly be on George Bush's shortlist of potential Supreme Court nominees, but on 21 November 2008, she was merely a District Judge. She started early this morning for an unusual hearing which was to begin promptly at 8.30 a.m. in Manhattan – in thirty minutes' time. In London, it is now 1.00 in the afternoon – a time when I would normally be having lunch. But today, lunch is going to have to wait. I am going to be in court.

Although I had arrived early for this hearing, two others were in the room before me – both outstanding lawyers, and both extremely well-known to me. James Lewis QC is an English barrister, a part-time judge, a Bencher of Gray's Inn, a first class lawyer and a great friend. James M. Webster III, better known as Jim, is a Partner of Washington DC lawyers Kellogg, Huber, Hansen, Todd, Evans and Figel, and a former Assistant US Attorney for the District of Maryland. He too is a man with whom I have built a close friendship over the course of recent years. And, finally, Colin Passmore, who guided me into the room, is the senior litigation partner of Simmons & Simmons, the man in overall charge of the matter of *United States of America – v – Stanley Stephen Tollman*. Colin was my point man through the troubles which dominate the latter chapters of this book. A fine lawyer, Colin is today the Senior Partner of Simmons & Simmons, a role which suits him well. He is also a good friend.

I had known Colin, James and Jim since the spring of 2002, and had spent more time with them in the almost seven years since than I had with some members of my own family. All very nice men – but... I was determined to correct the imbalance in my life between lawyers and family, and to correct it very soon.

However, I knew that what lay ahead would be very difficult for me, and for one very simple but significant reason. I had learned long ago that lying had no part in my life. My father always said, "Tell the truth and damn the consequences." And he was of course right. This was a lesson which I had learned from a young age. Two episodes from my youth, painful even now as I recall them, are perhaps to blame for my lifelong determination always to tell the truth.

When I was eight years old, in my first year at Marist Brothers Koch Street school in Johannesburg, a classmate sitting next to me produced a wonderful drawing of a motor car. A passing Brother spotted the artistic gem and asked me whether I had drawn it. I foolishly said that I had. This provoked a request from the teacher for a second. However, much as I tried to repeat what my schoolfriend had produced, the results were so appalling that the stupidity of my lie was exposed for all to see. This caused me profound embarrassment and much humiliation in the playground.

My second, and final, lie was ten years later. For reasons I still do not understand, I heard myself claiming to a group of friends that I was an excellent tennis player. Easily said, but not so easily demonstrated when called upon to make up a pair for some doubles. Although I had picked up a tennis racquet once or twice in my life, I was most definitely not an excellent player. Despite this, I stupidly had a go. I was so manifestly incompetent that all concerned knew that not only was I a terrible tennis player but I was also a shame-faced liar. Sadly, the ground did not swallow me up. The agony of that embarrassment made me vow to myself that I would never lie again. And here I am, sixty years later, having to put that vow to the test.

At the end of the meeting room which I had entered was a large screen. On this screen, I was already able to see the inside of courtroom 12A. But it was clear that things in New York were not yet ready for us. Colin ushered me to the side of our room in London, out of range of the camera which was beaming our own images across the Atlantic. The screens were, on either end, displaying images of two small groups of people who were not yet prepared for the fray. Colin indicated to me the parts of the room where I would be in shot, and the areas where I would be unseen. I worked out for myself the most advantageous areas – those where one could see everything which was going on in New York, but without being seen oneself.

I quickly realised that we might well have a little wait ahead of us. Although various figures were moving around and there was much whispering, nothing was really taking place. Besides, the key actors in this drama had yet to take their places.

Having brought nothing with me by way of distraction, I stared out of the window and across the skyline of the City of London, but my thoughts were elsewhere. I thought of my late father, and of the advice which I knew he would have given me, had he still been alive.

And before I knew it, I was transported not to New York at the beginning of the 21st Century, but to South Africa, almost a hundred years earlier.

BRAVE NEW WORLD

Logically, my story should of course begin in South Africa, the country of my birth, and the place to which my thoughts had taken me. My roots, however, are in Eastern Europe. And they are also in Lancashire, in the North-West of England.

So I will, if I may, go back a little further than my own arrival. To 1895, the year in which my father, Solomon Tollman, was born; and to a small town, then called Riteve. There have been various different spellings of this town over the years, and it is today known as Rietvas, in what is now recognised as the independent nation of Lithuania. But when my father was born, Riteve was a small town within the vast Russian Empire. It sat in a featureless landscape close to the Baltic Sea, and shivered for much of the year in cold winds from Siberia.

As the town miller, my grandfather was a prominent figure in Riteve. From a very young age, Solomon Tollman's back grew strong, helping his father by hauling heavy sacks of grain, and of milled flour. My father's physical and mental strength was to stay with him throughout his life. His mother was my grandfather's second wife, and a combination of brothers, sisters and half- and step-siblings meant that my father was one of no fewer than eighteen children.

Like many towns in Eastern Europe, Riteve was home to a substantial Jewish population. But Riteve was a friendly community, and the Jews co-existed happily with the other key section of the population – the Catholics. However, life in Riteve was not representative of life elsewhere in Russia. Conscription into the army of the Russian Empire was a very uncomfortable prospect for young Jewish men. It meant service for at least six years, and Jewish conscripts were not only prevented from observance of their beliefs, they were often pressed to convert to Christianity through starvation and other less subtle forms of cruelty. When my father reached the age of fourteen, his parents decided that he would not suffer these indignities, and instead hatched a plan to spirit him out of reach of the authorities.

Towards the end of 1910, leaving behind the relative prosperity of home and of family life, my father was smuggled initially to the German port of Memel, the northernmost ice-free port of the Baltic Sea, today called Klaipeda and also part of Lithuania. This involved thirty miles in a horse-drawn cart through low-lying and marshy ground, over muddy tracks which were often impassable in wet weather. Wrapped in warm clothing for protection against the winter weather, and laden with the weight of the gold five-rouble coins which had been stitched into his clothing, my father was placed on board a ship bound for Britain.

Solomon Tollman spent six months living in Britain with a Jewish family, before embarking on his true journey. In April 1911, he celebrated his sixteenth birthday. But just two months later, he claimed to be 17. This was in order to be able to buy a ticket – Steerage Class – on the Union-Castle Royal Mail Steamship *Braemar Castle* leaving London on 30 June 1911, bound for Cape Town, South Africa.

Union-Castle steamships were instantly recognisable lavender-hulled liners with red funnels topped in black. They ran on a rigid timetable between Southampton and Cape Town. The *Braemar Castle* was used regularly on the 'Cape Run' from her commissioning in 1898. During the First World War, she was to become commissioned by the United Kingdom government, first as a troop transport and later as a hospital ship. In that latter role she struck a mine in the Aegean Sea and was severely damaged.

We have become accustomed to travelling at 30,000 feet and 500 miles per hour, and to a world where nowhere is more than a day away. A hundred years ago, things were very different. The *Braemar Castle* was a four-masted ship with a single funnel and a single screw. She was the last intermediate steamer built for the Castle Line, with a speed of just 15 knots and a gross tonnage of 6,266 – about one quarter the size of a typical ferry operating today across the English Channel between Dover and Calais.

The ticket for my father's extraordinary journey is something of a family heirloom. It shows staging stops along the 'Cape Run' at Madeira, Grand Canary, Tenerife, Ascension and St Helena, before arriving in Cape Town, a journey which took almost a month. The ticket contains the *'Victualling Scale for the Voyage'*, shipping lines being required by law to indicate what *'Water and Provisions would be supplied by the Master or the Ship'*. My father's ticket spells this out:

TO EACH STATUTE ADULT, 3 QUARTS OF WATER DAILY,
EXCLUSIVE OF WHAT IS NECESSARY FOR COOKING ...
AND A WEEKLY ALLOWANCE OF PROVISIONS ACCORDING
TO THE FOLLOWING SCALE:-

$3^1/_2$ lbs	BREAD OR BISCUIT, NOT INFERIOR IN QUALITY TO NAVY BISCUIT
2 lbs	WHEATEN FLOUR
1 lb	OATMEAL
8 ozs	RICE
1 lb	PEAS
2 lbs	POTATOES
$1^1/_4$ lbs	BEEF
1 lb	PORK
2 ozs	TEA
1 lb	SUGAR
2 ozs	SALT
$^1/_2$ oz	MUSTARD
$^1/_4$ oz	BLACK OR WHITE PEPPER, GROUND
1 gill	VINEGAR
7 ozs	LIME JUICE
1 lb	PRESERVED MEAT
6 ozs	SUET
8 ozs	RAISINS
4 ozs	BUTTER

MESS, UTENSILS AND BEDDING TO BE SUPPLIED BY THE SHIP.

It is difficult to imagine what was going through my father's head as the *Braemar Castle* set sail for a new life on a new continent on the other side of the world. Although he knew that a much older half-brother was living in Cape Town, his surname was not the same as my father's, and they had never even met. My father knew simply that he would have a roof over his head for a while. With the sight of land fading out of sight behind the boat, the 16-year-old Solomon Tollman was getting further and further from everything he had ever known.

These were of course momentous times for South Africa. The previous year, the four previously self-governing Colonies – Cape, Natal, Transvaal and Orange River – had joined in a formal Union. The ceremony was to have taken place in May 1910, in the presence of the Prince of Wales, Heir Apparent to Edward VII. A month before this was due to happen, Lord Gladstone, the first Governor-General of South Africa, had left England to prepare for the ceremony. He travelled on another Union-Castle ship, the *Walmer Castle,* tracing a similar journey to that which my father was to take the following year. As the *Walmer Castle* passed the *Garth Castle,* a further ship of the Union-Castle fleet which was heading in the opposite direction and a day out of Cape Town, the *Garth Castle's* signal flags delivered the news that the King had died. The brief Edwardian Age was over, and the Prince of Wales had become King George V.

After four weeks, the *Braemar Castle* finally approached its destination, and the distinctive sight of Table Mountain came into view. My father was less interested in the fabulous scenery, however, than in getting to the address he had been given for his half-brother, Isadore Javits, an address to which he quickly made his way once the ship had docked.

He was welcomed into the home above the butcher's shop which was the family business. But his half-brother's wife came as something of a shock to my father. Kitty Javits, he discovered, was an Afrikaner, a South-African born Afrikaans- (or Dutch-) speaking white person. For a Jew to have married an Afrikaner was deeply shocking for my father, who later told me that he could only imagine how this news would have been received back in Lithuania. At the end of the 19th Century, South Africa was governed according to strictly Protestant principles. Jews and Catholics were barred from membership of the *Volksraad* (parliament) and from all military posts. Before the Boer War (1899-1902), Jews were considered *uitlanders* (foreigners) and anti-Semitism was known to be rife.

The truth was that a small number of Jews, including it seems Isadore Javits, settled amongst the white Afrikaans-speaking population, becoming known as *Boerejode* (Boer Jews). Amongst this group, intermarriage occurred and was accepted. In time, the Afrikaners were to prove almost schizophrenic in their attitude to the Jews. Pro-Nazi and overtly anti-Semitic Afrikaners were not uncommon at the time of Hitler, but when the Afrikaner-dominated National Party came to power in 1948, it abandoned anti-Jewish policies, despite its earlier antagonism.

But in 1911, any doubts that my father may have had at first meeting were quickly forgotten. There were too many other more immediate considerations. I have often thought how ill-prepared my father must have been for his arrival in South Africa. He was still so young, and how much education can he have gathered before he left his home, not to mention having to face the challenge of language in this new continent over the oceans? I will never understand how he was able to cope. But even more perplexing to me was how he was able to amass the body of wisdom upon which he, and those around him, relied during the very difficult years to come. Some of the most telling words I have ever heard were spoken by my father. I have little doubt that some of these he heard and then merely repeated. But there were others which he said to me over the years that I am equally certain were his own words rather than the words of others. I will never know where they came from. I often find myself repeating what he said to me. One of my favourites is, "First you get on; then you get honest; then you get honour." He was a remarkable man.

Having arrived at the home of Isadore and Kitty Javits, my father was swiftly put to work in the butcher's shop during the day, and allocated a corner of the floor at the back of that same butcher's shop in which to sleep at night. He was given a blanket but no mattress, and certainly no bed. Life was tough for my father, especially when he rather foolishly opened the family birdcage, allowing Kitty's canaries, her pride and joy, to fly away. After just under six months of ill-feeling and discomfort, my father could stand no more. He ran away.

My father and his half-brother were not the only Jews who had decided to seek a new home in South Africa. Neither were they by any means the only Lithuanian Jews. Although millions of Jews were emigrating to the United States, South Africa was also seen as a safe haven from the anti-Jewish pogroms, from general conflict within the Russian Empire, and from the anti-Semitism of the Czars. This period coincided with the development of the mining industry in South Africa, taking place first in the diamond fields of Kimberley and later in the gold belt of the Transvaal. The prospect of wealth made this strange land on the other side of the world attractive to those who were keen to put down roots and to succeed. In 1880, the Jewish population of South Africa had numbered approximately 4,000. But by 1914, it had grown to 40,000, many from Lithuania. Johannesburg may nowadays be abbreviated to Jo'burg. But at the start of the last century, it was sometimes referred to as Jewburg. My father felt sure that he would find a welcoming place somewhere else in South Africa.

So it was that he found his way to a small agricultural settlement in the Western Cape called Hopefield, named after the eponymous Mr Hope and Mr Field, two Cape Colony government officials. He found work there with a Jewish family who had recently arrived in South Africa, and who had a farm with an agricultural store. It was here that he would meet a man who would not only have an important influence on him but who, twenty years later, would be responsible for my middle name. This gentleman was an Afrikaner who had fought in the Boer War and who continued to call himself Colonel Stefan.

Colonel Stefan sold goods to agricultural stores, just like the one attached to the farm where my father was staying. My father struck up a friendship and, within a matter of weeks, was offered a job by Colonel Stefan.

Colonel Stefan supplied tools, machinery, tack and seed and was also building up a small collection of agricultural stores of his own. Within a year, my father was offered a small share of the business and thus became an enthusiastic junior partner in the venture. He also became something of a man about town, cutting quite a figure as he drove about in his cart, pulled by no fewer than four horses. As he travelled around, those he visited would often shout, *"Hier kom die Jood!"* Although this translates as "Here comes the Jew," it was in fact a friendly greeting, and my father's friendships grew with many local Afrikaners. Because of his line of work, he was also called a *smous*, a word meaning itinerant trader or pedlar in Afrikaans.

It was about this time that my father made the first Tollman investment in the hotel business by buying the Paternoster Hotel, more of which a little later. The Paternoster Hotel not only included the small hotel itself, but a farm, general store and a crayfish canning company as well.

As ever, the Jewish Diaspora meant that much of the Tollman family was on the move. At about this time, and encouraged by my father, other members of the family in Lithuania also undertook the same long journey to settle in South Africa. My father's sister, Rae, who by this time had become Mrs Groll following marriage to a cousin, moved to a village called Firgrove, a little to the south of Cape Town. My father's brother, Sam, chose Stellenbosch, just to the east, where my father helped him to buy the Commercial Hotel. My father was certain from the start that the Commercial Hotel would be a great success, a prediction that would prove to be correct. Even then, almost a hundred years ago, the Tollmans were already showing nous when it came to the hotel business.

In the meantime, my father continued to learn a lot about business from Colonel Stefan, many lessons of which he in time passed on to me. One particular story still springs readily to mind many years on. My father had developed a practice of calling at the stores which were under his supervision out of working hours in order to check on the books and on the inventory. He had dropped in one evening on a store and was looking at the books when he asked the manager whether there were any problems. "We did have a problem today," was the reply. "One of our account customers came in and picked up a saddle. We were so busy at the time that we didn't make a note, and we've forgotten who it was who took it. As a result, we are missing an expensive saddle and we don't know what to do about it."

When he got back, my father explained the problem to Colonel Stefan. "That's easy," Colonel Stefan replied. "There are 104 account holders at that store. Get the manager to send every account holder an invoice for the saddle. Everyone who didn't take the saddle will soon tell him so, thus revealing by elimination the one who did." My father passed this instruction back to the manager.

It was some weeks before my father saw that manager again. "Did everything work out with the missing saddle?" he asked. "Yes," said the manager, "…and no. We did as you suggested. All of the 104 account holders were invoiced. But only 65 complained to say that the invoice had been sent incorrectly. The other 39 just paid up!"

Apart from reflecting on the fact that this could well have been the most profitable sale of a saddle in the Western Cape, my father learned that day of the dangers of credit, and of the importance of checking invoices properly. These were amongst the lessons which he drummed into me from a very early age and which should have guided me safely through dangerous waters. But not only did I forget my father's important teaching at a crucial time, unforgivably I did so twice. Those mistakes were to bring me to the brink of catastrophe. As I stared into the abyss each time, my father's words rang in my ears. But I will come to all of that a little later on.

Colonel Stefan did not simply supply goods and equipment to the farmers. He also provided finance to fund their crops from year to year knowing that, come harvest, his lending would be returned with interest. The first ten years of my father's involvement with Colonel Stefan had been very good. But times were changing. The Great Depression was just around the corner, and the whole world was in trouble. In South Africa, most of the farmers had taken out Government second mortgages on their farms which could no longer be serviced, and the Government was foreclosing. My father, caught up in the overall collapse, lost almost everything he owned. He was left with the small hotel in Paternoster, and the crayfish canning company.

Lest readers might imagine that canned crayfish is a delicacy sought out by the world's epicureans, let me correct you. Canned crayfish is, to say the least, a highly acquired taste, with a smell which many find repugnant. This was a very basic food product indeed.

In the midst of financial turmoil there were, though, happier developments. My father met Evelyn Swerling, the woman who was to become his wife and my mother. She had been born in Manchester of Viennese parents who had emigrated to Britain around the turn of the century. But Lancashire had proved for them a difficult place in which to prosper. Mr and Mrs Swerling decided to take their two children – Sonny, aged four, and Evelyn, aged two – and move to a more promising land. Four more children were later born in South Africa.

The Swerlings carried to South Africa ideas which had been picked up in the textile industries of the North-West of England. My mother's Uncle Frank had built a small but successful business in Lancashire manufacturing raincoats, and her father had decided to copy his brother's initiative on the other side of the globe. He set up his raincoat business in Cape Town, confidently expecting to do just as well as Frank. The flaw in his business model was that Cape Town had only half as much rainfall as Manchester, and people who lived there simply did not wear raincoats.

The raincoat business duly folded, and my mother's family tried its hand at market trading instead, with a stall in the open market at the Grand Parade below Cape Town Castle. In between Indian and Muslim tailors, the Swerlings sold imported buttons. My mother often told me of the hours spent in the cold and rain, helping her father to count out the buttons. Life was tough, but the pennies earned through those tiny transactions were sufficient to enable my grandfather to open his own shop in Cape Town. Above the door was proudly displayed the sign:

B. SWERLING & SON
• SUIT LENGTHS AND BUTTONS FROM BRITAIN •

The shop made enough money to enable the Swerlings to buy a home in Sea Point, a little seaside town on the outskirts of Cape Town where, in the 1930s, the well-to-do had their homes.

My mother had, of course, arrived in Cape Town as a girl. Although Eastern Europe may have been in her blood, it was not in her memory and she viewed Eastern European men with something approaching disdain. In any case, she was just 19 when she met my father, who was then 35 years old. But this unlikely pairing worked. After a period of courting, they became engaged, getting married in 1929. No less a figure than the Mayor of Cape Town made a speech at their wedding.

CHICKEN FAT

The age of motoring had arrived, and Solomon Tollman's cart and four horses were replaced with a car – a Nash. In the early hours of 20 September 1930, my father was called upon to get out the Nash and drive my mother to the Booth Memorial Hospital in Cape Town, where I was born. Three days later, we returned to Paternoster, to what was to become my childhood home. Apart from me, the only other white people in the village were my father, my mother and the schoolmistress.

Even to this day, Paternoster remains a simple fishing village in the Western Cape, about 100 miles north of Cape Town. Recently, however, aspects of Paternoster have changed. Within the last five years, it has become something of a trendy destination for visitors, with smart restaurants and boutique guesthouses.

The name Paternoster has something of a history. Over the years, countless ships have foundered on the reefs that skirt the coast, and many have lost their lives as a result. Legend has it that the community owes its name to a group of shipwrecked Portuguese sailors who recited the Lord's Prayer in Latin – *Pater Noster* – discovering that they were amongst the lucky few, having reached the safety of land.

White-washed houses with corrugated iron roofs are scattered just above the shoreline of Paternoster, the parched land basking in the sun for much of the year. Beyond the shore, the wind-blown Atlantic stretches out to the horizon. Whales are often to be spotted out to sea in the cold Benguela current flowing northward from the Antarctic, bringing with it the nutrients which attract vast amounts of plankton and shoals of fish and, in turn, the creatures which feed upon them. Even today, bunches of salted mullet[1] are to be seen drying, strung up with ropes in the sun to create *bokkums,* the fish equivalent of *biltong.*

---

[1] Known locally as harders.

When was in Paternoster I lived barefoot, playing with my friends through the sulphur-yellow fields of colomba daisies. My recollections of those days are as vivid as if they happened yesterday. But one important thing is missing from my memories, and I cannot understand why.

I was an only child for just twenty-two months, because on 4 July 1932 my brother Arnold was born. Sadly, Arnold is no longer with us, having suffered a troubled and untimely death in August 2004, aged 72. Throughout the whole of his life, Arnold was extremely important to me, and in so many ways. Inexplicably, though, from the period of my childhood, but especially from the years in Paternoster, I have little or no recollection of him.

I do remember that Arnold was a very beautiful baby with wonderful curly blond hair. My mother was so proud of his looks that Arnold would be entered into beauty contests – where he always seemed to be placed second. Whether he was consistently pitched against the same impossibly beautiful baby who always snatched the crown from him, I do not know. But Arnold became known universally as the young man who "always comes in second."

I have photographs of that period, but Arnold does not appear in any of them. Perhaps that is why I have no recollection of him. In many ways, I seem to have played out my youngest years as an only child. My parents were both working and I was looked after by a coloured[2] nanny who took me to church on a regular basis – a curious experience for a Jewish boy. I was more than a little perplexed about this fellow called God who seemed to be the centre of attention but who never bothered to turn up, even though I had to.

The same, rather inattentive, nanny once took me to the circus, accompanied by my grandmother. Distracted, my nanny allowed me to crawl into a cage which contained a lion. My grandmother was understandably horrified, and her screams of "My Stan-a-lie!!" might well have been heard in Cape Town. Thankfully for all concerned, I managed to crawl out of the cage without so much as a scratch.

---

[2] The term 'Cape Coloured' has been in use since the 19th Century for members of what is sometimes called the only "truly original indigenous population" of South Africa, many descended from relationships between settlers, slaves and local tribes.

Our parents had strong ethnic similarities but their families were completely different from each other. My mother's were all English-speaking anglophiles and were concentrated in the Cape. My father's family, on the other hand, were overtly Eastern European, with friends who were largely Afrikaner. This contrast made for a very interesting life. But common to the whole family were the shared beliefs of good food and hospitality.

Leah Swerling, my maternal grandmother, outlived some of her own children, and died at the age of 96. She was always cooking food for me and, even though these were difficult times, there was always a rule that one's food should be as good as one was able to provide. One of the lasting impressions I inherited from her, and then from my mother, is a concept which, over the years, I have translated into the means by which I assess the character of other human beings. I will explain.

Rendered chicken or goose fat is very popular in Jewish cuisine, either for frying or as a spread on bread. This rendered poultry fat, known as *schmaltz*, was used by Eastern European Jews who were forbidden by *Kashrut*[3] from frying meats in butter or lard. Chicken fat was viewed as an essential, high-quality ingredient in many forms of cooking. Although by modern cholesterol-aware standards it may perhaps be viewed with horror, in the 1930s it was highly valued. My grandmother, and my mother after her, swore by chicken fat. Homemade chicken soup, even today, is a regular part of the Tollmans' family diet and, at the insistence of our regular guests, 'Bea's Chicken Soup' is an ever-present item on the menu of every Red Carnation hotel.

Over time, the words 'chicken fat' would, however, take on a completely different significance for me. It took a long time for the realisation to sink in, but one day I realised that I had developed for myself a personal measure of appreciation of humanity. This measure encapsulates the recognised qualities of chicken fat, but translated in my own mind as a metaphor for everything that really matters in a human being. In truth, the expression 'chicken fat' has

---

[3] The set of Jewish dietary laws, derived from the Torah's Books of Leviticus and Deuteronomy.

become more important to me than the dietary benchmark of even the most fastidious Jewish mother.

Chicken fat is not restricted to any particular gender, nor is it acquired as a result of age or experience. It is to be found amongst individuals from every walk of life, but those who are graced with this facility are, I would suggest, blessed with a rare and invaluable gift.

Do not get me wrong. I do not profess to be a faultless judge of humanity, and judging human character is in any case not what chicken fat is all about. I stress this important distinction because, although I have backed many people who have never let me down, there have also been some whose behaviour has been a serious disappointment to me. And I often think that I should have been able to work this out before the event, rather than – as was invariably the case – only when it was too late. Anyone who thinks my judgement of others is flawless needs to take a closer look at my track record. Almost the reverse is true.

With a number of very important exceptions, those in whom I have placed the greatest trust have also been my greatest disappointment. Throughout the whole of my life, there is no question that every major problem I have had has come from misjudging people and their intentions. But as I have already said, I should have known better. Without exception, I came to the realisation after the fact that these people never had any chicken fat. Had I bothered to work this out beforehand, I might well have avoided some of the most unfortunate (and expensive) chapters in my life.

For my own part, I myself have probably disappointed people. I have always tried not to disappoint, but sometimes I suspect that I may have let people down. I know I have weaknesses and I know them only too well. Sadly, I suspect that my weaknesses are merely the other sides of the coins which represent my strengths. For example, I have a tendency to be confrontational: to hit first and ask later – both physically and metaphorically. Nevertheless, despite my natural inclination to be confrontational, I know that I am utterly useless when it comes to confronting friends, probably because I never want to run the risk of breaking a friendship. It is precisely this weakness that has exposed me to all the worst things that have ever happened to me.

This is an uncomfortable admission to have to make because, to all intents and purposes, I am as fearless a person as anyone one is likely to meet. When, for instance, I was shown for the first time a court document headed *"United States of America - v - Stanley Tollman"* my reaction was simple. "Screw *them!*" On numerous occasions in business I have been prepared to jump blindly over a metaphorical cliff, hoping that I would find a root or branch somewhere to break my fall. In all aspects of my life I can be very tough. My maxim throughout my life has been, *Hit First and Continue Hitting!* But my strength evaporates if I have to get tough with a friend. I cannot do it. And I have numerous scars to prove this.

Notwithstanding sorry tales of misplaced trust, I have *always* been able to engage with all sorts of people, moving freely and without difficulty amongst the most diverse groupings imaginable. This facility, which I recognise to be a gift for which I am everlastingly grateful, has enabled me to discover the most interesting people, wherever they may be. These people – the people whom I would describe as *the* most interesting – rarely seem to have much in common with each other, besides the fact that they are really interesting. Some of this group have made a great deal of money. Others are penniless, but couldn't give a fig. Some have travelled the globe, whilst others have never left home. Amongst this group are professionals, artisans, academics, artists, doctors, writers, politicians, creatives and administrators. This is as diverse a bunch as you might imagine.

If I were to seek a distillation of what it is that enables me to group these people together, it is that from my perspective all these people are *seriously human*. They are people who understand life, and who make real connection with other human beings. They are also people who value life for what it is. They appreciate its wonder, yet they know too that it is tenuous. They know that life is something to savour and to appreciate, and not to waste.

I became aware of an ability to divine these people as long ago as the 1960s. In South Africa, I found that I was able to move comfortably through any section of society. I had friends from the Jewish community, but I had rather more who were Afrikaners. I had many black friends, American friends and English friends. I got to know many of the politicians, and I was on first-name terms with all and sundry. For some reason, there didn't appear to be an Indian living in Johannesburg who did not know me and who, even though I was only in my thirties, would address me as *D'ora*. To my embarrassment, I was told that this translated as something along the lines of 'the great one'. I thought of this more as a joke than as a compliment but I was assured that they were not trying to pull my leg. Who knows? We certainly got on well with each other.

It was about this time that the penny dropped that all the people with whom I really liked to spend time talking possessed a certain, indefinable, but common trait. Let me give you just one example of someone who represents the essence of what I am describing.

One of my lifelong friends is a man called Robbie Blank. He and I are almost the same age. Like me, Robbie is Jewish, but his father was born in Dublin, not Eastern Europe. Also like me, Robbie was born in South Africa. He is a man who throughout his life has been overflowing with ideas, with energy and with an ability to organise and to persuade people to get on with things. Had he applied himself to making money, without doubt he would by now be one of the richest men on the planet. But money has little fascination for Robbie, except as a means to make things happen. He is a truly wonderful man. At least once a week for the last 50 years, and regardless of where I am in the world, Robbie has telephoned me. I am embarrassed to admit that it is always he who telephones. I am not very good at making telephone calls. I almost never do it.

It is too common these days for people to define their own success by their career and job title. Often, this form of self-appreciation becomes almost delusional when people attribute value and, by extension, importance to activities which contribute not one jot to the greater good. I have little time for people like hedge fund managers, especially those who fail to realise that they are in the same line of business as pavement shysters offering punters the chance to 'Find the Lady'.

My father said many telling things to me. One of the most insightful was, "Be frightened of your own shadow." Those words have rarely strayed far from my mind throughout my life. And I hope that I have always behaved properly, maintained a sense of self-knowledge which has enabled me to keep my feet on the ground, and tempered optimism with modesty. Above all, I pray that I have conveyed my father's principles and guidance to my own children.

Returning, though, to the Stanley Tollman Chicken Fat Measure, this is the benchmark against which most people who come into my life are nowadays assessed. Many have a small amount only of chicken fat; most have none. But there are a tiny number of people whom one is honoured to meet in one's life who have chicken fat in spades. These are the people who, my family aside, make life worth living. These are the people who invigorate me with their ideas and with their conversation. These are the people who value life by their contribution to it, rather than by how much they have in the bank.

Kipling got there before I did:

If you can talk with crowds and keep your virtue
Or walk with Kings – nor lose the common touch,
If neither foes nor loving friends can hurt you,
If all men count with you, but none too much;
If you can fill the unforgiving minute
With sixty seconds' worth of distance run,
Yours is the Earth and everything that's in it,
And – which is more – you'll be a Man, my son!

I have always considered 'If' to be a masterpiece of observation. I cannot compete with the elegance of Kipling's language, but I am able to share his appreciation of the finest human qualities. Hence, my use of the assessment which I call Chicken Fat.

But there was not much chicken fat around when I was very young. I was unquestionably a child of the Depression, a slump which had hit South Africa even more severely than other parts of the world. Employment and business activity were almost non-existent and poverty was widespread within every section of the community.

The Paternoster Hotel had few visitors. Some of the visitors we did have, especially the long-term residents, were in fact members of my mother's family. I remember two salesmen – one in liquor, the other in farm implements – who stayed at the hotel for months on end. But in 1938, my mother had had enough. She packed up her things and told my father that she was taking my brother and me to Cape Town, to stay with her parents. There was no life for her or for the children in Paternoster. She simply could not take this any more, and she was *not* coming back. And she never did go back to Paternoster.

The Paternoster Hotel is still there, and there have been few changes to the establishment, although the lavatories are no longer outside. But times are nowadays changing in Paternoster, as no less an authority that the *New York Times* observed recently, in an article headlined Cape Town's Foodie Suburb:[4]

TWO years ago, Arnold Hoon, a chef from Johannesburg, was driving along South Africa's West Coast in search of lunch. On a whim, he and his wife, Annelise Bosch, followed an old wooden sign to Paternoster, a traditional fishing village about 90 minutes north of Cape Town.

What they found were whitewashed cottages overlooking Paternoster Bay, and a single restaurant, Voorstrandt, near a beach dotted with fishing boats. Soon, they were dining alfresco on fresh oysters and grilled lobsters, served with a crunchy green salad. "We never left," said Ms. Bosch, a former actress.

Last year, the couple opened their own tiny whitewashed restaurant, Ah! — one of several newcomers that have turned Paternoster into a popular draw for Cape Town's food connoisseurs.

Housed in a thatched guesthouse overlooking a pristine beach, the restaurant serves a terrific three-course dinner for 200 rands, or about

---

4   Cape Town's Foodie Suburb, *New York Times*, 30 March 2008.

$24 at 8.25 rands to the dollar. The menu changes daily and recently included lobster bisque with sesame and Parmesan phyllo twists, arugula salad with nectarines and Gorgonzola, and roasted quail topped with chipotle salsa.

Ah! also has two comfy rooms upstairs, decorated in vibrant turquoise, yellow and red for 350 rands a person, which includes a decadent breakfast of twice-baked cheese soufflé, and brioche French toast with caramelized apricots.

A handful of guesthouses have sprouted along the beach, adding to Paternoster's reputation as a foodie resort.

Suzi Holtzhausen, a chef from Johannesburg, recently opened the small Salt Coast Fine Foods and Inn, where she serves avant-garde fare in a white and blue-trim cottage. She uses local ingredients like suring, a yellow flower with a distinctive sour taste, to flavor soups and dagga (marijuana) in a rub.

A recent menu included veldkool soup (similar to asparagus), grilled snoek (a game fish) glazed with grape must (a fine syrup) and a seared loin of gemsbok (South African venison) in a chocolate shiraz sauce. The inn, set in a secluded compound, has two rooms.

Across from Salt Coast is the Noisy Oyster Restaurant, which serves modern South African cuisine. The chef, Brian Smit, changes the menu daily and might serve wok-tossed baby calamari with chermoula (a tangy North African marinade) and black mussels in white wine, garlic and turnips.

The ocean view from the Cape Dutch-style Oystercatcher's Haven guesthouse on the smooth boulders of the Cape Columbine Nature Reserve is spectacular. Just ask former President Nelson Mandela, who had dinner there in 2003 during a three-night stay.

"Mr. Mandela is known for his punctuality," said Wayne Attrill, the guesthouse owner. "He made his plane wait while he stayed on our deck for an extra 45 minutes. He just wanted to stare out at the sea for a while longer."

Even after the passage of seventy-five years, I still have the greatest fondness for Paternoster. Whenever I visit, the most beautiful memories come flooding back to me. In 1997, I was given a wonderful opportunity to put something back into the community which I left all those years ago, and at the same time to create a lasting memorial for my father.

An old fish factory in Paternoster had doubled up for many years as a makeshift community hall, but had been demolished to make way for new housing. Although it had been somewhat ramshackle, until demolition this unlikely venue had been the social centrepiece of the village. Its removal meant that there was no longer a venue for dances, wedding receptions or any other form of community gathering. The local council was offering to meet some of the costs of constructing a new community centre, but the community needed to produce the lion's share of the funding. Here was my chance, and I was absolutely thrilled to give Paternoster the 750,000 rand which was needed to make the project a reality.

On 28 March 1999, Bea and I attended the grand opening party of the Solomon Tollman Community Centre. We saw what a wonderful building had been created, and how important it was for the people of Paternoster. Since that day, the Centre has become an even more important part of the community, additionally housing a school where fifty local children are both fed and educated. At the opening, almost 1,500 inhabitants of Paternoster and their guests were treated to a three-course open-air feast. I said a few words, and my message was simple: "When I left Paternoster all of my dreams came true. Remember, everything is possible." What I did not know when I said those words then was that some of my nightmares were about to come true as well.

The Solomon Tollman Community Centre is located, fittingly, on land which is right across the road from the Paternoster Hotel. It blends in with the unique character of the town, local architect Jaco Visser echoing the white walls and flat roofs of the surrounding houses, with pathways made of seashells. Even the massive granite boulders which were present on the site have been incorporated into the design. It is a building which clearly 'belongs' in every way. I am proud of it, and I hope my father would be too.

SWAN STORES AND THE PALACE HOTEL

Arnold and I were very fond of our grandparents and, even though my mother had taken us away from Paternoster, it was good to move to Cape Town, notwithstanding of course the absence of our father. I can remember my grandfather working at the back of his shop – usually sorting buttons. The rest of his waking hours appeared to be spent reading. Although he had only spent a few years in Britain, he was very English in his pursuits. I thought of him as a typical English gentleman and a very nice and kind person.

If an important cricket match was taking place, the shop would be closed – this was a matter about which there was no argument. He regularly played cricket with us along the Promenade at Sea Point, and made us feel very much at home. And there was always a special welcome for me from my grandmother. As I was the first, and therefore the eldest, of what she would later proudly describe as her 20 grandchildren, my grandmother always considered me the apple of her eye. I say "describe as her 20 grandchildren" because, some years later, my wife asked me how my grandmother had managed to work out that she had twenty. I had to confess to never having thought about it much but we did the arithmetic and realised that the true number was in fact 16.

Faced with my mother's ultimatum of leaving Paternoster for good, my father had little alternative other than to sell the Paternoster Hotel and to look around for something else. In a classic case of a good turn being repaid, my father's brother came to our assistance. As my father had confidently predicted, my uncle had made a great success of the Commercial Hotel in Stellenbosch – in many ways thanks to my father. He now helped my father to locate and to buy something called the Swan Stores – a small department store – in Benoni, a small town situated on the Witwatersrand, about 18 miles from Johannesburg – but almost 1,000 miles from Paternoster!

The move to the Transvaal was inspiring for the family in every respect. Our possessions were packed up and shipped ahead and we then set out in the family car – by this time a Hupmobile – on the four- to five-day drive to Johannesburg, a journey made more passable by the fact that this car had a radio.

About 25 miles before reaching Benoni, we had to drive through a town called Vereeniging. Vereeniging is the Afrikaans word for 'uniting', being at the road and rail crossing points between the two old republics: Zuid-Afrikaansche Republiek and the Republic of the Orange Free State. Vereeniging is famous for the peace negotiations that ended the Boer War and is today a very important industrial centre.

As Mr and Mrs Solomon Tollman and their two young sons drove into Vereeniging that day in 1938, they discovered a line of 30 cars, each of which had a white handkerchief placed over the mascot which every car of the time had at the front of its bonnet. This extraordinary procession was the welcome from my father's extended family. Every single member of the Tollman family had turned out to welcome us to the Transvaal.

The concept of family created a huge impression upon us all from that moment onwards, and we made a point of staying in touch with everyone. I discovered that many of my relatives were in business, some doing very well. Three brothers, for instance, who were first cousins of my parents' generation, had together started a supply company under the name Tollman Brothers and Davis, providing poultry, eggs and cheese throughout South Africa. This business had become a great success in a very short space of time.

The yellow and dusty spoil dumps and the winding gears dotted across the landscape betrayed the principal activity of Benoni, which was gold-mining. My parents rented a house and realised immediately, gold or not, that the Swan Stores represented something of a challenge. Both of them found that they had to work around the clock, offering a remarkable level of service. It was not unknown, for example, for a single half-pound of butter to be delivered in person to a customer's home.

Benoni was largely populated by former British miners and by a large Jewish population which had fled from Europe. General Smuts said of Benoni, "Some of the most difficult passages of my life have been linked to the turbulent people of this little place." And in the years leading up to the War, there emerged in South Africa a movement called the *Gryshemde* or Greyshirts, a group comprising largely Dutch South Africans sympathetic to the Nazis. This group called for an end to Jewish immigration and promoted violence. I remember my father coming home one Friday night covered in blood following an attack on the synagogue in Benoni by the Greyshirts.

In his autobiography[5], Leo Lovell, the Member of Parliament for Benoni, recalled that evening in May 1938. Coming home he saw a man dressed like a stormtrooper standing on a large table surrounded by other similarly dressed men who were openly carrying *sjamboks*[6] and bicycle chains and waving flags which displayed the swastika. The speaker was shouting in Afrikaans, *"On Friday you get your pay. You're rich. But on Saturday you're poor again. Where's all your money gone? Into the pockets of the accursed Jew shopkeepers. While you grow poor, they grow rich."* These were uncomfortable times.

The Swan Stores had a wide and eclectic offering of goods which included food and drink, plus a vast selection of cheap products imported, invariably, from Japan. I remember that one of its specialities was its extensive, but slow-moving, stock of harmonicas. It was not long before my father was forced to accept that he could not really make any money running this business. It was time, once again, for us to move on.

His brother then introduced him to the Castle Wine and Brandy Company, which extended a loan which enabled my father to buy The Palace, a small hotel in Johannesburg. The Palace was opposite the Commercial Exchange, around the corner from Tattersalls, and two blocks from the Stock Exchange. My father and mother took possession in March 1939.

---

5 *For the Love of Justice*, Leo Lovell, Jewish Publications, South Africa 2009.
6 The *sjambok* is a traditional heavy leather whip made from the hide or penis of a hippopotamus or rhinoceros. It is sometimes seen as synonymous with apartheid, but its origins pre-date the arrival of the white man in Africa.

Johannesburg just prior to the start of the Second World War was a city with two distinct characters. Gold had been discovered more than 50 years before, and the city's essential roots remained those of a primitive mining town, with all that this entailed. But Johannesburg had become rich, and had grown into a settlement with a population of almost 400,000. It was still surrounded by evidence of mining, with mountains of excavated sand known as 'The Dumps' stretching in a line east and west for almost 60 miles along the Reef, as the old gold-mining settlements were known. But in places it was now a modern metropolis, with fine public buildings and spaces. The downtown area was a series of well-planned, wide streets with elegant buildings, set out in a grid. Trams and motor cars provided transport for a bustling metropolis, which sat on the Highveld of the Transvaal at an altitude similar to that of many European ski resorts, ensuring that even the warmest days were followed by cool nights. It was a great place in which to grow up.

Arnold and I loved our new home but it was only a matter of days before we had wreaked havoc at the Palace Hotel and it was decided that we should board at our new school. So it was that, at the age of eight, I started life at boarding school, taking my six-year-old brother with me. We went first to Marist Brothers in Koch Street, which was near the railway station and opposite Joubert Park, about a 25-minute walk from the Palace Hotel.

The Marist Brothers, or Little Brothers of Mary, are a Catholic religious order dedicated to the Christian education of the young. The Brothers' school in Koch Street was a grim building, cold and miserable. I remember distinctly the red polished floors throughout the ground floor and the general feeling of discomfort which accompanied the whole of my time there.

I was placed in the Middle School, but Arnold was separated from me and put in the junior dormitory. He was only six years old and was, in any case, small for his age, as witness his nickname 'Ticky' – the word South Africans used for the tiny silver threepenny bit. I remember spending many nights in the junior dormitory because Arnold was crying almost incessantly. Eventually – but only after five months – Matron concluded was that he was too young to be a boarder and recommended that he should be a day boy instead. I was therefore left on my own as a boarder, the only Jewish boarder in a Catholic school with many hundreds of pupils.

On 6 September 1939, the whole school was in the chapel at Koch Street when the Brother who was celebrating mass announced that South Africa had just declared war on Germany. This news was greeted with a ripple of excitement. After mass was finished, there was much singing of patriotic songs throughout the school, especially *There'll Always Be an England*. I gleefully joined in, but it was not long before I was approached by the Brothers and, for artistic reasons, was asked to stop. My days as a crooner may have been over – and for ever – but I have little doubt that the loss of my singing has meant that the world has been a more harmonious place as a result.

Two large turrets were built on a vantage point above the city, from which it was contemplated that German planes could be shot down. These turrets and their guns did not see a lot of action. Lack of local conflict notwithstanding, the impact of the War in South Africa was manifest by severe shortages. I do not think I have ever been so much in need of food. I remember even now the constant, gnawing hunger at school. My parents could not afford to give me pocket money, so there was no means by which I could supplement the meagre school diet. My mother would occasionally leave a paper bag for me at the school office in which were some dried apples and oranges, but this rarely staved off the hunger. As a result of that period of my life, I am now obsessive about ensuring that the fridge at home is always full.

In common with many, my parents were going through difficult times. Business was non-existent and my father struggled to pay the mortgage. My mother worked in the kitchen of the hotel and my father did everything else. They lived in two rooms of the hotel, my brother and I using whatever room was available at the time.

Whenever I came to the hotel, I found it was full of people in uniform – people who had come back from being 'Up North', meaning that they had been fighting in North Africa and were back on leave. Others were preparing to go back 'Up North'. Various family members who were in the forces treated the Palace Hotel as their headquarters, and came and went accordingly. I remember the sadness of cousins failing to return from the War. But one person who had made it back and was always at the Palace was my mother's younger brother, Frank. He was in his early 20s and had been invalided and sent home, and had been diagnosed as suffering from Hodgkin's Disease.

The piano became the centre of entertainment, with *Roll Out The Barrel* and *Wish Me Luck As You Wave Me Goodbye* being the standard repertoire. And it was at this time that I began to realise the true value of a hotel. Even if business was not good and one could make no money, there was always a roof over one's head and food in one's stomach.

It was during this time that I started to pick up the lessons of good hotel practice. My parents always made sure that there was lots of free food available for clients, who began to appreciate that one could eat at the Palace Hotel for the price of a beer. My mother spent all her time in the kitchen replenishing the food. On the rare occasions when I was able, I would come home from school to help her. As befitting the difficult times in which we lived, we provided inexpensive snacks such as freshly roasted peanuts and cucumbers which had been pickled in the old beer barrels. And we would regularly buy damaged cheeses at cheap prices as part of the free food offering. My mother roasted the peanuts and it was then my job to salt them. There were often complaints that I had been a little too heavy with the salt. My answer was simple. "The more salty the peanuts, the more thirsty the customers." We sold a great deal of beer.

In the restaurant we would serve steak and eggs, with grilled sole available for an extra ten pence (10d)[7]. My mother was a skilful cook who had learned at the knee of her own mother. The dining room of the Palace Hotel attracted a regular and faithful clientele of bookmakers, stockbrokers and racehorse trainers, all of whom were there simply because of my mother's food.

---

[7] A sum of money from pre-decimal currency – £.s.d. (pounds, shillings and pence).
There were 240 pence to the pound.

At around the beginning of the War there was a new influx of Jewish refugees into South Africa. My father and my uncle started to pick up dark stories from some of them as to what was happening in Europe. Together, they made a desperate attempt to get other members of the family out of Europe, especially my father's younger brother, Gideon, who was a rabbi. It was concluded, however, that my grandfather, who by then was in his 90s, could not survive such a journey. In any case, this was never to be.

I remember coming into the hotel at about this time, which must have been April 1939, to find my father lying on his bed, crying. I had not seen my father cry before, and would not see him cry ever again. He had just received a cable telling him that his father had died. I was never to meet my grandfather. I was never to meet my grandmother, either. At 84, she too was too old to leave her home.

Nothing was heard in South Africa for two years but, when it was, my father, my Uncle Sam and Aunt Rae kept the detail to themselves. All we were told was that my grandmother and my Uncle Gideon had died. My father never, ever, spoke about what had actually happened.

In 1972, and well after my father had died, we took the family to Israel. I was, of course, always profoundly aware of the fact that I was Jewish, but I had been isolated from many aspects of Jewish life and its traditions. In reality, I had never lived at home until I left school. And my understanding of the fate which befell my father's family during the war was patchy to say the least.

My father, my Uncle Sam and my Aunt Rae had never spoken about what had happened to the rest of their family in Riteve in 1941, and the rest of us therefore assumed that it was not something about which we should speak. Looking back now, I can understand why they dealt with things in the way in which they were able, but I am almost ashamed that it took so long before I was to gain a proper understanding for myself. Our visit to the Holocaust Memorial on Mount Zion in 1972 revealed that an outrage had taken place in Riteve, although what we learned then is inconsistent in detail with what we have learned since. Forty years later, I am still trying to piece together the true story.

In 1897, when a census was conducted, the population of Riteve numbered just 1,750. Of this total, the number of Jews in the town was recorded as 1,397 – in other words, 80% of the population. By 1923, although the size of the town was very similar, the number of Jews had decreased to 868. When the German army invaded Russia in June 1941 there were between 800 and 1,000 Jews living in Riteve. Within weeks of the invasion, the vast majority of these people had been murdered.

On 22 June 1941, the German army had invaded the Soviet Union. Importantly, some weeks earlier Hitler had decided to adopt new measures in his war against the Jews. He ordered Heinrich Himmler, the SS supreme commander, to take whatever steps were necessary to annihilate Jews within the Russian Empire. As a result, Himmler's Deputy, Reinhard Heydrich, formed four units specifically for this purpose. These were the *Einsatzgruppen,* the feared SS paramilitary death squads whose task it was to move from town to town in the occupied areas and, in accordance with the specific instructions of the *Führer,* to execute "Jews, gypsies, racial inferiors, asocials and Soviet political commissars". The *Einsatzgruppen* were assisted by large numbers of Lithuanian collaborators.

In every Jewish community the *Einsatzgruppen* followed a similar procedure. The Jews were forced to assemble in a central place, whence they were taken by a heavily-armed escort to a killing site not far from the town or village. In some cases, the Germans used anti-tank ditches or shell craters as graves, but in many sites mass graves were dug beforehand. The victims were forced to hand over any valuables, take off their clothes and either stand in front of the graves or lie in them. They were then executed.

Writing about the actions of the *Einsatzgruppen,* the author Gitta Sereny said[8]:

> *An SS signal concerning these "actions" was found amongst German army records after the War. Addressed to the security police, Rega, from the Commander of the Security Police (and SF) Eastern Zone, and entitled "Executions", it requests "immediate information regarding*

8   *Into That Darkness,* Pimlico 1974.

number of executions categorized as (a) Jews; (b) Communists; (c) Partisans; (d) Mentally ill; (e) Others."

The reply ... states that executions up to February 1st 1942 were: (a) Jews, 136,421; (b) Communists, 1,064 (amongst them 1 Kommissar); (c) Partisans, 56; (d) Mentally ill, 653; (e) Poles, 44; Russian POWs, 28; Gypsies, 5, Armenians, 1. Total: 138,272; of which women 55,556; children 34,464.

By early 1942[9], behind the front from Rega and Minsk to Kiev and the Crimea, they had killed well over 500,000 Jews; two thirds of them, as we can see from the signal, women and children and nearly all by shooting in previously dug mass graves.

In most cases, and Riteve is no exception, there were few surviving witnesses and the story is necessarily incomplete and confusing. On 23 June 1941, fire destroyed all but a few houses in the town. Some say this was because the fleeing Russians had set fire to the town, others that it was the result of a bombardment by the Germans – an unimportant distinction. The Jews of Riteve fled into the surrounding countryside. But directions had been given that, on pain of death, they were not to be given assistance, and should be sent back to their homes.

The most murderous of the four *Einsatzgruppen* squads was *Einsatzgruppe A,* which operated through the Baltic region. Riteve, being close to the German border, was one of the first settlements to suffer at the hands of *Einsatzgruppe A.* When the Jews of Riteve returned to their fire-ravaged town, plundering paramilitaries of *Einsatzgruppe A* were there to greet them. The various accounts of events conflict in detail, but their conclusion is always the same.

The first to die were the communal leader, Bere Zaks, and his wife. Both were shot. Rabbi Shmuel Fondiler was escorted into the community hall, alongside the synagogue, accompanied by a substantial number of other Jews. There he was taunted and his beard was either singed or cut in half, depending upon which account one reads. He was then forced to shred a Torah scroll and deface other sacred artefacts, before being harnessed to a cart laden with

---

[9] The signal in question does not indicate the length of the period in question, but would appear to start from the date of the invasion of Russia. In other words, seven months.

rubbish which he was made to haul like an ox. One account says that he had a heart attack and died. Another, that he was shot dead. The accounts agree that the next step was the torching of the community hall whilst many Jews were still inside. All perished, including my grandmother, my uncle and all my other relations. It was the record of this act that my family and I discovered whilst at the Mount Zion Holocaust Memorial.

What happened to the remaining Jews of Riteve is unclear. Some appear to have been sent to nearby Telz, where they were murdered. Others were murdered closer to home, and others still transported further afield. In various ways, the lives of the Jews of Riteve were systematically extinguished.

There exists a memorial to the Martyred of Riteve, listing each family whose members were killed by the Germans in the summer of 1941. It does so by listing the name of the head of the family only. It contains the entry:

TOLMAN, RABBI YECHIEL AND FAMILY

Yechiel Tolman was my father's younger brother, whom the family knew as Gideon, and who had become head of the family upon the death of my grandfather. In some versions, the name Tollman is spelled just as we do today, with two l's. In fact, Tolman and Tollman were interchangeable in our family until fairly recently.

Notwithstanding the horrors in Europe, as far as South Africa was concerned the turning point in the war was the decisive outcome of the battle of El Alamein. After this, in the middle of 1943, the Allied forces invaded Sicily thus launching the Italian campaign. Things for my parents improved dramatically, as business in South Africa started to pick up across the board. The Palace Hotel filled up with residents, and there was a strong demand for food and drink. This meant that prices were able to rise for the first time in many years, even though there were still shortages. Those drinking in the bars knew that a tot of whisky was likely to be rationed to a quarter of its usual size, but the customer was still prepared to pay the price of a whole tot simply to get it. Over the next few years, my parents' fortunes improved dramatically.

Meanwhile, Johannesburg was still on the alert for air-raids, and the sirens would sound frequently. At school in Koch Street, a warning of an air-raid would mean that the boys were split into two groups. Those who were able to reach their home within 15 minutes could go there. The rest had to go down to the cellar out of harm's way. Although the Palace Hotel was in fact a 25-minute walk from school, by covering the distance at a run I had discovered that not only would I have time to get back there during one of these alerts, but would get a meal as well. This was a big result. I usually went home with three or four friends in tow. For the record, every single one of those many air-raid alerts proved, thankfully, to be a false alarm. And, no, they were not set off by schoolboys in need of some decent food!

In 1942, as a 12-year-old, I was sent to a Boy Scout camp in Margate for three weeks (Margate in South Africa, that is, not the one in Kent). The troop of Boy Scouts concerned was the 1st St Patrick's and comprised a group of about 50 14-year-old boys. Not only was I the only 12-year-old in the party, all the others were Irish Catholics, who soon discovered that they had a Jewish boy amongst them. On the first day I arrived, I was awoken roughly in the middle of the night and pulled out of bed. This incursion was in order to mount an inspection of my private parts, to view my circumcised penis. They then proceeded to drop molten candle wax onto the end of my John Thomas. This was just the painful start of a week of anti-Semitic bullying. I quickly realised that if I was going to survive I would have to stand my corner. During those three weeks, I fought virtually every other boy in the group.

I do not think I have ever actually started a fight myself but, over the years, I always seemed to be in one. It became clear that I needed to become rather more proficient in fighting, and a man called Harry Isaacs, a customer at the Palace Hotel, gave me boxing lessons. I improved significantly. So significantly that, aged 15, I was entered into a competitive fight in the Southern Transvaal against an opponent who was a foot shorter than I was. The prognosis looked good. However, short though he may have been, he matched me pound for pound and I was soundly thrashed. Nevertheless, thanks to Harry I had learned skills that would stand me in good stead in the years ahead, especially when, many years later, we opened the Colony Club in Johannesburg, which could on occasion be a very physical place.

GROWING UP AND STEPPING OUT

In 1943, I moved up from Marist Brothers, Koch Street to Marist Brothers College in the Johannesburg suburb of Observatory, a school where I was to stay until 1948. The school at Koch Street had been a city-centre location with almost no grounds. But Marist Brothers, Observatory was a very different kettle of fish with extensive grounds, playing fields and even a swimming pool. It was a paradise.

Marist Brothers was a rigidly Catholic school in terms of its approach to education, but it was, to say the least, eclectic in terms of its intake. Many of my schoolfriends were Chinese and Lebanese and, in later years, included a handful of other Jewish boys. Irrespective of our family traditions and faiths, all of us were required to attend daily Mass. This did, though, have the compensation in those deprived times of offering modest additional sustenance in the form of a mouthful of the communion bread and a sip of wine.

Our day-to-day diet at school was dull and unrewarding. A typical wartime meal comprised hard tack biscuits, corned beef and beetroot salad. By the time I moved to Marist Brothers, Observatory in 1943, however, my parents' fortunes had improved to the point where they were able to pay me pocket money. When supplies were available, I was able for the first time to buy a little extra food.

After the war ended, my parents purchased a beautiful house sitting in an acre of ground in the well-to-do Johannesburg suburb of Lower Houghton. They were proud of their new home and its swimming pool. This was in many ways their first real home – and ours too! Arnold and I had rooms at the top of the house.

My three closest friends from boarding school all came from comfortable backgrounds. One was from Natal; another, a Lebanese friend, was from Brits, a town close to Pretoria; and the third was from the Orange Free State, where his family owned a farm. The day

pupil to whom I was closest was a boy from Johannesburg called
Raymond Eskapa. Raymond has a very interesting surname which
means, quite simply, 'escape'. Raymond's ancestors were amongst the
Jews who survived the expulsion from Spain at the end of the 15th
Century at the hands of the Spanish Inquisition and its evil architect,
Father Tomas de Torquemada.

On 30 July 1492, a decree ordered the expulsion from the country
of the entire Jewish community, some 200,000 people, within just four
months. This was the ultimate fire sale, as Jews were forced to sell
their homes and businesses at absurdly low prices. Tens of thousands
died while trying to reach safety. Rumours spread that fleeing refugees
had swallowed gold and diamonds, and many were knifed to death by
robbers hoping to find treasure in their stomachs. And captains of
Spanish ships charged Jewish refugees exorbitant sums, before
rewarding them by throwing them overboard once at sea.

Raymond and his late wife, the well-known author Shirley
Eskapa, would in time rank amongst the family's closest and life-long
friends. Over the years they have always been very important to us.

With our final year at school in sight, in July we all went to
Durban for the holidays in order to lie on the beach and to get some
action in the waves. By now, I should have been at ease with the
world, especially by comparison with what had gone before. I should
have considered life to be both rosy and settled. But building
inside me was a feeling of inadequacy, and I could sense that I was
becoming desperate to be someone else. I needed, I thought, to
be like the others. My friend from Natal was a young man called
David Duchen, arguably my closest friend at the time and who
went on to become captain of the South African squash team. His
father operated a mining concession in Natal as well as running a
general store. Together, the two of them appeared to be the perfect
father-and-son combination.

It was at about this time that I started to reflect on my own life, and
my relationship with my own father. Indeed, I began to think that all
my feelings at the time were somehow linked to my relationship with
my father, in relation to which I had an underlying sense of uneasiness.

As time progressed, I sensed that my father was becoming frightened of my ambition and was clearly troubled by the company which I chose to keep. He told me that he was worried that some of my friends were what he described as 'wheeler dealers', and were a bad influence.

My father was a proud man who commanded huge respect from his friends. Known universally as 'Tolly', he was used to dealing with difficult situations. The Palace Hotel was, on occasion, a very rough place. This did not worry him. He had a highly effective right hand which led him, on one occasion, to be charged with assault. But these were calm and dispassionate acts, born of need. He did have a fearsome temper but he rarely displayed it, almost to the point of reserving it for the occasional disagreement with his eldest son.

Although he clearly had the capacity to give me a sound beating, that only ever happened once. One of the residents of the Palace Hotel was an elegant gentleman called Bill who was one of those who had "come back from Up North" and had been invalided out of the forces through injury. He impressed my father, who ended up giving him the job of creating a new bar at the Palace Hotel, to be called simply 'Bill's Bar'. This was to be decorated (at some expense) in an elegant style to reflect Bill's taste and 'savoir-faire'.

On the day that the decoration was completed, Arnold and I were coming back from school and, as we passed the City Hall, we spotted a mechanical ostrich on a pole. Passers-by were being encouraged to donate a few coins "For the War Effort". Those who did so were rewarded by the sight of the ostrich shooting up the pole in front of them. We thought that this was a simply wonderful idea and concluded that the Palace Hotel needed something similar. We returned to the Hotel, where we secured a couple of bags of chicken feathers from the kitchens before retiring to the freshly-decorated Bill's Bar as the place we had chosen to glue together our own 'ostrich'. That was the point at which disaster struck, the chicken feathers seeming to acquire a life of their own. They shot all over the bar, and settled gently on *every* surface, including walls and ceiling. Everything had just been painted and the paint was not yet dry. In seconds, Bill's Bar was transformed from an elegant drinking haunt into something resembling a poultry shed.

When my father discovered what we had done, he chased me around the hotel in order to let me have it. I suffered the first and only beating from him when he managed to find some old electric cables with which he whipped me mercilessly. But I deserved it. I remember my mother's younger sister, Bertha, who was staying with us at the time, applying Vaseline to the weals on my back and saying, "He shouldn't have done this"; to which I responded, "It wasn't his fault."

My father gained a reputation as an honourable and straight-talking man, who at all times lived his life in accordance with the Ten Commandments. But he was also a complex character. He would happily listen to or tell a dirty joke with friends, but he would never, do so if I was present.

Some years later, when I had become successful in business, I bought four or five small buildings in Johannesburg. I converted these to ten flats, the intention being to lease them, with the rent generated providing income for my parents during their retirement. These were architect-designed flats in Ferndale in the desirable Randburg district of Johannesburg, and the whole exercise had been well-planned and skilfully-financed. The first my father knew about it was when I took him, as a surprise, to show him and my mother the flats which I had built in order to provide for them. My father's reaction? He said nothing. Not a word. In some curious way, he resented what I had done.

It is fair to say that my parents had a very different approach to life from that which I chose to adopt as my own. Because I had boarded during school time, and during the holidays had always been sent away to stay with relations, I never really lived at home until I left school. So it was that I became a member of the family proper for the first time at the age of 17 – when I was almost a man. I was independent. Worse, I was opinionated. And my opinions did not chime with those of my father. I disagreed, when I was in fact expected to conform.

My mother insisted that we all ate together in the evening, and she was right to do so. Eating together is an essential part of family life. But conversation around the Tollman dinner table often became animated. Then it became heated. Then downright adversarial – often concluding with either my father or me storming off. But only words were ever exchanged. There were never blows, and the arguments were always swiftly forgotten. But my father saw me as something of a rebel – a common assessment, I suspect, of most first-born sons.

Inevitably, politics was at the heart of most of our disagreements. My father was a staunch conservative. He knew Jan Smuts[10] personally, and was a dyed-in-the-wool supporter of everything for which he stood. He was, however, not a racist and did not approve of the National Party's advancement of the policy of segregation. Nor did he approve of the formalisation of *apartheid* which took place when Smuts was voted out of office in 1948. But neither was my father a liberal, and he held traditional views about South African society and those within it. His last word in our arguments was often to call me a *Kaffir boetie* – meaning someone who fraternised or sympathised with the cause of the black community. In 1973, the word *Kaffir* would be made actionable in South African courts under the offence of "unlawful, intentional and serious violation of the dignity of another". But that was many years later.

The Palace Hotel provided very basic accommodation. It was never decorated and it had bare wooden floors throughout. None of the rooms had private bathrooms and each morning the corridors were lined with the chamber pots which the guests had placed outside their doors.

It is fair to say that I was never exposed to taste or style but, despite this, I always seemed to know what I wanted. I do not know how or why. I never set foot outside South Africa until 18 months after I was married, and there were no magazines and precious few books from which one could learn. I seemed to have an instinctive taste, which I always felt was struggling to get out.

---

[10] Jan Christian Smuts (General Smuts) (1870-1950) played important roles in the South African War and in both World Wars. He was twice Prime Minister of South Africa (1919-24 and 1939-48). He also helped to draft the United Nations Charter.

In 1940, my youngest brother, Ivan, had been born, who came to be known by me simply as 'Kid', given the ten-year gap between us. Kid spent all day, every day, with his nanny, a white lady called Flo. They lived together at the top of the house and my mother rarely went up to see him, instead receiving reports from the nanny. My mother seemed almost uninterested in her three sons. She never, for instance, came to see me at school, restricting her visits there to the occasional bags of dried fruit left for me in the school office. My mother appeared less interested in her family than in her poker, her friends, and in getting dressed up.

But it would be quite wrong to assume that she was a bad woman, or even that she somehow failed as a mother. She was neither of these things, and was in fact an immensely kind and thoughtful woman. I became very close to her during her later years.

The first 20 years of married life had been a long and inexorable grind for her – misery and slog, night and day. When things became easier for my parents, my mother found that she had a little freedom for the first time to enjoy herself, and she did just that. She was at last having a good time. In many ways, this was linked to the fact that she now had a home – for the first time in 20 years of marriage. Until then, my parents had lived 'above the shop' in a couple of hotel rooms. But from 1946 onwards, she was able to enjoy herself.

It would be especially wrong to judge her harshly. She had married young to a much older man from a very different background, and the early years of marriage had been a struggle. But, deep down, she was full of life and she was the kindest person; always there for her children, getting books from the library if we needed them, or buying us the best tickets for the cinema.

But it was only during the last years of her life that I really understood the extent to which my mother cared for me. When my father died, she lent me everything that she had in order, as I will explain later, to enable me stay in business. She had been widowed, aged just 55, and her cash not only represented the entirety of a lifetime of hard graft, it was also all she had to live on for the rest of her days, which she expected to be rather greater in number than

God in fact allowed her. Yet she put everything on the line for me. Not because she trusted me to pay her back, but because she loved me.

When I had children of my own, I became very aware of the difference in the approach of my mother to her grandchildren and that of my wife's mother, the children's other grandmother. My mother barely had even a passing resemblance to the stereotype of an Eastern European Jewish mother. She was highly anglicised in her appearance and in her approach to life.

My wife's mother would be around the whole time, helping with the children's growth and upbringing at all stages, and enforcing a little discipline where necessary. In other words, she did all the hard work. My own mother drifted in from time to time, never needing to say harsh words and usually bringing sweets and small gifts. Needless to say, my children thought very highly of their paternal grandmother. And I adored her too.

I mentioned earlier that I do not have any memories of Arnold at Paternoster. Thinking about this more carefully, my memories of Arnold do not really kick in until he left home in 1952 to go to university in order to train as a dentist. Until then, we may have been physically close, even sharing a room, but it was when we started to go our separate ways that, ironically, we began to get much closer. We built a remarkable bond between us that was to last until he died. We could not have been closer.

Arnold was in every way my baby brother, and the periods of separation in our lives – for instance, me as a boarder at Marist Brothers and him as a 'Day Dog' – made no difference. We shared everything, but in the rough-and-tumble way that brothers usually do. I remember, for instance, the time we stayed with our grandparents in Cape Town. We slept in bunk beds there; me in the upper bunk, Arnold in the lower. Every night without fail, I would wake up in the middle of the night and kick Arnold out of bed, and he ended up just sleeping on the floor. It sounds cruel, but it was just a little bit of fun. That sense of fun stayed with us throughout our lives. Sure, he annoyed me from time to time, as brothers do. But there was never anything to it. I remember playing cricket with Arnold one day on a public beach, when I realised that he was wearing my new cricket trousers. "What are doing with those?" I remonstrated. "Get them off!" And he did, there and then; much to the amusement of the several hundred others who were also on the beach at the same time.

The trouser incident took place at Cape Town. This was because, once the Tollman fortunes had improved a little, we spent family holidays in Muizenberg, a beach-side suburb of Cape Town and a place where many of the mining barons had chosen to build their summer retreats. Muizenberg was also a popular destination for Jewish families. A small house on the seafront was owned by Cecil Rhodes, and it was there, in the now famous 'Rhodes Cottage', that the great man died in 1902.

I completed my matriculation at Marist Brothers, Observatory, in preparation for university. Academically, my performance was like the curate's egg – good in parts. I scored well in English, History, Geography and Science. But in Maths, Trigonometry and Geometry I was lousy. My performance in sport was more consistent. I competed for the school in both cricket and rugby, and I also ran for the school in athletics. Whilst playing rugby, aged 17, I received a kick to one of my knees. After the game was over, I found that I could not walk properly. I was diagnosed as having a torn cartilage and was swiftly operated upon. In the United States 30 years later, my knee was examined by Dr Richard Steadman, a well-known sports doctor who developed his skills through repairing injuries sustained on the ski slopes of Vail. All he would say, rather unhelpfully, was, "I would never have operated."

I think it may have been owing to the fact that I disagreed constantly with my father that I got into the habit of arguing with everybody else as well. This led me to become a very active member of the school debating society, at which I developed some skill. In the year in which I matriculated, I won the school prize for debating, possibly assisted by the fact that my parents had donated the Cup.

Although I seemed to be in more than my fair share of scraps, I was very popular at school and it was clear that I was on course in my final year to become a prefect. But that was not to be, and the unsettling course of events led me to experience, not for the last time, feelings of injustice.

At the back of my classroom, a few days before the school was due to announce its list of prefects, one of the teachers discovered that someone had carved the initials S.I. into a desk. My initials, lest you are in any doubt, are S.S.T. I was nevertheless accused of having carved the initials S.I. into a desk. Truthfully, I denied the charge. I do not know to this day who carved those initials, or when, or why. All I can say with certainty is that my denials fell on stony ground. As a result, I was passed over for the role of prefect. I had been entirely innocent of the charge, for which there was no evidence whatsoever. And yet the school had punished me. Whatever happened to the presumption of innocence? In a small way, I was scarred for life.

Painful lessons like these notwithstanding, I enjoyed my school days enormously, and I continue to take pleasure in watching the progress of some of my fellow pupils. Joel (later to become Lord) Joffe was in the the same class as me, and became a famous human rights lawyer as well as a businessman. He defended Nelson Mandela in the Rivonia trial of 1963/64, when Mandela and others were accused of sabotage. Writer and broadcaster Pat Rogers – another contemporary of mine – appears, I am pleased to see, to be working as hard as ever. It is good to read about someone of one own's age somewhere other than in the obituaries. A year or so ago, Pat was remarking with sadness on the decline in the number of Jews in Johannesburg, given the contribution which they had made to the economy over the last century. Another of my school friends was Mandy Moross, another Jewish pupil at Marist Brothers, who later completed an MBA (with distinction) at Harvard Business School. He will feature in my story a little later on.

But back in 1948, I was beginning, mentally, to move on from school and to step out into the big wide world. This was the time when I was definitely growing up. My horizons were widening. Saturday nights became party nights. My mother gave me dancing lessons. My friend David Duchen invited me to holiday with him and his family in Natal. His parents took me out one day and offered to treat me to a new shirt. This was not any old shirt that they had in mind but a shirt from South Africa's top shirt maker, priced at the princely sum of £1. I chose a shirt in blue. And David's parents bought two of them for me – both in blue. I was thrilled, and I treasured that gift, looking after those shirts carefully for a very long time indeed. Those two blue shirts gave me a real interest in good clothing and this act of generosity and the interest that it spurred in me would lead, some years later, to my being voted the best dressed man in South Africa.

David Duchen and I were inseparable but, as so often happens with friendships, we ultimately went our separate ways. David emigrated to Australia where he became a huge success in the pharmaceuticals industry. I caught up with him there in the 1970s and we were able to pick up almost as though we had seen each other the day before. True friendships last a lifetime.

Upon matriculation, I went rather grandly with three of my friends to dinner at the exclusive Criterion Hotel restaurant run by the famous hotelier, George Petousis. The chefs of the Criterion had a terrific reputation and the food was as wonderful as we had expected. During the course of the meal, George himself came to our table and offered his three young diners a bottle of wine on the house. A modest gesture for him, but a gift of memorable significance for its recipients. We were so impressed by this action that I suspect that all four of us still remember it even today.

In later years, George was to become a client of mine, as a regular visitor to the Colony Club, where he often arrived late but then made up for it by staying until we closed the place. In the 1960s the family sold the Criterion and moved to Cape Town where his son, Francois, developed the famous Vineyard Hotel in Newlands, perhaps the favourite destination of English tourists to the Cape. Both George and Francois have now sadly passed on, and the Vineyard is in the hands of George's grandson – who, pleasingly, is also called George Petousis.

Upon leaving school, I chose not to opt for full-time higher education but to study off-campus three nights a week at the

University of Witwatersrand, and at the same time to seek an apprenticeship. Known to all as 'Wits', the University of Witwatersrand is located in Braamfontein in North-Central Johannesburg. It is considered by many to be the leading English-speaking university in the country. My university studies were for a combined course of chemistry and biology based upon the 'B' I had received at matriculation in Physical Sciences.

Without much inspiration, I was struggling with three choices – whether to become a lawyer, a doctor or a pharmacist. I chose pharmacy, and I signed up as an apprentice to a pharmacist called Geoffrey Albert George Glucksman. Mr Glucksman's chemist shop was just three blocks away from the Palace Hotel and, on the face of it, represented a stable foundation on which to base my career. Stable it most certainly was not.

Mr Glucksman's wife had chosen to have an affair with Mr Glucksman's best friend. As a result, Mr Glucksman decided to sue his friend for alienation of affection. The Courts were unpersuaded and Mr Glucksman lost. Unhappy with the justice being offered by the Courts, Mr Glucksman chose another route. He shot and seriously injured his best friend and then turned the gun on himself – this time fatally. This did not augur well for the future of my apprenticeship at the Maritime Pharmacy.

Glucksman had a manager at the pharmacy called Mike Chafkin, whose future was every bit as uncertain as mine. However, Glucksman also had an accountant, an individual called Manny Vallet, who arranged for Mike Chafkin to buy the pharmacy from the estate. This in turn enabled me to stay and to work for Mike instead. I was employed from 8.00am to 6.00pm with an hour for lunch and, as an apprentice, I earned £9 a month.

By sheer coincidence, Mike Chafkin was to play a more involved role within my family than I had imagined. My mother's cousin and her husband had moved from London to Durban, where they had bought a hotel. The move to South Africa had in large part been prompted by the wish that their daughter, Anne Proops, should broaden her life. In particular, they hoped that she would meet someone whom she would marry. Although very pretty, Anne, who was two years my senior, could never seem to nail the playboys of Johannesburg, any one of whom was her primary target. After a succession of failed attempts, Anne met Mike Chafkin, who became crazy about her. Mike was a nice enough guy, but an unlikely substitute for the sort of men my cousin was originally targeting. Anne decided, though, to accept second best and she and Mike became married.

I had always helped out at my parents' hotel. I was very used to moving the bar crates and to maintaining the cellar underneath the hotel. I also regularly helped my mother in the kitchen and I felt I already knew more than a little about the business of entertaining.

During lunch breaks from the Maritime Pharmacy, I would run back to the Palace Hotel to help my mother in her now bustling kitchens. The fame of her home cooking had spread far and wide and diners were queuing up for her Lancashire Hot Pot. At the same time, the dining room plates had been replaced by 'surplus' platters on which the food was served. These platters, being bigger than the plates they replaced, meant bigger portions. This went down well with the guests. A Dover sole was not a Dover sole at the Palace Hotel unless its head and its tail overhung the edge of the platter.

For one hour's part-time work a day at the Palace Hotel, I earned £5 a week, more than twice as much as I would earn for a full-time, 45 hours a week, position at the Maritime Pharmacy. And every Friday night, horse-racing took place at the race track at Viljoensdrift, near Vereeniging. The tote at the racecourse was operated by none other than Manny Vallet, assisted by his articled clerk, Wally Segal. I helped them out, earning £5 a night, plus tips from happy horse owners and from the occasional successful flutter of my own. Thus, aged 18, when all my friends were on an allowance from their parents of £20 per month, I found myself with a pocketful of ready cash.

My mother, as a present for leaving school, took me to Levenson's, Johannesburg's top men's store. She paid for a grey pin-striped suit; a blue suit; a Daks sportscoat (Daks was the UK's premier brand); suede shoes; ties; and an armful of shirts. When I returned home, my father took one look at my new wardrobe and accused me of being a *moff*.[11]

I was not yet 19, I had money in my pocket and I was now well-dressed. The next thing I needed was a car. My parents had taken out an insurance policy at my birth, to provide for the costs of higher education. The £250 which the policy delivered upon maturity was about to come my way, and I took the view that nothing would broaden my education more than ownership of a car. A cousin owned a Chevy Fleetline, and two of my friends in Johannesburg had MGs. However, the £250 was only enough to buy me a Ford Prefect 10. This car did not *drive*, it chugged. For about nine months, it was the bane of my life. It was only after my uncle, a GM dealer, replaced the Ford Prefect with a brand new Vauxhall that I was saved from embarrassment. The quality of my girlfriends improved overnight.

After my days spent filling prescriptions and helping out in the kitchens of the Palace Hotel, I had little energy and enthusiasm for my studies. Dissecting frogs and learning about the life of plants became less and less interesting, and I started to miss classes at about the same time that my social life became more active. I came home later and later, often in the early hours. I remember on one occasion I returned home at 6.00am, and was on the stairs, when I passed my father, who was on his way to work. He congratulated me for getting up so early.

There is no doubt that my own personal horizons were expanding by the time I reached 19. I met two young Englishmen who lived a couple of blocks away – brothers called Mossie and Toddy Berman. Their father was in shipping, and financed the movement of goods between the UK and South Africa.

The Bermans dressed beautifully and had a permanent table at the Carlton Hotel, the best restaurant in Johannesburg. They oozed style and charm and had impeccable manners. They knew their way around London and the South of France, and – from my inexperienced perspective – everywhere else in the world that was exotic. This was 1950, and the Bermans had just returned from Miami Beach, having travelled right across the United States. These

---

[11] 19th-century slang for hermaphrodite, sometimes used to refer to a flamboyant homosexual.

guys were seriously in touch with life – and they took a liking to me, taking me under their wing and regaling me with wonderful stories.

At about the same time, I became aware of a small but active community of Americans in Johannesburg, comprising largely ex-servicemen who, post World War II, had sought new opportunities in South Africa. Every Sunday morning, the Americans in Johannesburg held a volleyball game at the Automobile Club, one of the city's great country clubs. I was invited to play and I joined in with enthusiasm.

Of particular note amongst the Americans were the three Wilson brothers, the two eldest of whom – Hack and Roy – became very good friends of mine. Hack Wilson had married Stella Cohen, the daughter of Sam Cohen who, in 1929, together with his British partner, Michael Miller, had created OK Bazaars, a nationwide chain of general stores. Hack had brought the Pepsi Cola franchise to South Africa and set about creating bottling plants to produce not just Pepsi but also Canada Dry. Within a short space of time, he was supplying his beverages throughout Africa.

His brother, Roy Wilson, coupled movie star looks with an extraordinary personality. A former major in the US Air Force, Roy had become a war hero. Despite a large disparity in our ages, we got on really well together. I started to be invited with the Wilson brothers to Johannesburg's best homes.

This period generated a new spirit in Johannesburg, people coming from all over the world attracted by the great wealth of South Africa. I found it all very exciting. But it left me with an enormous sense of personal insecurity. Everyone else appeared to know where they were going. They had a definite sense of purpose. I, on the other hand, had absolutely no idea what I was going to do with my life. The only thing that was perfectly clear to me was that my future did *not* lie in a chemist's shop. I had realised some time ago that I was simply not cut out to be a pharmacist. But the last thing my father ever wanted me to do was to go into the hotel business. He hated it so much.

By this time, the Palace Hotel had employed a manager, a man who was some sort of distant nephew, who had a connection to one of the families from my grandfather's first marriage. This man called my father 'Uncle'. A bachelor, he always had Saturday evenings off. There were various things that had to be done in the hotel on those evenings, so I helped out. These duties cramped my style, as Saturday evening was when one took a girl to the cinema. My response to this dilemma was to take the girl to the cinema and sit with her as the lights dimmed. When the film started, I then excused myself "for a few minutes" and rushed back to the Palace Hotel. I would cash up, lock up the money and then lock the three bars, before rushing back to the cinema to catch the closing credits. The arrival in recent years of the DVD has meant that I have been able to catch up on the middle sections of many of the films from the Fifties of which I was familiar only with the beginning and the end.

My interest in clothing continued to develop. Mossie Berman introduced me to his tailor, and I started buying shirts from Jermyn Street shirtmakers Hawes and Curtis, who had a branch in Johannesburg. As a result, I acquired a quite different and more sophisticated look. Michael Bloomberg, whilst working at Salomon Brothers in New York 20 years later, is credited with the expression, "Dress British. Think Yiddish." But I was there long before him.

I was now wearing wonderful clothes. But, apart from the look, I was living in my parents' beautiful home; and I had cash. Every night, I was taking out a different girl.

I was also developing some rather finicky tastes. I did not drink alcohol. Instead, I insisted on freshly-squeezed orange juice with water. I started to eat out at the Carlton Hotel. I was learning all the time, absorbing those things which I considered to be important. I learned how to order food and wine. I also learned about cooking and I took these lessons back to the chefs at the Palace Hotel, teaching them, for instance, how to char-cook steaks properly. I even developed some new dishes for the hotel, some of which proved extremely popular. My greatest success was with a fillet steak, cooked in butter and served with a cream and brandy sauce.

It was clear that my natural inclination towards hospitality was coming to the fore. I found myself helping my mother to present the platters more attractively. I suggested the introduction of beetroot, cabbage salad and other types of fresh salad. Radishes, spring onions and other forms of crudités were presented in a bowl on the diner's table. Salads were served separately on a side plate. From the perspective of the 21st Century, these look like modest developments but, in the years just after the war, believe me these were innovative.

In 1948, as a reflection on the improving fortunes of the Tollman family, my father had bought a new car, this time a Chrysler. On special dates I was allowed to borrow the Chrysler. This was, I suspect, something of a thank-you from my father for the contribution I made to the hotel.

My father always used to say, "The world is full of willing people – some willing to work, the rest willing to let them." In my case, my father never had a doubt over my willingness to work. In fact, I was useful to him in many ways, it having long been my practice to get up at 5.30am to go to the market to buy fruit and vegetables. But I was now able to help in other ways as the enterprise grew and as we found ourselves developing closer and closer connections with the bigger clients. Every Johannesburg bookmaker belonged to the same club, which was named after the world-famous English bloodstock auctioneers, Tattersalls. The Club's full title was 'The South African Tattersalls Subscription Rooms', but it was known universally simply as Tattersalls. It was just around the corner, and it housed all the bookies in one big room. Tattersalls operated every day of the week except race days, and to a man its members chose the Palace as the place for refreshment. We offered a daily set lunch for an inclusive price of half-a-crown[12].

In part as a result of the popularity of my 'fillet-steak-cooked-in-butter-with-cream-and-brandy-sauce', we found ourselves unable to buy sufficient fillet steak. What was more, Johannesburg hotels were not allowed by law to bring in meat from outlying districts of the city. In addition, in a world still affected by wartime rationing, we continued to struggle to get hold of spirits too, especially whisky. So, in the hope of sourcing scarce ingredients, I would take the car out and make trips up through the Reef towns – the old gold-mining towns which were 40 miles or so away from Johannesburg.

---

[12] Half-a-crown referred to the pre-decimal currency of two shillings and six pence. There were eight half-a-crowns to a pound.

I visited liquor stores and butchers, buying up whatever spirits and fillet steaks I could lay my hands on. These were the days of price controls and I usually ended up having to pay extra – under the counter, of course. On one illicit run, I was chased by the police, thankfully outrunning them.

It was about this time that I realised that I had to make some big changes in my life. I was missing virtually all my lectures and there was never any time to sleep. Something had to give. I decided to leave Mike Chafkin and the Maritime Pharmacy and, more importantly, abandon my apprenticeship. Instead, I got a job as an unqualified pharmacist at a big 24-hour chemist in Orange Grove. This job provided some very useful benefits, notably the 400% increase in pay to £50 per month and the face-to-face contact with customers. The latter meant that I could chat up girls and get some dates. And I could also work until 9.00pm for extra money.

But my university work continued to suffer. I passed my first year exams, but in the second year I heard myself telling my mother, untruthfully, "I don't have college today." The truth was that I was trying to work out where to go with my life.

On my 21st birthday, in September 1951, my parents unexpectedly threw a wonderful party for me. It was a perfect evening. They had hired a band, and the tiers of the house and its balconies were beautifully decorated and full of people. My mother had a great deal of style. It was a fantastic party. 'Toute Johannesburg' was there.

Toute Johannesburg may have been there but, family aside, no-one at my party was of particular significance to me. This was because, although I had had a succession of dates in recent years, I was now 21 and had never had so much as a serious crush on any girl. But all that was soon to change.

Other changes were also afoot. Somehow, almost imperceptibly, something in South Africa was stirring. Universities, and especially Wits, were becoming radicalised and there was much talk of freedom. Nelson Mandela, writing about this period, said:

> *"I had no epiphany, no singular revelation, no moment of truth, but a steady accumulation of a thousand slights, a thousand indignities and a thousand unremembered moments produced in me an anger, a rebelliousness, a desire to fight the system that imprisoned my people. There was no particular day on which I said, Henceforth I will devote myself to the liberation of my people; instead, I simply found myself doing so, and could not do otherwise".*[13]

---

[13] *Long Walk to Freedom*, 1994.

BEATRICE LURIE

After my memorable 21st birthday party, life continued. I gave my parents a little more help at the hotel, cashing-up on Saturday nights and going with my father on Sunday mornings to take stock and order for the week ahead, before returning home together for Sunday lunch. But I continued working in the chemist's in Orange Grove. And, of course, most nights were spent on the town.

Just after I had left school, my friend David Duchen had called me one evening and asked me to go with him to the ice rink, which was situated in the southern suburbs of Johannesburg. Unsurprisingly, I was no ice skater and this invitation held little appeal for me. But I agreed to go along with David for the ride.

David had also invited another friend who was a year or two older than we were, and who was accompanied by a girl of 14 whose name was Beatrice Lurie. My only memory of her that day is that Beatrice Lurie was very young. I, on the other hand, considered myself a sophisticated man of the world and a lad about town. I took little notice of her.

A little over three years later, I was to meet Beatrice Lurie again, briefly. By now, she was 17. We were both attending an engagement party for her cousin, who was marrying a mutual friend. We exchanged polite small talk, and she told me that she was just about to embark on an overseas tour which had been organised by the National Union of South African Students. This meant that she would be out of the country for several months. Once again, I hardly gave her a moment's thought, at the time or after the party.

About three months later, in February 1952, I attended the 21st birthday party of a girl called Val Bayliss, who had been going out with a friend of mine. Much later, I would get to know Val well because she was to marry Edward 'Tubby' Block, the younger brother of Jack Block. Jack Block headed a famous Kenyan family which ran

Block Hotels, which included the Norfolk Hotel and Treetops Hotel, both of which were to acquire international reputations, but for two very different reasons.

The Treetops Hotel is situated in the Aberdare National Park in Kenya. When opened in 1932, it was built literally as a tree-house, offering guests the opportunity to view wildlife in close proximity, but in complete safety. From the original, modest two-room tree-house it has grown over the years into 50 rooms. The original structure was burned down by guerrillas during the 1954 Mau Mau uprising, but the hotel was rebuilt. It was whilst staying at the original Treetops in February 1952 – the very same month as Val Bayliss's 21st birthday party – that the young Princess Elizabeth heard of the death of her father King George VI, and of her accession to the throne.

The Blocks were to become great friends, especially Jack, who operated a night club in the New Stanley Hotel in Nairobi, which took bookings from many of the cabaret acts which we brought to Africa when later we opened the Colony Club in Johannesburg. Jack would in time become an Israeli citizen, and his reputation meant that he came to the attention of the Popular Front for the Liberation of Palestine. On New Year's Eve 1980, the Norfolk Hotel in Nairobi was bombed, killing 16 people and injuring more than 100.

But back in 1952, one of the other guests at Val Bayliss's party was Beatrice Lurie, who that very day had returned from the student trip to Europe. She had just broken up with her boyfriend of four years. I asked her to dance and, before the evening concluded, I asked her for a date.

The week of the party, an event occurred which resulted in one of my most treasured photographs – even though it was taken before Bea and I had even gone on a date together. Not only am I not in the photograph, I had nothing to do with its creation. The image shows Bea dressed in a majorette's uniform posing with none other than the former world heavyweight boxing champion, the Italian giant Primo Carnera. Bea had been chosen as the lead majorette in the Johannesburg students' charity Rag Week celebrations, which were opened by the 6ft 6in, 300lb Carnera, known universally as the

Ambling Alp. And the photo opportunity was therefore the equivalent of Beauty and the Beast.

For our first date, I took Bea to lunch at a restaurant called His Majesty's Cellar, which was located in the basement of His Majesty's Theatre – at the time Johannesburg's leading theatre. She appeared suitably impressed, later admitting that this was the first time anyone had invited her out for lunch. I asked her out again the following Saturday night. Over the next few months, we went out together a couple of times a month.

In July, I had arranged to meet up with friends in Durban. July in South Africa is of course a winter month. However, because it is situated on the east coast, and benefits from the warm Agulhas current from the Indian Ocean, Durban is the winter vacation spot of choice to many South Africans. In fact, KwaZulu-Natal has arguably the finest climate and the best surfing in the country.

But the reason I was meeting friends in Durban in July 1952 was not surfing, but the Durban July Handicap, South Africa's premier horse race, which has been held since 1897 at Greyville Racecourse. This is the biggest betting race of the year in South Africa, attracting casual and serious punters alike.

I discovered that Beatrice Lurie was also planning to go to Durban at the same time, not for the horse racing but to play in the Natal Tennis Championship. She told me that she "played a little tennis". But it was only later that I was to learn what a wonderful tennis player she really was, and that she had won numerous provincial tennis tournaments. The Luries were in fact very serious tennis players. Bea's brother, David Lurie, had played in the Wimbledon Championships in both 1950 and 1951.

Bea knew that I was driving to Durban, and asked me whether I might give her and her friend, Lee, a lift. I was happy to help, thinking that the long drive to Durban might pass more swiftly with a little company. I had already agreed to give a lift to the 14-year-old sister of a friend, and welcomed the prospect of some adult company in the trusted Vauxhall. My hopes were swiftly dashed.

By the time we set out for Durban, I considered that Bea and I had become good friends. We had dated regularly, and had as close a friendship as I had ever had with a girl. I say friendship rather than relationship deliberately, as I had never had a relationship with any girl. I had naturally expected Bea to sit in the front of the car alongside me. But when the time came to set off, Bea and her friend jumped into the back seat, meaning that the 14-year-old had to sit next to me. Thus began perhaps the longest journey of my life.

Johannesburg to Durban was a six-to-seven hours' drive, and I swear that the two girls in the back never stopped yapping for a moment of that journey. The noise behind was, in stark contrast to the near silence in the front. That journey was annoying, awkward and never-ending.

When – eventually – we arrived where we were all staying, the Butterworth Hotel in downtown Durban, to cap it all Bea announced that she would not be going out when she was in the city. She explained that the strict discipline of her self-imposed schedule whilst playing in a tennis tournament meant that there would be no socialising. I was left to my own devices.

Whilst I squired Durban's young beauties, Bea stuck faithfully to her regime, and the two of us would only see one another briefly to tell each other what had been happening. This arrangement would no doubt have continued until the finish of the tournament, had divine intervention not occurred when Bea pulled a muscle in her back and had to withdraw.

Although I was still sore about being expected to play the role of chauffeur, I asked Bea to join me for dinner that evening. And, as we were in Durban, I decided to take her to the famed Oyster Box Hotel & Restaurant in Umhlanga, then about half an hour's drive outside the city, today just 10 minutes on the motorway.

Although KwaZulu-Natal is the home of the Zulu nation, in the 1950s the area around Durban was predominantly populated by descendants of English settlers, who had been encouraged to the country to work in the coal mines, the other key component being large numbers of people from India. Catering, as it was, for this

Anglo-Indian amalgam, the Oyster Box had the unique feel of a colonial outpost. I loved it.

Bea admitted that she had never tasted oysters before but was persuaded to order half a dozen. So far, so good. But, the second that one was in her mouth, she decided that oysters were most definitely not for her. She promptly spat the oyster on to the floor. This rather indelicate manoeuvre – one which which was especially inappropriate for a young lady – was observed by most of our fellow diners. Our romance was very nearly over before it had even begun.

Fifty-four years later, in 2006, I was given the opportunity to buy the Oyster Box from Ken O'Connor's Trust, which owned the property. The ownership, with 11 Trustees, was complicated, but our desire to preserve and to build on the traditions of the Oyster Box was welcomed by almost every Trustee. In order to preserve the unique characteristics of the Oyster Box and its colonial past, but at the same time ensuring that the hotel met the demands of the 21st Century, we ended up demolishing and rebuilding the vast majority of the property. Our daughter, Toni, oversaw the two-year, R500 million project, under Bea's guidance and inspiration. Nine hundred guests, including IFP leader Prince Mangosuthu Buthelezi and Zulu King Goodwill Zwelithini, attended the Oyster Box's re-opening party in October 2009.

Distaste for oysters notwithstanding, our dinner in 1952 was a much more low-key affair. When the meal was over, I drove Bea back to Durban, pulling the car to a stop at the beachfront. We got out and sat astride the wooden fence at the top of a sandy bank leading down to the beach, and looking out to sea. We were laughing and telling each other jokes. One of my jokes required a little theatrical gesturing. As I raised my arms, I lost my balance completely and toppled over, tumbling down the bank and landing in a crumpled heap on the beach. As I tried to recover my composure and my dignity, I realised that Bea was laughing hysterically.

There is no doubt that this is the moment when it all began.

Over the following 48 hours, Bea and I realised that something had happened between us. Two days later, the two of us drove slowly

back to Johannesburg, this time with Bea in the front seat. When we
arrived back, my parents were waiting for me to tell me the sad news
that Uncle Frank had died in Cape Town. My mother's brother had,
of course, been unwell since he had been discharged from the army
almost 15 years earlier, but Frank was just 34 when he died. My
mother and I set off at once for Cape Town and for the funeral.

We were in Cape Town for four or five days, during which time I
wrote and posted my first letter ever to a girl. When it arrived, Bea
showed it to her mother whose response was direct and to the point:
"I hope he doesn't have any ideas!"

Whilst away, I also bought Bea my first gift to a girl, choosing
Mitsouko cologne by Guerlain. When I got back from Cape Town, I
went to see her. She thanked me for the gift and we chatted. As I was
leaving, I said, "I'll see you on Saturday night." "No. I can't," she
replied, "I'm going out on Saturday night." Surprised, almost hurt,
I said, "But I thought something had happened between us?"
Bea responded firmly, "Perhaps. But I don't believe in simply going
steady. Either we have an arrangement, or we don't." And thereby
hangs the tale.

In the post-war years, before air travel became commonplace,
although a certain amount of travel to other countries within Africa
took place regularly, this was not considered by South Africans to be
foreign travel. Foreign travel was a description restricted to the
infrequent and extended journeys taken by South Africans which
began with the boarding of a ship of the Union-Castle Line. This
meant that one was 'going overseas', beginning with a stop in Europe.

In late 1952, my parents, who had been talking of making a world
trip for a very long time, decided to take time out, travelling initially
to Europe, where they would spend three months, before heading
across the Atlantic to the United States and Canada. In all, they
would be away from home for six months. Part of the planning for
this trip included, I was informed, the closing-up of the family home
whilst my parents were away.

These announcements required me to reflect urgently, and
profoundly, on my life and on my future. My parents were about to

embark on a world trip. I was losing my home, albeit temporarily. I had just met a girl with whom I knew I wished to spend the rest of my life. And I had no feasible way of making a living which would sustain even me, let alone a wife and, who knows, a family. My parents may have been about to embark on an ocean voyage, but it was I who was 'all at sea'.

Bea and I had discussed the idea of getting married, but until now we had kept such thoughts to ourselves. We discussed what we should do in the light of my parents' news, and Bea suggested that we should begin by telling her parents of our plans to get married. Thus it was that one Saturday in late 1952, ten days before my parents were due to sail, I drove nervously to the Lurie home.

The Luries lived in the highly desirable Johannesburg suburb of Houghton, and had done since the early 1930s. Bea was a third-generation South African, and had been born in Johannesburg in 1933. Her father had also been born in South Africa, in Port Elizabeth. But her grandparents were from Europe, and had arrived in South Africa from Lithuania during the 19th Century. They were amongst those Jews who joined the Boers on their Great Trek into South Africa's hinterland.

The Tollmans and the Luries were very different families. Apart from my generation, my family was foreign born. Moreover, my father and other members of his family and his friends spoke Yiddish when they were together. The Luries, on the other hand, had all been born in South Africa and spoke English, although Bea's father also spoke Taal, the Afrikaner language.

The Tollmans were in the hotel business, whereas the Luries were traders, especially of hides and skins – even having a branch in the Congo, whence they sourced crocodile skins which they supplied to the smart shops of Paris. Many of South Africa's traders at that time were of Lithuanian origin and operated from the markets of Johannesburg's New Town, buying and selling meat, fish, poultry, cheese and eggs, and of course hides, skins and handbags.

In time, I was to learn that the Luries are a very large family with an immensely long recorded history which claims ancestry direct from King David. Amongst Bea's family tree are remarkable names such as Karl Marx, Yehudi Menuhin and Felix Mendelssohn.

I also learned that, as a child, Bea had lost an uncle who was very important to her. David Lurie – not to be confused with Bea's brother of the same name – was an exceptional scholar at the South Africa College School, Newlands and had in 1920 been selected to go to Lincoln College, Oxford University as a Rhodes Scholar. He had qualified as a doctor and, in 1934, had returned to South Africa to work as a registrar in the Department of Surgery at the University of Witwatersrand. He was enlisted into the Army during the War, and was tragically killed near Cairo in 1943, aged just 40. A Research Scholarship at the University of Witwatersrand bears his name today. Almost 70 years after his death, Bea still speaks often about her Uncle David.

Reuben Lurie, Bea's father, was everything as far as I was concerned. A man for all seasons, he was as happy in the company of leading Afrikaner politicians as he was with the medical men of the time. He dealt comfortably with international businessmen but also with the street traders of New Town. Whomsoever's company he was in, he spoke their language.

He was also a hugely successful businessman, and had built a company called Protea Holdings which was listed on the Johannesburg Stock Exchange. Protea had acquired the licence to a number of major international concessions, mostly linked to the medical profession. Seimens, DuPont and Squibb Pharmaceuticals were amongst Reuben's portfolio, as was the provision of x-ray equipment to hospitals throughout Africa. Protea also had concessions for other non-medical goods such as Wilson Sporting Goods.

Reuben Lurie was a man of great taste – well-read, well-travelled and with an encyclopaedic knowledge of fine wine. He was always immaculately dressed in tailored suits from Savile Row. His interest in literature was matched by his enjoyment of classical music and by his appetite for the finest things in life. He was a true renaissance man and could converse on almost any subject. Talking to Reuben Lurie was always an enlightening experience. Like me, he read biographies and, like me, he enjoyed learning about history. In many ways, we were interested in the same sorts of things. He also subscribed to a number of overseas magazines such as *US News & World Report*, and these he often shared with me, helping me to broaden my own interests and the horizon of my ambitions. He had a highly developed international perspective and an interest in global issues.

Rueben did a lot of business in Europe before the War and, whilst on a trip to Hungary, he developed a friendship with the Gabor sisters – Magda, Zsa Zsa and Eva – before they became internationally famous. Some members of Bea's family took the view that Reuben Lurie was a little too friendly by half with the Gabor sisters! Poland was another European market which he developed after much effort, and only after going to live there on his own for a while.

In all, he spent over two lonely years of his life in Poland, building relationships within the country's glove industry, and providing high quality African hides. But these business relationships almost got him into very serious trouble when he found himself in Poland during the summer of 1939, having gone there to collect some unpaid bills. When he became stranded almost immediately, there was great uncertainty as to his fate. Amongst Bea's most prized possessions is a letter which her father wrote, and somehow managed to send, during those days of uncertainty. Thankfully, he was able to secure a seat on what proved to be the last plane out of Poland before the Germans invaded in September 1939.

Having decided to tell Bea's parents of our plans to get married, I had arranged to meet her father first in order to tell him the news. I was understandably a little nervous. I remembered that when I had offered Bea a lift to Durban, Mr and Mrs Lurie had sent for my old school friend, Raymond Eskapa, whom they had known since he was about 14. They had demanded of Raymond a character reference for "this Stanley Tollman". I am sure, though, that their request did not have marriage in mind.

Nevertheless, months later Reuben Lurie and I now had a good rapport, developed through the extended conversations which always took place between us when I arrived to collect his daughter. These were lengthy not because Reuben and I were especially talkative, but because I was invariably kept waiting for Bea to get ready to go out. This was necessary because Bea, whose mother used to make most of her clothes, nearly always demanded a final, last-minute, fitting session during which various finishing touches were made to her outfit.

My conversations with Reuben were never awkward or difficult. On the contrary, they were always easy and fascinating. With my pharmaceutical background, he and I would often have long talks about developments in medicine, and inevitably we would touch on the sporting news of the day. From the day we met, he and I got on incredibly well and Reuben Lurie and I enjoyed an extremely close relationship for over 20 years until, in 1974, he died of shingles, aged 74. I still miss him.

I still miss Bea's mother too, but not for the same reasons. The lady who was to become my mother-in-law was a rather different kettle of fish. Although Reuben had welcomed unequivocally the news that I wanted to become his son-in-law, Blanche Lurie seemed a little concerned as to what trouble this young man was going to get her daughter into. Although she was herself married to a man who seemed to have a perpetual glint of excitement in his eye, she was very straight-laced.

I imagined from the almost baleful gaze with which she observed me that she wasn't entirely sure that marriage was a good idea. And her concern was probably well-placed. Over the years, I have certainly managed to create a good deal of grief for Bea and for all those around me. I just hope that this grief was more than outweighed by whatever happiness I have also engendered.

Fathers want everything for their children. I always say to my own, "When you no longer have your father, think of what he would have said to you now. He was one person that wanted nothing more from you than that you did your best. For him that was always good enough." Throughout their lives, I have told them to make sure that, on balance, their life would be judged at least 51% positive.

Perfection is neither achievable nor desirable. I am pleased to be able to report that their personal score has always proved to be in the positive and by rather more than a single percentage majority.

Having told my future in-laws of our plans, the next question was, "How to tell *my* parents?" This was difficult. We were not at all sure how pleased they would be with this news coming so close to their overseas trip, but we knew that we had to say something before they went. Bea and I talked it through and decided that we needed some advice. We decided to go and see my mother's youngest sister, Bertha, who was rather closer to being a pal than an aunt. Bertha had married an older gentleman during the War who became known to me as 'My Uncle Max'. Bea and I went together to their flat. Bertha and Max were thrilled with the news and were in no doubt as to what we should do. "Face it straight. Front it out – and soon." And that is just what we did.

Looking back now, I try to imagine what my parents must have really been thinking. Here was I, aged 22, having never so much as brought a girl home before. As far as they could see, I had an indifferent attitude to finishing my education and I had no prospects whatsoever. They were themselves within days of a major overseas trip. And I chose this time to announce that Bea and I wanted to get married. In their position, I have often wondered what my reaction would have been to this announcement.

Thankfully, my parents' reaction was completely supportive, and they were clearly very happy with the news. They did, however, ask for one condition: that we would wait to announce the engagement until they had returned from their overseas trip. That was tough. But of course we went along with it.

Our close friends all knew that we were privately engaged, and the next six months were very difficult for me, made much worse by the fact that my brothers and I had to move out of the family home! One can perhaps understand why my parents would not want to leave three young men alone for six months in a house which they both treasured, but it was rather inconvenient – for me at least.

Arnold was by this time away at medical school and was largely unaffected. And Ivan was at boarding school. But I was forced to spend the next six months camping in various rooms at the Palace Hotel. This did, of course, mean that I could keep an eye on the business whilst my parents were away.

With marriage on the horizon, I realised that it was time to sort out a few things. I met with Mike Chafkin, who by now had married my cousin Anne, and he asked me to return to the Maritime Pharmacy. I agreed a salary of £75 a month. In addition, my father had agreed to pay me £50 a month to keep an eye on things at the Palace Hotel, additionally allowing me use of the Chrysler whilst he was away. After a few weeks, the Luries offered me the use of their guest room on the occasional night. This meant that after dropping Bea off I would not need to drive back to the city to return to the Palace Hotel.

A month or so after my parents had left, I was invited by the Lurie family to join them for the family celebration of Rosh Hashanah, the Jewish New Year. The entire Lurie family would be gathered for this occasion with uncles, aunts, nephews, nieces and cousins from both sides of the family. The previous evening, when I was collecting Bea from the house, an aunt who had arrived early for the gathering said to me, "Would you please have a haircut, Stanley?"

Remember, this is 1952, a decade before The Beatles and the Rolling Stones, and the perception at that time as to what constituted long hair was not at all what it would become in the 1960s. I was nevertheless very proud of what I saw as a good head of hair and wore it in a somewhat floppy style. I had developed, with more than a little pride, the art of flicking it back. I politely told Bea's aunt that I had just had a haircut and that I did not propose taking another one in the near future.

I did not fully appreciate the significance of this exchange until the following day when I returned to the Lurie home. One of Bea's uncles, Uncle Solly, had a particular dislike of 'long' hair to the point of irrationality, possibly influenced by the fact that most of his own head was shaved. But this rather extreme perception appeared to have been adopted by much of the rest of the family as well. When I was ushered that night into a very large room, around the edges of which the whole of Bea's extended family were standing or seated, I politely said, "Good evening everybody," and wished the assembly a Happy New Year. The reaction to my entrance is still seared into my memory. It could not have been colder nor less welcoming. Not one person came across to introduce themselves, and the frozen silence in the room was broken only by a couple of extremely reluctant grunts. Bea was very upset by the whole episode. However close I may have become to Bea's parents, I still had a mountain to climb in terms of building a relationship with the rest of the Lurie family. I am pleased to report that I later successfully scaled the familial equivalent of the North Face of the Eiger, because Uncle Solly and I were to become the best of friends.

Disagreements were not restricted to my domestic life. In the days after my parents set sail, and in respect of a number of matters, I discovered that I did not see eye-to-eye with the manager at the Palace Hotel. There were confrontations between us which resulted in his announcement that he would be leaving as soon as my parents returned from their trip. I decided that this was no bad thing as I had my own plans. I had worked out that my future did not lie in higher education and had stopped going to lectures altogether. I made up my mind that it lay in the hotel business and that I would make this clear to my parents upon their return.

In June 1953, my parents got back from their overseas trip. In keeping with the practice of the time, they arrived laden with gifts for everyone in sight. Every relative and every member of staff received something. Bea got a blue cocktail dress for the engagement party and I was given a dinner jacket, in readiness for the forthcoming wedding.

As soon as the time was right, I made the announcement of my intention to pursue a career in the hotel business. To describe my parents' reaction as one of horror would be an understatement. They had found themselves in the hotel business almost by accident, and neither of them liked it. My mother could not wait to get away from it, and my father thought that it was quite simply not a good business for me to enter. They were both implacably opposed to my idea and desperately tried to dissuade me. But I made it absolutely clear to them that my mind was made up. I was determined to be a hotelier. It was no longer enough for me to help out from time to time. I wanted formally to join them in the management of the Palace Hotel. Very reluctantly, they realised that I was not to be shaken from my view, and there was no point in continued resistance. There was a new partner in the venture.

My first major management contribution to an improved Palace Hotel involved the restaurant. A friend of mine had just qualified as an architect, and I asked him to design an upgrade for the restaurant and for the lounge. The ultimate plan was to make the restaurant bigger, but the first stage of the redevelopment had the reverse effect. The restaurant had become an immensely popular place, but it had reached the limits of activity by virtue of its size and food offerings. Next to the restaurant was an area with a large piano, around which soldiers used to meet and to sing. It was already extremely popular, but not as profitable as I felt it should have been.

The first stage in the redevelopment meant, however, that the number of tables in the restaurant fell from 15 to just eight, albeit temporarily. Takings dropped proportionately and my parents, especially my father, expressed the view that my rash actions would bankrupt us. His fears were compounded when, as part of the next stage of the plan, I removed a wall – a particularly ill-conceived idea. What I considered to be an unimportant internal wall was in fact structural, and the whole building was in danger of collapse. Things looked dark indeed.

Once I had dealt with the structural emergency, I then sought help from my friend Robbie Blank, who was introducing a series of highly innovative materials and products into South Africa, most of which were based on plastic. From the perspective of the 21st Century it is difficult to imagine that plastic was ever viewed as both exciting and chic. But our introduction of Robbie Blank's plastic chairs into the restaurant at the Palace Hotel was an unbelievable success, and the redevelopment eventually proved to be a true money-spinner.

Focused now entirely on the hotel, I worked all day, seven days a week, and my father was able to take it much easier. My mother, too, was able to come into the hotel far less frequently.

Although the food in the restaurant was just as good as it ever had been, we went through a period when the shout, "Where's Mrs. Tolly?" became frequent and worrying. Such was the reputation of my mother's cooking, and the fear of its loss so troubling, that something had to be done about it. My father asked my mother to make a point of arriving surreptitiously at the hotel at 1.05pm every day, at which time she would conduct a slow and visible walk through the restaurant, creating the impression in our clients that she was still harnessed to the oven. Having completed this leisurely perambulation, she would then put her coat back on and go home. Everyone was happy.

In the meantime, I was the jack-of-all-trades, running the kitchen, acting as both *maître d'* and head waiter, and running the hotel itself when the restaurant was not open. The success of the hotel was almost overwhelming and the restaurant at the Palace became known as *the* establishment at which to eat. Our diners regularly included lords, ladies and millionaires. Although merely a 30-room hotel, it was immensely successful, returning an annual profit of around £50,000. For the early 1950s, especially at a time of almost non-existent tax, this was a great achievement.

From this point on, my life started to become more interesting. By dint of hard work, I was able to run a successful hotel, and also to go out and have fun. Bea and I went out dancing and to dinner parties, and we became regular clients at Ciro's. Although the two venues were completely independent of each other, the unashamed inspiration for Ciro's Johannesburg had been the world famous Ciro's in California. During the 1940s and 1950s, Ciro's Los Angeles was one of the hottest nightspots in the world, hosting performers and guests such as Frank Sinatra, Judy Garland, Marilyn Monroe and Humphrey Bogart. At the time, Ciro's Johannesburg was without question the city's top night spot, with a resident orchestra led by Sam Sklair. So well-known were Bea and I in Ciro's that when we arrived

Sam Sklair and his orchestra would invariably start to play our song – *Singin' in the Rain*, from the film of the same name which had been released the previous year. Almost sixty years later, *Singin' in the Rain* is now the ringtone on my mobile phone.

Two stories from Ciro's in the 1950s are worthy of a mention, although I will vouch only for the truth of the latter. The first story is Bea's, which I have heard her repeat often during our married life. It once again concerns my hair. (Somewhat ironic these days, when much of it has departed my scalp, never to return.) Bea alleges that one night whilst we were dancing at Ciro's, shortly after we had become engaged, she became aware that she had been facing in the direction of a wall for quite a time. She turned around and spotted an American girl, who she was convinced had been making eyes at me – and that I had been responding accordingly. She took me outside at once and, despite my unequivocal protestations of innocence, refused to believe me. Instead, she said that she hoped that my hair would disappear, along with my good looks. When Bea cuts what little is left of my hair nowadays – something which incidentally she has done throughout the whole of our married life – I remind her of that curse.

Whether or not the first story is the product of a fertile mind, the second concerns an incident at Ciro's one evening when I indeed committed a *faux pas* of which I am embarrassed even today. This stemmed from my misinterpretation of the contents of the refrigerator at Bea's home. To explain, the Lurie family's approach to food was one of disinterest, and the fridge at the Lurie home invariably contained very little. In fact, only two things could be guaranteed to be inside at all times – a bottle of milk and a Ball jar[14] full of caviar. I had assumed that caviar, in common with milk, was clearly a staple in some households, even though it did not feature in our own fridge. What I did not realise at the time was that Reuben Lurie was very friendly with a diplomat from the Black Sea region from whom there appeared to be a constant supply of caviar. Not only did I not know this, I also had no clue as to how much caviar cost. One night at Ciro's, in a party of about eight of us, I shouted to the waiter, "Caviar for everyone!" This proved to be a wonderful idea

---

[14] A proprietary brand preserving jar made of glass.

– until the bill arrived. The successful novelist Shirley Eskapa, a lifelong friend and the wife of my old schoolfriend Raymond Eskapa, was one of those in the party that evening. She often reminded me of the shock of picking up her share of the bill which I had so carelessly generated for us all.

Sadly, Shirley is no longer with us. She died in August 2011, aged 78. She had been married to Raymond for almost 60 years, and all that time she had been a writer. In Johannesburg, Shirley had been an active member of the white women's anti-*apartheid* resistance organisation, the Black Sash, and had been someone of interest to the secret police. Raymond eventually persuaded her that they should both leave the country of their birth, and they went first to Geneva and then to London. Bea and I miss Shirley a lot.

With my parents' return from their overseas trip, we were now at last able to announce to the world what our friends had known quietly for some months: that Bea and I were engaged to be married. My mother and father threw an engagement party at our home, but I discovered much later that my actions that evening almost cost me my marriage altogether.

My parents were keen that the engagement party was properly organised and wanted to greet their guests in person, expecting Bea and me to stand with them in the welcoming line. Bea was happy to do so but, for reasons which I can no longer remember, I point-blank refused. Bea promptly burst into tears and disappeared to the bathroom with a friend for what seemed like a very long time.

It was only many years later that I learned from that friend what had happened in the bathroom, and how close Bea was to calling off the wedding in the light of my appalling behaviour. Eventually, though, she felt able to go ahead with the wedding because, ironically, of the trust which she placed in my father. "Stanley's father is a decent human being, and I am going to go ahead with the marriage in the expectation that Stanley will grow up to be like his father." I hope she has not been disappointed.

THE PLANTING
OF OUR FIRST ACORNS

The success of the Palace once the war was over meant that my father and I were able to repay completely the loan from the brewers which had enabled the hotel to have been bought in the first place. This meant that we were now a 'Free House', no longer tied to any one brewery.

Towards the end of 1953, I had a visit to the Palace Hotel from a man who was to have an enormous impact on my future commercial life. The visitor was a gentleman called Mr Myburgh, one of the bosses of Ohlsson's brewery, responsible for South Africa's second most popular beer – Lion Beer. He had booked into the Palace with a couple of colleagues for lunch.

At the end of the meal he called me over to his table to introduce himself and to tell me how much he had enjoyed the food. He went on to tell me that Lion Brewery was completely rebuilding the Nugget Hotel, on the site of the original hotel in Nugget Road. The Nugget was situated in the commercial part of town, but across the road from a park, close to the Johannesburg suburb of Village Main. Amongst other things, the area was home to a number of engineering, media and other businesses. The South African Broadcasting Corporation was based there, as were the publishers of the magazine *Drum*. The *Drum* had been created two years earlier as *African Drum* by former test cricketer and author Bob Crisp and Jim Bailey, an ex-RAF pilot and son of financier Sir Abe Bailey. A family magazine aimed mainly at black readers, it would later become famous for its reporting of township life under apartheid.

Given the potential of the neighbourhood, Lion Brewery was of the view that, once refurbished, the Nugget Hotel would be a great success. Mr Myburgh had observed what a wonderful job had been done at the Palace Hotel, and he offered us a lease on the Nugget as a brand-new, 22-room hotel, but one without furniture, fixtures or fittings.

My father, with whom I discussed this, thought this was a good opportunity and I agreed to talk to Bea. The Nugget could clearly be an opportunity of great significance to the future Mr & Mrs Stanley Tollman. Once again, Robbie Blank was called upon for ideas and he and I sat down to plan how we would develop this hotel. After much consideration, Bea and I concluded that the Nugget represented a real opportunity for us.

The two of us entered into a long lease with the Lion Brewery, and thus became the new proprietors of the Nugget Hotel. We had rolled the first of our metaphorical dice in a life-long partnership which would bring us love, exhilaration, happiness, despair, success, friendship, treachery, satisfaction, disappointment and any other emotion or experience you might care to mention – with the possible exception of boredom.

On 7 March 1954, Bea and I were married. I was 23 years old and Bea was just 20. By the standards of the time, our wedding was a major event. My mother decided that she wanted us to pull out all the stops, to create something which, in fairness to her, was not really her style. She and the Luries agreed that the wedding reception should be held at the Carlton Hotel, Johannesburg's top venue. Three hundred and fifty people were invited and, well over 50 years later, the detail of that day remains etched in my memory.

Bea's parents insisted on picking up the bill, and they also gave us 10,000 shares in Protea Holdings as a wedding present, a gesture they repeated for each of their children. That share certificate was at the time worth about £7,500 – a great deal of money. Looking back, however, I realise now that I did not at the time appreciate the true value of this piece of paper. In fact, I admit that I did not really think about it much at all. I was perhaps more taken by the envelopes containing cash which we received from most of the guests to our wedding. Gifts in the form of money are of course a traditional part of most Jewish weddings, and Bea and I received an awful lot of cash that day.

The Luries were founding members of the Reform community in Johannesburg, Bea even teaching at the Reform shul and also singing in the choir. She was a wonderful singer; a coloratura soprano whose voice was so beautiful she was persuaded to enter competitions. Amongst the competitions which she entered was the Johannesburg Eisteddfod where she sang wonderfully. So well, in fact that she came second. Many people would have been delighted to have been ranked second in such an important competition. But it says more than a little about Bea's perfectionism that she reached the conclusion, having not won, that there was little point in continuing to sing competitively. She never did again.

Although the Luries were stalwarts of the Reform Synagogue, my parents, and indeed our entire family, were from the Orthodox community, which viewed the breakaway Reform Synagogue as being worse in many ways than the Catholics. When I arrived on that wedding day at the Reform Synagogue I was surprised to see Barnett Swerling, my mother's father, sitting outside. "Come on Beryl," I said, using the name by which the family always called him. "Let's go in." And I gestured to him to come with me. With a pained expression he shook his head and said to me, "I can't go in *there*." I sat with him outside the Synagogue for a few minutes before saying that I, of course, had little choice. Eventually, kissing me on the forehead, he wished me well. As I went in, he remained firmly outside. Once we were married, Bea joined the Orthodox Synagogue, much to the satisfaction of my parents' families. And Bea and I continued to worship at the Orthodox Synagogue until my father died twelve years later, after which we stopped attending.

My own relationship with Judaism is far from straightforward. Remember, I did not spend my formative years in the bosom of a Jewish family but largely within the confines and discipline of a Catholic boarding school. Traditions which are commonplace to most Jews were never ingrained in me. The one thing, however, that my father always told me was that I should live my life in accordance with the words of the Ten Commandments. Over the years, I have endeavoured faithfully to adhere to those principles. And Bea and I have tried to teach our children to do the same.

The cash which we received as gifts at our wedding provided the capital which Bea and I used to fit out and furnish the Nugget Hotel. Apart from the striking design which had been provided courtesy of Robbie Blank, I also sought assistance from an engineer with whom I had developed a friendship. Eric Marthinusen was 20 years older than me but we got on extremely well. I knew that he had developed a system for the fast freezing of food, and one day he and I devised an idea which I felt sure would make money.

Whilst at school, I had been invited by a Portuguese friend to spend a weekend in Lourenço Marques, today called Maputo, the capital city of Mozambique and a favourite playground for South Africans. Whilst I was in Lourenço Marques I remember the excitement of eating the Mozambique national dish, *Prawns Piri Piri*, which combines the fabulous local Mozambique prawns with the piri piri chillies from that part of the world. The remaining ingredients are olive oil, garlic and lime or lemon juice. Despite its many natural resources, and a surprising fact for a country that enjoys almost two thousand miles of coastline, South Africa does not produce prawns at all. *Prawns Piri Piri* was, therefore, a very special and exotic treat, and I felt certain that it would go down a bomb in Johannesburg.

Eric Marthinusen and I decided that a fast refrigeration plant should be built in Johannesburg close to the Nugget Hotel. We would then arrange to have prawns driven the five to six hours from Mozambique direct to the refrigeration plant. Until that point, prawns were not served in Johannesburg because the deep frozen prawns of the time became very soft upon thawing and were unsuitable for the sort of cuisine we had in mind. My friend Roy Wilson backed the establishment of the plant in Johannesburg[15] and *Prawns Piri Piri* were introduced to the restaurant of the Nugget Hotel. This was an overnight sensation and meant that the restaurant at the Nugget became a huge and immediate success, with people lining the stairs to the first floor restaurant as they waited for a table to be free. There was a little initial difficulty because some of our less sophisticated diners complained that the prawns were a little tough, but not everyone had worked out that one had to remove the shells.

---

[15] Subsequently a plant was built in Mozambique itself and the prawns were transported already fast frozen.

Within a year, restaurants serving *Prawns Piri Piri* had sprung up all over Johannesburg. But by then the Nugget's reputation was established.

A small point of clarification. I said earlier that I had not left the country until after I was married. But I have now admitted to a trip to Mozambique whilst I was still at school. There is no inconsistency, however. As I explained a little earlier, South Africans did not consider they had left the country and gone overseas unless and until they had crossed the ocean. Visits to other African countries did not count.

Having put the Nugget on the map with *Prawns Piri Piri*, we then made a second name for ourselves by serving the best fish in Johannesburg. Until then, fish had always been pan fried. Attempts to grill fish, especially on the bone, had rarely been successful. Restaurants never seemed able to ensure that fish was properly cooked. Either it was overcooked and therefore too dry, or the meat closest to the bone was still almost raw. Typically, the fish involved was a wonderful southern hemisphere white fish called kingklip. The ingredient was fabulous, but the end result rarely did justice to the raw material. Our solution was simple, involving the addition of a knob of butter inside the fish during the grilling process, with the fish being placed in the oven to finish off. This ensured that fish served in the Nugget were always perfectly cooked, a technique many of our restaurants use even today.

At the end of the Nugget's first year of trading, the accountant informed my father that the business had made a very great deal of money – £10,000, no less! My father told the accountant not to tell me, though, explaining that the information would go to my head. I think that he had misjudged me. Even in those days, it was not the money which fascinated me. Throughout my career, I have always wanted to build things – to create. In many ways, the money has merely been a by-product.

Indeed, the first and only thing I did with the money we made in the first year at the Nugget was to spend £2,000 on a new car for my parents. Bea couldn't believe it. Not only did we not have a new car, we didn't even have a car at all, just a station-wagon which I used to collect the vegetables each day, and which always smelled of cabbage. Bea was getting used to the way my mind worked, which was perhaps not always as she would have liked.

A year earlier, for instance, just after the opening of the Nugget, an incident occurred of which I am far from proud. By way of mitigation, I would say that my actions displayed my unswerving pursuit of excellence. More likely, though, they revealed an unattractive side of my character – or at least that is what my mother-in-law thought at the time.

Remember, this was a time long before Bea ever really became fully involved with the hotel kitchens, which had always been my responsibility. On the day in question, Bea and her mother happened, however, to be occupying a corner of the kitchen, where they were engaged in the writing up of clients' bills. This was well before the arrival of computer systems, and the meticulous calculation and preparation of bills all had to be done by hand.

As I walked into the kitchen in order to check on the food, I passed a waiter who was on the point of taking a plate out to a customer. On the plate was something which I thought immediately was nothing other than a travesty. "What's that!" I shouted. "Call that a monkey gland steak?"

A point of clarification may be required here for non-South African readers, who will be relieved to know that a monkey gland steak, a favourite of South Africans since the 1950s, has nothing whatsoever to do with monkeys. A monkey gland steak is a thinly-beaten fillet steak which is served with a liberal coating of a sauce made from tomatoes, Worcester sauce, chutney and other ingredients. It can look wonderful or – as in the case of the offending article before me at the Nugget – it can look dreadful.

"Call that a monkey gland steak!" I was so upset that I picked up the steak and threw it, plate and all, at the stoves, where it smashed into smithereens, splattering the chefs with the sauce which they had just sent out to a customer. A deathly silence followed, which was broken by my mother-in-law saying rather pointedly to her daughter, "Bea, I think I am going to take you home."

For the first six months, Bea and I had worked literally night and day. And every other member of the family pitched in. The Nugget had developed a very good night-time trade and my mother, father and mother-in-law gave us a huge amount of help.

To complicate matters, Bea announced that she was pregnant and we knew that arrangements had to change – and quickly. It was unthinkable to me that Bea and I could have a child and carry on living in two rooms over the shop, just as my family had done so often over the years. This was no way to contemplate bringing up a young family. I decided that we would have to get an apartment in the northern suburbs of Johannesburg. But apartments were at the time very hard to come by. However, a customer of the Nugget Hotel ran an estate agency and he offered to help. The result was a two-bedroomed apartment in Rosebank, meaning that Bea and I were able to move out of the Nugget.

To describe life at the time as hectic would be an understatement. We now had two hotels, both of which were doing good business and both of which made substantial demands upon all concerned. But this was not to be the limit of the challenge. To cap it all, at a lunch one day at the Nugget, Ted Sceales, the head of Chandlers Union Breweries, the third biggest brewery in South Africa, approached me with a proposition. He told me that they were rebuilding a hotel in Craighall Park, in the northern suburbs, close to the new and affluent district of Johannesburg called Hyde Park. This was an attractive area with huge open spaces and, although close to the city, the hotel was considered to be out of town. It had only 17 rooms but it had a large restaurant with a dance floor. Chandlers had looked at the restaurants at the Palace and the Nugget and believed that I was the person to run the rebuilt hotel. I discussed this proposal with my father and we concluded that we should take this on as well as the other two hotels. This represented an opportunity to realise the dream of creating a world-class restaurant in Johannesburg, close to an area where most of the affluent lived. I got ready to open my dream restaurant.

The rebuilt hotel was christened the Hyde Park Hotel. Although it was technically in Craighall Park, Craighall did not have the same cachet but the hotel at least faced onto the suburb of Hyde Park.

We named the restaurant The Colony after the famed New York restaurant which I had read about on our honeymoon, and which had been described as 'the most famous restaurant in the world'. The Colony in New York had originally been a Madison Avenue speakeasy, where the liquor was stored in an elevator which could be shunted down into the basement if the prohibition enforcement officers visited. But it had been taken over by the legendary Gene Cavallero, who cleaned up the place and opened an entrance to the very same restaurant, no longer from Madison Avenue but from fashionable East 61st Street. It had then been 'discovered' by the Vanderbilts, and the clientele at lunchtime was the original 'ladies who lunched', with women diners outnumbering the men by six to one.

I had also read that the most important reason for the success of The Colony in New York was that Gene Cavallero was completely committed to the business and was always on hand to greet patrons personally and to make everyone feel both special and welcome. I took this to heart.

I starting by preparing as well as was humanly possible for the opening of The Colony. I worked for months on the menus. In Johannesburg in the 1950s there was a vibrant international community comprising entrepreneurs, hustlers and go-getters – every single one of them looking for opportunities in the City of Gold. I came up with the idea of having a menu containing 42 dishes, all of which were priced at 25/-[16]. Although this was a full price for a meal, in 1955 it also represented great value, the reason being that, for one price, guests could eat as much or as little as they wished. Diners could also choose to eat as many dishes from the menu as they wanted, and all for the same fixed price.

The food on the menu featured everything up-market which was available in South Africa. A few examples were smoked salmon, asparagus, mixed hors d'oeuvres, chicken liver paté, fillet steak, grilled

---

[16] One pound five shillings in pre-decimal currency.

kingklip[17], curry served in a coconut shell, duck in cherries, grilled farm ham on the bone and flaming lamb skewers. There were usually three soups available and these, and indeed everything else on the menu, were always of the highest quality.

And the wine? Although South Africa is today viewed as one of the world's great wine-producing countries, in 1955 it was not even a wine-*drinking* country. Those wines which were consumed were almost all imported. And in that our wines were no exception. But the choice of our wine offering *was* exceptional. Our wine list featured famous names like Dom Perignon, Château Lafite Rothschild, La Tâche, Romanée-Conti and Château d'Yquem.

I had decided that my restaurant would have continuous music from 8.00pm to 1.00 am Tuesdays to Fridays. On Saturdays, local Sunday observance laws required us to close at midnight. In order to provide continuous music, we needed two bands. I turned first to Bea's uncle, Arthur Harris, who had created the first South African-based record company, Truetone Records. I gave him a brief and he put together a five-piece band for us. For the second band, I approached the musical director for Sam Sklair, the regular band at Ciro's, to form a second group, but this time with a drummer.

Having decided on my music, I then picked some of the best chefs who had worked for my parents at the restaurants at both the Palace and the Nugget. I now had my kitchen complement. Finally, I turned my attention to the decoration of the restaurant and chose a black and white theme with a red carpet. The restaurant at The Colony became Bea's first decorating assignment, expressing its monochrome scheme with the use of black and white squares, even commissioning black and white fabric from which the curtains were made.

We already had responsibility for two hotels in the city and we were now gearing up to open a third. We decided to employ a couple as resident managers at the Hyde Park Hotel and my mother suggested that we should engage her youngest sister and her husband. At the same time, I hired a manager for the Nugget and a manager for the Palace. The Hyde Park duly opened for business with my aunt and uncle as managers, and its restaurant welcomed diners with a

---

[17] Kingklip is the Afrikaans word for a delicious eel-like seafish found in South African waters.

tremendous fanfare. The Colony restaurant, with its new menu, was a great success and it was soon booked out every night. In the middle of all this, our first child – a son – was born. Wynn arrived on 8 July 1955. We were now really running, and I was having to arrive five days a week at The Colony fully dressed to act as host for the evening. My work there rarely finished before two in the morning but this did not excuse me from having to pick up my father at precisely 8.45 the following morning to go together to the office at the Palace.

Wynn's arrival meant, of course, that Bea was away from the hotel for a while but she gradually returned to work, helping my aunt to supervise the kitchen at the Hyde Park. Everything seemed to be going well until, a few weeks later, I arrived one day at the Hyde Park at 4.00pm one Friday to discover that the bar was closed, with people waiting outside it. I was informed that my uncle was still on the green at his bowling club! As is so often proved to be the case, there are many plus points of involving family in business. But these are heavily outweighed by the minuses if things ever go wrong. The break-up with my aunt and uncle was acrimonious and very painful.

My father decided that we should replace my aunt and uncle with my mother's cousin, Alfred Proops and his wife. (Alfred and Fanny were the parents of Anne Proops, who had married Mike Chafkin.) Alfred had been born in England and was a man with a pleasant enough personality. In my view, though, he was completely unsuited for what I was trying to achieve at the Hyde Park. He was not, and in my mind never could be, a world-class hotelier. My father realised that I could not work with Alfred, and he did not press the suggestion. It was about this time that my father, who had been trying to hold the reins until then, appeared to recognise that not only was I a young man in a serious hurry, but I was a young man whom he could restrain no longer.

I remember that my father came over to the Nugget one day and found that I had done something of which he did not approve. He shouted at me there and then – right in the public area of the hotel itself. But this was the last time he shouted at me. I think he realised that it was neither a good nor a productive thing to do. In any case, shouting was not even his way, and he never once shouted at my brothers. His normal method of expressing disapproval was what I used to call his 'deep freeze', a much more effective method. The 'deep freeze' is something which I have used over the years to great effect with my own children. But I can never sustain the *froideur* anything like as well as my father could. I think it is because I have a naturally explosive temperament, one which I have to try to control. But any inclination I have to temper passes as quickly as it arrives.

The last words my father ever said to me were spoken as he was wheeled off for an operation from which he never recovered. He looked at me and, referring to the incident that day at the Nugget, said simply, "I am sorry that I shouted at you."

Having thought about the management of the Hyde Park at some length, my father told me that he had concluded that the only way that I would get it right at the hotel would be if Bea and I moved into the property. This was very difficult. Bea and I had recently moved from Rosebank into a beautiful garden apartment in the suburb of Illovo. I did not savour the idea of breaking the news to her. But, without a murmur of disagreement, Bea accepted that this had to be. And with Wynn just six months old, we moved into the Hyde Park. Bea worked in the kitchens and I was front of house.

This moment represented a crucial turning point for Bea and me. I concluded that in order to pursue the business career which was now clear in my mind, we should sell the two city hotels and concentrate our energies entirely on the running of the Hyde Park and The Colony – with one exception. The experience of decorating both The Colony and the new apartment had made both Bea and me realise that she was really good at interior design and, for her, a new career was born. Bea took over responsibility for decoration, and I never decorated anything ever again. Our daughter Toni has inherited her mother's flair for decoration and both she and Bea keep me at a distance, although they do tell me that I am a wonderful adviser.

In 1956, having tried out a few local acts to entertain guests in The Colony, I decided we needed instead to adopt a more international approach. Although some of our acts had gone on to achieve levels of worldwide fame, this was not the same as booking artists of true international standing. I decided to set my sights further afield and on one of the great entertainment centres of the world – London. Leaving Bea in charge, I made my first overseas trip to London where I fulfilled a long-held ambition and stayed at the Savoy Hotel. I had grown up with dreams of the world's most famous hotel, and of Auguste Escoffier, the Savoy's legendary chef of past years. Now, at last, I would experience the hotel for myself. I would also able to meet up with Arnold in London, where he had now completed his graduate studies en route to becoming a dentist. He had also got married. Before setting up in practice in South Africa, he was spending a year in England whilst he finished his training, and he was living in Dolphin Square.

When I arrived in London, in my pocket was an introduction from our local entertainment agent in South Africa addressed to the Grade Organisation, where I went to meet Leslie Grade. Leslie Grade was the brother of Lew Grade, the Russian-born English impresario and media mogul. Lew Grade had become one of the biggest figures in the world of popular entertainment. When, aged just 11, he had been asked the question, "What is two plus two?" he had famously replied, "Are you buying or selling?"

Lew and Leslie had grown up in London together with their third brother, who became Bernard Delfont. (They had each been born with the surname Winogradsky – Lew and Leslie adopted Grade, Bernard chose Delfont.) The three of them had attended a school in Bethnal Green, east London, where Yiddish was spoken by almost all the pupils. Leslie, whose son is Michael Grade, was Britain's foremost talent agent. At the time I went to see him he was booking the ITV variety show, *Sunday Night at the London Palladium*, hosted by Tommy Trinder, later to be hosted by Bruce Forsyth. This show was broadcast every week by Lew Grade's ATV. Over the years, the programme featured everybody who was anybody from the field of popular entertainment. Leslie provided a wonderful entrée to this world.

Over the next three years, The Colony featured great cabaret, with many of the big names of the period travelling to South Africa at our behest – names such as Petula Clark, Roy Castle, Dickie Valentine, Anne Shelton and Alma Cogan. Typically, a performer would arrive with an accompanist. With performance fees and travel and accommodation expenses, there was often a significant outlay of cash. In order to reduce the cost to The Colony we created a cabaret circuit within Africa. We contacted friends in Nairobi who owned the famous open-air Equator Club, other friends in Brazzaville, Leopoldville, Salisbury in Rhodesia, Blantyre and later in Durban. We succeeded in turning this circuit into a proper business and occasionally I would promote a concert at the City Hall in Johannesburg along with the artist, who would then get a share of the box office take.

The Colony quickly gained an international reputation for the quality of its food, its entertainment and its unique atmosphere. In those years, every night at The Colony was just like New Year's Eve. Bea often says that she would give everything to have one more night at The Colony as it was then. As the *Rand Daily Mail*[18] wrote about us at the time:

> *All the best people wine, dine and dance at The Colony. At least Trevor Bailey and the other MCC stars did last cricket season. That's why a cordial invitation is extended to Ian Craig's Australians to motor out to Craighall, Johannesburg's flash suburb, and do so this season – if they think Trevor Bailey is one of the best people!*
>
> *Funnily enough, Stan Tollman, The Colony boss, was in Britain a few days ago and stumbled across Bailey, who said: "Let's dine and I'll show you how London serves a crayfish thermidor." Afterwards, the famous English cricketer had to give "best" to The Colony.*

Because The Colony became *the* place to hold one's wedding reception, we worked many of our Sunday nights. And on Monday we ran gourmet dinners with spectacular food and wines to match. The competitive effect of all of this on the Johannesburg hospitality business was remarkable. Leading restaurants brought in

---

[18] *Rand Daily Mail*, 11 October 1957.

international chefs and our competition stiffened. Johannesburg night clubs gained a worldwide reputation. At one point, The Colony was just one of six top night spots where one could dine and dance, with two or three offering international cabaret as well.

The Colony was, however, the only venue in the northern suburbs. This meant we were closer to people's homes. We also had extensive parking. When we created The Colony, the hotel had a terrace which was enclosed in glass, but we covered its walls with travel posters and opened a separate restaurant called The Hydeaway. This offered breakfast, lunch and dinner but with a totally different menu to that offered by The Colony. Apart from her prowess in decorating, Bea had also shown an enormous talent for cooking. She spent hours perusing cookery books and magazines from around the world and she taught all our chefs – who were nearly always black or Indian – new ways of cooking. Almost without exception, these chefs showed the most incredible talent and, over the years, displayed greater proficiency than international chefs who had turned up in South Africa and whom we occasionally employed.

There were, however, exceptions to this rule, Monsieur Raymond Oliver being one of them. Burt Fellows, co-editor of South African Gourmet, wrote in 1957[19]:

The event of the week was the visit to The Colony of Monsieur Raymond Oliver, international celebrity and French culinary ambassador.

While Monsieur Oliver and Mr Stanley Tollman talked shop over a glass of the recently introduced Taylor's Cream Sherry, I went through the comprehensive menu. Knowing Monsieur Oliver's liking for fish, I ordered Trout Meunière. In recent years South African trout has rightly become renowned. The cold waters of the Magaliesberg are conducive to forming a firm flesh on the prince of fresh water fish. The famous chef ordered Pigeons Saumi, a speciality of The Colony. Monsieur Oliver invented a famous dish, Pigeons Rainier III for the ruling monarch of Monaco but paid tribute to the quality and serving of pigeon at The Colony. He was particularly impressed with the meatiness and gamey flavour of the domestic bird, and congratulated the chef.

19 *Rand Daily Mail,* 1 November 1957.

The restaurateurs exchanged menus and recipes. Monsieur Oliver was pleased to hear that Mr Tollman and I had dined at his internationally famous Grand Vefour restaurant in Paris and he invited Mr Tollman to spend a month in his kitchens. The offer was accepted.

At around this time I started to write a regular weekly column for the *Rand Daily Mail* which appeared every Friday and which talked about the latest in food and drink, and in which I recounted my experiences from my visits to Europe. Here is a smattering of my contributions from that period:

In the last three years the number of restaurants, clubs and dinner-dansant restaurants in Johannesburg has more than doubled. At various places of entertainment throughout our fair city we find 'big names' appearing nightly. As the demand for more and better entertainment increases, so the standard of food, wine and service improves in establishments throughout the city.[20]

Having just returned from London, where one can today eat as well as anywhere 'at a price', nostalgically one thinks of fish at Wheelers, Simpsons of the Strand for roast beef, Le Coq d'Or where Henri Sartori still greets one at the door and one has baby poussin on the open spit. The Savoy Grill is still supreme and the grouse incomparable.[21]

Various words have been written of late of what I shall call the 'platter' controversy. Certain people are of the opinion, because food is served in a restaurant on a platter, it should hold liberal portions. Being the originator of 'platters in restaurants', our original intention was to provide space in which to serve a sufficient portion of food, leaving enough room to add vegetables and salad without creating a 'stew'.[22]

When Raymond Oliver, culinary ambassador supreme, visited our city recently, he passed on to Derek Goodman a famous lobster recipe which has added to his international fame (Raymond's, not Derek's). This lobster in champagne is done in the following way. The meat of the tail is carefully removed and sliced, soaked in champagne – La Residence 'Gout Americain' is recommended – and placed back in the shell.

[20] *Rand Daily Mail*, 15 November 1957.
[21] *Ibid*, 18 October 1957.
[22] *Ibid*, 8 November 1957.

*The meat is covered with camembert cheese from Stellenbosch, and
mashed potatoes are placed around the shell in the pan, and baked lightly.
A wonderful dish!*

*When a certain international celebrity visited The Colony recently,
he sampled some of our newly imported Red Beluga Caviar (Red for
beyond the Iron Curtain, not colour). His favourable comments made me
decide to serve this delicacy on New Year's Eve.*[23]

In 1958, Wynn, who was now three years old, was joined by a
sister, Toni, who was born on 13 October. Having disposed of the
Palace and the Nugget and therefore with only one hotel to manage,
we had much more free time during the afternoon to spend with the
children in leisure and later in school activities. I had always shown a
capacity for horse-riding and, over time, became interested in polo.
This interest led to our owning a stable-full of horses and polo ponies.
This in turn meant regular admonishments from my father, who told
me that, whilst I slept, the horses were still eating. These words fell on
unreceptive ears. Until, that is, I got a polo ball in the mouth during
a game, which required 16 stitches in my palate. If I am honest, my
enthusiasm for the game waned a fair amount as a result.

This was an extraordinary period of our lives. A period during
which we met many new people, a great many of whom became our
lifelong friends. It was an exciting time. We were at the heart of
Johannesburg's riding set, a group which was more English than the
English themselves, and which made The Colony their place.

After Bea and I had been living at the Hyde Park for some
months, two things happened at about the same time. First, having
sold the other two hotels, my parents embarked on another overseas
trip. Second, Bea and I decided that it was now time to buy a
house in order to create a home for ourselves. We located a rather
run-down house in Melrose which was overgrown with creepers
but which had great potential. It sat in two-and-a-half acres of
land and had a tennis court and a swimming pool. However,
notwithstanding the pool, the tennis court and the fact that the
house was spacious, the accommodation itself was very basic.

[23] *Rand Daily Mail*, 13 December 1957.

Unquestionably, though, it had potential. The only issue was whether we could afford to exploit that potential.

It was at this point that the shares which Bea's parents had given us as a wedding present six years earlier suddenly came into their own. We sold these and used the cash that we had realised in order to buy the house. But it needed a great deal of work and our budget was already exhausted. For the first two years that we lived there, we closed off the sitting room and didn't use it in order to save money. And we used the handymen from the hotel in order to complete the necessary refurbishments elsewhere. When my parents returned from their overseas trip my father was shocked to discover that we had moved out of the hotel. He thought that the business would deteriorate if we were not living over the shop. My father was right about many things in life but, on this occasion, I am happy to say he was proven wrong.

The new house in Glenhove Road, Melrose transformed our lives. Having become accustomed to life within the physical constraints of hotel rooms, we now found ourselves with a dining room, a bar with a playroom, a nanny's room and sufficient bedrooms for the children of a growing family to have one each. The house provided a wonderful base for our family. In the middle of the grounds was a huge Eastern Plane tree with vast spreading branches under which we put a table and lots of chairs. Every Sunday we would invite friends for lunch at which we would always serve delicious food and often a braaivleis – the Afrikaans word for grilled meat. This would, of course, be cooked outside on coals, the Afrikaans word for barbecue, braai, coming from the the word for roasted meat itself. There would always be a wonderful lunch under the tree followed by lots of tennis, swimming and great company.

One of the entertainers whom we had hired to perform at The Colony was the late Roy Castle, who became a great friend, and who sent us a thank you for lunch under the plane tree in the form of a brass bell which arrived accompanied by a note which said:

"Nail this bell to yonder tree,
and when it rings just think of me."
Baie Dankie Stan and Bea[24]
Love R.C.

We have that bell to this day.

Unless there was a wedding reception, The Colony was closed on a Sunday. On Sunday evenings, therefore, we regularly held parties at the house where our visiting performers often entertained our guests. We also had a 16mm movie projector and the playroom would be converted to a private cinema, screening the latest movies.

In February 1959, a young Englishman called Mickie Most appeared at The Colony, in his first ever appearance in South Africa. Mickie had been born Michael Peter Hayes, the son of a regimental sergeant-major from Aldershot. He had decided to change his name, emigrate to South Africa and become a pop star. Mickie Most and the Playboys appeared at The Colony several times en route to no fewer than 11 Number One singles in South Africa. But after just three years, he returned to the United Kingdom, where he gave up performing, instead becoming one of the world's most successful pop managers and producers. Within a very few years he discovered the Animals and Herman's Hermits, and had produced hit records for artists such as Donovan, The Seekers, Jeff Beck and Nancy Sinatra.

Later in 1959, we brought Jean Sablon to sing at The Colony. Jean was one of the most widely acclaimed male French singers of all time, whose popularity rivalled that of Maurice Chevalier. He had been born in the outskirts of Paris in 1906, and into a very musical family. His sister, Germaine, was in London with Charles de Gaulle during the Second World War, from where she had made popular *Le Chant des Partisans*, a song which was to become an anthem of the French Resistance.

Before the War, Jean had been a regular performer at a Paris cabaret called *Le Boeuf sur le Toit*, where he had become a close friend of Jean Cocteau and where he had joined forces with Django Reinhardt and Stéphane Grappelli to perform, and to make his first

---

[24] Baie Dankie is Afrikaans for 'Thank you very much'.

jazz records. A frequent visitor to *Le Boeuf sur le Toit* was the Prince of Wales, who became a firm fan of the trio.

In 1937, Jean made his first visit to the United States, where he became known as 'The French Troubadour' and 'The Latin Lover'. He spent two years there, singing on stage and on the radio, and featuring on the CBS Hit Parade, where he ranked higher than Frank Sinatra. In America, he also realised for the first time the significance of the microphone. When Jean Sablon died, James Kirkup wrote in *The Independent:*

> Sablon made the great discovery that a mere technical tool, a microphone, could be humanised. He made it part of his body. He made love to his mike, cradling it in his hands like a lover's face, stroking it, whispering words of love to it, smiling at it with his ironic yet tender smile. He used it not for vulgar volume, but to refine the artistry in the delivery of the most banal lyric. He was the first popular singer to know how to conduct a personal relationship between his voice and his mike. It was amplification as art.

Mr Kirkup went on to admit that he had seen Jean Sablon perform during a season at the London Palladium in 1948, and had been so moved that he *"had wept through the performance"*.

Frequently referred to as the French equivalent of Bing Crosby, Jean Sablon later worked with the likes of Cole Porter and George Gershwin, and his records sold in millions around the world. Having worked extensively on Broadway, Jean Sablon had become a legend in the United States as well as Europe and was well-known to the international community in Johannesburg. The demand for tables at The Colony was unprecedented. We found that we had to open on Monday night in order to accommodate demand. Seating guests at The Colony during the residency of Jean Sablon was a nightmare, one which was repeated each and every day. Everyone wanted tables close to the performing area and some guests offered waiters extraordinary tips in the hope of improving the table which they had been allocated.

Jean Sablon was originally booked for two weeks, but we extended the stay twice and he ended up performing for four full weeks. During that period, our reservations book looked like a Who's Who of Africa and even 'Monty' himself – Field Marshal Montgomery – turned up one evening, taking pride of place at what we considered the 'King of Tables', the table by the fireplace. During his residency, Bea and I took Jean and his manager, together with Roy Wilson and his wife, to the game reserve at the Kruger National Park near Lourenço Marques. This trip cemented a friendship which was to last for the rest of Jean's life. He came back to South Africa for a second visit, and later Bea and I would visit him at his home in Cannes-La-Bocca whenever we were in France. The last time we saw him was a few months before he died, in 1994, aged 87.

NEW HORIZONS

Jean's residency at The Colony was, without question, the most profitable we had achieved with any entertainer, and by a very considerable margin. In fact, we had made so much money that we were able to approach the breweries and buy the freehold of the Hyde Park Hotel together with its adjoining land.

I thought this would impress my father. He and I had disagreed about the pricing of the Jean Sablon residency, which we both knew was likely to be a great success. He had wanted to charge an additional five-shilling supplement, whilst Bea and I insisted on sticking to the standard all-inclusive price of 25 shillings, which included dinner with its 42 dishes. "You could have bought the freehold on two hotels if you had charged the five-shilling supplement," was my father's attitude. And perhaps he was right.

Nevertheless, Bea and I had been married for just five years, and we were already the proud owners of a prime piece of income-generating real estate. It was against this backdrop that we decided to take our first trip to the United States and Canada. My mother had a cousin who lived between homes in Ontario and Florida and whom my mother had not seen since 1948. Although the cousin was much older than us, Bea and I decided to visit. This was March 1959.

We started by taking a South African Airways Douglas DC6 to London. This was a four-engined propeller-driven aircraft with a range which required us to stop twice en route in order to refuel. Whilst in London, we booked a few new acts for The Colony and then travelled on to Paris to visit Jean. It was from Paris that we then took our first flight on a jet-engined aircraft – a Boeing 707 on its recently-introduced transatlantic jet service to New York. This was exciting stuff. We were, though, to be brought sharply to earth very soon indeed.

We were booked to fly onwards within a couple of hours on an internal flight to Miami. However, when we landed at Idlewild Airport (later to be renamed John F Kennedy) we did so in the middle of what we were later told was the worst snowstorm for 30 years. Having passed through immigration, we were informed that there were not only no flights to Miami but to nowhere else either. Worse, there were no available hotel rooms. Neither were there any taxis. I am not sure what the expression being stuck up a gum tree is really all about but, whatever it is, this felt very much like it.

Thankfully, we had been given a number of introductions to people in New York by various American friends in Johannesburg. One such introduction was to the owners of the "21" club, at that time one of the most famous restaurants in New York, if not the world. "21" was not a club in the true sense of the world but an establishment where, until the proprietors considered you suitable, you would not even be allowed through the front door. I called the club, spoke to one of the owners and explained our predicament. "Hang fast," was the reply. "And don't worry. We'll have a car at the airport for you within the hour." Remarkably, they did just that.

I had read a great deal about "21". I knew that the club had originally opened as a speakeasy in Greenwich Village in the Prohibition era, but had subsequently moved to 21 West 52nd Street from which address it had it had acquired its name. It had been established by two cousins – Jack Kreindler and Charlie Berns – who had the good sense to realise that prohibition could not last for ever, and decided to relocate to the basement of an elegant old brownstone building in an otherwise exclusively residential area.

Preparing for the time when they could sell alcohol legitimately, Jack and Charlie studied everything there was to know about fine wines and liquors, but until 1933 they were forced to continue illicitly. Although raided by the police on numerous occasions, the two were never caught. As soon as a raid began, a system of levers was used to tip the shelves of the bar, sweeping the liquor bottles through a chute and into the city's sewers.

When they were able at last to trade openly, their preparations paid off, and they soon let it be known that there were two types of customers who would not be welcome at "21" – actors and journalists. The reaction from these two groups to being banned was remarkable, with celebrated actors and journalists alike almost *demanding* to be allowed entry. The owners relented in the case of actors – the more celebrated the more accommodating Jack and Charlie were – but in the case of journalists, especially gossip columnists, they stood firm. "21" took the view that the privacy of their patrons was of prime concern. There is little doubt that this helped to make the reputation of the club. Celebrities flocked to it and, with the exception of George W Bush, every President of the United States since Franklin Delano Roosevelt has dined at "21".

Bea and I were driven into Manhattan through the snow, amazed that someone was willing to be so helpful to complete strangers on the basis of an introduction from others. What was even more amazing, given what we had been told about there being no hotel rooms free anywhere that night, was that the car drew up at a hotel only a block away from "21", which was expecting our arrival. We were shown to our room, where we were able to freshen up, before heading off to the table at the "21" club which we knew was being held for us.

We were dropped off by the driver outside the famous Iron Gate which, even today, is the trademark of "21". We passed through, and then climbed the exterior steps past a dozen or so life-sized statues of jockeys, their racing colours obscured in part by the snow. Entering the bronze doors of "21" itself was an absolutely unforgettable experience. Benjamin Franklin once said, "The taste of the roast depends on the handshake of the host." Nothing more apposite could have been written about the man who greeted us that evening and who would, over the years, become one of our closest friends. Jerry Berns, brother of one of the founders of "21", had taken to the restaurant business like a duck to water. When he died in 2007, aged 99, it was said about him that he was the only person on the New York restaurant scene, other than Joe Baum[25], who really had

---

[25] Joe Baum was the restaurateur and innovator credited with America's first themed restaurants, including The Four Seasons Restaurant, Windows on the World, Quo Vadis, Tavern on the Green and the Rainbow Room.

the ability to understand customers and treat them in the way in which they wanted to be treated. He had a remarkable ability for matching names to faces, and for making people feel at home.

It was clear to Bea and me that "21" was a restaurant like none we could imagine. It had no fewer than three regular dining rooms and three bars, and the restaurant's scarlet-jacketed waiters were just the public face of a team which was 250-strong. Two Cadillac limousines were always on hand for VIP guests, and the restaurant featured both a barber's shop and a tailor's shop.

Three hours after landing at the airport in a blizzard, we found ourselves sitting at a table in the middle of the most remarkable and vibrant restaurant in the world. Around us, every table was vibrant in red and white checked tablecloths and, even though the weather outside was frightful, every table was occupied. Each of the bars was four-deep with people. The buzz of excitement was almost tangible. My eyes glanced down to a brass plaque which revealed that we had been seated at Table 30 – Humphrey Bogart's no less – and the table at which he had become engaged to Lauren Bacall in 1944. A few hours ago we had felt as though we had been condemned to purgatory. Miraculously, we were now in heaven.

The next morning the car was sent to pick us up once more, this time to take us back to the airport. The snow had cleared and we were able to fly down to Miami and get our first glimpse of Miami Beach. Even then, the Berns' hospitality continued. Jerry and his wife, Martha, telephoned the very next day to ensure that we had made it safely to our destination and to enquire about the date of our return to New York. During the course of that conversation, Bea must have mentioned that we were about to celebrate our fifth wedding anniversary. Without hesitation, Jerry and Martha said that they would throw a party for us upon our return. Bear in mind that I am just 28 years old and Bea is 24. And the owners of the most famous restaurant in the world are offering to throw a party for us? This is heady stuff indeed.

In Miami and in Palm Beach, we met so many people whose names were known internationally that Bea's hands shook almost constantly from nerves. It was overwhelming. The introductions that we had been given in South Africa seemed to open every door. We were invited out to parties and to the finest shows and introduced to fascinating people wherever we went. We were invited to a performance by Jan Peerce, the great American tenor and one of the stars of the Metropolitan Opera Company. Imagine the honour for two young South Africans when we were then invited to have dinner with him after the performance. This was an extraordinary trip, one in which we also made some remarkable friendships.

We then went on to visit cousins in Hamilton, Ontario, just outside Toronto, and although we had thoroughly enjoyed our experiences in the United States, generally speaking most of the people we had met were significantly older than us. But when we got to Canada we were able to get together with people of our own age group, for the first time meeting various cousins and their friends. By this time, we had been away from South Africa for about a month and in many ways we were looking forward to getting back home. But on our way back, we stopped of course in New York for two events, one planned, the other unforeseen, before going on to Washington, and to our journey home.

The planned event was the party which the "21" club threw for us on 4 May 1959 to celebrate our fifth wedding anniversary, and to which no fewer than 150 guests had been invited. We still have the menu from the dinner that evening which is signed by many of those who were present. It contains the names of some of New York's most famous families. The menu also displays the wonderful cuisine of the time which "21" offered its guests:

Amuses Bouches

---

*Borscht en Gelée
avec
Perles du Volga*

Coquilles St Jacques

---

*Agneau de Printemps
Bouquetière*

Salade de Saison

Fromages Assortis

Gateau St Honoré

New York had seen us satisfy all our restaurant dreams and more besides. We had even lunched at the original Colony and met its renowned owner, Gene Cavallero, about whom we had read so much. But New York had one remaining surprise for us. On our last night there, we decided to drop in to El Morocco, the Manhattan nightclub on East 54th Street which was famous for its blue zebra stripe motif and for its associations with the rich and famous. When the time came for us to leave, Bea and I were passing a table when I almost fell over a man whom I had never expected to see in New York. This was John Schlesinger. Not, I hasten to add, the film director famous for *Midnight Cowboy* and *Far From the Madding Crowd* but the remarkable son of the legendary I W Schlesinger, one of South Africa's most famous industrialists.

The 5ft 2in Isadore William Schlesinger was, ironically, an American salesman from Manhattan's Lower East Side who, in 1896, had chosen to emigrate to Cape Town in the middle of the Gold Rush. Acting as a salesman for America's Equitable Life Insurance, he sold policies to the gold miners and anyone else who would listen, earning a record US$30,000 a year in commissions – an absolute fortune in the 19th Century. Encouraged by this success, he first set up his own insurance company in South Africa and then turned his hand to real estate. He brought the chain store, the cafeteria and the American-style drugstore to South Africa, as well as buying up most of South Africa's nascent movie industry, both production and distribution. He then moved into catering and to the hotel and restaurant business. When he died in 1949, I W Schlesinger was involved in nearly every sector of the South African economy.

John Schlesinger had inherited the business upon his father's death, at the tender age of 26, along with an American passport and a Harvard education. John had a reputation as a playboy with a love of speedboats and a keen eye for judging beauty queens. Even though I found him drinking in the small hours in a Manhattan nightclub, I was aware that, nine years into the role, John Schlesinger had lived up completely to his father's legacy. Nevertheless, John unquestionably enjoyed the good life. He asked us to stay for a little while because he wanted to introduce me to his new best friend, Mr Jack Daniels – a moment fraught with danger. Until this point in my life, I had been thoroughly uninterested in alcohol. Perhaps it was the excitement of New York, or the fact that I had not seen a bottle of Jack Daniels' bourbon before, that persuaded me to have one or two – or perhaps even more. John became from that night a very, very good friend and I would not wish to blame him too much for the introduction to the evils of drink. But there is no doubt, from that very moment on, that I developed a taste for Jack Daniels which was to become somewhat excessive.

When we met him, John was 35 years old and had already been married with two children, but his American wife had won a legal separation from him that year. John had been a bombardier with the US Air Force during World War II but had renounced his American citizenship two years before his father died and was now unashamedly South African. Even then, he was looking a little sad, because he was trying to divorce his wife and, at the same time, trying to play the field. We nevertheless had a most enjoyable evening with him, even though it meant that I woke up the next day suffering a hangover of some magnitude. I had never before drunk bourbon and I had never before had a hangover. As we left New York that morning on the train to Washington Bea refused to sit next to me. And I didn't blame her. I wished I could have been somewhere else too.

When we got back to South Africa, John made contact with us once more. He introduced us to a new way of life, one consistent with his standing. He was, after all, running one of South Africa's three largest enterprises, and he showed us facets of life in South Africa of which we had been completely unaware. He invited us on to his yacht and we met and moved in the company of a different set of people. My father, and indeed some of my old friends, felt a little left behind.

John had everything going for him but he was not the spoilt offspring who wasted the family fortune. His working day started without fail at 8.30am and even on vacation he ran the business from an office in his converted Fairmile motor torpedo boat. He rationalised his father's businesses, selling off a number that were not central to the group's activities. As *Time* magazine said in 1963, "John Schlesinger, after 14 years of stewardship, has fooled everyone. He has not only preserved his father's empire, but has also given it a new and imaginative direction." At about that time, he also decided to demolish the Carlton Hotel in Johannesburg, one of my favourite haunts from the past and the place where our wedding reception had taken place. But he only took that decision in order to build a new 23-storey office building to house the Schlesinger enterprises. He clearly had continued growth in mind.

Interestingly, when the British Government was on the point of granting commercial television licences in 1954, Lew Grade, the impresario, decided to recruit the most impressive consortium that he could muster in order to apply for a licence. His consortium included John Schlesinger and Dick Harmell, John's right-hand man in South Africa. But this grouping was considered to be *too* influential and the application failed.

Despite his massive achievements, John's life ended quite miserably. In 1961, he hired a friend of mine called Mandy Moross to run his businesses. Mandy and I, as I have already mentioned, were at school together. After Marist Brothers, Mandy went on to graduate from Witwatersrand University, and then to complete an MBA at Harvard Business School. Following this, he went to England to work for Imperial Chemical Industries before returning to South Africa to join Anglo-Transvaal Consolidated Investments.

When Mandy joined the Schlesinger organisation, his business dealings were initially greeted with acclaim. In 1971, Management Magazine voted him 'Businessman of the Year'. However, he seemed to me to have taken his eye off the ball, and by the time that the Schlesinger companies were sold three years later to the Anglo-American Corporation of South Africa, one of the Oppenheimer family companies, it was at a bargain basement price.

John nevertheless took the Oppenheimer money and went to live in Rome. On leaving South Africa, he donated the entirety of his substantial art collection to the University of the Witwatersrand. John then married an Italian lady with whom Bea and I did not get on at all. And we were not alone in this view; dislike of his new wife was a commonly-held view by most of his old friends. When John realised how we felt about her, he cut us out of his life completely. Perhaps I should have been more understanding of his situation, but his actions were incredibly hurtful. I, in particular, felt that John had let me down terribly. And it did not have to be that way. Sadly, throughout my life I seem to have encountered disloyalty with alarming frequency. I have always been loyal to ideas, to ideals and to friends and John was incredibly important to me. In my personal experience, the words "You can count on me!" are among the most misused in the English language. I have heard them far too often in my life. And far too often they have meant nothing at all.

It wasn't, by any means, just Bea and I who felt let down. Until he subsequently divorced his Italian wife, John spent several years in the social wilderness, losing many of the friendships which had been so important to him. He then fell out with Mandy Moross, whom he had subsequently made a partner in his business interests and who, according to John, proceeded to lose a lot of John's money in the City of London.

I saw John occasionally during the twilight years of his life. He had moved back to the United States where Bea and I would see him socially from time to time. And although we made up with each other as best we could, it was never the same. He had married for a third time – this time to a Vietnamese woman. When he died in 1992, he was by then estranged from both of his children from his first marriage. His wife asked me to deliver the eulogy at his funeral. I found myself standing in front of John's coffin, surrounded by people whom I did not know, but who I was certain were not from John's life as I knew it to be. I felt incredible sadness. This was a man with an extraordinary personality, with every advantage and with a great deal to offer. He was also a man who appeared to be determined to play out his life productively. Sadly, though, he wasted his life completely. He had so much to offer.

But I have moved on a little too far. Back in 1959, although we had only visited the East Coast in our visits to New York, Miami and

Washington, I had been bowled over by the USA. To my mind, there existed an extraordinary contrast between the confidence and vibrancy of the United States and, on the one hand, the constraints of life in South Africa and, on the other, the austerity of post-War England, where things were only just beginning to recover. Although I had fallen totally in love with London, where the way of life seemed to reflect the way in which I wished to run my own, I could feel that the United States was enticing me. Without knowing it, I had laid the early mental foundations for what was to become, 20 years later, my greatest misadventure.

I felt my unsettlement most profoundly upon my return to South Africa, where I now had the sense of no longer belonging in my home country. It was different for Bea, for she came from a family that belonged, and she was clearly a belonger. But she was also something of a rebel; or at least she always had the capacity within her to be a rebel. It was against this backdrop that our new-found relationship with John Schlesinger was, in many ways, unsettling. John always tried to absorb people. Was he a good influence? Decidedly no. Did I learn from my relationship with him? Absolutely I did.

1961 was an ominous year for South Africa, a year in which most white South Africans viewed events which were taking place as the beginning of the end, although time would show that it would take another 30 years before they were fully played out. Nelson Mandela recounts the story of March 1961 thus:

Sharpeville was a small township about thirty-five miles south of Johannesburg in the grim industrial complex around Vereeniging. PAC[26] activists had done an excellent job of organising the area. In the early afternoon, a crowd of several thousand surrounded the police station. The demonstrators were controlled and unarmed. The police force of seventy-five was greatly outnumbered and panicky. No one heard warning shots or an order to shoot, but suddenly the police opened fire on the crowd and continued to shoot as the demonstrators turned and ran in fear. When the area had cleared, sixty-nine Africans lay dead, most of them shot in the back as they were fleeing. All told, more than seven hundred shots had

---

[26] The Pan Africanist Congress of Azania (PAC) was a South African liberation movement: a breakaway from the ANC. Today it is a minor political party.

been fired into the crowd, wounding more than four hundred people, including dozens of women and children. It was a massacre, and the next day press photos displayed the savagery on front pages around the world.

The shootings at Sharpeville provoked national turmoil and a government crisis. Outraged protests came in from across the globe, including one from the American State Department. For the first time, the UN Security Council intervened in South African affairs, blaming the government for the shootings and urging it to bring about racial equality. The Johannesburg stock exchange plunged, and capital started to flow out of the country. South African whites began making plans to emigrate. Liberals urged Verwoerd to offer concessions to Africans. The government insisted that Sharpeville was the result of a communist conspiracy.

In Cape Town a crowd of fifty thousand met in Langa township to protest against the shooting. Rioting broke out in many areas. The government declared a State of Emergency, suspending habeas corpus and assuming sweeping powers to act against all forms of subversion. South Africa was now under martial law.[27]

The fuse had been lit. But still the band played on...

Into these turbulent times, on 7 August 1961, Brett, our second son – and third child – was born. All of our children are special to us, but Brett has always played a particularly important part in our lives. Our eldest child, Wynn, was, and still is, incredibly bright and my father adored him. Toni is number two – and was a very sensitive youngster. As a toddler she would never stop crying. In fact, so often and so loudly did she cry that she was almost throttled by her nanny; metaphorically speaking, that is.

At about the time that Brett was born, I decided to develop the land adjacent to the Hyde Park Hotel, building a small shopping complex with offices above. Simultaneously, I added a wing to the hotel itself and built a swimming pool. The Hyde Park became the first in what was in time to become a long line of Tollman-created boutique hotels, and 20 years before that term was ever used. Every bedroom in the Hyde Park was decorated differently. Our guests loved it, and the Hyde Park quickly established a reputation as *the* hotel of

[27] *Long Walk to Freedom*, Abacus, 1994.

choice for every visiting movie star or celebrity. Marlene Dietrich, Maurice Chevalier, Diana Dors, Tony Martin and Cyd Charisse all stayed with us there.

We had managed to mine a lucrative seam of fashionability within Johannesburg. Everyone flocked to the Hyde Park, and there was never a night without at least one personality or celebrity present among our customers. One of my perhaps less tasteful additions to The Colony at this time was that of the cigarette girl who was in fact a male dwarf. No bouquets from the politically correct! More seriously though, I also acquired the South African rights to import "21"-branded Cuban cigars. Charlie Berns, Jerry's brother and one of the two co-founders of "21", had spun off '"21" Brands'. I became his South African franchisee.

But the world was about to change, because 1961 was of course the start of the Swinging Sixties. In London, Hélène Cordet, the blonde Greek-born cabaret star, had opened the Saddle Room, Britain's first discothèque. She had achieved notoriety with gossip of an extra-marital relationship with her lifelong friend, Prince Philip. Rumours notwithstanding, there is no question that Hélène Cordet had close connections with Europe's royal families, many members of which flocked to her discothèque in Hamilton Place, Mayfair.

Royalty aside, when it became known that the Saddle Room was so packed that Bob Hope had been turned away on three consecutive nights, the discothèque's place in social history was assured. If the Saddle Room needed a further stamp of approval, it came one October night in 1962. Four young men with mop-top haircuts, northern accents and an odd line in tailoring came to the door. One of them was holding a 45 rpm vinyl disc which he said the four of them had recorded, and which they had released as a single that very day. Hélène allowed them to come in and told the girl at the turntable (this is before the days of disc jockeys) to put their record on. Thus it was that *Love Me Do*, the first record by The Beatles, graced the turntables of the Saddle Room.

But a year earlier, a very different recording artist had appeared in person at the Saddle Room – a man whose one single hit record would transform the concept of popular dancing. Chubby Checker sang *Let's Twist Again* and he and Hélène Cordet together demonstrated the Twist on the Saddle Room's dance floor. London had officially started to 'swing'.

But not everyone was uncritical. George Melly, for instance, acknowledged that the Saddle Room was "the most fashionable discothèque in London" but he was not impressed by "all the flabby jowls and bottoms wobbling about on the dance floor. When danced by the young, the Twist is certainly immensely erotic," he said, "but when danced, and danced badly, by the middle-aged, it becomes obscene."

Back in South Africa, we excavated a large area underneath the hotel and created our own discothèque. We called this The Stable, emulating the success of the Saddle Room. And it was not long before the queues outside The Stable, night after night, rivalled those outside the Saddle Room and outside discothèques in New York City. Our equivalent of Chubby Checker was one of our visiting cabaret artists from London, who personally demonstrated the Twist for the patrons of The Stable. She was still young, but the remarkable Alma Cogan was already the highest paid female entertainer of that time and looked certain to be a major public figure for decades. She threw legendary all-night parties at her apartment in Stafford Court, on London's Kensington High Street, at which the guest list would include the likes of Noël Coward, Sammy Davis Jr, Audrey Hepburn, Princess Margaret, Roger Moore and Michael Caine. I was invited to one such party at which The Beatles were playing poker. Alma's untimely death in 1966 at the age of 34 robbed the world of a great entertainer.

The food offering at The Stable was simple but delicious – hamburgers in a style we had learned from the "21" club in New York City. The Stable was quite different from The Colony and remarkable in its own way. Tales of the nightly goings-on at The Stable are both colourful and legendary. Two events in particular stick in my memory. The first was the visit from Liberace, who was performing in Johannesburg and had decided to visit The Stable on his evening off, and who became a family friend. The other was the night when Harry Oppenheimer, one of the world's richest men, learned to dance the Twist. I wonder what George Melly would have made of it.

We added to the Hyde Park in many other ways too. We acquired a licence for the first ladies' bar in South Africa. Until then, women had been allowed to drink in a lounge but not in a bar. And we built a new fish restaurant which we called The Contented Sole. The shopping complex opened with ten retail outlets and a series of offices above. The whole development was the result of almost seven years' work, and was unquestionably our pride and joy. In 1962, the Hyde Park was valued for insurance purposes at R1 million[28], worth approximately US$1.5 million. Aged 32, I felt that I had arrived.

At about this time, when my mother and father were holidaying in Durban, Ted Sceales, who was now the Managing Director of SA Breweries, offered me a second hotel. In 1956, SA Breweries had taken over Chandlers Union Breweries, Ted's previous firm, following the South African Government's introduction of a heavy tax on beer. South African Breweries had taken over not just Chandlers, but Ohlsson's too, both of which companies were struggling for business in the wake of a slump in beer sales. Ironically, it was this enforced consolidation of the industry which enabled South African Breweries (SAB) to rationalise, cut costs and become one of the most efficient brewers in the world.

Ted's offer this time around was of a small hotel in the City of Johannesburg called the Salisbury. I took him up on his offer. I felt that I was ready now both to handle the Hyde Park and to emulate the success we had achieved at the Palace. I thus took over the Salisbury, installing a traditional and comforting restaurant specialising in dishes like roast beef and featuring tables with red tablecloths.

Within the next two years, I picked up two or three more small hotels, and at each I introduced pub-style restaurants. At the same time, I opened two liquor stores in Johannesburg. On my letterhead I added the words, *"A Division of the Tollman Organisation"*. Some organisation! But I was very proud of this new message.

---

[28] The Rand, a decimal currency, was introduced to South Africa on 14 February 1961, but it would be ten years before Britain would also go decimal.

In London in 1962, I was invited to a party hosted by Monty Berman and his wife. Monty was a famous theatrical costumier based in Irving Street, off Leicester Square. Amongst many within the entertainment industry with whom he forged friendships were Cubby Broccoli, Richard Burton, Roger Moore, John Mills, Bernard Delfont and Lew Grade. In 1967, his business became part of Lew Grade's Associated Communications Corporation (later rechristened ATV).

At the Bermans' party, I was introduced to the Welsh film actor Stanley Baker and his wife Ellen. Over dinner, I talked at length to Stanley, who had been born and brought up in the Welsh mining village of Ferndale, in the Rhondda valley. He had grown up alongside that other great Welsh actor and film star, Richard Burton, and the two had been great friends since childhood. By the time I met him, Stanley Baker was already a hugely successful movie star. The previous year, he had turned down an offer from Cubby Broccoli to star in a series of three films about a British secret service agent called James Bond. As he was unhappy about signing up for three films, the part in *Dr No* went instead to Sean Connery. And the rest is history.

During dinner, Stanley told me that he and his partner, an American movie producer called Cy Endfield, had recently acquired the movie rights to an exciting new film which they hoped soon to put into production. Cy, who would go on to produce films such as *The Graduate* and *A Bridge Too Far*, hoped to raise the money from Joseph Levine, a well known American producer who had made a lot of blockbuster films. The film rights which Stanley had acquired were based on an event that took place in the Anglo-Zulu War in 1879, in which 139 British soldiers successfully defended a mission station at Rorke's Drift against an assault by 4,000 Zulu warriors. This extraordinary event had resulted in no fewer than 11 of the soldiers being awarded the Victoria Cross, the largest number by far ever to be awarded at any one time. To put this number and the significance of Rorke's Drift into context, only 1,356 Victoria Crosses have ever been awarded since the decoration was created. During the whole of D-Day only one Victoria Cross was won. Similarly, during the whole of the Battle of Britain only one VC was awarded.

Stanley wanted to come to South Africa to undertake a reconnaissance. I invited him to come to the hotel and I offered whatever assistance I could. Stanley duly arrived with his unit manager, Bob Porter, a man who had worked for many years with Stewart Granger. At that time, South Africa was a very different country from that which we know today. Apartheid was in full swing and the bureaucracy of the time was elaborate and mystifying. I helped Stanley as best I could. He used the Hyde Park Hotel as his base – a home whilst away from home.

Zulu was made the following year, 1964, in The Royal Natal National Park, near the original site of Rorke's Drift. Stanley played the part of Lieutenant John Chard, a down-to-earth Royal Engineer who found himself fighting alongside the men of 'B' company of 2nd Battalion, 24th Regiment, under the command of Lieutenant Gonville Bromhead, who was played in his first major role by a young Michael Caine. Both Chard and Bromhead had been awarded the Victoria Cross for their spirited leadership in defending the mission against overwhelming odds.

During the making of the film, the crew used the Hyde Park as its base, and everyone who came to South Africa used the hotel as a staging point en route to the filming. Two of those from whom Stanley Baker sought advice were King Cyprian Bhekuzulu Nyangayezizwe ka Solomon, the King of the Zulu nation himself, and Prince Mangosuthu Buthelezi. In each case, they were great grandsons of King Cetawayo, whose subjects fought the war against the British invasion of which the assault on Rorke's Drift was a part.

Prince Buthelezi was subsequently asked by Stanley to participate in the film itself, acting the part of his great grandfather, King Cetawayo. When, more than 40 years later, we took over and refurbished the famous Oyster Box Hotel in Umhlanga, KwaZulu-Natal, we were immensely proud that the opening was conducted by none other than the Zulu King, Goodwill Zwelithini. It was King Goodwill's grandfather who appeared in *Zulu*. We were equally honoured that a speech was delivered at the Oyster Box opening that day by the then 80-year-old Prince Buthelezi himself.

Other *Zulu* stars like Michael Caine and Jack Hawkins spent many happy hours at the Hyde Park Hotel and at our home. Because the set itself was in Natal, they also needed access to the Port of Durban, and I introduced them to a friend who had started his first hotel in Durban, the Astra, where he had opened a nightspot. This was a young man of whom the world was later to hear more than a little – a certain Sol Kerzner. During this period, the Bakers became firm friends of Bea and me, so much so that when our fourth child, Vicki, was born on 10 January 1963, Stanley became her godfather.

In December 1964, Stanley Baker had predicted an ultimate world gross of US$9 million for his movie, although some observers thought that this was optimistic to say the least. Twenty-five years later, however, his prediction proved uncannily accurate because, by the end of 1989, the world gross had exceeded US$10 million, a gratifying return on a picture which had cost just US$1.8 million to make. Sadly, Stanley was not around to see that his prediction had proved to be so reliable.

In 1975, Stanley had been reunited with Cy Endfield and Bob Porter to make a film called *Zulu Dawn*. However, before production could begin, Stanley, who had smoked all his life, was diagnosed with lung cancer. In February 1976, he underwent an operation to remove the cancer. He appeared to be recuperating well and, three months later, he was awarded a knighthood in Harold Wilson's resignation honours list. But he did not live long enough to have the honour conferred by the Queen. He contracted double pneumonia after swimming at his Spanish villa against his doctors' advice. He died on 28 June 1976, aged just 48.

Stanley was from Ferndale in the Rhondda valley, which is where his ashes were scattered. At the ceremony, one of Stanley's old school friends from Ferndale noticed that a man whom he knew had been born in Maerdy, the next village to Ferndale, had also attended the ceremony. "What are you doing here?" he said to him. "You're a Maerdy man, and Stanley was a Ferndale boy." "It's like this," replied the man, whose parents were from the Caribbean. "Someone had to represent the Zulus at this funeral!"

Ten years earlier, after the success of *Zulu*, Stanley and Cy Endfield made another film in Southern Africa called *Sands of the Kalahari*. This ill-fated endeavour was based on a story about a plane crash in the desert hundreds of miles from civilisation. Stanley, who had always intended to star, wanted to do so alongside Richard Burton and Elizabeth Taylor. Sadly, neither actor took the part and, as replacements, Stanley hired George Peppard and Susannah York. One day, Stanley called me from Namibia where the film was to be shot and where he and Cy were scouting for suitable locations. He told me that George Peppard was about to arrive in South Africa and wondered whether I would be kind enough to look after him for a little while until things were ready in Namibia to start shooting. "Of course I will," I told him.

George Peppard was a highly successful Hollywood actor who had starred in films such as *Breakfast at Tiffany's*, *The Carpetbaggers* and *The Blue Max*. I met him at the airport and spent the next few days showing him Johannesburg until he was called to report to Windhoek[29] for the start of filming.

George and I had hit it off together during the time he had spent in Johannesburg, and it therefore came as no surprise when he telephoned me late one night a few days later. He was, however, not phoning for a chat but was in a state of anguish, saying that he couldn't make this film because, "The director has absolutely no idea what he is doing." He walked off the set the next day and arrived back in Johannesburg. He then spent a few more days with us, but refused to return to the set unless the director was replaced. Given that I knew that the film was being directed by Cy Endfield himself, I thought this was an unlikely prospect. But I nevertheless agreed to speak to Stanley Baker. As expected, Stanley told me that this demand was unjustified and completely impossible to meet. The part would have to be re-cast. I reported the not unexpected outcome to George, who was resigned to returning home to the United States. I took him to the airport and saw him off.

It may have been an unhappy episode as far as the film was concerned, and for George's reputation as an unreliable actor, but he

---

[29] The capital city of Namibia.

and I had become pretty good friends during this time. In fact, we had struck up a relationship which would prove to last until George died in 1994. His part in *Sands of the Kalahari* was taken by Stuart Whitman. Sadly for all concerned, the film was not a box office success.

In 1964, we bought the Oxford Hotel to add to our portfolio of properties. This was situated in Rosebank, five minutes from where we lived, and it was a hotel which I had admired for many years. Bea created a restaurant for the Oxford which we called the Blue Fox. This featured a huge cane wheelbarrow, decorated in blue and white. It also had two tents which were erected within the restaurant itself and which could be kept either opened or closed. The grand piano was painted white. Smaller wheelbarrows would be pushed to the diners' tables filled with fresh vegetables and salad items. Salads were made for diners at their table. The menu offered dishes which at the time were considered exotic. These included turkey breast with oyster sauce. And the Blue Fox became famous for offering the best char-grilled steak South Africa had ever seen.

The following year, 1965, Bea and I went to Los Angeles for the first time. Amongst people we met there were a couple who had been introduced to us by the owners of "21" club. They had suggested that we look up their niece, Doris, whose mother was a Kreindler, and who had married Arthur Glick, the owner of a clothing factory in California. We made contact with them, only to discover that the Glicks were having a party. We were asked whether we would like to come.

When we arrived, we discovered that the guest list read like a *Who's Who* of Hollywood. I was introduced to the likes of George Montgomery, a polymath if ever there was one – equally at home as a painter or sculptor as well as being a working stuntman and an actor starring in Westerns. We met Lloyd and Dorothy Bridges and struck up a friendship which would subsequently prove to last for life. And we met once again my new best friend, George Peppard.

At the Glicks' home, friendship was clearly in the air that evening. Despite the fact that Doris was hosting this party and had a lot of very important guests to look after, she and Bea managed to find enough time together that evening to sow the seeds of a friendship which would prove to be one of the strongest Bea and I have ever made.

A few days later, George Peppard invited us to a great dinner party which he threw with his soon-to-be second wife, the actress Elizabeth Ashley, his co-star in *The Carpetbaggers*. One of the other guests around the dinner party was the great Henry Fonda. Sadly, the marriage of George and Elizabeth Ashley was to prove short lived, and George went on to wed three more times!

Bea and I returned home from California via New York, where Jerry and Martha Berns held an 11th wedding anniversary party for us at "21". This was just as glamorous and as beautiful a party as they had given us six years earlier, but by now our friendship had been reinforced by a visit they had paid in the intervening years to South Africa. Bea and I had taken them for a trip to a game reserve near Lourenço Marques. And shortly afterwards, Jerry's partner, Pete Kreindler – like Jerry, a brother of one of the founders of "21" – made the same journey to visit us and go on safari together. Jerry and Pete and their families were together viewed as the First Family of the restaurant industry in the United States, and it was a great honour to welcome them to Africa.

Upon our return to South Africa, my parents set off, almost simultaneously, on another of their world trips. This culminated in July 1965 with a visit to New York City. Whilst there, they were wined and dined, and generally and comprehensively entertained by many of the friends whom we had made over the years, both in Johannesburg and in the United States. In addition, Bea and I had organised an evening for them. *Fiddler on the Roof* had opened on Broadway and Bea and I had taken it in when we were in New York ourselves. We had enjoyed the show so much that, when we knew that my parents would be in Manhattan, we bought them tickets.

Fiddler on the Roof was a wonderful show, set in Tsarist Russia in 1905. When my parents got back to South Africa I asked my father whether he had enjoyed it. "What was there to enjoy?" he replied in all seriousness. "There was nothing to enjoy. I came from a place just like that!"

Bea and I had business to attend to in Cape Town which meant that we were able to meet the boat upon which my parents returned from their trip. We then took the Blue Train back together to Johannesburg. I thought then that my father did not look particularly well. Over the next few months he saw a number of doctors. In November, he was diagnosed with a prostate problem, requiring an operation. Following this, my parents took an apartment for three months' recuperation in St James, which is near Cape Town and positioned between Table Mountain National Park and the sea.

On Christmas Eve, I called my father to tell him that we had that week opened a new liquor store next to the Hyde Park Hotel. This was at a time of great significance for the sale of alcohol in South Africa because, four years earlier, the government had lifted the prohibition on the sale of 'European liquor' to Africans. Until 1961, *apartheid* rules had meant that blacks had been restricted to drinking sorghum or maize beer only. The Government, moreover, had held a monopoly on the sale of alcohol to blacks. Now, for the first time, non-whites had been allowed legally to buy liquor openly from a liquor store.

This was, however, the time of high *apartheid* and, although blacks could now buy alcohol from a liquor store, they could only do so using a separate doorway. Notwithstanding this restriction, we were the only liquor store in that part of town and, given the excitement about the relaxation of the rules, we had a seriously bumper day. I was desperate to tell my father of the day's takings. He was restrained in his response, and came out with a line which over the years I have repeated endlessly to managers of my own businesses: *"Don't tell me what you take. Tell me what you make!"*

Pointers on good management aside, the relationship between alcohol interests and *apartheid* in South Africa is very interesting. *Apartheid* was, of course, formally introduced by the National Party in 1948, even though the Liquor Act banning blacks from consuming 'European liquor' was enacted as long ago as 1928. But the National Party received a great deal of its support from the Afrikaner-dominated wine industry. In the Cape, the wine industry was the

Party's financial backbone. Represented by powerful voices in Parliament, wine was completely exempt from tax, which provoked claims of unfair competition from the brewers. The response from South African Breweries, now the largest brewers in the world, was simple. In order to protect their interests, they entered the wine industry themselves, buying Stellenbosch Farmers' Winery (SFW) in 1960. Today, SFW markets about a third of all wine produced in South Africa.

During the first weeks of 1966, my mother reported that my father continued to be weak, and did not appear to be recovering well at all. We were nevertheless reassured by the fact that he had specialists on hand to help him. Bea and I had been invited to Cape Town by John Schlesinger to attend the launching of his new yacht, which had been built for him in South Africa. We were pleased to accept because this would give us an excuse to see my father and establish how he was doing, but without appearing to interfere. It was, however, a shocking experience. He had changed beyond recognition, and his weight loss was frightening. I arranged for him to return as soon as possible to Johannesburg where we had access to doctors whom we knew.

My parents returned the following week and I met them at the airport. My father had immense difficulty in walking. The doctors checked him into hospital immediately for tests and, as my mother and father had sold their house in Johannesburg, we arranged for them to stay in one of the suites at the Hyde Park Hotel. Tests on my father's blood showed that his red and white blood cells were completely out of balance. Upon further examination, it was agreed that he was suffering with an internal haemorrhage, which his doctors in Cape Town had failed to diagnose. I remember well that we had Helen Shapiro appearing at The Colony that very week, and that I had to struggle to put on a brave face throughout it all. On 12 March 1966, my father was operated on to address the haemorrhage but, weak as he was, he died on the operating table. He was 70 years old.

Although I had been managing the business for many years, I found it incredibly difficult to cope with my father's death. In the short term, I had to settle the estate. He and I had owned the business 50:50, originally as S. Tollman and Son but, because my uncle was also S. Tollman, we had changed the name to The Solomon Tollman Company. My father had bequeathed his share of the business in equal parts to each of his three sons. This meant that I now owned around two-thirds of the company with Arnold and Ivan owning one-sixth each.

My father's death had a huge impact on my emotional state. It was a very long time before I was able to bring myself to go to the cinema or to a party or a dance. Instead, I threw myself completely into the business and its development. Others must have recognised that I was under self-imposed stress because, at a family dinner one Sunday night, my mother and my brother ganged up and together metaphorically jumped on me. Out of the blue, it was suggested that Arnold should abandon his very successful dental practice and join me in the business.

I loved Arnold very much indeed, and I knew that working together would be a joy. Nevertheless, despite my feelings about him, I resisted vigorously the suggestion that he should join me in the business. I did so because I knew just how unhappy my father would have been had he been around to hear this suggestion. My father was immensely proud of the fact that Arnold was a professional. And in any case my father always viewed the hotel business as being no place for one of his children to work, given the requirement to work at night and the fact that hotels were sometimes very rough places to be. The idea that two of his three sons would both be in the hotel business would have had him spinning in his grave.

It was, however, clear that my cause was already lost. After many fruitless protests, I bowed to the inevitable and agreed that Arnold should join me. It was clear that he couldn't wait to be involved in the business. What I did not realise at the time, however, was that Arnold was *already* involved in the hotel business, but in a manner in which perhaps he should not have been. I was perhaps the last to know that Arnold was having an affair with an attractive blonde girl who wore mini skirts and high-heeled red boots, and who worked in the bar at the hotel. Shortly afterwards, Arnold announced to the world that he was leaving his wife and four young children, and moving in with Sandi Philip, the racy cocktail waitress. It was only then I discovered that Arnold had been having an affair with Sandi for 18 months. And this liaison might have continued still longer in secret, had it not been for the fact that my mother saw Arnold in a car with a blonde and had it out with him.

A few of the people my father had dealt with over the years would not release the estate without the discharge of loans in respect of charges on property until replacement collateral had been provided. Reorganising the securities which were in place at the time of my father's death was not straightforward. I was having great difficulty in getting the release of my father's signature on various loans, including those from Barclays. This meant that the loans would all need to be paid off or refinanced, and all of them within a year. I suddenly had a requirement for a substantial amount of additional working capital in order to pay down these liabilities. It was not possible to borrow commercially in order to do this and, for a while, it looked as though I would be faced with having to dispose of assets in a distressed manner. This would have been disastrous for me. But this is when, as I explained earlier, my mother came to my help, extending an unsecured loan which in fact represented the whole of her savings, but saving my hide. I am happy to say that I was able to repay her within a short period of time.

In 1967, having settled my father's estate, an opportunity arose which would enable me to change my direction in business. I was given the chance to buy the Moulin Rouge, a recently-constructed hotel in a district of Johannesburg called Hillbrow, which had been open for just six months. The Moulin Rouge was a 170-room, fully air-conditioned hotel which had a great deal going for it

Hillbrow was an upwardly mobile suburb, a ten-minute drive from the City, which was full of apartments and shops. It was in many ways the Johannesburg bohemian quarter, if such a thing existed. It was full of cafés, ethnic restaurants and nightclubs, and the nightlife there was both vibrant and very busy. We added a swimming pool, bar and entertainment to this recently constructed hotel, and the response was phenomenal. We were hugely successful in attracting business from a number of airlines, including Iberia, Varig, Sabena and UTA, which quickly elected to put their crews up overnight in the Moulin Rouge. The hotel was at all times of the day and night full of attractive people, and lovely girls were always to be found lying at the side of the pool. The bar and the restaurant were packed from the moment they opened until the moment they closed.

Because of our success, Arnold and I now divided up the nights when each of us would work to ensure that we were better able to cover the enterprises which we now ran. These were part of a series of operational adjustments which were taken at the time which proved to have much greater significance for us. Until then, our key focus had been our restaurants, ably supervised from the beginning, as indeed they are today, by Bea. But the acquisition of the Moulin Rouge had the effect of propelling us beyond restaurants, and properly into the rooms business. Realising that there was real money to be made there, we became hoteliers. The transformation was both rapid and smooth.

Having said that, I would not wish to diminish the importance of our restaurants, which to this day remain Bea's pride and joy. Both of us, of course, are involved each and every day, seeking out new ideas and dishes from around the world to add to our restaurants. But it is Bea who is the overall inspiration for our kitchens, and our restaurants and hotels always feature a number of Bea's own recipes, which are often our customers' particular favourites. Typically, we will test and develop a dish at home before teaching it to the chefs.

The Moulin Rouge was in fact such a success that in the first year of operation it made R150,000 profit (at the time circa US$200,000). In no time at all, we were able to pay off the loans we had taken out in order to buy the hotel. The Moulin Rouge represented the first of a series of hotels which we acquired in rapid succession. Early in 1968, we bought the 120-room Maxim's Hotel, five miles from the Moulin Rouge. Bea hung 12 cages of singing canaries in the restaurant of Maxim's, not realising precisely how much cleaning this would necessitate. Later that year we acquired the Crest Hotel, a 300-room hotel which, like Maxim's, was also in Hillbrow. We created a bar in the form of the nose-cone of a Boeing 747, the jumbo jet's maiden commercial flight having recently taken place. Everything was going swimmingly.

To cap it all, at the end of the year, I got a call from Cyril Hoffman of Hoffman Constructions, one of Johannesburg's busiest builders. He told me that Hoffmans had never before built a 5-star hotel, but that they had a site located in downtown Johannesburg, just around the corner from the Law Courts and the Post Office. He said that they would love to build a 5-star property for us.

Bea and I jumped at the opportunity to create a hotel which had the potential to be the finest in Johannesburg. Fifteen years before the Trump Tower, we decided to call this new hotel the Tollman Towers, so proud were we of this opportunity. We chose to build a hotel which featured suites only – 150 of them, six suites a floor, in a building of 26 storeys. Although we had endless ideas for this new venture, Bea, who was still only in her mid-30s and would be in control of design, had never before designed a hotel from top to bottom. Fearlessly, she undertook this giant project with the assistance of just two secretaries. What's more, she managed the whole thing in a little over 12 months from concept to completion.

Whilst the construction was underway, I became the subject of the regular 'Pen Portraits' column in the quarterly magazine *The Epicure*[31]. This was written by Percy Baneshik, a well-known South African journalist who had dropped out of school and had taught himself to write, and in whose memory a public lecture is given each year at the English Academy of Southern Africa.[30]

Percy Baneshik's profile of me contained the following:

Still in his middle thirties, yet already the OC[32] of a chain of hotels, bottle stores and 'character' restaurants, Stanley Tollman, heading the Solomon Tollman group of companies, is an enthusiast buoyed along on the tide of his work by comparative youth.

[30] The English Academy Percy Baneshik Memorial Lecture.
[31] *The Epicure* magazine, April-June 1969.
[32] I think he meant 'Officer in Charge'.

A leading feature of his enthusiasm is a genuine connoisseurship in food and drink, acquired through avid reading and personal exploration around the world of the great places of eating and drinking. Added to that, there is his taste for the best in entertainment. Stanley Tollman has had no ordinary influence on the development of the 'floor show' in South African restaurants.

Stanley launched the principle of cabaret in an outlying hotel, and it increased the wear on the beaten path out along Jan Smuts Avenue that was already a feature of Craighall topography.

The cabaret attractions included some of the most celebrated performers of their time – Jean Sablon, Dickie Valentine, Petula Clark, Alma Cogan, Roy Castle, a whole parade of artists of whom some, unknown when Stan booked them, have become top-liners today. Some became permanent friends.

In its train, this brought more show people to the Hyde Park, not to perform but to stay. Luxury accommodation was built in 1963, to provide a setting for stars like Marlene Dietrich, George Peppard, Maurice Chevalier, Trini Lopez.

Stanley has acquired more hotels since – the Oxford, with its elegant Blue Fox restaurant; the Salisbury; the Great Britain; the Club (now a bottle store); the Central, Maraisburg and Moulin Rouge.

Now Stanley is a keen traveller, moving about the world in search of new hotel-keeping notions. A slim, trim figure, he keeps a keen, slightly hooded, eye on the operations of the Tollman Group from a suavely decorated office above the Hyde Park Off-sales bottle store.

And the secret? His wife, Bea, says it is his genuine interest in food and wine. "He would rather spend his last money on a good meal than on anything else," she says.

The Tollman Towers thus became one of the highest buildings in Johannesburg. Each of the suites featured its own fully equipped bar and refrigerator, air conditioning, and direct dial telephones. Forty years on, in the era of wi-fi and flat screen multi-channel television with endless entertainment options, the Tollman Towers' offering of four-channel radio may seem somewhat pedestrian, but in the Sixties our new hotel was absolutely at the cutting edge. (By the day in 1972 that television was introduced in Johannesburg, the suites at the Tollman Towers were already equipped to receive transmissions.)

The opening at the end of 1969 was a major event and, for the first few years at least, it was not uncommon for people to walk through the lobby simply in order to see it. Many more visited the Assegai Bar on the 24th floor, with its panoramic views right across Johannesburg, the building being one of the tallest in Africa. The Tollman Towers was voted one of the top 10 hotels in the world, the first time any hotel in Africa had ever been recognised in this way. Even today, we meet people all the time who remember the Tollman Towers and who reminisce about the times they stayed with us there. It was a truly memorable place.

Just before we opened the hotel, Arnold and I decided briefly to put aside our golden rule that both of us could not be away from the business at the same time. We had decided to make a quick trip to the United States in order to market the Tollman Towers to the American travel industry. On this occasion, we decided to fly via Brazil, rather than Europe.

The night before we left, my mother came up from Cape Town to Johannesburg to say goodbye to us. In the three years since my father had died, I had become very close to her, speaking on the phone almost every day. Notwithstanding our closeness, when I parted company with her at the Moulin Rouge, she bade me a surprisingly emotional goodbye and handed me a letter to read on the plane. We said our goodbyes in the lounge of the hotel, but as I was walking through the lobby to leave, she ran after me and threw her arms around me, something she had never done before. Looking back, it is clear that she was deeply troubled about her health.

Arnold and I left on the morning of Sunday 5 October 1969, the plan being to stay in Rio de Janeiro that night and then fly on to New York in the morning. We were staying at the Hotel Copacabana Beach, and had that evening been invited out to dinner in Rio by a couple of friends. When I got back to my hotel room after dinner, I found that as many as half a dozen messages had been pushed under my door asking me to phone Bea urgently. When I got through to Bea she told me that my mother, who had suffered all her life with high blood pressure, had complained of a pain in her head and had been taken into a local nursing home for observation. Once there, she had suffered a massive aortic aneurysm and had died. She was just 59.

This was a devastating blow. My mother had a long history of suffering from hypertension, but was being treated for her high blood pressure. But I found out after she died that she had stopped taking her medication, because she said that it did not agree with her. But the manner in which she had said her goodbye led me to believe that she had had some form of premonition.

My mother was buried in West Park Jewish Cemetery, in a plot adjacent to my father[33]. Here I was, still in my 30s, and my parents, with whom I had worked so closely, were both now gone. Not only was I now an orphan, I was responsible for three families and 12 children, my brothers, just like me, having four children each. I felt very much alone.

Arnold and I of course spent a great deal of time together – in fact, we worked in offices which were linked. But, since Arnold had left his wife and family, unless we were at work, he and I rarely saw each other.

My relationship with Ivan was less complicated, but no less worrisome. Ivan is the nicest man but, even before my parents died, I had always needed to keep an eye on him. He had run away to Israel to join the army when he reached the age of 18. Upon his return to South Africa, Arnold and I had made sure that he was looked after with various jobs. But being one of the nicest people one could ever hope to meet does not mean that someone will necessarily be a star at business. Irrespective of the time of day, Ivan always looked sleepy and he acquired the nickname Pablo, in keeping with his apparent ability always to be in *siesta* mode. Alternatively, Arnold's nickname for Ivan was quite simply, '*Oy vey!*'[34].

In fairness, one job which Ivan did very effectively was operating the lighting at The Colony whenever we had artists performing there. But this success contrasted markedly with his performance when put

[33] Plots H1261 and H1262 West Park Jewish Cemetery, Johannesburg.
[34] A Yiddish exclamation of dismay or exasperation.

in charge of one of our fully-stocked liquor stores, which he 'closed-up' one evening without locking the front door!

Some years later, I brought Ivan out of South Africa and set him up as the Beverly Hills area representative for Trafalgar, a job in which he was both well-liked and effective. He retired when he reached the age of 60 and now he occupies himself by buying and selling small buildings and apartments in California. Ivan is an extremely nice and loyal human being who wrote to me on my 70th birthday to thank me for the positive impact on his life which I have had over the years. I was pleased to read that letter, and I often think of Ivan and his family.

My mother did not live long enough to see the opening of the Tollman Towers, and the fact that that my parents were not there with us on that momentous day was a matter of huge regret to me. At the opening, we dedicated the property to them with a brass plaque proudly positioned at the front door. When, some years later, we were to leave South Africa under unhappy circumstances, we removed that plaque from the building. It is now installed in the lounge at the Milestone Hotel in London. For readers who may be interested in seeing it, it is to be found alongside a window in the lounge. It carries the message:

THIS HOTEL IS DEDICATED
TO THE MEMORY OF
SOL AND EVELYN TOLLMAN

As I write this, I recognise that God has been kind to me, having already clocked-up a decade more that the allotted span of three-score years and ten. I take nothing for granted. My father and Bea's father lived to similar ages – 70 and 74. But whereas my mother died suddenly at 59, Bea's mother had the first of numerous pacemakers inserted at the tender age of 42 but still managed to live a further 45 years, dying at the age of 87.

The letter which my mother had given me to read on the aeroplane concerned my drinking. Ever since John Schlesinger had introduced me ten years earlier to the pleasures of Jack Daniels at the El Morocco Club in New York, I had drunk nothing else. Since part of the hotel business often involves having drinks with customers at the end of the day, I found that I was having half a dozen drinks each and every evening. Alcohol did not affect me in any visible way and, after my father had died, I found myself drinking more and more. My mother's letter reminded me how disappointed my father would have been to see me drinking so much. After she died, I responded in two ways. I started to drink less frequently. And I switched from hard liquor and moved on, instead, to what was to become my life's great pleasure – drinking good wine. This fascination led me in 1998 to buy a vineyard in South Africa from Peter Finlayson and his partners. But more of that later.

The Tollman Towers was accredited as the first 5-star hotel and restaurant in South Africa. At the time, the South African government required 'non-white' guests to be in possession of a foreign passport before being allowed to eat in a 5-star restaurant. This meant that we were required to turn away black South African diners. However, and consistent with our long-standing policy, we always honoured bookings from blacks, foreign passport or not. Universally, they were welcomed into our restaurant. Although this approach was out of step with the prevailing social and political climate, Bea and I had never been supporters of apartheid and, as time progressed, we found it increasingly difficult to stomach.

Politics notwithstanding, Africa was in our blood, as it will always be. At about the same time as the Tollman Towers was nearing completion, the family made its first financial commitment both to conservation and, tellingly, to travel. We bought a small game reserve on the edge of the Kruger National Park which was called Sohobele. This was next door to the Timbavati Game Reserve, where six years later Ranger Chris McBride was to discover the world famous 'White Lions of Timbavati'. Sohobele was the most beautiful property, and the family fell in love with it. It became the catalyst for my passion for preserving the remarkable fauna, flora and landscape of the world's most stunning continent. In time, we developed a safari business at

Sohobele which was the stepping stone for countless safari operations in later years.

As we opened the Tollman Towers, I was approached by a man called David Abramson, who headed something called National Growth Fund-Sats. David Abramson was quite a celebrity at the time, especially in financial circles. He was just 33 years old and was already being written about as an "intellectual financial empire builder and visionary with global ambitions". Sitting in a swish office on the 19th floor of Johannesburg's African Life building, he had demonstrated such acumen that investors had flocked during the spring of 1969 to take up shares in National Growth Fund-Sats' parent company, National Funds Investments Ltd (NFI). No less than R236 million had flooded into the company during that period, making it the second biggest mutual fund in the world outside the United States.

David Abramson told me that National Growth Fund-Sats was planning to put together a new company with the accent on all aspects of tourism, and that he wanted me to head it. He hoped to use our hotel business as one of the component parts of the new venture, the other being a small tour company called Trafalgar Tours, which had been around for about 20 years and which each year carried a few thousand South Africans and Australians on coach tours around Europe. He valued our business at R3.5 million, give or take.

He had not of course included in his assessment the properties I had built alongside the Hyde Park Hotel, which meant that, by my calculations, I seemed to have made around R5 million. However, since I was now 39 and I had been worth about R1 million when I was 25, this didn't seem to matter hugely. I was much more concerned with the disposable income which I had in my pocket. For me that was all that mattered. Other people, however, took the view that being successful before you had reached the age of 40 meant that the local community looked up to you. It reminds me a line from the song *If I Were a Rich Man* from *Fiddler on the Roof*, "When you're rich, they really think you know." But I was just about to prove that 'they' would have been very wrong indeed to think that I knew what I was doing.

MY FIRST BIG MISTAKE

On 5 February 1970, a week before my deal with National Growth Fund-Sats was to be consummated, Bea and I were listening to the news on the radio when it was reported that David Abramson of NFI had resigned, and with immediate effect. The following morning, shares in NFI were suspended at the request of the Company, and an announcement was made to the effect that an investigation was underway into share allocations which had accompanied the successful public offering the previous Spring.

What all this meant may in part have been uncertain. But there was no doubt at all about one thing. The architect of our corporate transaction had gone away, and with him our deal.

This dark cloud did, though, have one highly propitious silver lining because, during negotiations, I had developed an excellent relationship with a man called Nick Tarsh at Trafalgar Tours. Nick had been one of the key players in the story which was the Overseas Visitors Club – or OVC as it had been universally known. The Overseas Visitors Club was created in Cape Town in the early 1950s by Max Wilson and Chone Dredzen, two young South Africans. The business had subsequently migrated to Britain.

Chartering a Union-Castle Line ship, Max and Chone brought their first contingent of young colonials from South Africa to Britain for the princely sum of £30, which included one week's lodging at the OVC headquarters in London's Earls Court. Accommodation was provided initially at 3 Templeton Place, a war-damaged and otherwise dilapidated property for which Max had paid just £4,800 in 1954, intending to use it as somewhere he and a few South African friends could stay when in London. In 1958, the Club moved to what was to become its 'spiritual' home thereafter – 180 Earls Court Road. In the late Fifties, Earls Court was becoming a home-from-home for every young citizen of the old British Empire – or Commonwealth as it was of course now known. To a man and to a woman, these young people seemed intent on travelling the globe. The accents to be heard in the Earls Court Road were predominantly those of Australians, Kiwis and South Africans.

The OVC was a fascinating place. In time it became a group of five hotels with a total of 600 rooms, five restaurants and seven bars. It even included a night club where a singer called Gerry Dorsey appeared for a fee of £15. But this was before Gerry Dorsey changed his name to Engelbert Humperdinck. The OVC had two other essential features – a *poste restante* office and a branch of a travel agency called Trafalgar Travel, which had its own very interesting story. It is important that I provide a little background to this particular travel agency because, many years later, Trafalgar was to become one of the mainstays of the Tollman family fortunes.

Trafalgar was originally started in 1947 by a demobbed soldier called Bill Nunn. During the War, Bill had worked in Army intelligence, but back on Civvy Street he was hired as personnel director for a large engineering works, and found himself organising morale-boosting social functions for the workforce. This was a challenging brief, given that wartime rationing was still very much in evidence. But Bill realised that times would change, and that there was a very real opportunity to create a new business. Thus it was that in 1947 he established a company called Industrial Recreational Services (IRS) with the objective of organising group travel and entertainment for British industry. Looking back, this may today seem an unusual concept, but Bill's organised visits to places like Ramsgate, Margate or Brighton, with groups of up to 500 people travelling together on a dozen coaches, were very successful.

In 1949, IRS moved its offices to 139 Grand Buildings next to London's Trafalgar Square, a location which was to provide the company with the name Trafalgar. And in 1957, Max Wilson bought a stake in Trafalgar, as did a South African conglomerate called Mosenthal. The business was thus brought alongside the Overseas Visitors Club, and a branch of Trafalgar was set up within the OVC itself at 180 Earls Court Road, run by a man called Alastair Duthie.

Finally, to cement its South African connections – an augur for the future of the enterprise – in 1961, Trafalgar's first overseas office was opened, in Johannesburg.

The Overseas Visitors Club had a huge notice board across one entire wall carrying *Personal, For Sale* and *Wanted* notices of the kind one might expect to see in the window of a village shop. It was on this board in 1962 that Contiki founder John Anderson pinned up a notice which said:

SMALL GROUP OF YOUNG AUSTRALIANS AND
NEW ZEALANDERS TOURING EUROPE (CAMPING)
12 WEEKS, 15 COUNTRIES, TOUR COST £100,
FOOD KITTY 25/- A WEEK EXTRA,
DEPARTING 29 APRIL –
'ONLY TWO SEATS LEFT!'
PHONE JOHN AT FRO 2418[35]

This rather unprepossessing notice became the basis upon which John Anderson was to found Contiki Holidays – more of which later.

Max Wilson was the brother of Boris Wilson, a famous South African politician and human rights activist. Together with Helen Suzman, Boris Wilson was one of 12 Members of Parliament who, in November 1959, broke away from the United Party to create the Progressive Party, arguing, "We felt that we had been sent to Parliament to fight the racist policy of the National Party, and that the United Party wasn't doing the job properly." The Sharpeville Massacre took place just four months later, precipitating a State of Emergency and the banning of the ANC and PAC. The following year, a general election was called and the Progressive Party, seen by many as representing a threat to the maintenance of white power in South Africa, was almost wiped out at the ballot box. Helen Suzman alone survived. She stood for the next 13 years as the Progressive Party's sole representative in Parliament, in the face of unremitting hostility. A remarkable woman, she never once wavered from her condemnation of apartheid.

[35] In London in 1962, telephone numbers always referred to a particular telephone exchange by its three initials, followed by four digits. The two Earls Court exchanges were called FREmantle and, in this case, FRObisher. All one needed to remember for any London telephone number was the exchange plus just four digits. Those were the days.

I had discovered Max Wilson's erstwhile colleague, Nick Tarsh, to be a polished operator and a man of many parts. Originally from Liverpool, he was educated first at Clifton College in Bristol, where he became the school's first Jewish head boy, and later at Cambridge where, in between his studies of law and economics, he found time to become a rugby Blue. Fresh out of university, he had joined the OVC and had quickly progressed to become part of the management of the Club.

In 1959, it was decided to abandon the name of the Overseas Visitors Club and to lead instead on the name 'Trafalgar' which had thus far been restricted merely to the OVC's travel agency. Henceforth, the OVC would be called Trafalgar Tours. Subsequently – in January 1964 – Nick Tarsh, together with his partners Neil Herman and David Lawson, had bought out Max Wilson and Chone Dredzen, the syndicate of three thus becoming Trafalgar's new owner.

Nick had accepted the logic of David Abramson's plans, even if Mr Abramson was no longer around to implement them, and he realised the benefit of becoming part of a bigger tourism business. Thus it was that he and his partners sold Trafalgar Tours to us for £150,000. This was 1970, and the offices of Trafalgar Tours were then in Bressenden Place, in London.

In those days, it was very difficult to buy overseas businesses from South Africa because of the extremely rigid exchange controls which were operating at the time. I nevertheless approached the Government in Pretoria to make the case that the acquisition of Trafalgar Tours was very much in the interests of South Africa. I was delighted when this assertion was proved correct, for not only did Trafalgar increasingly take South Africans abroad for vacations, it also brought large numbers of overseas visitors into the country. The timing of this acquisition followed hard on the heels of the opening of the Tollman Towers and life felt good, if a little hectic.

It was at about this time that I was approached by Bea's brother, David Lurie, and his partner Murray Maclean. The pair had together made a success of an old engineering company, turning it into a mini conglomerate. David and Murray were two examples of an emerging trend in South Africa called the 'Whizz Kids'. (Sadly, however, most of them ended up as 'Was Kids'.) David and Murray were connected with the investment guru Jim Slater who later went on to build Slater Walker Securities with the British Conservative politician, Peter Walker.

In 1970, by means of a combination of share ownerships through Slater Walker and Abercom Holdings (David Lurie's and Murray Maclean's holding company), Jim Slater, David Lurie and Murray Maclean controlled a small, publicly-listed investment conglomerate. This was called Cape General Investment Company, which owned a number of businesses in the Cape Town area. David and Murray suggested a plan whereby Tollman Hotels and Tourist Industries (THTI) would be reversed into Cape General, the resulting combined business maintaining its listing on the Johannesburg Stock Exchange.

Cape General Investment Company had a rather mixed bag of businesses which included a finance company, a Datsun/Nissan franchise, the Datsun motor racing team and various other assets. The company had a very distinguished board of prominent local directors which included a member of the House of Lords. Regrettably, it had a dearth of cashflow. Due diligence was conducted but by Cape General rather than by us. They were, of course, the public company and, largely because Bea's brother was involved, I felt comfortable. And I believed everything I was told. All seemed to be going well until, at the last minute, David and Murray said that they felt that the Net Asset Value of the combined operation was insufficient. This observation led to David Lurie persuading me to inject into the company, as an addition to the combined operation, the R1.3 million worth of property in the form of shops and offices which I had built next to the Hyde Park Hotel.

After the deal was completed, I went down to Cape Town, where Cape General's offices were located, and took advantage for the first time of the chance to review the various companies to which I had become joined at the hip. To my horror, I discovered that, with the exception of the finance company, every single company was in trouble. I had been sold a complete can of worms. Worse, I had knowingly been sold a complete can of worms. I was subsequently informed that Jim Slater, referring to Cape General, had gone as far as to tell David Lurie and Murray Maclean to "get rid of that piece of crap".

When Bea learned how bad things were at Cape General and the fact that we had been duped, she had a falling-out with her brother which was so fundamental that it was to contaminate completely and forever the relationship between them. David Lurie died in 2005, aged 77. Despite the passage of 35 years, the pain of that betrayal had not faded, and he went to the grave with his actions neither forgiven nor forgotten.

The falling-out of David and Bea was, to say the least, awkward, made no less so by the fact that one of his children had almost become part of our own family. David had divorced his first wife and there were three daughters by the marriage. The eldest daughter, Cathy, came to live with us following the divorce, and we treated her in the same way we treated our own children. She lived with us right up until the time we left South Africa in 1976.

At my 60th birthday celebration at *L'Ami Louis* in Paris in 1990, Wynn, Toni, Brett and Vicki all stood up and, as part of their combined presentation, said together how lucky they had felt that Cathy had moved in and become "our fifth child". Cathy lives in London now, and is married to Anthony Alt, an investment banker who is a big wheel in NM Rothschild. I spoke at their wedding. Cathy is a highly-strung lady, and the early years of her marriage were, shall we say, a little tempestuous.

When, as will be revealed, Bea and I were arrested in London many years later at the behest of the Unites States Department of Justice, we were told by our lawyers (wrongly, as it transpired) that we needed to find four people urgently who would stand surety for us, each of them speaking for £250,000. Our business would not be acceptable to the Court, nor would our children be allowed to provide guarantees. A number of friends were, therefore, approached for help, and these included Cathy and Anthony. They came round to see

us at the apartment and we explained the problem. I noticed as we
spoke that Anthony appeared to be responding rather strangely to our
request. They went away to think it over, but we felt sure that they
would help. After all, this was simply a surety, and no cash or other
assets would be tied up. Besides, in the light of everything that we had
done for Cathy and her sisters over so many years, and knowing full
well as she did that we would be the last people in the world to
abscond and leave her in the lurch, this was not such a big ask.

The following day, however, Cathy said no, explaining that she
and Anthony couldn't "because of Anthony's reputation". "You must
remember, Anthony is an investment banker. It would not be seen to
be right." And for good measure, she reminded us that we had not
helped her mother (Bea's former sister-in-law and a woman whom
neither of us knew) when she had asked us for 1 million rand to
support an investment proposal which she was touting.

At a time of great hurt for us, that refusal of help was amongst the
most hurtful things which happened. When our differences with the
United States were finally settled, and when the coast therefore was
clear, Cathy told us how wrong they had been to refuse our cry for
help. But I am afraid that her attempts at rapprochement were not
greeted with great enthusiasm. The relationship between us is
damaged beyond repair. Sadly, this is not a unique situation, as I will
describe later. As Elizabeth Taylor once said, "You find out who your
true friends are when you're involved in a scandal."

Back in 1971, it was of course impossible to carry on working
with David Lurie and Murray Maclean, and we ended up buying out
their shares in the expanded business, which meant that we ended up
owning 70% of THTI. It took us 18 months of day-and-night slog to
clean up the mess which was Cape General, selling up or closing
down all that we had acquired through the merger. In late 1971, the
now re-named company, Tollman Hotels and Tourist Industries
Limited, was listed on the Johannesburg Stock Exchange. Ironically,
1971 had been a good trading year for us, and we ended up making
R750,000 profit. The share price went up to R1.30, meaning that our
shares were worth about R5.5 million. In other words, I was back to

where I had started before David Lurie had raised his head. But money has never been a measuring stick as far as I am concerned. Much more importantly, I had lost almost two good years of my life.

In 1972, Trafalgar was in partnership in Australia with a man called Dino Philippides, a man of many parts. Partly into real estate, in addition to having a sole Trafalgar agency for Australia, Dino was also an agent for Brisbane Travel Operators. Additionally, he handled Express Asia across Australia, by means of six branches. His 50% share of our Australian Trafalgar enterprise was owned through his company, Australian Express. But Dino loved the idea that he might become a director of a public company. So I negotiated to buy Australian Express from him, which he sold me for AU$350,000 in cash and shares. Not only did we now own the whole of Trafalgar Australia, we also owned Australian Express. In the first year, we made £150,000 profit from this investment. As the exchange rate was two Australian dollars-plus to the pound at the time, this meant that the investment had paid for itself in just one year. This type of investment was to become something of a habit, and buying businesses and then making them more efficient very quickly has stood me in very good stead over the years.

Having gained control of the Australian enterprise, we then opened new offices for Trafalgar in New Zealand, Canada and New York. By 1973, both the UK and the Australian travel companies were doing very well indeed. We had lived in Glenhove Road for 16 years and had seen our family grow up there. But we now decided that we had outgrown our home and that it was time to look for something new. Bea had seen a house called *Dias Doradas* (Spanish for 'Golden Days'), situated in two-and-a-half acres of land and located in the district of Sandton, later to become Johannesburg's most fashionable suburb. *Dias Doradas* was not only a house with a Spanish name, but also had something of a Mexican feel about it. We spent the next year designing and extending in order to accentuate the Mexican character of the house. Bea scoured both Mexico and Spain for tiles and for antique furniture and she created a wonderful home, complete with tennis court and swimming pool.

Bea's only concern about the new property was that she felt we had tempted providence by moving into a property with such an optimistic name. At this time, however, everything in our business life appeared to be going very well indeed. In fact, we were in such a strong financial position that we found we were able to dictate interest rates to banks, which were keen to meet their monthly targets.

We had become extremely well known in South Africa, and not just amongst the business community. We began to acquire a level of recognition normally reserved for movie stars. I remember clearly having been approached in 1959 by Walter Boxer, the head of United Artists in South Africa. Walter asked whetherI would allow Bea to accompany him to the African première of *Some Like it Hot,* which featured Marilyn Monroe, Tony Curtis and Jack Lemmon. He was aiming for some of the Tollman glamour to rub off on him in the photographs from the red carpet. And around that time our buildings too attracted great interest. The Tollman Towers had become legendary, Dias Doradas was voted House of the Year, and we continued to add further hotels and businesses to our expanding company. Even our holiday time was looking up for us. We upgraded to a large flat in Sea Point, Cape Town, where we spent a few weeks each year. Everything on the horizon looked fine.

Or so we thought.

ONCE BITTEN, TWICE SHY?

As we arrived for our holiday in Sea Point in 1973, I received a telephone call from Nick Tarsh. He wanted to know whether Bea and I might be prepared to meet one of his old partners from the days of the Overseas Visitors Club. The man he wanted us to see was none other than the co-founder of the OVC himself, the near-legendary Max Wilson.

As we already knew, Max was a man with both entrepreneurial spirit and vision. He had not only made some exceptional chartering arrangements to move young vacationers around the globe, but had bought a number of hotels during his OVC days. Having sold his stake in OVC, Max had concentrated on his interest in property, especially hotels, and was now a director of a company called Court Hotels, based in London. We met Max and his charming wife in Cape Town and, over dinner, he outlined his idea. This involved our enterprise, THTI, taking control of Court Hotels, a public company which owned various properties in London. He explained his thoughts as to the linking of the two stand-alone investments, and did so very persuasively. His ideas fell on receptive ears, for the timing was right.

At around this time, Bea and I were becoming even more fearful of the direction in which South Africa was going under *apartheid*. The Government had recently tried to ban 'Africans' from working as telephonists, barmen, barmaids and receptionists in 'White' hotels[36]. At a personal level, I had had a number of run-ins with the government because we were serving black guests. I was asked to explain why I considered it acceptable for blacks to be served at 5-star hotels. I had responded robustly, and the vigorous defence of our policies which I had put up had held good, but for how much longer, I wondered? Bea and I both felt certain that things were going to get worse in South Africa before they got better.

"Labour Ban 'A Heavy Blow' to Hotels": Johannesburg Star, 21 February 1970 – front page.

Our overall approach to our personal and business lives had in many ways become anathema to the bigots who were ruling our country at that time. Black friends would often be invited to our home for dinner, and we employed a significant number of blacks in managerial positions. In our hotels, blacks worked shoulder-to-shoulder with white employees, even in skilled positions – skills which we had often taught them. Able staff were always promoted as appropriate, irrespective of race, and many of our people succeeded in breaking through the impositions which the regime had tried to impose, often through rule or legislation. We were frowned upon by the authorities.

A recent experience from our travels had also had a big effect upon us. During our US trip, we had attended a dinner in Washington, before which our hosts took us to one side and asked us to tell their friends that we were English. Under no circumstances, they told us, should we admit to being South African.

Against this backdrop, the idea of acquiring hotels and other assets in a different part of the world had some real appeal to us, and we felt our fellow directors would share our view. And they did. One of our directors, Fred Allen, who had been introduced to us by Bea's brother, David, was especially keen to get into London, because he wanted to move there.

Although Bea and I could still remember the pain of our Cape General debacle, we now had the benefit of an accountant and financial advisor on our board – a man called Zell Rangecroft. Zell was a partner in the Johannesburg accounting firm of Kessel Feinstein.

Zell and I flew to London, together with Bea, in order to meet up with the two individuals who would be conducting our own due diligence of any possible deal. We felt sure that we were not going to make the same mistake twice. Older, wiser, and with professional support, we felt like the intelligent 'A' team which was setting out to do a job which was well within our ability. This time, we felt certain that we would do it well. But I should perhaps have remembered my father's words,

"If you want to play with the Gods you better get used to the thunder and lightning."

Max Wilson's partners in Court Hotels were two men whose names meant little to me at the time we were introduced, but which are now etched into my brain; but not, I hasten to add, in the section reserved for fond memories. They were called Jack Dellal and Stanley van Gelder.

Although I may have made a good deal of money by most people's estimation, in those days I was still financially very naïve. No business school for me. The closest I had ever got to an MBA was my father's approach to accounting theory. This he conducted on the back of a cigarette pack, two simple questions being the key: "How much did you take?" and "How much did it cost you to take it?" If, having subtracted the answer to the second question from the answer to the first, there was a positive remainder, then you were in business. It was no more complicated than that.

Court Hotels was not, however, run on the back of a cigarette packet. (More's the pity, I might later conclude.) The company had a complex and very interesting balance sheet. This fact was brought to the attention of the rest of us by Zell Rangecroft, who was known to be a brilliant accountant, and by our in-house finance man, Pierre Pfeiffer, who had a reputation as an overall financial whizz. (Although South African, Pierre's father had been the head of a Swiss bank, I should perhaps have thought twice before trusting Pierre, who had been an original director of Cape General in the Slater days. Perhaps he was not as much of a whizz as both he and I assumed him to be.) The others who were involved in the due diligence, and whom we had travelled to London to meet, were Nick Tarsh, the London-based THTI director, and Irishman Seamus O'Byrne. Seamus was a protégé of mine whom I discovered when he was working as a manager at a nightclub in Salisbury, Rhodesia[37]. I had brought him down to The Colony, which eventually he ended up running. Seamus was now part of the Trafalgar Tours team.

Court Hotels operated the Queens Hotel in Crystal Palace and the Regency Hotel in Queensgate, but it also had an odd mix of

[37] Salisbury, Rhodesia is today Harare, Zimbabwe.

properties which included a slice of Cadogan Gardens and a large chunk of Overstrand Mansions in Battersea. These were owned by a subsidiary called Comfort Flats. Max Wilson did an effective selling job and the due diligence team passed the deal. The company had a £6 million bank overdraft at Keyser Ullman, secured by £6 million receivables from hotels. These Max had pledged to Keyser Ullman. What we did not know was that the £6 million figure for receivables included income from hotels which the company had actually sold! As to the cost of the overdraft, it is difficult after the passage of so many years to recall precisely what level of interest rate Court Hotels was paying on its debt, but it was well under 10%. Measured against the prevailing interest rates of the early 21st Century, that guide level may sound usurious, but the world had become used to paying at those levels and whatever rate Max had told me that he was paying was not exceptional for the time. But all that was soon to change.

The idea was that we would buy a controlling stake in the company in two tranches. Most of the stake which we were to buy came from those to whom we were speaking, notably Dellal and Van Gelder. Before we arrived on the scene, these two held 20% of the equity of Court Hotels. This they sold to us in two equal parts.

In order to finance this deal, we had been introduced to a merchant bank in the City of London called Charterhouse Japhet, which was based near St Paul's Cathedral and adjacent to Paternoster Row. As I looked at the street sign, I viewed the reference to Paternoster as a good omen, considering where I had spent my earliest days. The investment banker whom I dealt with at Charterhouse Japhet was a very personable man called Richard Reynolds. His Chairman was Malcolm Wells. Charterhouse Japhet also conducted its own due diligence on Court Hotels. All concerned expressed the view that everything was in good shape. From this we took great comfort. Not for the first time nor, sadly, for the last (as you will see later), I placed my complete and misguided trust in others.

They say that lightning never strikes twice in the same place. Similarly, sensible people are supposed to learn from their mistakes and not to repeat them. Perhaps I do not deserve to be described as sensible. I say this because, apart from the cash we invested, I was somehow persuaded, as part of the deal, to divest both Trafalgar Tours and Australian Express from THTI and, as part of the deal, inject them into Court Hotels. I even borrowed £2 million from Charterhouse Japhet to finance the package. Worse, I blithely ignored my father's advice of yesteryear, and provided the bank with a personal guarantee to boot. This meant that we had two lots of bank debt: one to Charterhouse Japhet – the cost to us of financing the deal – the other to Keyser Ullman, representing the company's existing borrowings. We also had loads of both company and personal security at risk. I kick myself even now when I think about it.

Instead of demonstrating that I had learned the painful lesson of four years earlier, the days ahead would reveal the opposite – I had fallen into the same trap for a second time. And on this occasion there was no looking back. As the old saying goes, "Folly enlarges men's desires while it lessens their capacities."

Here I was, stars in my eyes, imagining myself as an international operator. I was wining and dining at the best tables in the finest restaurants in London, and enjoying the lavish hospitality of others. I had spent most of my nights in London at Annabel's in Berkeley Square, stupidly deluding myself into thinking that I had made it to the big time. I was doing what the big boys did. Or so I thought.

However, what I was not aware of at the time – and perhaps I should have been – were the sinister reputations of Messrs Dellal and Van Gelder. Nor did I know of the three years which Max Wilson had spent in jail for fraud. What I discovered only after the event was that Max was a chancer who, aged 19, had been sent to prison for the embezzlement of trust funds. Although he subsequently paid all the money back, even his old friend and close colleague, David Gevisser, wrote of him years later, "Max produced money-making ideas at a great rate, but was often unable to manage them into profitable practice." These days, I always say to those who are prepared to listen, "Always do business as if the person you are doing business with is trying to screw you because, if he isn't, you will be pleasantly surprised."

Before the end of September 1973, I had signed the Court Hotels deal. Just one week later, on Friday 6 October, Syria and Egypt launched a surprise attack on Israel, starting what was soon to become known as the Yom Kippur War. Overnight, the world had changed. Everything had just gone crazy.

Within days, the Organisation of Petroleum Exporting Countries (OPEC) increased the price of a barrel of oil by no less than 70%. Twenty-four hours later, provoked by the fact that the United States had decided to back the Israelis, OPEC then proclaimed an oil embargo which lasted almost six months. By the end of the year, crude oil prices had risen by 400%. The world was in crisis, and the conditions in Britain, the home of Court Hotels, were amongst the worst anywhere.

The Yom Kippur War had started during a period when the British Government was attempting to square up to the industrial might of the UK's coal miners. But with North Sea oil yet to come on stream, OPEC's decision had left Britain more dependent than ever upon coal. The miners knew this and, within a matter of days, called for industrial action. A formal State of Emergency was declared in Britain and the Bank of England announced the biggest credit squeeze in living memory. Minimum lending rates went up to a record 13%. I received a call from Max Wilson to tell me that the company's interest rates were no longer under 10%, nor anything close to that figure. Our interest rates had been increased by the banks to a breathtaking 25%.

This dreadful development haunts me even after the passage of 40 years, and its implications were such that I find myself repeatedly telling my managers that they must at all times be concerned about risk. I say to them, "Always look at the downside risk. And don't bet it all. No matter how sure you are, hedge it." Thinking of Court Hotels, I then continue, "I did, and looked what happened to me. If you always calculate and protect against your downside risks, the upside takes care of itself." In reading on, you will soon discover that, in 1973, I had not only bet it all, but I had failed to protect against the downside. I was horribly exposed.

Max told me that he was doing everything he could to find a way of collecting the outstanding mortgages so that we could manage the overdraft. Court Hotels had sold a number of properties and had outstanding debtors running into millions of pounds. These would reduce the Keyser Ullman overdraft, but only once these debts had been collected. Two of our people, the due diligence team of Nick Tarsh and Seamus O'Byrne, joined the board of Court Hotels. Max would remain in the Chair and manage the company as well as running the real estate side of the business.

However good a plan this might have been, it was never to be fulfilled, and for the least expected of reasons. In December, Max called me to say that he had suffered a heart attack and would not be able to work for some time. Max was a man not much older than I was, and this news was a terrible shock. It was of course appalling for Max and for all those close to him, but it was almost as big a body blow for me. As my mind was racing on the other end of the telephone, I found myself struggling to come to terms with what this meant for Max – and for me. Before I could say anything, he announced that he would be resigning at the next board meeting. I finished the call by saying that I would come to London and see him in the New Year and that I would discuss everything with him then. I signed off by wishing him well.

As 1974 began, a three-day week came into operation throughout Britain, with factories and businesses limited to electricity on either Monday, Tuesday and Wednesday or Thursday, Friday and Saturday. Shops were limited to power either in the morning or in the afternoon and had to choose when to be open. The following month, the miners voted for an all-out strike, precipitating the first of two General Elections which were to take place that year.

The worldwide crisis had a devastating impact on business activity and on stock markets, triggering a stock market crash which was to last for two full years, during which time the Dow Jones Industrial Average lost over 45% of its value. In London, the effect was even worse, with the London Stock Exchange's FT 30 losing 73% of its value. The UK economy had seen 5.1% growth during 1972.

But by 1974, Britain had gone into recession. The UK's property market collapsed.

I had come to London in January as I had promised and I had seen Max, who told me that his health was such that his doctors had told him he must stop work altogther. He would instead be handing things over to a sidekick called Michael Lewis. I fully understood his position, but I was nevertheless gravely concerned. Max was the one with the relationships with the bank and with the debtors. He also knew all the ins and outs of the company. It was no exaggeration to say that we had done the Court Hotels deal for three reasons – because of Nick Tarsh's relationship with Max Wilson, because of Max's real estate expertise, and because of the promises and reassurances that had been made to us by all concerned. I had placed at risk a successful business in South Africa in order to buy Court Hotels and here I was, three months after completion, with the business climate deteriorating by the hour and with the secondary banks in trouble.

To make matters worse, I had absolutely no relationship with Keyser Ullman. It was, of course, part of the deal that the Keyser Ullman directors Dellal and Van Gelder would sell me their shares in Court Hotels, resign from the company's board and disappear into the setting sun. They had clearly seen the writing on the wall. As far as their personal involvement was concerned, they had escaped by the skin of their teeth. They were now 'out'. And I was 'in' – right up to my neck. And if I was in, so indeed were the two banks themselves – Keyser Ullman, who had lent money to Court Hotels, and Charterhouse Japhet, who had lent me money in order to buy out Dellal, Van Gelder and others.

For some, the nickname 'Black' Jack may summon up the image of a pirate, but it was in fact acquired by Dellal as a result of his penchant for the London gaming tables. Dellal, already an established property speculator, had in 1972 made £58 million when he sold his bank, Dalton Barton[38], to Keyser Ullman. Following this takeover,

---

[38] Following the takeover, the Dalton Barton element of the combined operation remained at its base in Hyde Park House, Knightsbridge. The old Keyser Ullman operated from Throgmorton Streeet, and later Milk Street, in the City.

Dellal continued to speculate in property on his own account, as well as becoming Keyser Ullman's Deputy Chairman.

He was widely blamed for many of the activities which led to the secondary banks crisis of the period, which had its roots in the cheap money policy of Edward Heath's Government. Those who took advantage of the low interest rates in 1973 were not, however, as had been intended, industrialists who would create jobs and growth. Instead, it was largely property developers who borrowed heavily from the banks simply in the expectation that property values would keep on rising. A policy aimed at strengthening UK industry prior to entering the European Economic Community instead created conditions which, looking back from the perspective of the banking crisis of 2008, provided the closest historic parallel in Britain. Margaret Reid, a *Financial Times* journalist, writing as long ago as 1982, penned the definitive account of the crisis, in which she made the telling comment, "If the effectiveness of defences against a new major banking crisis[39] were to be diminished through ignorance of what occurred in 1973-75 so that the whole thing could occur again before all the necessary lessons had been completely learned, then Marx's dictum that history repeats itself, first as tragedy then as farce, would be all too abundantly borne out."

Stanley van Gelder was one of those who gave evidence in 1979 to Department of Trade Inspectors appointed to investigate the collapse of a Keyser Ullman client, Ferguson & General Investments, better known as Dowgate & General Investments. Referring to the events of 1973, he said, "We lived in a tremendous, a most optimistic, world at that time. What you bought for a million pounds one day, you sold for two the next, and that person sold for three the day after."

During this period, Keyser Ullman had embarked on a bizarre lending spree. In giving evidence himself to the Department of Trade Investigation into Dowgate & General, Jack Dellal said, also referring to 1973, "At that time, we had a lot of money and the City were telling me, 'Lend it out. Lend it out.'"

---

[39] Margaret Reid, *The Secondary Banking Crisis 1973-75*, Macmillan 1982.

Lend it out he may have done, but in 1975 Keyser Ullman had to write off £82.5 million of doubtful debts which, taken together with earlier provisions, meant that they had written off a total of £119 million as a result of its irresponsible lending. The Bank of England had to step in to deal with the secondary banks crisis overall, with support from the clearing banks organising a rescue fund called the LifeBoat, which provided additional capital to those in distress. For the bankers, Christmas 1974 was not a happy time, nor one spent with the family. The idea of a lifeboat was 'floated' (forgive the pun) at a crisis meeting four days before Christmas Day, and the LifeBoat Committee was established and met for the first time a week later. Keyser Ullman started to receive support loans from the LifeBoat six months later, in July 1974. By the Spring of 1975, Keyser Ullman had drawn down some £65 million in emergency monies.

The banks may have been up to high finance but, at a personal level, with Max Wilson out of commission, my focus was on much smaller issues. My crisis was every bit as acute, but in microcosm. I sat down and analysed Court Hotels' books. I discovered that the so-called asset sales were in reality worthless. They had effectively been debt-funded, but with Court Hotels itself being the lender. There had been virtually no interest payments made against these mortgages during the six-month period prior to our takeover of the company and all of the loans were in default. Amongst other things, these had represented the sale of ten apartments in Cadogan Gardens, Chelsea, disposed of for about £45,000 each to a previous partner of Max Wilson, who had provided not a penny by way of deposit. The disposals were not only debt-financed but that debt was not being serviced. They were not really sales at all. The company's books had been fixed accordingly.

For the second time in my life, I had been sold a can of worms. Worse, for the second time in my life, those selling their stake knew that they were selling a can of worms. How this fact had gone unnoticed during due diligence was totally beyond me. And how it had also escaped the notice of our merchant bank I will never know.

I was 43 years old and thought that I had already learned a few things about life. I had not got to where I was in my career without the inevitable ups and downs in business. But nothing which had gone before had prepared me for the 18 months which were to follow. These were without question little short of hellish.

For the next six months, I commuted between Johannesburg and London. After taking the evening flight out of Johannesburg, I would spend a day in the London office before taking the evening flight back to Johannesburg again. The fundamental problem was that there was simply no cash coming out of Court Hotels. In order to service the UK debt, I was having to make payments out of the South African company. By October 1974, I realised that, unless I could come to some accommodation with the London banks, I would effectively destroy a highly successful company in South Africa which represented my life's work. I called on a close friend, Johannesburg solicitor Monty Koppel, and he and I flew to London, together with a South African investment banker in support, having made appointments with Charterhouse Japhet and Keyser Ullman.

I saw Charterhouse Japhet as being reasonable people. They were after all my bank and I considered them to be my friend. Perhaps for this reason, I did not at the time fully appreciate what was going on. I knew that the whole world was of course experiencing unprecedented market conditions, and I was not alone in being unable to service debt. I could not afford to service the debts of Court Hotels. As these were debts which I had, of course, assumed as a result of the deal, I felt sure that Charterhouse Japhet, reasonable people after all, would understand. I was not, therefore, suspicious when they asked for my agreement to send one of their bankers to South Africa to look at the best way of sorting things out. I saw no problem with this and, against Monty's advice, I suggested that the Charterhouse Japhet banker come out to South Africa in the New Year. Another stupid move. In agreeing to let them come to South Africa, I had made yet one more big mistake. The Charterhouse Japhet loan was secured not by South African assets, but by the assets of Court Hotels. My naivety was in not understanding this fact.

The man Charterhouse Japhet subsequently sent to South Africa to look at our businesses was called Derek Edmundson, who moved into our offices in Johannesburg, and worked with some of our people in analysing the company's activities.

The day after our meeting at Charterhouse Japhet, one of their people accompanied the three of us when we went to see Keyser Ullman. A few months earlier, I had never heard of Keyser Ullman. Now, my company owed this bank £6 million, even though I personally had borrowed not so much as a penny from them. To make matters worse, the Keyser Ullman debt was not being serviced, nor had it been serviced for months – long before we had even arrived on the scene. Max Wilson had known this, but he was no longer around. And 'Black Jack' Dellal and Stanley van Gelder knew it, but they were now out of the picture too.

There is a widespread belief that Dellal, whose private investments continued to derive finance from the bank itself, was a prime culprit in the near disaster at Keyser Ullman, which went on to achieve the dubious record of making the largest loss in British history. In its 1975 Report & Accounts, Keyser Ullman noted that the bank had lent a great deal of money to companies in which directors of Keyser Ullman had a personal interest. In this, they were referring in large part to the bank's loans to Court Hotels. Jack Dellal told the *Financial Times*' Margaret Reid that the loans to Court Hotels were made "in line with the principle of providing finance to customers one was well acquainted with". Lending money to oneself seems a very questionable interpretation of that principle.

Demonstrating Teflon-like qualities, Dellal himself walked away from the debacle virtually unscathed, having disposed of his personal holdings – including of course Court Hotels – just before the crash.

I suspect that few people have had the unfortunate experience of finding themselves in a room with a bunch of hard-nosed bankers whose attitude had changed as fundamentally as had that of the bankers whom I found in London in late 1974. One minute I had been wined and dined as their very best client. The next, I was being viewed as something deeply unpleasant in which they had all somehow managed to tread. Unless you have experienced this sort of treatment at first hand, it is perhaps difficult to appreciate. Let me say simply that there are a small number of lessons in life which I would not recommend as essential learning. This is certainly one of them.

I would like to be able to say that when I walked into Keyser Ullman's offices in Milk Street that day I met a gentleman. I cannot, though, tell a lie. I was not received by a gentleman, but instead by someone called Ian Stoutzker, a man of about the same age as me. When I walked into his office he refused even to shake my hand, and for the first time in my life I felt the brunt of someone treating me with total contempt. I tried to explain that it was not I who had borrowed the money and that I was every bit as much a victim as he. I pointed out that two of his own directors had been on the board of Court Hotels, and Keyser Ullman itself was largely to blame, not Stanley Tollman. Dellal and Van Gelder were unquestionably aware that interest payments were not being made on the loans which the company had extended to various third parties. However, all of these protestations fell on the deafest and rudest of ears. He simply didn't give a damn. This was a man in trouble, and he just wanted his money.

The Charterhouse representative also spoke up, reiterating everything I had said. Together, we then asked for time to try and sort things out. Begrudgingly, Stoutzker gave us six months, effectively freezing the loan in the interim. "Property and money are easily interchangeable," Stoutzker had said in an interview 12 months earlier.[40] Events were soon to prove this to be one of the most stupid statements ever made.

Keyser Ullman was the City finance house which had bankrolled Cavenham, the international food group which had been run by Sir James Goldsmith. A series of remarkable deals had transformed Cavenham, a near bankrupt company, into one of Britain's biggest trading groups, and had earned Keyser Ullman substantial fees in the process. But Keyser Ullman had got greedy, so Jimmy Goldsmith took his business to Hambros. Another high profile client was Tiny Rowland's London-based mining finance business, Lonrho.

[40] Maurice Barnfather, "Flurry of deals pitches Keyser into the big bank league", *Industrial Management & Data Systems:* Volume 73 Issue 1.

Keyser Ullman's history was inextricably linked to the Keyser family, and the two men who ran the business day-to-day had strong 'family' links. In the early 1970s, the bank had become very active in corporate finance generally, largely under the direction of Dellal and Van Gelder, but under the hands-on management of its two managing directors, Roland Franklin, and the man whom I had just had the displeasure of meeting, Ian Stoutzker. Franklin was very much part of the family as, by definition, was his sister, who just happened to be the wife of the other Managing Director. Ian Stoutzker was thus Roland Franklin's brother-in-law. Cosy? I think not.

As I left the offices of Keyser Ullman that day, I was a changed man. The meeting with Stoutzker had been so unpleasant that I resolved, once out of the mess in which I currently found myself, I would never again allow a bank to take away my dignity. Thirty-five years on, I am happy to say that I never have, and I never will.

Within days, the very offices in which we had met that day were to be the backdrop of a meeting at which history would be made. The non-executive Chairman of Keyser Ullman was Sir Edward du Cann MP, a former government minister who, at that time, was the Chairman of the influential Conservative backbench grouping, the 1922 Committee. Following two defeats for the Conservative Party at the polls in both the February 1974 and October 1974 elections, there was widespread dissatisfaction with the leadership of former Prime Minister Edward Heath.

On 15 October, five days after the second election, Edward du Cann had convened a meeting of the executive of the 1922 Committee in those very Keyser Ullman offices on Milk Street, thinking that it would be safe from the prying eyes of the media. At this meeting, it had been decided that the Committee would press Edward Heath into holding a leadership election. Du Cann's hopes for privacy were, however, hopelessly dashed following a tip-off, and press photographers were waiting for the conspirators to leave. This led to the group being dubbed the 'Milk Street Mafia'. The *Daily Express* splashed the story under the headline, *"ALL SO SOUR IN MILK ST.* – Du Cann's secret band run for cover."* This fateful meeting triggered a sequence of events which would result in Margaret Thatcher becoming leader of the Conservative Party, with all that that subsequently entailed.

But whilst this was taking place, the secondary banks crisis led Keyser Ullman to the brink of collapse. Sir Edward du Cann himself had authorised a £17 million loan to a man called Christopher Selmes, a 28-year-old so-called entrepreneur; a loan which was secured on a worthless guarantee. Selmes fled the country with the loan undischarged and Du Cann resigned. Both Roland Franklin and Ian Stoutzker resigned in July 1975. Somewhat ironically, five years later Keyser Ullman was bought by the Charterhouse Group, owners of Charterhouse Japhet. Keyser Ullman and Charterhouse Japhet were combined and the Keyser Ullman name was dropped.

Back in October 1974, following my meeting with Stoutzker, I had returned to South Africa with a very heavy heart, struggling to think of a solution. The only advice which I had received was to put Court Hotels into administration and hope to be able to retain Trafalgar and Australia Express by buying them back out of the business. This meant that the banks would be left with every other asset in the business in order to discharge the liabilities to them. But, no matter which way I examined it, there was no way that this plan could possibly work. Trafalgar and Australian Express would not survive for even two days whilst in administration. Once confidence in a travel company is lost, the business is doomed. There is a great deal of evidence to support this view.

I am an eternal optimist and I am never, ever, prepared to give up. I can stand at the edge and look right over the top. Even then, when I can see the bottomless chasm in front of me, I am not prepared to wait patiently until I fall off or I am pushed over. There is no such thing as the inevitable. I would rather fling myself over the edge, in the confident belief that I will catch a root or a branch to pull myself back up. On only one occasion have I ever found myself helpless: unable to change the course of events. But that story comes much later on in this book.

As we desperately sought investors who might buy the company, or at least some of its assets, we spent the next few months meeting, talking and pleading with anyone who was prepared to listen. But we were not the only ones with something to sell. By any measure, London was a fundamentally destabilised marketplace. One man's problem could very well prove to be another's opportunity. In the midst of the state of emergency which characterised both the British economy and the fortunes of Stanley Tollman, I knew in my bones that something would come up which would fix everything. I had a little time to solve the problem. Not much. But a little. I resolved to keep my eyes and ears open. I felt sure that something would come along, and come along it did.

Business may have been slow for most at that time, but not for everyone. For those involved in the insolvency business, life was hectic. One such individual was Martin Spencer, at that time a partner in accountants Stoy Hayward, and a liquidator of numerous bankrupt businesses. I became aware that amongst the assets of which he needed to dispose was a hotel in Great Cumberland Place, a Georgian crescent close to London's Marble Arch. I went to see Martin at his offices in Wigmore Street, and he showed me the detail of what was on offer. The Montcalm was being comprehensively refurbished, but the refurbishment was not complete and the hotel was short of being finished by about £100,000. The lease of the property was for sale for £25,000 but, in order to open for business, the first thing any new owner would have to do was to complete the refurbishment.

Even though I had myself been frantically trying to offload hotel properties in London and was not in the market to buy, I realised that the Montcalm Hotel was a real opportunity. Sadly, though, the acquisition of the Montcalm could not simply represent a marvellous addition to the wonderful company which Bea and I had lovingly built over 20 years from hard graft. There was no escaping the fact that our South African businesses had been starved of cash and therefore crippled, perhaps fatally, by the investment in Court Hotels.

Appreciating the reality of the situation in which we now found ourselves, we nevertheless pressed on with the idea of acquiring the

Montcalm. I approached Denis Brown, a friend who had financed various enterprises over the years, including our acquisition of the Moulin Rouge. His operation was willing and able to advance us the £125,000 which we needed to buy the Montcalm and finish the work. We thus acquired our first 5-star property in London, albeit not yet finished, but for a very affordable price. I always say to those around me, "No matter what problems you have, careful thought and time will sort out all things. Be out there, never shirk a journey, choose your goals and wait. You always get your time and chance."

We tackled the work at the Montcalm as swiftly as we could and by March 1975 we were ready to open for business. I was the victim of a diary clash and had to be away on business in Australia at the time of the launch. So, in the same way she has done all our married life, Bea stepped up to the mark, flew to London and handled the opening of the hotel on her own. Thankfully, she was supported by many of the London-based friends whom we had made over the years. Amongst those present were Stanley Baker, Graham Hill, Diana Dors and Max Bygraves. It was, so I am told, a very memorable occasion and the Montcalm was given an outstanding launch.

We had inherited an architectural design for the rooms at the Montcalm which was for its time highly innovative. Bedrooms were arranged on two levels, with the sleeping area upstairs and an area downstairs where guests could conduct business. In many ways, the rooms had the characteristics of a suite, but in miniature. This feature, coupled with Bea's finishing designs, produced a wonderful hotel which was an instant hit. Not only did guests love it but the location of the Montcalm could hardly have been better for the time.

The offices of the Grade Organisation, of ITV, and of EMI and Chrysalis Records were all just around the corner, and the Montcalm became *the* place to stay in London. Our guest list included rock and movie stars, television personalities and top models. Rod Stewart became so attached to a comfortable chair in the Montcalm reception that he seemed to become part of the furniture. It became known as the 'Rock & Roll Hotel', and everyone who was anyone stayed at the

Montcalm, including the members of ABBA, The Beatles and the Rolling Stones. Not only were the rooms great, so was the food. We worked very hard at the restaurant, which really took off. It was written up extensively, and was soon one of the busiest in London. We became the venue for every trendy event. Rock stars from Jethro Tull to the Bay City Rollers would launch their latest albums at the Montcalm, and world light-heavyweight boxing champion John Conteh, one of the greatest sporting celebrities of the time, staged his pre-fight press conferences with us. The Montcalm was most definitely on its way. Without ever consciously attempting to do so, we had in effect replicated what we had created at the Hyde Park Hotel in Johannesburg.

It was around this time that I met a man for whom I developed a substantial respect, and who was to become one of our closest friends. Nicky Kerman was a London restaurateur, responsible for establishments such as Scott's, Drones and Sheekey's. He approached us about using our basement at the Montcalm. Together with his business partner, movie producer David Niven Junior, Nicky attracted investment from dashing industrialists James Hanson and Gordon White, and film star Michael Caine. Together, they opened a discothèque in the Montcalm's basement, which they called Dial 9.

Despite the success of the Montcalm, our overriding preoccupations remained the unloading of the original Court Hotels deal and at the same time hanging on to our travel businesses. With these goals firmly in my sights, I was travelling constantly in order to meet with bankers and possible investors, and I was rarely in my office. Meetings instead took place in hotel lobbies, where it seemed as though the whole world had a deal for me. One meeting, in May 1975, was, however, quite different all from the rest.

Bea and I travelled, together with Monty Koppel, to Chicago to see Jay Pritzker, who I can honestly say was one of the most exceptional businessmen I have ever met. Together with his brother, Robert, Jay had built a conglomerate which had made them both multi-billionaires. Amongst other things, they had major interests in Braniff Airlines, *McCall's* magazine and Ticketmaster, as well as casinos in Las Vegas and Atlantic City. In many ways an intensely private man, Jay Pritzker endowed the Pritzker Architectural Prize, often described as architecture's Nobel Prize, which carries a $100,000 annual award.

Jay Pritzker trained as a lawyer and accountant, and began buying small companies whilst still in his twenties. But he was best known for the deal he made in 1957 in a coffee shop called Fat Eddie's at Los Angeles International Airport. Whilst waiting for a flight, he had noticed that Fat Eddie's seemed to be unusually busy and that the hotel of which Fat Eddie's was a part had no vacant rooms at all. Despite their obvious success, the hotel and coffee shop were nevertheless both up for sale. There and then, Jay Pritzker made up his mind to buy them both, writing his offer of $2.2 million on a napkin. Little did the owner, Mr von Dehn, know that he was about to give his name to one of the world's most successful hotel chains. Mr von Dehn's first name? Hyatt. And the rest is history.

Jay Pritzker's relationship with the authorities, especially the US Internal Revenue Service (IRS), was uncomfortable to say the least. The IRS had challenged the inheritance from his late father. Prior to his death, his father had settled everything into trusts on behalf of his children and grandchildren. The IRS, calling the trusts a sham, sent Jay Pritzker and his brother a bill for $53 million. The Pritzkers stood their ground, and in 1994 settled with the IRS for less than 20% of the money which had been claimed.

To say that I enjoyed my conversation with Jay Pritzker would be an understatement. Regrettably, however, it was clear both to him and to me that there was no meaningful deal which would work for both of us. A gentleman to a fault, he went as far as to say to us, "Would a million help?" This was said seriously, but I did not take him up on it. I valued him much more for his friendship than as a source of charity. From that day onwards, I considered him a real friend, and I saw him regularly over the years until he died in 1999. He was one of the world's great entrepreneurs and he was also a thoroughly decent human being.

We headed back to South Africa from Chicago, stopping off overnight in London on the way. As we arrived at the Montcalm, I got a telephone call from the children, who were at home in South Africa. They had been approached at the house and had been pressurised by a journalist, who had wanted them to say something. They had said nothing at all, but the following day they saw posters at the news stands in the neighbourhood which carried the headline, *"Tollman brothers flee South Africa"*. I called Arnold in Johannesburg, but he had not yet seen the newspaper. Bea and I returned home to experience our first taste of cruelty from the media – a taste to which I will never become accustomed, much less acquire. The entirely fictitious story had been splashed on the front page of the newspaper. Monty Koppel wrote the strongest possible letter of complaint. The newspaper's response? A one-inch retraction on page seven.

On our arrival back in South Africa, we discovered that the rumour mill had been at work. Endless chit-chat from people who knew little or nothing about us nevertheless began to create real problems. A story spread that our bars were no longer able to offer some of the most popular liquor brands, presumably because we could no longer afford to buy them in the first place. The irony was that stories of this kind had a danger of becoming self-fulfilling. Suppliers, believing what they had heard and thus worried about our ability to pay, withdrew the credit that we had enjoyed for years.

Meanwhile, the constant travelling, pressure of work, anxiety and excess drinking finally took its toll on me. My blood pressure was sky high and my doctor told me to go to bed for a week. I had never in my life before been ill enough to have to stay in bed, let alone be off work for a week. Thus began a lifelong battle with high blood pressure, a complaint which dogged my mother before me. However, although I may have chronic and often uncontrollable hypertension, Bea says that I am really no different even today from how I was ten, 20, 30 or even 50 years ago. My friend and doctor, Isadore Rosenfeld, begs to disagree.

During my week in bed, I received a telephone call which did little to lower my blood pressure. This was from my banker,

Malcolm Wells, the Chairman of Charterhouse Bank. He was not, however, telephoning from his office in the City of London, but from Johannesburg airport. And he was not arriving there but about to board a plane to go back home. He told me that he had been in South Africa for a week, something which we had known nothing about. I was still recovering from the surprise of all of this when he said, "You remember that I told you that if we ever decided to turn from being your friendly bankers to being your unfriendly bankers, that I would let you know? Well, I am just phoning to tell you that that is now the case." With that, he was gone.

I put down the telephone and picked it up again immediately. I dialled Arnold and asked him to tell Derek Edmundson to leave our offices at once. All we had done by giving this man access to the company was to enable him to prepare a document for the sale of the business. I then demanded a meeting with Edmundson the following day, together with Monty and Arnold. Edmundson admitted that he had been meeting with representatives of Southern Sun Hotels, a subsidiary of South African Breweries, now known as SAB Miller, which was, even then, one of South Africa's biggest companies. Southern Sun Hotels was now headed by one of my closest friends, Solly Kerzner.

Solly, five years younger than me, was an extremely bright and able businessman who had already established a reputation as a very tough and a hard negotiator. Notwithstanding this reputation, we had over the years extended numerous favours to Solly, helping him with the development of his business in a great many ways. We had every reason to believe that he was a good friend. Not, we thought, someone who would stab us in the back.

Sol was the man who had owned the Astra Hotel in Durban which I had recommended as a base on the coast when *Zulu* was in the course of being filmed. Sol had been born in the poor Johannesburg suburb of Troyeville and, like me, of Jewish immigrant parents who were in the hotel business. Unlike me, he trained as an accountant before joining the family business. My financial skills were picked up in other ways. In 1962, Sol had bought the Astra which he subsequently added to by building two more hotels in Durban called the Beverly Hills and the Elangeni. In 1969, he had struck up the partnership with South African Breweries to establish Southern Sun Hotels.

Whatever one might think about Sol Kerzner's ability as a hotelier, it is impossible to deny that he is a showman. A few years later, he would go on to negotiate a deal with Bophuthatswana's so-called 'President', Lucas Mangope, which granted him an exclusive gaming licence in the nominally independent Bantustan[41] and the rights to build a giant casino. Bophuthatswana had been declared independent by South Africa's *apartheid* government, although it was never recognised by any other country. Because of its 'independence', Sol Kerzner was allowed to provide not just gaming but also topless revue shows.

Such entertainment was anathema to many in South Africa, especially the *apartheid* government of the time with its strong Calvinist traditions. But with Bophuthatswana being just an hour away, the people of South Africa who did not share such Calvinist sensitivities travelled over the border in droves, attending musical performances and major boxing matches. Sol succeeded in persuading a great many performers and sportsmen and women that although playing in South Africa was inexcusable at the time, playing in 'Bop' was all right.

Solly would go on to create Sun City, a resort situated near the city of Rustenburg. This was a Hollywood-style 'Lost City' featuring four hotels and two golf courses created by Gary Player – one with crocodiles in the water feature at the 13th hole.

But the thin veneer of respectability gained by so-called 'independence' was over time eroded, and Sol was accused of propping up Bantustan dictators and profiting from *apartheid* policies. Many artists and sports stars refused to play in Bophuthatswana, and the song *(I Ain't Gonna Play) Sun City* became an anti-*apartheid* anthem. Eventually, in 1996, Bophuthatswana was brought back into South Africa, when it became the North West Province.

---

[41] A Bantustan was a territory set aside for black inhabitants of South Africa and South-West Africa (Namibia) as part of the policy of *apartheid*. Ten Bantustans were established in South Africa, and ten in neighbouring South-West Africa (then under South African administration).

Twenty years earlier, though, Derek Edmundson told us that Southern Sun were prepared to make an offer for the South African businesses. He also told us that if I refused to meet Southern Sun and start negotiations with them, Charterhouse Japhet would have no hesitation in taking down the whole house of cards. Nice people to do business with.

All of this may have started with Edmundson knocking on Southern Sun's door, but Solly and his partners had quickly realised the opportunity which our properties represented. We had, for instance, just opened a new hotel at Johannesburg Airport which Bea had designed from top to bottom. It had been widely recognised for its stunning design, its décor and its furnishings, and had been an immediate success. We were also building a second Tollman Towers, this time in the Main Parade in Durban. This promised to be even more amazing than the acclaimed Tollman Towers in Johannesburg. Southern Sun was now extremely keen to get its hands on our 5-star portfolio of properties because, quite simply, it had nothing even remotely to compare with them.

With the gun to our head, and with no enthusiasm whatsoever, we met Solly, who was accompanied by various Southern Sun Hotels executives. Following some detailed talks, we then carried out the necessary due diligence in South Africa. Having done this, we all then flew to the UK to look at the London properties. We met Keyser Ullman once again, this time under the auspices of Charterhouse Japhet. Once more, Keyser Ullman refused even to acknowledge my existence. I somehow bit my tongue and together we examined a number of alternative methods which might be adopted which would go some way to meeting the needs of the various parties in the room. This was perhaps not the easiest of meetings – certainly not the shortest – but it was by no means hopeless, and it was clear that something could be done.

However, upon our return to South Africa, Southern Sun advised me that they had decided that they were not prepared to go ahead with a two-country deal, expressing the view that it was all too complicated. Amongst other things, they stupidly took the view that the Montcalm was not a proper asset because it was only leasehold. They had no interest in London, but they were still prepared to consider the airport hotel and the Tollman Towers hotels in Johannesburg and in Durban.

Whilst we were thinking things over we got a call from Derek Edmundson who asked Arnold and me to go to Charterhouse Japhet's Johannesburg lawyers' offices, but without Monty Koppel. "Just bring Bea," was all he said. As requested, I went to the offices with Bea and with Arnold and we were ushered into a room and asked to sit together at a round table. Edmundson came in, accompanied by his lawyers.

On the table he placed two documents. One was slim – just a few pages long. The other was an inch thick. Edmundson held up the slim document. "*This* is a very simple document. If you agree to our terms and conditions this can all be very easy." The terms and conditions he had in mind were that we would hand total ownership and control of everything to Charterhouse Japhet, and for nothing. "By the way," he added, "if you choose the simple route, there is one further condition. You must discharge Monty Koppel as your lawyer. The alternative," he went on, "is *this*." At this point he picked up the thick document. "In this we accuse you of everything." Then, looking directly at Bea, and in as intimidating a manner as he could muster, he said, "This document accuses you of everything in the book. If you don't surrender, we will throw this at you."

At this point Bea, who had noticed a familiar figure lurking in the adjacent room, calmly looked up. "*What* is Sol Kerzner doing here skulking in the doorway?" she demanded. Derek Edmundson replied, "If you sign here today, Sol Kerzner is ready to take over immediately." At this point, I was reminded of what my father always used to say about bankers: "Nothing but bookmakers in striped pants." I am not a person who takes threats lightly or easily. In this, Edmundson had seriously misjudged me. Enough was enough.

I stood up, saying to Bea and Arnold, "Come on. Let's go." The three of us left the office and did exactly what Edmundson did not want us to do. We went straight to Monty Koppel's office and told him what had happened. Furious, Monty picked up his coat and walked right over to Charterhouse Japhet's lawyers. The receptionist told him that they were all in a meeting. Monty barely broke stride, barging straight into the meeting and giving all concerned a severe talking to, accusing them of reneging on numerous promises. In between various protestations from them, he was able to work out that they were now preparing an application to the court to place our company into liquidation.

Monty acted quickly. Within hours, we were joined by two of South Africa's top lawyers and advisers, Joe Rabinovich and the legendary Mervyn King, who would later go on to become a judge in the South African Supreme Court.

The following day, Charterhouse Japhet attempted to place our company into administration, only to discover that we had got there first. Monty had succeeded in the appointment of an administrator whom we knew reasonably well. Against a highly complex backdrop, our main company, THTI, was going into administration. This way, there was now a chance that we might get something out of it. Had it been left simply to Charterhouse Japhet and their lawyers, you can be sure that we would most certainly have got nothing out of it at all.

After we left Monty's office that day, we walked over to the Tollman Towers, our pride and joy. Walking through the front door and standing in the lobby, I looked up and saw the plaque on the wall in memory of my parents. Not knowing what the future held in store for us, I removed the plaque from the wall and we left.

The following morning, we once again met Monty, Joe and Mervyn. They all appeared quietly confident, which made Bea and me feel a great deal better. Although the other side had employed the firm reckoned to be the best white-shoe lawyers in town, someone passed the remark that our team was from the first division whilst their team was from the third. How true that remark turned out to be.

None of us was at all concerned about any allegation of impropriety. The suggestion that they would throw the book at us was as preposterous as it was insulting. I, for instance, had drawn no salary for 18 months and on a number of occasions I had actually paid bills myself on behalf of the company, knowing that I was unlikely ever to be paid back. I had to do this because the company's credit had quickly disappeared. These were very difficult times, with rumour after rumour spreading in a small community. Local banks and suppliers listened to gossip which was often completely unfounded and, failing to realise that their own actions were in fact helping to create the very situation they feared, withdrew our lines of credit. Not realising that these actions were destroying a highly successful business, our suppliers were withdrawing credit in every direction, many insisting on cash on delivery. The resulting need for enhanced liquidity placed even greater pressure on the cash flow. Arnold handled the suppliers, a thankless and immensely difficult task because our credit was entirely exhausted. From that moment onwards, I have always recognised the central importance of liquidity.

With an administrator in place, our negotiations with Charterhouse Japhet and Southern Sun came to an end. When they realised that they had been totally out-manoeuvred by our team they had no choice but to request a meeting. One Sunday morning, we were all invited to the boardroom of Werksmans, Solly Kerzner's Johannesburg lawyers, to see if anything could be sorted out. These offices were well known to me. The senior partner and founder of Werksmans, the veteran Natie Werksman, knew me well. And David Schneider, one of the firm's partners, had been my personal lawyer for many years and was a very close friend.

As we arrived at Werksmans' offices, Natie called me into his room for a few words before the meeting. He advised me not to make too much of a fuss, telling me that it was in my best interests not to object to anything. Once it was all done, Southern Sun would see what they could do for me. In other words, stop barking and they will throw you a bone.

After months of hell, it was fair to say that all concerned were both emotionally and physically exhausted. I knew that we could not fight indefinitely, and that I had to try to find a way of bringing this to an end. Given what Natie had said, I tentatively floated the idea of making a deal whereby I would hold on to one of the hotels plus some money. But the kind of bone that Southern Sun had in mind clearly had a great deal less meat on it. Proving the old adage that no good turn goes unpunished, the helping hand which we had given Sol Kerzner over the years clearly counted for nothing. Natie was dismissive of my suggestion, rejecting it out of hand. He explained that Southern Sun's idea of something which could be done for us was to contemplate whether to offer Bea a job as a designer.

These fruitless, and frankly insulting, initial exchanges over, we went into the meeting proper. My team were uncompromisingly tough, giving way on nothing at all. The meeting took some time and concluded without agreement, but we were still talking. It was only after several days of negotiation that a deal was negotiated whereby we were left with just three out of our twenty-something hotels in South Africa – including our beloved Tollman Towers in Johannesburg. Everything else went to Southern Sun and SA Breweries. The price of all these assets and of the goodwill attaching to them met the settlement of the outstanding debt to Charterhouse Japhet. Realising what a great opportunity these assets represented, the bank cannily took a share in the businesses rather than cash. Years later, when the company was subsequently floated, the value of the Charterhouse Japhet stake meant that the bank had realised a significant profit on the whole of its Tollman 'adventure'. Would that the same were true for me.

I will take a moment to reflect on Sol Kerzner's life since those unhappy days, although I think that a more objective assessment might be provided by an independent commentary. As you can imagine, my own relationship with Sol never recovered following his actions in 1975. Instead, I will leave you with extracts from a recent report from South Africa's *Sunday Tribune*[42].

Sun sets on Sol's empire

DIMINUTIVE powerhouse Sol Kerzner, 77, has been a colossus in the business world for as long as anyone can remember.

The hard-drinking, much-married, chain-smoking mogul with a blue collar background confounded sceptics at every turn to build a multi-

---

billion rand global holiday resort empire. Midas-like, everything he touched turned to gold. Like him or loathe him, he was both envied and admired.

But, as he and his fourth wife Heather, 44, head for the divorce court, it seems personal happiness has again eluded him. This week it was announced that he had retired as the executive head of Kerzner International.

Those close to Kerzner say the blow dealt the hotelier by the death of his son and heir, Butch, in a helicopter crash in 2006, was one he never fully recovered from. Kerzner lost his second wife, Shirley Bestbier, to suicide. His next trip down the aisle, with one-time Miss World Anneline Kriel, led to divorce after five years. His marriage to Heather tottered on for 12 years, culminating in divorce papers being filed in the UK in November.

On the surface Kerzner led a charmed life, but in reality his empire was crumbling and Heather wanted out of a marriage that had become increasingly lonely as her husband jetted from one part of the world to the next, shoring up deals and trying to stave off creditors. In December, television show Carte Blanche revealed that Kerzner had parted with resorts worth billions in transactions with giant Canadian property company Brookfield. He exchanged these assets for a mere $175m (R1.4bn), with the proviso that the buyer took over $2.3bn of debt.

The erosion of Kerzner's portfolio started in 2005, when he and Butch decided to buy out minority shareholders and delist the company from the New York Stock Exchange. Their timing could not have been worse. They incurred $3.6bn in debt just before the Great Crash of 2007.

But back to my story, and to July 1975. I was almost 45 years old and, for almost as long as made no difference, I had been known to be a millionaire. But not only had I lost both my money and my most valuable asset – my reputation – I also came to the realisation that I had lost a lifetime's work, thanks entirely to my flirtation with London. I took comfort, though, in the fact that I had made the best of an impossible situation. I approached the future in the hope that my few remaining assets might represent a solid base – if a small one

– upon which I could rebuild the family's fortunes. I could not afford to look back. I had to look forward.

With the awfulness behind us, and leaving Bea and Arnold in Johannesburg to look after the hotels, I persuaded Monty Koppel to come with me to London to see how we could best sort out Court Hotels. We still had some serious problems to deal with. Thus it was that after 18 months of non-stop travel, with everything which that had entailed, Monty and I arrived at the Montcalm Hotel to set up camp for the duration.

Monty began by hiring the services of a lawyer called Lionel Lipkin, a South African who was practising in London. Together they began holding a series of meetings with Keyser Ullman's in-house lawyer, Bruce Fireman. The objective of these meetings was to find a means by which both parties might get out of the mess in which they found themselves. But the meetings did not start easily and, over the weeks which followed, they became more and more acrimonious. They culminated in a demand from Keyser Ullman that I should resign immediately as Chairman of Court Hotels. Monty refused. With the talking effectively over, Keyser Ullman called an extraordinary general meeting, with the sole purpose of removing me from the board.

Unsure as to what was going to happen, we decided to protect what we thought to be a promising asset, but which no-one else did. Taking on its liabilities, we bought the Montcalm out of the company for a consideration equivalent to its book value. This meant that we were able to buy it for £2.00, in addition, of course, taking on the liability for those debts associated with it.

The day of the EGM arrived and I asked Monty what we were going to do, knowing full well that Keyser Ullman were going to move for my removal from the board and for the appointment of a liquidator for Trafalgar and Australian Express. He said little by way of response, but seemed quietly confident. And well he might have been, for things did not go exactly as Keyser Ullman had planned.

The meeting had been convened at the Regency Hotel, in Queensgate. As the meeting was called to order, Lionel Lipkin stood up. He wished to make clear to Keyser Ullman and to the meeting that 21 days' notice was of course required for the convening of an extraordinary general meeting. This point was not disputed, but no-one could understand why Lionel was making it.

He went on to point out that Keyser Ullman had in fact assessed incorrectly the number of days' notice which they had given, explaining that the period of time which they had allowed was not 21 days but was in fact 20 days. They had simply not counted up the number days correctly. In other words, inadequate notice had been given and the meeting had not been properly convened. Red faces all round. The supposed meeting collapsed, amidst chaos, embarrassment and more than a little fury. The extraordinary general meeting never took place. And Stanley Tollman remained in charge.

At this point, I must introduce another character into my story, one who plays a small but ultimately important part in the saga of Court Hotels, but whose association with me proved to be much more significant. For the time being, I will introduce him only in a provisional way, but will tell more in the chapter which follows.

I had met Ken Bates before, entertaining him when he made a visit to South Africa. Ken was a former associate of Fred Allen, who you may remember was the director of our company to whom Bea's brother had introduced us. Although Ken was a man of some substance, he was clearly more than a little eccentric. He said that he owned a bank in Ireland, but freely admitted that at one time he, together with his wife and children, had lived in a caravan. He had not been accompanied to South Africa by his wife, but by a mistress and by a business associate called Freddie Pye. I found Ken to be a man with an outgoing personality, who was brimming in confidence. Although it was clear that he and I were completely different in character from each other, his buccaneering nature struck a chord with me.

In 1973, I had taken a call from someone who in the past had worked for David Lurie (Bea's brother), but was now working for Ken Bates, who it seemed had investments in South Africa. Ken had acquired a company called Union Townships, and was interested in buying a property business which we owned. We agreed to sell this company in exchange for shares, and I joined the board of Union Townships. Thus began my business relationship with Ken Bates.

I sought advice from him about the Court Hotels problem during 1974, and he had offered not just advice but his help in sorting things out. He even joined the board of Court Hotels. When the South African debacle was over, and I had arrived in London with Monty to work full time to clean up the mess, Ken asked to step down from the board. In fairness to him, he had tried his best to help to sort things out, but he had concluded that without a substantial improvement in the London property market, which remained in the doldrums, nothing other than a large injection of cash would solve the problem. But cash was in very short supply – unless you were either an oil-rich Arab sheik or Adnan Khashoggi.

Following the chaos of the extraordinary general meeting that never was, Ken Bates flew over to London from Ireland, having agreed that he would approach Keyser Ullman and try to buy Trafalgar for £500,000. His argument to Keyser Ullman was simple. If liquidators or administrators were to be appointed, confidence in the travel businesses would disappear instantly. If so, this part of the Court Hotels operation would be worthless. This is a theory which has proven correct time and time again. After years in the industry, I have never seen a travel company survive administration or liquidation unless rescued swiftly by a white knight. For a travel business to try to pick up the pieces by itself simply never works.

Nick Tarsh had already attempted to mount a management buyback, but could not raise the money. And there was no-one else interested in the business. Keyser Ullman had a stark choice. In the case of our travel operations, with no other immediate buyers, it was a clear choice between the liquidation of a business with few tangible assets and goodwill which would disappear overnight, or Ken Bates' offer of half a million in cash.

Good sense prevailed. Ken Bates and Freddie Pye acquired 60% of Trafalgar and Australian Express, and the Tollman family acquired the balance. Nick Tarsh stayed on as Managing Director, with Ken Bates as Chairman and me as Deputy Chairman. With the travel companies out of Court Hotels, and with the Montcalm safely in our hands, we fought no more. Court Hotels was no longer our problem. We breathed a huge sigh of relief, and Keyser Ullman did what it could with the remaining property-based assets, taking a hit against its loans.

It was at this point that Monty informed me that his wife was threatening never to talk to him again, assuming she could still remember what he looked like. He and I decided that it was about time we returned to South Africa. It was now the first week of December 1975. It had taken us three-and-a-half months to sort out London, but I now felt that I had come out of all of this in respectable shape, and with a foot firmly in the door outside South Africa.

Before I had left London I had asked friends to see if they could find us an apartment. Eddie and Sally Leigh had a clothing business which often organised trade shows at the Cumberland Hotel in Marble Arch. They lived in Bryanston Court, an elegant apartment block in London's Bryanston Square. Bryanston Court was where Mrs Wallis Simpson had once had a first floor flat in which she used to entertain Edward, Prince of Wales. Within weeks, Eddie and Sally called us to say that they had managed to obtain a four-bedroomed apartment in Bryanston Court itself. What's more, because these were the days of rent control, the lease was very cheap. For a man who was now obliged to count the pennies, this was wonderful news. The gods appeared at last to be smiling down on me.

The gods may have been smiling down on me in London, but when I arrived back in South Africa, I had a sharp reminder that I should take little for granted. It seemed that whilst I had been away, everything which could have gone wrong had gone wrong, including a serious burglary at home. I learned that there had been a spate of jewel robberies in Johannesburg by a 'gentleman burglar', who had been visiting from London and targeting particular homes in places such as Sandton. It was at this point that I was reminded of Bea's fear of tempting providence by moving into a property with such an optimistic name.

But there was little skilful or elegant about the so-called Raffles' work at *Dias Doradas*. Our safe had been smashed out of the wall into which it had been built and carted off, together with all of Bea's jewellery. She had lost all my mother's diamonds and the jewellery which she had been keeping for the children. To add insult to injury, although we were well-insured, the insurance company had read the negative publicity about the Tollmans' financial problems, and had refused to pay, implying that it was a put-up job.

Although the burglar had been obliged to work under cover of darkness, the insurance company had no such inhibitions. They, it seemed, were perfectly prepared to commit daylight robbery. We were eventually forced to settle for just 25% of the value of the stolen jewellery. In a lifetime of insurance, this was the only claim we had ever made and yet the insurers reneged. So much for insurance. The list of other people's graves on which I could happily dance was growing.

During this dreadful period, the press were really nasty. As if losing your money were not bad enough, to have journalists crowing about it was appalling. Many of the so-called friends we had made over the years no longer felt the need to call. All the positions in society which we had held had disappeared, not to be renewed. Everyone, it seemed, had run for the hills. Bea's mother and sister stood by us, as did a handful of friends. Doris and Arthur Glick from Los Angeles were kind enough to send cheques, saying that they hoped it would help. It did. And one local friend lent us 10,000 rand. Otherwise, no-one offered anything – neither family nor friends.

I had returned to South Africa with trepidation, having been away from the family for longer than I had either planned or cared to imagine. Apart from the burglary, what else, I wondered, had happened whilst I had been away? I found that Bea and Arnold had been through all kinds of trauma as they tried to keep business and family together. I realised, and not for the last time, that I had a life to rebuild from scratch.

The thing which I had held most dear – my reputation – was in tatters. I had also lost all my money. Bea and I sat down together and talked. After a while, I told her that I had come to the conclusion that our future no longer lay in South Africa – certainly not in a South Africa stained by *apartheid*. We had to leave. And, as it had always been our intention to educate our children in England, and as we now had a base in London, this was the time for us to go.

So it was that we left South Africa. Wynn was already at Rugby School doing his A-levels. We took Toni, Brett and Vicki with us, together with the US$12,000 which represented our total wherewithal, and we moved to London. Arnold stayed behind in Johannesburg to look after the three remaining hotels.

THE SIREN CALL

Moving to London was challenging for all of us. Although I had managed to secure business footholds from which time might allow us to rebuild our fortunes, the first 18 months were tough – financially and in other ways. Cash was extremely tight, and living in London meant coping with both the English weather and with life in an apartment, or flat as we had to learn to call it. For many years, we had lived in large houses with grounds. London was a completely new experience, with disadvantages as well as obvious benefits.

Cost-cutting applied to almost every aspect of our lives, with the exception of the children's education which was sacrosanct as far as Bea and I were concerned. Our son, Brett, joined his elder brother, Wynn, at Rugby School. Toni went off to study at the Sorbonne in Paris. And Vicki stayed with us in London, where she attended the Francis Holland school in Regent's Park.

Overall, though, we found London to be a welcoming place, despite its obvious constraints. Over the years, we had struck up both friendships and acquaintanceships in South Africa with people who lived or worked in England, and these relationships were now rewarded, sometimes in the most unexpected of ways. I had noticed that Bruce Forsyth was doing a one-man show at the Talk of the Town, and thought it would be fun for the family if we all went to see it. Bea and I had been introduced to Bruce when he had visited South Africa with *Brief Encounter* star Trevor Howard, and we had got on really well. Little did I expect, though, what was to happen when we arrived at the theatre.

The Talk of the Town was a London institution. Previously called the London Hippodrome, it had housed a famous circus variety theatre. Over the years, this had featured, amongst a great many other things, polar bears, elephants and a youngster called Charles Chaplin. In 1958, it had been converted into a world-class theatre restaurant, and renamed. The brains behind this project were those of Charles Forte, Bernard Delfont and Charles Nesbitt. Talk of the Town patrons were able to wine, dine and dance whilst enjoying exceptional entertainment. Very much like The Colony, when I think about it.

On the night that we chose, we were being ushered to our seats, having arrived a little late. So late, in fact, that Bruce Forsyth was already on stage. Without warning, having noticed us arriving, he stopped the performance. Not, in case you might imagine, to admonish us for our tardy arrival, but to welcome us. "These people, ladies and gentleman, are the Tollmans. They are from South Africa. I would like everyone to welcome them please." And welcome us they did. It was an unexpected moment, and one which I will always remember.

At this point in my story I will reintroduce Ken Bates – this time in a little more detail. Much has been written over the years about my friendship with Ken and my alleged business relationships with him. Some of what has been written has been accurate. Most, especially in the context of my involvement with Chelsea Football Club, has been absurd invention. In setting the record straight, I may have to puncture a few perceptions, but I think it is time that the truth was out. I read recently, for instance, in a story about Ken rather than me, that Stanley Tollman was a man given to wearing a dark brown mink coat, even in the summer. This would be eccentricity bordering on madness! Not only have I never owned a mink coat, of whatever hue, I have also never worn one, especially in the summer. How can people write such rubbish?

Ken Bates is about one year younger than I am. When he was 18 months old, his mother died and he was abandoned by his father, to be cared for in a West London council flat by step-grandparents. His first job was working in the ticket office at Paddington Station. Bored, he tried to get into the Army but was refused because he had a clubfoot. He decided instead to train to become an accountant. In his late teens, he was reconciled with his father and, abandoning his accountancy course, moved to the

North of England to work with him in a quarry business near Manchester.

The world was engaged in massive post-war reconstruction, and the quarry prospered. Ken began supplying ready-mixed concrete to the building trade, a business which was booming. Aged just 22, he married Theresa, the daughter of a wealthy Irish country squire, and within a year had bought his first Bentley.

The young Ken Bates' savvy approach to business came to the attention of the City. He was approached by an investment bank, and in January 1965 he floated on the Manchester Stock Exchange a public company called Howarth, a Burnley-based construction and property development business. In the same year, aged 34, he became chairman of Oldham Athletic Football Club. Football was a lifelong passion for Ken, and his clubfoot had not only prevented him from joining the Army, it had also stopped him from pursuing his dream of becoming a professional footballer.

During a business visit to the Caribbean in 1966, Ken saw opportunities to make huge advances in land values and to do so in a tax haven, avoiding Britain's 90% income tax. In 1968, he moved himself, his wife and his five children to Little Wickham's Cay, a small island in the British Virgin Islands. But his adventures in the BVI were complex, and ultimately not wholly satisfactory, so Ken looked far and wide for new opportunities.

One of the places he looked at was the Irish Republic, and in June 1971 he bought an off-the-shelf Irish company called the Kildare Bank. Two months later, the Kildare Bank was renamed the Irish Trust Bank, with premises in Dawson Street, Dublin. During the first year of operations, the bank attracted well over 1,000 savers in the Republic of Ireland, the UK and the United States. Exploiting Ken's Lancastrian and football connections, these savers included the likes of Bobby Charlton and George Best. The Irish Trust Bank looked as though it was in business.

It was during his 'Dublin years' that I got to know Ken Bates, and to observe the manner in which this extraordinary man went about doing business. There is little doubt that he was different from other people, but being different is not in itself a negative. I soon began to realise that Ken's skill, imagination and energy were qualities which on balance I admired, however uncomfortable I might on occasion have felt about his behaviour.

I observed at a distance the goings-on in Ireland, especially when the Irish Central Bank applied to revoke Ken's banking licence, citing the fact that he had failed to mention his directorship of Howarth when he had applied for the licence in the first place. How or why he failed to point out the fact that he was a director of a public company, goodness only knows. As it was, Ken bowed to the inevitable and resigned as a director, to be replaced by Freddie Pye. Freddie, whom I had of course met in South Africa, was another colourful character, a former professional footballer, wrestler and scrap metal merchant. Over the years, he was also Chairman of both Stockport County and Wigan Athletic football clubs, as well as Vice-Chairman of Manchester City.

Even though he had stood down from the board of the Bank, Ken carried on working in Dublin. His relationship with the Irish Trust Bank continued, albeit in a very different way. But in 1975 the bank got into difficulty about its lending and, at the beginning of 1976, the Central Bank applied to the High Court to close it down.

Whilst the court hearing was going on, Ken entered the Bank's premises in Dawson Street and, pushing past a female assistant, seized a sack of documents. "You can't do that," someone shouted at him as he was leaving. "See you in court," was Ken's reply. Sadly, his appearance in court was rather sooner than I suspect that Ken had contemplated. Half an hour after he had removed the documents, the judge hearing the Central Bank's application issued a warrant for Ken's arrest for contempt. This rather dramatic sequence of events was reported extensively in *The Irish Times*.[43]

All credit to Ken that he volunteered himself to the courtroom that afternoon, pointing out that the papers he had taken were in fact personal documents. Sadly, though, his contrition was not enough to save the Bank, which the court ordered to be closed. Ken had to look for opportunities elsewhere.

[43] *The Irish Times*, Wednesday 24 March 1976.

It was around this time that I began to develop a closer relationship with Ken. We agreed to form an informal partnership in relation to future deals, and to work together to build the travel businesses which we owned jointly. The rest of the time, each of us worked independently on what was, for both of us, our brand new lives. For my part, as I was trying to sell the three remaining hotels in South Africa, I travelled to Johannesburg a few times. But I also I endeavoured to earn some income out of both the travel business and the hotels, gradually trying to build a life again.

Part of that new life was a renewed interest in the United States. In December 1976, Monty Koppel offered us the use of a friend's flat in Palm Beach, Florida for a month, including the use of a car. Monty was a joint owner of something called Lion Country Safari which was located at Loxahatchee, some 15 miles inland from West Palm Beach, and he had reasonably extensive connections in Florida.

We had visited Palm Beach 12 years earlier and remembered it as a very clean and beautiful place with some of the biggest mansions we had ever seen. Palm Beach was quite unlike anywhere else in the world that we had visited, and its ability to stand apart was well-known. In March 1946, just six months after the end of the Second World War, *Life* magazine carried the following report[44]:

Palm Beach. Having survived another war, its cosmopolitan society plunges into one of its gayest seasons.

"In the first winter after the Second Great War," some future historian will write, "several million Americans devoted themselves exclusively to the pursuit of happiness. The famous watering places like Miami Beach and Palm Beach in Florida were even more crowded than in the days of the last previous boom (1925-1929). Prices rose astronomically. Sometimes it seemed as if all the fabulous wealth of the New World was being flushed through pari-mutuel machines at race tracks, through cash registers of hotels and bars ..."

All this was true last week. But if the future historian is a heedful recorder, he will stop right there. He will be on the verge of a terrible mistake. Palm Beach is nothing like Miami Beach. By last week, there had gathered in Miami Beach a fantastic collection of Broadwayites, columnists, black marketeers, war profiteers, Hollywood actors and producers, all with swollen pocketbooks and a frenzy to spend. Against such people, Palm Beach would bar the windows of its chateaux, and get out the shooting irons of its illustrious grandfathers.

In fact, Palm Beach this winter would like nothing better than to shut off the three bridges which connect its 30-mile-long spit of land with the mainland and bar all visitors and newcomers. Yet Palm Beach is changing. Its isolationism is gradually yielding.

Thirty years later, we found the Palm Beach residents to be much more friendly. On arriving with Brett and Vicki (Wynn and Toni were both spending the Christmas vacation with friends), we were welcomed by Monty's friend. This man was known to all and sundry as BJ Harris. He was a very successful local businessman, and I recall even now how incredibly kind he was to us. In common with most residents of Palm Beach, BJ was not a native Floridian. He was in fact the archetypal southern gentleman, hailing as he did from Louisville, Kentucky – the birthplace of the then heavyweight boxing champion of the world, Muhammad Ali.

Although we had been impressed by Palm Beach in 1964, this time we fell totally in love with the place. We were taken aback by the beauty of the island, with its wonderful houses, beautiful gardens and pristine hedges. But we were also completely at one with the peace, quiet and overall gentility of the place. We knew almost from the moment that we arrived that we would some day spend much more time there.

Bea and I were walking one evening on our way to meet BJ for dinner at Palm Beach's best restaurant, La Petite Marmite in Worth Avenue. We found ourselves staring sadly into the windows of all the beautiful shops. I say sadly, because there was nothing in these shops which we could afford to buy. We felt like poor relations, up from the country, noses pressed in envy against the window panes.

When our month in Palm Beach was up we said goodbye, promising to return. Never for a moment, though, did we imagine that within ten years we would have rebuilt our fortunes to such an extent that we would own not only one of the most beautiful houses in Palm Beach, but one of its best hotels as well.

Returning to London, I applied myself with even greater determination to those opportunities which I knew were within reach, notably the Montcalm hotel and the travel businesses. In the latter case, I settled down to work with Ken Bates in order to realise the full potential of Trafalgar.

Throughout the whole of 1976, Bea and I would often think about Palm Beach, and every time we agreed that it would be a wonderful place to spend more time. We had unquestionably been hooked by the seductive charms of Florida and, for that matter, the United States. At the beginning of the following year, our finances were such that we were able to buy an apartment in South Palm Beach for just $177,000 fully furnished. We had secured our foothold in paradise.

GETTING OUR LIVES BACK
PART II

November is the time temporary residents start to drift back to Palm Beach for the winter season. Daytime temperatures are dropping to a comfortable 80°F or so, and at night it is possible to sleep without the necessity for air conditioning. A perfect time of year.

November is not, however, the perfect time of year to be in the City of London, however comfortable the surroundings of Simmons & Simmons might be. My thoughts were drawn away from the window and back to the reality of 2008. I noticed that the screen for the pending video conference still displayed signs of preparation and little else. I decided to preserve my strategic position, out of sight of the camera.

I considered the people in the room in London, and wondered how I had come to know them in the first place. After a few moments' thought, I realised. We were all gathered together for this fateful morning in a gloomy London quite simply because of the place from which my thoughts had just departed. Palm Beach, no less. Let me explain.

One of Bea's closest friends is Kate Ford, the widow of Henry Ford II. Kate, whose maiden name was DuRoss, married Henry in 1980, and the two of them had lived togther in Palm Beach until his death in 1987. Kate lives there to this day, although she also has an apartment close to ours in Eaton Square in London. Henry and Kate also owned Turville Grange, a wonderful country house near Henley on Thames which we often used to visit.

One of Henry's personal lawyers, now Kate's lawyer, is a great friend of ours. Frank L Chopin practises today in Palm Beach, and has acted for us there. More importantly, though, he has over the years become Kate's companion and our close friend. Not only was Bea very fond of Kate, she also liked Frank a great deal, as did I. Kate and Frank, both separately and together, used to spend a lot of time at our home in Palm Beach, and we would sometimes go on holiday together. And the four of us would occasionally be invited to join Max Fisher on his yacht.

Frank is no country lawyer, even though he hails from New Orleans and practises in Palm Beach. He has been involved with some major pieces of litigation, is hugely experienced and has wonderful contacts in legal circles all over the world. Perhaps his most important local client was Earl Smith, who was the Mayor of Palm Beach for six years in the 1970s. Appointed to the post of US Ambassador to Cuba at the time when the Batista government fell and Fidel Castro came to power, Earl Smith had the extraordinary distinction of receiving appointments from no fewer than four US Presidents – Roosevelt, Eisenhower, Kennedy and Reagan. A leading financier, accomplished sportsman and prominent Republican, Earl Smith was a remarkable character, and Frank Chopin's close association with him did a great deal for Frank's own reputation in Palm Beach.

In late 2001, it became clear that Bea and I had a problem with the authorities in the United States – a problem which was to result seven years later in my waiting here at Simmons & Simmons for this fateful video conference. I had become increasingly unhappy about the situation, and recognised that we needed help. Having reached that conclusion, we had sought advice from Frank.

Frank was angry with us that we had not spoken to him before. He took the view that we had been burying our heads in the sand. And if we had known then what we were later to discover, he would have been right to say that. But, as we explained to him, nothing we had ever done could possibly have led us to conclude that we had a real problem. In any case, I saw Frank as a friend rather than as a lawyer, and I hadn't wanted to say anything to anybody. I wanted to keep these worries from other people. Not because I had anything of which I felt ashamed, but I didn't want to get others involved. I just didn't want to bother them. Besides, until that point, the 'warnings' which had been passed on to us by our advisers were, as they repeatedly told us, of little consequence. At worst, we should expect a slap on the wrist. All that changed, though, as I will explain shortly.

Frank heard what we had to say, and swiftly concluded that we needed help, and the very best help we could find. Or, to be more accurate, we needed the best help *he* could find, given that we knew little about these things. I was already being advised in the United States, and Frank offered to come with me to New York to assess the work of the team which was in charge of my affairs. But Bea was not being represented, and Frank said that that must be corrected, and swiftly.

Frank accompanied me to Manhattan to meet the legal team which had been looking after me for over two years in relation to the enquiries which spilled over from the investigation of Monty Hundley. Morvillo Abramowitz was widely regarded as the best criminal defence firm in town, if not the country. Bob Morvillo was nominally in charge of my business, but it would be a few months before he played any sort of decisive role – sadly, not a constructive one. When I originally instructed the firm, I also met Elkan Abramowitz whom I found absolutely charming, but he was never involved on my account. The day-to-day work was in the hands of a man called Jack Tigue. Frank thought little of the work which they had done for me. He interviewed Jack Tigue, and adjudged him in particular to have done a lousy job. For practical reasons, though, he did not recommend that I should change attorneys immediately, although that decision was to come sooner than expected.

In the meantime, though, Frank recommended that, in addition to appointing a US lawyer for Bea, I should think again about my own US representation, and also get some powerful advice close to our new home in Europe. After all, he said, if there is going to be a fight, Europe is where it should be fought.

Bea and I had recently moved back to Europe. Although we had lived in the United States for some years, the responsibilities of the travel business and Red Carnation meant that both of us needed to be in Europe, with the United States becoming once again a place of recreation only. We had bought a place in Geneva, close to Vicki and her family and to the Hotel d'Angleterre, which had recently become part of Red Carnation.

Given that US tax was at the heart of everything, the first introduction Frank made for us was to the Washington, DC law firm of Williams & Connolly, and to the senior partner there, Brendan Sullivan. Bea and I flew with Frank to Washington to meet Mr Sullivan, and exchanged pleasantries. He was a nice enough man, although I was not hugely impressed. But Frank said that this was precisely the right firm for Bea. So it was that Bea instructed Gerry Feffer, a top litigator and a partner of Williams & Connolly, to act for her. Gerry had in the past worked not only in the US Attorney's Office for the Southern District of New York, but had been Deputy Assistant Attorney General, Tax Division. If indeed we had a problem concerning tax, we knew that problem was now on the desk of the US Attorney for the Southern District of New York. Gerry certainly had the right background.

Gerry Feffer also had a number of very high profile clients. These included President Clinton himself, whom Gerry had defended in the context of the Whitewater investigations. He had also acted for Leona Helmsley, the hotel heiress who famously said, "Only the little people pay taxes!" This comment was reported by Helmsley's housekeeper at her trial for tax evasion in 1989. Referrring to Leona Helmsley, Gerry admitted openly in court that his client was "a tough bitch", but then asked the jury to leave judgment on that count to a higher authority.

Frank Chopin also agreed to help us find the best legal brains in Europe. His mind jumped immediately to London, a city where he had worked extensively in the past. From the start, Frank's professional guidance has been invaluable. His advice, and his help in finding and securing a dream team of lawyers and advocates has been remarkable. He laid the foundation stones which were to prove successful in the final outcome. Throughout, his recommendations were clear and unequivocal. The three Ds were his mantra. Defy. Deny. Defend.

Frank was, of course, well aware of the distinction which the British legal system makes between the role of the barrister and the solicitor. The responsibility for advocacy and specialist legal advice are on the whole the preserve of the barrister. The day-to-day handling of any particular piece of litigation is, however, the responsibility of solicitors, typically organised these days into large firms, sometimes employing hundreds of people.

Frank knew that we would end up by appointing solicitors who would, in turn, hire the services of good barristers. But he decided to seek some initial guidance from the barrister whom he considered was best qualified in London to offer the kind of advice which Bea and I were likely to need. Frank had done some serious research and was pleased that this led him to the door of a man already known to him.

Clive Nicholls QC[45] was, rather disturbingly, a man of similar age to me and therefore himself well within the territory of what most people would consider to be retirement age. Educated at Trinity College, Dublin and at Cambridge, Clive had been called to the Bar as long ago as 1957. He was now the head of a specialist set of chambers at Three Raymond Buildings, Gray's Inn. Clive had an unparalleled track record in the field of international crime and had been a key figure in many high profile cases. Frank Chopin was kind enough to fly across the Atlantic with our interests at heart and met Clive at his chambers on 21 February 2002 in order to review the mess in which we had all, by now, concluded that we were. I appreciate that I have not yet explained the nature and extent of this mess. But all will be revealed soon.

Clive Nicholls confirmed that Frank was right to be concerned for our welfare, and considered that Bea and I should be preparing for the onslaught. He recommended that Frank should approach Simmons & Simmons as the best firm to act for us.

Thus it was that the man who greeted me as I arrived that morning was brought into our lives, for Frank picked up the telephone to Colin Passmore, Head of Litigation at Simmons & Simmons. And it was Colin who soon carefully pieced together for us the human machinery which we would need in order to be ready for the fight which was to come. Unsurprisingly, Colin instructed Clive Nicholls to be part of the team.

---

[45] Queen's Counsel, the senior tier of British barristers, often referred to as Silks by virtue of the silk gowns which they wear in court.

Clive, realising the amount of both work and skill which would be needed, suggested that another of the barristers at Three Raymond Buildings should be hired to assist. At this point James Lewis was brought on board. When this happened in early 2002, James was simply Junior Counsel. It was not until Maundy Thursday[46] of that year that James's name would appear for the first time on the lists of Queen's Counsel, when he became James Lewis QC.

James had been called to the bar a full 30 years after Clive Nicholls, but that was not the age difference between the two men. James had started his professional life as a soldier, coming to the Bar later than most, but this late start had not prevented him from carving out a formidable reputation. Just like Clive, James had been involved in some extremely high-profile international cases.

Frank's visit to London was followed shortly by a trip for Gerry Feffer who, arriving at Heathrow from Washington early one morning en route to see Clive Nicholls, was standing in line for immigration. In a second line alongside him he spotted a familiar face, that of Chris Todd, a partner of Kellogg, Huber, Hansen & Todd, an up-and-coming Washington law firm. Chris had also been an Assistant US Attorney for the Southern District of New York, although a few years later than Gerry. Chris was accompanied by Jim Webster, a fellow partner of Kellogg, Huber, Hansen & Todd.

As the three men edged towards the immigration desks the exchanges between them were friendly, but only as complicated as one might expect at 7.00am after an overnight flight during which someone appears to have stolen a whole night's sleep from you. But this chance meeting would in time prove fortuitous.

Gerry had his meeting as planned with Clive Nicholls, during the course of which the conversation got around to the fact that I needed to review my own representation in the US. Chris Todd's name was mentioned by Gerry as someone who was worth considering. What he did not know was that Chris Todd's name was, by the most bizarre coincidence, already pencilled into Clive's diary for later that day.

Chris and Clive had never before worked together but, even so, they knew each other very well, and for the oddest of reasons. Many

---

46 Maundy Thursday is the Thursday before Easter and, until 2005, was the day each year on which new Queen's Counsel were appointed.

years earlier, Clive had been working in New York, acting for the US Attorney's Office for the Southern District, and for an Assistant US Attorney called Sarah Gold, today an attorney with Proskauer Rose. This was Clive's first time in New York, and he was disappointed at the end of an intensive week's work not to have seen very much of Manhattan. Sarah Gold had said, "This is a job for one of my colleagues!" At which point, she had produced Chris Todd, who escorted Clive on a whirlwind tour of the Big Apple. This started in Harlem, and progressed through every speakeasy and Irish bar imaginable before ending up at the Helmsley Palace. Clive and Chris hooked up at lunchtime on Friday, and eventually parted from each other at lunchtime on Saturday. During this time, their company had been lubricated by fine liquid and great conversation, much of which stemmed from the fact that they had both studied at Cambridge University. From that moment onwards, they were great friends.

The rendezvous with Clive was purely social, involving champagne, chocolates and a look at Clive's new book[47]. Gerry Feffer's name was mentioned, but only in passing. But almost as soon as Chris and Jim got back to Washington, Chris got a call from Frank Chopin asking him to return to London to meet me. Within days, I had hired Kellogg, Huber, Hansen & Todd to represent me in the US. And that explains the presence of Jim Webster, the third individual in the room with me that morning at Simmons & Simmons.

Having reminded myself as to how the team before me had been assembled, I then tried to identify the very beginning of this whole horrible process. This time, I did not have to look across the Atlantic at all. The events which were the trigger for all of this took place, ironically, only a few miles from where I was standing now, but 30 years earlier. Was the Montcalm really that long ago?

---

[47] *The Law of Extradition and Mutual Assistance – International Criminal Law: Practice and Procedure* 1st Edn. 2002 Oxford University Press.

FATE INTERVENES

In May 1977, we had rented an apartment for three months in the hills outside Cannes. Whilst there, I got a telephone call from a friend who asked me to meet a man called Bob Hausman, who was the President of Loews Hotels. Loews was of course well known to me, and this approach sounded interesting.

Loews Hotels was part of a family conglomerate of businesses which had been pieced together by Brooklyn-born brothers Laurence Tisch and Preston R 'Bob' Tisch. I fixed a meeting with Bob Hausman, during which he expressed an interest on behalf of Loews in buying the Montcalm hotel. Since the 1940s, the Tisch brothers had been acquiring a series of disparate interests which included hotels, movie theatres, cigarettes, oil exploration and watch-making. I had met Laurence Tisch in South Africa some years before, when he had visited and stayed in one of our hotels, and had been very impressed by him. He donated millions and also raised fortunes for education at New York University and for the arts, the Tisch galleries at the Metropolitan Museum of Art being named after him.

The Tisch brothers had purchased a large stake in the Loews chain from MGM in 1959 and within a year had gained control of the company. But they will be best remembered for their controversial purchase in 1986 of a quarter of the shares in CBS, ostensibly to defend it from the clutches of corporate raiders. However, they themselves sold assets, fired news reporters and otherwise cut costs before selling the business on to Westinghouse in 1995 at a substantial profit.

But back in 1977, I realised that the possible sale of the Montcalm represented a very real opportunity. Not only did I agree to meet Bob Hausman, who was later to become Chairman of Loews, but I entered into negotiations with him, and also with a Loews executive called Sandford Freedman.

Remember that at the time we bought the Montcalm, in March 1975, it was not only difficult to sell a hotel, it was almost impossible to give one away. The Montcalm had been comprehensively rebuilt at someone else's expense, even though it needed the fit-out to be finished. We had managed to pick up a long lease on the hotel for £25,000 and the fit-out then cost us a further £100,000. Considering that the total cost for the purchase and fix-up of this hotel was therefore just £125,000, you will appreciate the scale of the gain which was achieved when we agreed to sell the Montcalm to the Loews Corporation for close to $5 million. We had owned the hotel for just two and a half years.

At the time when we disengaged from Court Hotels, I had given Seamus O'Byrne a stake in the Montcalm. This meant that Seamus received a substantial windfall, sufficient to trigger his retirement from the hotel business. He moved back to Dublin, the city of his birth, where he opened a successful wine bistro called Dobbins, in partnership with his brother, John.

After the completion of the Montcalm transaction, Bob Tisch organised a dinner party in London to celebrate. The Tisch brothers also owned the Churchill Hotel in Portman Square, where they took a private room, and extended an invitation to all their American friends whom they knew to be in London at the time. The Tisch brothers were very well connected in business, entertainment and politics. In 1986, for instance, Bob was to become United States Postmaster General as part of the President George H W Bush administration. But at his party that evening I was introduced not to a politician, but to the legendary Lew Wasserman, the unchallenged master of Hollywood.

Hollywood today is dominated by multinational corporations, but at the time that Bea and I met Lew Wasserman for the first time, 'Tinseltown' had been run for many years by a series of larger-than-life, publicity-seeking individuals such as Jack Warner, Samuel Goldwyn and Louis B Meyer. Although a much more private individual, Lew Wasserman's name ranked alongside these figures.

In fact, he outlived them and ultimately outgunned them, becoming known as 'The Last Mogul'.

Born in Cleveland, Ohio to Russian émigré parents, Lew Wasserman grew up in a difficult neighbourhood, and began his career in entertainment as an usher in a movie theatre. His big break came when he moved to Chicago and became a talent agent for the Music Corporation of America (MCA). MCA moved its headquarters to Beverly Hills in 1937, and Lew rose quickly in the organisation as it worked to create a monopoly of motion picture, stage and radio talent. His early clients included Bette Davis, Betty Grable and Ronald Reagan. In 1941, he negotiated one of Hollywood's first $1 million movie contracts for Reagan with Warner Brothers Studios. Despite what was to prove a lifelong friendship with Ronald Reagan, Lew Wasserman was a Democrat and would in time become one of the earliest backers of Bill Clinton.

As MCA President, he wielded huge power and influence in Hollywood, with corporate tentacles reaching every aspect of the entertainment business. His agents were known as the 'Men in Black' because, like him, they always wore the Wasserman 'uniform' of dark suit, white shirt and dark tie.

But in 1962, he became involved in a lengthy battle with the US Department of Justice over what were perceived to be MCA's monopolistic practices. Some very ugly exchanges culminated in a showdown between Lew Wasserman and the then Attorney General, Robert Kennedy. In order to avoid criminal indictments for alleged anti-trust violations, MCA divested itself of its talent agency almost overnight and instead bought struggling Universal Pictures. In doing so, Lew snatched victory from the jaws of apparent defeat, for another glorious chapter in the Wasserman story was about to be written.

Under his direction, Universal Pictures was transformed into Universal Studios, the largest and busiest lot in Hollywood. Although in the early days it was not itself a prodigious generator of its own product, Universal Studios became a finishing school for many of today's best directors, including Steven Spielberg, George Lucas and

Ron Howard. These relationships blossomed, and with them blockbusters, including *Jaws*, *Back to the Future* and *E.T.* In 1990, Lew sold Universal to Matsushita Electric in a deal worth $6 billion, with his own share amounting to half a billion dollars.

Lew and his wife, Edith, had a small house in Belgravia, and were regular visitors to London. It was little surprise, therefore, that they should be at Bob Tisch's party at the Churchill. I struck up an immediate and easy friendship with Lew that evening, and we continued to see each other on and off over the years, in time becoming very close friends. Lew was a quiet dynamo of a man, at one and the same time gentle but tough. It was not difficult to see why he had been so successful. Larry King said that Lew Wasserman would fill any room with his presence, a view with which I would wholeheartedly concur.

Nine years after that dinner in London, in July 1986, Bea and I were amongst the guests at Lew and Edie's 50th Wedding Anniversary. This was held on the Universal backlot where *Back to the Future* had been filmed two years earlier, and where a set had been created to give the impression of downtown Cleveland as it would have been in 1936. It featured the Palace Theater where Lew ushered, and the Mayfair Casino where Lew and Edie first met. Chasen's, the West Hollywood restaurant, provided the catering, serving its famous chilli as well as potatoes stuffed with Beluga caviar. Bob Hope, Audrey Hepburn and Charlton Heston were amongst the guests, and Rosemary Clooney and the great lyricist Sammy Kahn serenaded the hosts with a customised version of *My Way* – *"For 50 years, through laughs and tears, they did it their way."* Bea and I were honoured to be seated at the very next table to Lew and Edie, a table which we shared with Danny Kaye, Walter Matthau and our close friends Isadore and Camilla Rosenfeld. Our memories are of an incredibly happy occasion.

The sale of the Montcalm should have been an equally happy occasion for us. However, the longtime friend who had called me to suggest that I should meet Bob Hausman fell out with me over what he considered should have been his commission on the sale. I paid him a 5% introductory fee, which meant that I gave him £125,000. Expressed another way, he had earned as much for one telephone call as we had originally *paid* for the hotel in the first place. Believe it or not, however, he considered that this was not good enough, and demanded more. Another friendship down the drain.

Some months after the sale was completed, Bob Hausman approached me again, this time suggesting that we should go into partnership together and build a hotel group of our own in the United States. Bob said that he would remain at Loews, and pass on all opportunities which came across his desk but which did not fit the Loews 'acquisition template'. He explained that these were often interesting opportunities, and that there was money to be made.

Bob Hausman had joined the Tisch brothers in 1967 following an invitation from Bob Tisch. At the time, he owned and ran a chain of pancake houses branded Aunt Jemima. Bob Tisch, like Bob Hausman, was a member of the Metropolis Country Club in Scarsdale. At the Club one day, he approached Bob Hausman and asked him whether he would like to come into the hotel business. He sold his restaurants and became an integral part of the hotel company that would that year acquire the Loews name when the Tisch brothers bought Loews Theaters.

Bob Hausman handled the negotations for Loews to open a hotel in Monte Carlo and, in doing so, became a friend of Prince Rainier and Princess Grace. When she died in 1983, Prince Rainier asked Bob Hausman to become Chairman of the Princess Grace Foundation USA.

Bob Hausman told me that one of his Loews management team, a man called Monty Hundley, whom I had met briefly in connection with the sale of the Montcalm, would be prepared to leave the corporation and that he would provide the management expertise necessary to build the partnership. Bob was seeking strategic advice from me, plus a little financial backing.

My initial response was lukewarm, as I was heavily involved elsewhere and was in the mood to shed responsibilities as opposed to setting up new ventures. At the time, I was also thinking seriously of retiring. Most importantly, I was now actively involved with Trafalgar, and was keen to apply my energies to developing our travel businesses. However, Hausman assured me that I need not have anything to do with the day-to-day running of the business, but could in many ways act like a silent partner, providing investment and being on hand for strategic advice. Besides, there was a team of highly-qualified accountants and lawyers which had already acquired a substantial body of experience. These guys could handle it. My role would be the occasional raising of finance, and the provision of a little advice.

I have already mentioned that we had become attracted by the United States as a recreational base, and that we had bought an apartment in Palm Beach in 1977, the first of a number of US homes. So we were not averse to the United States. On the contrary. And an additional consideration was that Brett had left Rugby and was now studying at the Cornell University School of Hotel Administration at Ithaca, in up-state New York. Upon graduation, he was keen to join a hotel group in the US. With Brett's career in mind, Hausman's request that I back the new US business venture was given more careful thought than it would otherwise have received.

After substantial consideration, the deal which we struck was as follows. Bob Hausman, Monty Hundley and I would each be minority shareholders, although Bob would be a sleeping partner. Bob Hausman and I had day-to-day responsibilities elsewhere, and he and I would therefore be non-executive with the new venture, offering help from a distance. Monty Hundley would become a full-time executive with the business, which was named simply Tollman-Hundley, because Bob Hausman's contract with Loews prevented him from being openly involved. Hausman was nevertheless not only the creator of Tollman-Hundley, but a key figure in the development of the corporation for its first eight years, after which time he stepped away for family reasons. He died in April 1997.

And thus it was that, in the very best of faith, I signed up to my involvement with Tollman-Hundley, a venture which was founded in 1978, which I entered with few expectations, and which would in due course propel the whole of my family to the edge of destruction.

MONTE CARLO 14

At about the time of the sale of the Montcalm, Nick Tarsh's contract at Trafalgar came up for renewal. He demanded an eye-watering increase in his salary to retain his services. Ken Bates and I, now actively overseeing the venture, were not in the mood to be blackmailed. We chose not to meet his demands, electing instead to re-hire someone whom Trafalgar had in fact fired five years earlier.

Ironically, even though Ken and I were about to travel to Australia to visit our investments there, finding a rapid solution to the Nick Tarsh problem worked incredibly well. This was because the man we wanted to persuade to return to Trafalgar was in fact now living and working in Melbourne. Ken and I visited him there. He was an impressive young man called Mike Ness, who had trained as an accountant in South Africa. He had been fired by Dino Philippides a few years earlier for having had the temerity to order a radio for his company car without proper sanction. He had been a loss to the business, and we persuaded him to re-join us. Mike would in time prove to be a very important figure in the worldwide development of the family's travel businesses.

After seeing Mike Ness, amongst the other things Ken needed to do in Australia was visit his sugar farm, which was near Cairns, Queensland. I went to Cairns too, planning to do a little fishing myself whilst Ken worked. We checked into the best accommodation Cairns had to offer at the time, a place which I believe was called the Tradewinds Motel. A world-class establishment this was not. Cairns was then the back of beyond, a fact underlined by its hospitality offering – or lack of it.

Imagine our surprise, therefore, to discover in the motel bar that evening that the only drinker there was none other than the Oscar-winning actor, Lee Marvin. He and I started talking and I discovered that, just like me, he was there for the fishing.

Ten years earlier, a Cairns game-fishing captain, operating 30 miles out to sea, realised that he had hooked into a very large fish indeed. A spectacular leap revealed that this was a gigantic black marlin, the ultimate game-fishing species. After a long fight, it was brought in to the boat, weighing in at no less than 1,064 pounds. Until that time, Cairns had not been viewed as a game-fishing destination, certainly not one for thousand-pound black marlin. That single fish changed everything, putting Cairns on the tourist map, especially when Lee Marvin and others made the pilgrimage each November in pursuit of a fish reckoned to be the world's finest and most challenging prey.

Lee became completely obsessed with catching his ultimate trophy fish, one even bigger than the thousand-pounder of 1966. And he was successful. Three years before I met him, he caught a black marlin which weighed-in at a staggering 1,218 pounds, a photograph of which is included in this book. And a 15 foot-long cast of an even larger fish (1,232 pounds) hung on a wall in a specially-constructed room at Lee's home in Arizona.

Knowing that I had to be up at the crack of dawn for the charter boat I had booked, I went to bed early, wishing Lee luck for the morning. When I arrived at the dock the next day, my skipper asked me whether I would mind sharing the boat with another fisherman who had been unable to find a boat for himself. I happily agreed, and was joined by my fellow drinker from the night before. Thus it was that Lee Marvin and I went fishing together for the first time but not, I am pleased to say, for the last. Over the years which followed, we fished together regularly. Lee, who died in 1987, was the all-American hero – a good-looking, decorated war veteran who became an Oscar-winning Hollywood star. He is buried at Arlington National Cemetery.

Ken Bates, who was the majority shareholder in Trafalgar, had taken offices in the building which was above what was known at the time as the West London Air Terminal. This was situated at 25 Buckingham Palace Road, where passengers flying with BOAC were able to check in for their international flights, a short walk

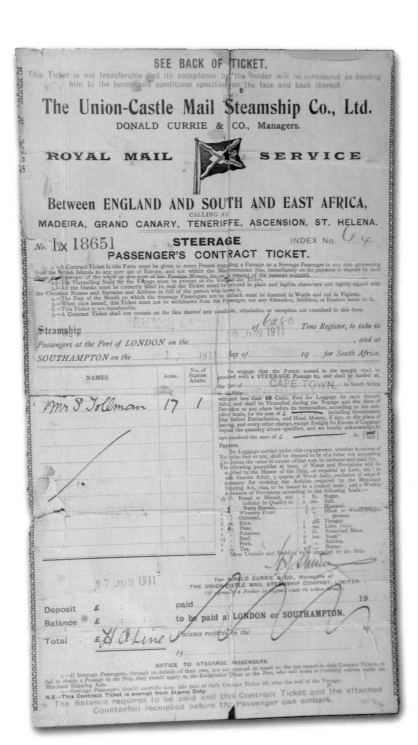

My father's ticket to a new life

SS Braemar Castle

My mother's parents, Barnett and Leah Swerling

The family
From the left: Arnold, my mother, Ivan, my father and me

Bea's father, Rueben Lurie

Beauty and the Beast
Bea and World Heavyweight
Boxing Champion,
Primo Carnera

Young love

The night Bea and I got engaged
Ciro's, Johannesburg, 1952

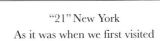

"21" New York
As it was when we first visited

Our 11th Wedding Anniversary, 1965
"21" New York

Jean Sablon at The Colony, 1959

A night at The Colony
From left: me, Bea, Sid James, Arnold, Ellen and Stanley Baker

Bea attends the première of *Some Like it Hot*,
Johannesburg, 1959

Left: Visiting Venice 1963, whilst aboard John Schlesinger's yacht

Senior management from our Johannesburg hotels, 1961
Bea, who was pregnant at the time, is absent

The liquor store I built alongside the Hyde Park Hotel
with my office above

First ladies' bar in South Africa, Hyde Park Hotel, 1960

Friends and family celebrating Alma Cogan's residence
at The Colony. Alma is third from right

Bea and the children, 1966

Proof that I was once a polo player

Our pride and joy. The Tollman Towers, Johannesburg, 1970
The 'T' on the side of the 27-storey building was so big that it was
visible to aircraft landing at Jan Smuts airport

Dias Doradas, our 'House of the Year', 1972

Our farm in Connecticut

Bea and me with our two youngest, Brett and Vicki,
at Naivasha, Kenya

Bea with George Peppard at Sohobele,
our first game reserve, 1970

My father's portrait is a constant reminder of an exceptional man

away from Victoria station. Although Ken's offices were there, Trafalgar's operations remained at Bressenden Place, also in Victoria, where they had been since 1969, and no doubt still would be, had it not been for redevelopments in the vicinity of Victoria station. We are now in Waterloo.

Ken and I were talking together one day in his offices in Buckingham Palace Road when he told me that his bank was calling in a loan on his sugar farm, and that he desperately needed £25,000. With the Montcalm deal done, it was possible to write him a cheque. Ken, in an extraordinary act of generosity – which I have to say was a side of his character which he showed on many an occasion during our 30 years of friendship – insisted on giving us 50% of the sugar farm. This was to prove a more than generous gift. Within two years, the City of Cairns compulsorily purchased the land on which the sugar farm was situated. And they did so for a very large sum of money indeed.

The following year, 1978, Ken and I decided to move to Monte Carlo. Because both of us were always on the move, and knowing therefore how unlikely it would be for us to be there at the same time, we jointly acquired a beautiful duplex penthouse with just two bedrooms. The apartment was situated behind the Dolls Museum, overlooking the sea. Bea furnished it with some of the beautiful things which we had kept in store from our house in Johannesburg. Later that year, our daughter Toni got married in Monte Carlo at the La Vigie Beach Club in a wonderful two-day celebration.

At about the same time, we also rented an apartment at 641 Fifth Avenue, New York. This building, known as Olympic Tower, had been developed by Aristotle Onassis, and had been completed only two years earlier. It overlooks the spires of St Patrick's Cathedral right across 51st Street. With our apartment in New York, and our homes in South Palm Beach, London and Monte Carlo, in just three years we had come a long way from the dark days of 1975 and our tragic South African losses.

During the next four years I divided my time between my investments in the hotel businesses, working with Mike Ness and Ken

Bates on Trafalgar and its subsidiaries, and visiting Palm Beach, New York, London and Monaco. The Tollmans' lives became something of a non-stop international commute, because Bea and I always travelled together from place to place, something which we try to do even now.

My informal partnership with Ken was to play a major part in rebuilding the family fortunes. Between 1978 and 1980, Ken and I together pulled off five deals which in total netted us even more than our South African empire had ever been worth.

Toni was married and Wynn was in New York, but as Brett and Vicki were still growing up, they would spend the summer with us, usually in Monte Carlo. During this time they became very friendly with Stephanie and Albert, the younger children of Prince Rainier and Princess Grace. Our lives seemed to be a continuous pattern of travel, work, socialising and seeking new opportunities.

During this period, Ken Bates and I acquired together an extraordinary cattle station called Lorella which was situated in Australia's Northern Territories, and which we visited on a couple of occasions. This was a property covering more than one million acres, and was about the same size as the whole of the US State of Delaware.

We also made a 29.9% investment in Grey-Green, a British publicly-listed transport company. But the family who owned the majority of the shares refused to give us a seat on the board. We sat on our stake, but not for very long. In 1978, Ken had invited me to a Chelsea football match and, whilst there, I met an interesting businessman called Tom Cowie (later to become Sir Tom Cowie). He already had various motor vehicle related businesses, and was clearly a man who had his eye on growth. Ken and I sold our stake in Grey-Green to him, realising a profit of around £1 million – a lot of money at that time – and Tom went on to take over Grey-Green and make it one of the cornerstones of his expanding empire.

At the time that Ken and I disposed of our Grey-Green stake, he and I had a wager as to what our profits for the year would turn out to be. I am not a gambler by inclination. Quite the reverse, as will be revealed later. However, Ken and I nevertheless shook hands on a deal whereby the loser of the bet would take the winner and his wife wherever in the world they wanted to go. I won. And I chose the Hawaiian Islands.

And so it was that Bea and I found ourselves, with Ken and Pam, his then wife, in Hawaii on 7 March 1979, the occasion of our 25th Wedding Anniversary. Unbeknownst to Bea and me, Ken had made special plans. He had arranged for a chauffeur-driven vintage Rolls-Royce to take us on a tour of the island, a tour which culminated in lunch on the beach. Everything was graciously and beautifully executed, with great taste and enormous generosity. It was a memorable day, and we have the album to prove it. Ken has been married three times himself. His first marriage, to Theresa, lasted 20 years and his second, to Pam, for 13. He is currently married to Suzannah.

At around the time of our anniversary in Hawaii, we sold the flat in Palm Beach and bought a small house right next door to *Mar-A-Lago*, which was shortly to become Donald Trump's mansion. *Mar-A-Lago* is Spanish for Sea-to-Lake, and was built in 1927 by Marjorie Merriweather Post and her husband Edward Hutton. It was bought by Donald Trump in 1985 at a cost of $10 million. He renovated the property to include no fewer than 58 bedrooms – and three bomb shelters! It sits in 17 acres, a huge estate by the standards of Palm Beach.

Our house was a more modest affair, sitting in only an eighth of an acre. But with Bea's clever design following a rebuild of the property, we ended up with a five-bedroomed house, plus pool, which could accommodate the whole family.

In 1981, I became aware that Arthur Frommer's world famous travel business was in trouble, and I was very keen to save it if possible. Arthur was an American, and a lawyer by training. A graduate of both New York University and Yale, he had been Editor of the Yale Law Journal for a while. He was drafted into the US Army during the Korean War, but had been posted to Europe. Whilst there, in 1955 he wrote and published a guidebook called the *GI's Guide to Travelling in Europe*. He followed this up with a civilian version two years later, entitled *Europe on Five Dollars a Day*.

Arthur's fascination with travel led to further publications and thence to a tour operation which he called $5-a-Day Tours, Inc. In 1969, he built a hotel in Amsterdam on the site of the Weaver's Guild, Nooderstraat which he called the Arthur Frommer Hotel. As part of my attempts to save Arthur, we bought the hotel, providing him with much-needed cash. Sadly, even this was not enough to save his business from going under.

In the following year, 1982, I achieved a lifetime ambition with the acquisition of a beautiful 210-acre farm in Litchfield County, Connecticut. (We subsequently bought up five or six smaller, adjoining farms, and we now own about 400 acres in total.) I had always wanted to own a special farm and this was very, very special. On some of the land we continued to grow corn, or maize as it is known elsewhere in the world. But, in time, we also grew some of the best vegetables I have ever tasted, and we kept a veritable menagerie of farm animals. We had hayrides. We bred horses. We had a stream running through the estate from which we caught trout. We also had a lake. *Rebecca of Sunnybrook Farm* had nothing on us. Our Litchfield County home was little short of paradise. In the years which followed, we built a house for each of our children within the estate. Litchfield County represented the lungs which we all needed when spending time, as we knew we would, in Manhattan.

Meanwhile, back in the UK, seeds of a possible endeavour were germinating which would lead ultimately to the parting of the ways for Ken and me. In truth, I suspect that the 'soil' into which these seeds were planted had been well-prepared with the creation of Tollman-Hundley Hotels, which I later concluded had made Ken feel somewhat left out.

Ken had retained many of his football connections, especially from the North-West. One his friends was Malcolm Allison, the former manager of Manchester City. At a party one day, Allison introduced Ken to a lady called June Mears, the wife of Brian Mears, who was then the Chairman of Chelsea Football Club.

The two of them got on well together; so well that June Mears invited Ken and his then wife, Pam, to Stamford Bridge. Thus began a great friendship between the Bateses and the Mearses, and Ken found himself invited to Christopher Mears' 21st birthday party in 1981. Birthday celebrations were, though, a little muted because Chelsea had just been relegated to the Second Division, and were in financial trouble. Ken offered to help, writing out a sponsorship cheque for £18,000 on the spot.

In fact, Chelsea Football Club was in a dire position. Not only was there the team's dismal performance on the pitch, attempts to redevelop Stamford Bridge had ended in complete disaster, and the very existence of the Club was in doubt. At this point in the story, the name of Martin Spencer, the insolvency expert at Stoy Hayward, is reintroduced. But this time only because he had an assistant called John Papi, a Kuwaiti, who decided that he had something which could well be of great interest to Ken Bates.

John Papi had clearly researched his prospective prey accurately, because when he took a taxi to Ken's office one day in November 1981, he had something in his briefcase to put on the table which he felt was certain to create interest. In essence, he suggested that Ken should take over Chelsea for just £1, provided that he also assumed responsibility for the Club's debts, which were running at £600,000.

From the perspective of the 21st Century, it is difficult to imagine that these are real numbers. How could one possibly purchase a leading football club for so little money? But 1981 was a long time ago, Chelsea was at its lowest ebb, and the sporting world had yet to experience the revenues which professional football would soon generate. Caveats notwithstanding though, Ken was still very keen to make this deal, which was completed in early 1982.

Ken told me about it shortly afterwards, but said that he would like to pursue *this* venture on his own. During the time that we had invested together, our normal rule was that we would share each other's discoveries – risk and return – 50:50. But I knew that Ken had always had a love affair with football and, more recently and especially, with Chelsea FC. I was very happy for him that he had

achieved one of his lifetime ambitions. It was around this time that
Ken decided to leave our jointly-held apartment in Monaco, meaning
that Bea and I were now sole occupiers.

Ken asked me to join the Chelsea Board, which I did in
November 1982, but that was it. Nothing more. The endless
speculation that I was somehow the secret owner of Chelsea was
simply untrue. It was a massive red herring; encouraged it seems by
those who were happy that the bloodhounds were pursuing a false
scent. True, I did buy shares in the club, but only when there was a
public offering. Other than a few enjoyable hours' entertainment
every so often at Stamford Bridge, I took nothing out of Chelsea. And
I was happy to help Ken when he decided to sell. I took a call from
him at home one evening in 2003, when he told me that he was with
Roman Abramovich at Harry's Bar, and that Abramovich wanted to
buy the club. Ken needed to be able to speak for more than 50% of
the shares in Chelsea, and asked me whether I would sell my shares
to make up the numbers. I told him that I was happy to go along, if
that was what he wanted.

The highlight of my time at Chelsea came very soon after I
joined the Board. This was the 1983/84 season, which Chelsea began
in the Second Division. Ken later wrote about this in his book,
Chelsea… My Year [48]. I feature extensively in this volume, but almost
entirely in relation to meeting up for lunch, usually at Harry's Bar or
the Chesterfield Hotel.

In fact, the reference to the Chesterfield in diary entries dated
1984, as Ken's were, is significant, because this is precisely the time
when I was negotiating with Sir Max Joseph, ultimately buying the
Chesterfield Hotel out of Grand Metropolitan Hotels. The
Chesterfield would in time become the foundation stone of Red
Carnation Hotels and an important part of the family fortunes. And
around this time I also bought a small hotel in Beaulieu, France, and
another in Neuilly-sur-Seine, Paris creating a collection of four
European hotels, including the Frommer in Amsterdam.

In Chelsea… My Year, Ken makes reference to the wonderful
Harlequin Great Dane which he always wanted and which I gave him

---

[48] *Chelsea… My Year,* Ken Bates, Chelsea Football Club 1984.

when he bought The Grange, his country home near Beaconsfield. He named this huge beast 'Tolly'.

And there is another reference in Ken's book which I would like to mention. It is an entry dated Saturday, 12 May 1984. This was a momentous day. Chelsea had just ended the season as champions, and had been promoted to the First Division. I was in the United States that day, working, and I was extremely interested in the final scores of the season. Remember, this is long before the days of the internet and instant access to sporting information wherever one might be. Ken's entry for that day includes the following:

I rang Stanley Tollman in New York to tell him the result. He called me a sadistic bastard: he had been waiting for three hours for my call and thought we must have lost!

In 1983, Ken bought a company called Marina Travel, which he described as "a big thing in Scotland". Marina Travel may have been a big thing in Scotland, but we soon discovered that this acquisition was an absolute disaster. Part of this company was in far worse condition than had been disclosed to us. After just four weeks, we had to walk away from the deal, but by then it had already cost us £5 million – £5 million which Trafalgar itself did not have.

Today, Trafalgar is a profitable business providing holidays for around 250,000 people per year. But at the time of the Marina Travel acquisition, Trafalgar was a very different creature. It provided holidays each year for just 25,000 people and made only a modest profit. Unsurprisingly, therefore, Bea and I resented the money which we had to produce simply to keep Trafalgar afloat. Marina Travel was a very painful experience.

Against this backdrop, Ken told me one day over lunch at Harry's Bar that he wanted out of Trafalgar in order to concentrate fully on building up Chelsea Football Club. In fact, he wanted out of everything. In the light of the Marina Travel debacle, we both recognised that this was a sensible decision, but I have often surmised what was really going on in Ken's mind.

Trafalgar may have been the catalyst for our separation, but the division of interests cut right across the board. We could have dealt with Trafalgar in isolation, but I think that the fact that I was spending more and more time in America upset Ken, and he was in some way jealous of other partnerships. Given that I had made it very clear that I had no intention of going back into the hotel business, he must have found my partnership with Monty Hundley both difficult to understand and, I suspect, disappointing to him.

Within a very short period, we concluded the terms of our split, Ken and I dividing up the various assets which we owned jointly. Trafalgar had very little financial worth at that point beyond its reputation and was perceived by both of us to represent small change. Apart from the injections of cash which we had already made, we all knew that Trafalgar would have to be rebuilt from the ground up.

Ken was asked to give evidence in the Tollman-Hundley trial, which he gave by means of a videotaped deposition which was taken on 17 September 2003 at the American Embassy in London's Grosvenor Square. In answer to a question about what business deals he and I had done together whilst I was living in the United States he said, "In the event I can't recall that we acted in any, because I think Stanley was in a new country, building a new career, and I suppose business-wise I became irrelevant."

Ken is a very interesting man. A bully with a soft side. He can be great, but he can also be awful. Others who know Ken have a similar appreciation of the man. As David Mellor, former Conservative Cabinet Minister, once said, "Ken is someone who calls a spade a shovel and he does not suffer fools gladly. In an argument or a fight he does not take prisoners. Take him on at your peril. He can be rude and swear like a trooper. He does like to be the centre of attention and puts you down, but you have to appreciate that beneath all that he is a nice, kind, spontaneous man. I have only fond memories of my relationship with Ken."[49]

Life with Ken was rather like the opening lines from *A Tale of Two Cities* – the best of times but often, almost simultaneously, the worst of times. If I review the hours and the days which we spent together, I

---

[49] Brian Woolnough, *My Chelsea Dream*, Virgin 1998.

have some of the best memories imaginable. Sadly, there were also some deeply unhappy moments. Throughout the period I knew him closely, though, which was 30 years, I was always completely loyal to him. The fact that he was able to achieve what he did in life despite having a clubfoot revealed the strength and determination that was to be the hallmark of his whole career. But his overall behaviour in relation to the Tollman-Hundley investigation and the subsequent trial was, I may say, a little questionable. He and I have not spoken since.

People have told me that I should never have worked with Ken. With the benefit of considerable hindsight, that would have been a mistake. I have no bitterness towards Ken. On the contrary, I have reason to be grateful to him. Through Ken, we were able to get Trafalgar back and it was this business which would ultimately become the cornerstone of the Travel Corporation and the family fortunes.

I will, if I may, allow Ken, speaking in his own words, to close this period of my life, as well as this particular chapter of my book:

> *"I will leave it to others to decide whether I am good at fighting. Someone once said that Ken Bates likes a good fight and, if he has not got one, he goes looking for one. That is not true. I am a good friend and a bad enemy."*

GETTING OUR LIVES BACK
PART III

In the offices of Simmons & Simmons in 2008, I thought of the evidence which Ken had given five years earlier, and of his videotaped appearance on the screen in the courthouse in Manhattan. I wondered whether it was the same vast televison monitor on which I would shortly be appearing myself.

Back in 2003, I am told that Ken's video contained a head-and-shoulders shot of a familiar bearded figure who was in typically uncompromising form. Upon being asked the nature of the 'social relationship' which he admitted that he and I had enjoyed following the disbandment of our partnership, he answered quite simply, "Eating and drinking."

I could sense from what I learned from others who saw this performance that Ken seemed more than a little exasperated by the whole exercise. Knowing the man, he would certainly have had little time for the circus which he saw before him in London, where the video had been recorded.

The venue for the recording of Ken's submission had been the United States Embassy in Grosvenor Square. Apart from a couple of stenographers, there were also two Assistant US Attorneys, an officer of the FBI, an officer of the IRS, four defence attorneys, and even one of the defendants themselves. That's 11 people, including the stenographers, most of whom had flown from New York at someone else's expense expressly to ask Ken what he clearly considered to be some damn silly questions.

I thought about the answers he had given to those questions. I thought too about his vagueness and supposed lack of recall. And I thought about his preposterous refusal to accept that he had ever met Sanford Freedman. Freedman was Tollman-Hundley's Harvard-educated lawyer, and was the defendant who had crossed the Atlantic to appear in person in front of Ken in London, presumably in the hope that his presence might jog the Bates grey matter. But Ken's memory was not to be jogged. He admitted to having been my guest at the Sandpiper Bay Resort in Port St Lucie, Florida, but repeated that he could not remember meeting Sanford Freedman there. As my grandchildren would probably say in such circumstances – "Whatever."

I mused further on Ken Bates' comments, largely because thoughts of the Sandpiper Bay reminded me of Prince Rainier, more of which later, but I concluded that there was little point in conducting a mental post mortem of Ken's answers. It was all far too late for that.

My thoughts did, though, drift once more to what Ken had said about the significance of him and me meeting at the Sandpiper Bay Resort. He told the court that I had announced then that I wanted to end our business relationship because I had chosen to throw my lot in with Monty Hundley, rather than with him. My own recollection is, shall we say, somewhat different. Apart from never saying to anybody that my commitment to Monty was in some way the single most important business relationship of my life (which it demonstrably was not), my recollection is that Ken himself initiated the break-up of our partnership. This followed the very expensive mess he had got us into over the acquisition of Marina Travel.

But all this was history. It was a chapter of my life of only passing relevance to the events which had led up to the court appearance which I was about to make. Of much more importance now was not the chapter of my life which had been closed with Ken, but the sequence of events which followed. With the ending of the Tollman/Bates partnership, a page had been turned decisively. With Ken no longer a part of my life, I had chosen not to look over my shoulder at the past, but to look forward firmly into the future.

I began to make emotional and financial commitments to a country whose achievements, whose lofty aspirations and whose way of life I admired hugely. Sadly, though, I did not appreciate at that point in my life that, for all its high-minded idealism, the United States of America is a nation that tolerates behaviour within the executive branch of its government which is worthy of the mob. That painful realisation came much later.

In the early 1980s, there was little I yearned for more than the pursuit of life under the Stars & Stripes. But, as I reflected on that memory in the November morning in London in 2008, I was forced to accept that those dreams had sadly turned into a nightmare, one from which it seemed I might never awaken.

THE LAND OF THE FREE

Although there had been substantial preparatory work, as a venture proper Tollman-Hundley only really got going with the acquisition in 1979 of a management contract for the Prince George Hotel in New York. This opportunity was introduced to me by my old friend George Kaufman.

I met George for the first time in New York in 1978. He is a graduate of both Ohio State and New York Universities, and a Korean War veteran. For almost 50 years, George has been a prominent figure in the world of New York City real estate. Amongst other things, he is the President of the Midtown Real Estate Owners Association and a member of the Real Estate Board of New York. Through his company Kaufman Realty Corporation, he has been involved with the ownership, management and development of major commercial and residential properties of all kinds, but almost always in the New York City area. George is a very sweet guy who has always been incredibly kind to us – with one notable exception, which I will explain later.

Today, George is perhaps best known for his exceptional work in regenerating the Astoria Studios in the New York City borough of Queens. Originally built in 1920 as a studio close to the Broadway theatre district, the studios produced a number of well-known movies, including the Marx Brothers' *The Cocoanuts* and *Animal Crackers*. It was at that time branded simultaneously as both Paramount Studios and Astoria Studios. But, when Paramount moved all its operations to Hollywood in the 1930s, the studios became known simply as Astoria.

George undertook to transform and revitalise the now re-named Kaufman Astoria Studios into a major East Coast facility, capable of competing for business with the Hollywood studios, bringing feature film and television production back to New York. This is a monumental objective, but one towards which he has already made great strides.

The Prince George is a remarkable building, and first opened for business in 1904. Nowadays it is on the *National Register of Historic Places*. In its time, the Prince George was a leading New York hotel, but changing tastes and years of wear and tear meant that in 1979 Tollman-Hundley discovered a hotel in need of some serious work. This meant that Bea was able to go back to her first love, and she set about the redecoration of the Prince George. Situated close to Madison Square, the hotel was in a part of Manhattan which was no longer fashionable. That did not mean, though, that it was without striking features, notably a 5,000 square foot ballroom rich in neo-Renaissance detail and with a heavily ornamented ceiling. Within the budgetary confines of a mid-priced hotel, Bea managed to redecorate in a manner which was complementary to the extravagant decoration of a bygone age. She did a wonderful job.

Tollman-Hundley also located its own offices within the Prince George from which to operate the company. My son, Wynn, was also given an office there, the idea being that he would look for deals for the company. But this never really worked out.

My relationship with Wynn, my eldest child, is perhaps the greatest failure of my life. As a child, it was clear that Wynn had incredible potential, but it was equally clear that he was someone who was not at ease with the world. He went to St Stithians College, a Methodist Church school which is situated in Randburg, an area just to the north of Johannesburg. The school song of St Stithians is, *"Here their ship once anchored and here its course was set."* In Wynn's case, however, the ship seemed neither to be anchored nor set on the right course.

St Stithians is primarily a boarding school, but Wynn was unable to make it as a boarder and, very much against my wishes, he became a day boy. Upon matriculation, he was entered into Rugby School to do his A Levels. But things did not go smoothly there, either, because he started to develop terrible headaches. Bea and I took him to New York, where he had every test possible to find the source of the headaches. But the doctors could never find the reason.

He nevertheless managed to complete his A Levels, and then went to the London School of Economics & Political Science – the LSE. He had a very good mind and he understood finance extremely well. He had always had a leaning towards economics and had wanted to work in investment banking. In 1977, through my friendship with Jay Pritzker, Wynn was introduced to Salim 'Cy' Lewis, the imposing senior partner of Bear Stearns, New York. Wynn joined the investment banking division of Bear Stearns under Sig Wahrsager, who took him under his wing. Wynn found an apartment in New York at 55th Street on the East Side.

On our visits to New York, we discovered that Wynn had become very much a part of the swinging New York scene. Talked of as one of the city's 50 most eligible bachelors, he was always welcome at Studio 54 and at Xenon. During the 1970s, these were two of the world's best-known nightclub/discothèques. Studio 54 was located at 254 West 54th Street, and its opening night had been graced by the likes of Michael Jackson, Mick and Bianca Jagger, Liza Minnelli and Salvador Dali. And the list of those unable to get in was just as impressive, including, as it did, Woody Allen and Frank Sinatra. At its prime, the nightclub's flamboyant owner Steven Rubell became well-known for hand-selecting guests from the huge crowds milling around outside, mixing beautiful 'nobodies' with glamorous celebrities. 'Studio' as it came to be called, was notorious for its hedonism, the balconies were known for intimate encounters and drug use was rampant. Studio closed forever in 1980 with one final party entitled, 'The End of Modern-day Gomorrah'.

Wynn fell prey to the culture of drugs, late nights, and correspondingly late mornings. Bea would often telephone, hanging on the line for ages just to make sure he had got up in time for work. His mentor, Sig Wahrsager, sadly died of cancer in 1985, and Wynn left investment banking and moved to the currency trading side of Bear Stearns. But he could never arrive for work on time, and he was fired. He subsequently joined trading company Ladenburg

Thalmann & Company, working for another friend of mine, Stephen
Weisglass, who believed that he could sort Wynn out. Sadly, he was
wrong. Wynn was fired once again for failing to come to work on time.

Wynn's attitude to life had a profound effect on all the other
members of the family, but I think that no-one was more affected
than Brett. At this point I am able to harness the thoughts of a close
friend, who can talk with the objectivity of an outside observer. I can
do this by borrowing a few paragraphs from a letter written in support
of Brett, which appears in context a little later on in this book. In the
meantime, this is what George Kaufman had to say in 2004:

*Brett has had an extremely challenging, if not impossible, relationship
with his elder brother, Wynn, who chose a very different path from that
expected of him.*

*As a child, Brett was bullied by his brother, and tormented by his
brother's unwillingness to conform. Wynn was given a job in the family
business, with disastrous results. He regularly turned up at the office late,
and often drunk. To make matters worse, he then developed a drug
problem, and eventually had to be asked to leave.*

*Wynn became the black sheep of the family, turning his back not
only on the family business, but on his parents and on his brother and
sisters. His alcoholism became steadily worse and his behaviour more
extreme and antisocial. Brett, who for many years lived close to his
brother, tried endlessly to help him. Each time, he was rebuked. Brett has
for twenty-five years been tortured by Wynn's behaviour, hoping against
hope to rebuild bridges between Wynn and the rest of the family, but
throughout he has been doomed to failure.*

*The pressures on Brett were intolerable. He has always felt a
powerful duty to step into the breach – to become for his parents both the
son his brother never was, as well as their second son too. His naturally
sensitive instincts and personality have been obliged to develop an
uncomfortable outer shell of toughness in order to cope.*

Wynn marches to his own band, and in his own time. His office in the Prince George was right at the entrance of the Tollman-Hundley office suite. On my visits to New York, I would always approach his door nervously, hoping to find him in. But I rarely found him there. On most occasions, his office was locked. Around this time, he added drink to his problems. Thirty years later, drinking continues to be a problem for him.

In the middle of the 1980s, Wynn left Tollman-Hundley to pursue other ventures, usually with the next up-and-coming tycoon, and one of these deals proved very successful. This involved an IT company in Norway in which both he and Bea invested. This was subsequently floated on the Norwegian stock exchange, creating a bonanza for Wynn and, to a lesser extent, for Bea. He also had one or two other notable successes, including finding the Milestone Hotel in Kensington for Red Carnation in 1998. But, no matter how many times we have tried to bring Wynn fully within the family, it has never worked.

A few years ago, on a visit to South Africa, Wynn suffered a bad car accident and has stayed there since in order to recuperate. He has never married and his erratic behaviour means that he has great difficulty in maintaining long-term relationships. I am aware of two girls whom he should have married, but in each case he destroyed their relationship.

We have spent hours with Wynn and all of us have worked hard, but to no avail. Relationships between parents and children are often not straightforward, and sometimes, regardless of effort and for whatever reason, they do not work out. But Bea and I are left with a profound sense of loss as far as Wynn is concerned. To this day he has no meaningful relationship with any other member of the family. I wish so much that things had worked out differently.

My other great regret in life was allowing myself to be persuaded to get involved with Tollman-Hundley. But this was a steady seduction. In the beginning, I had merely dipped a metaphorical toe in the water, never expecting it to be a big deal. But the three-man partnership of Hundley, Hausman and Tollman began to grow quickly. After just five years of trading, Tollman-Hundley had developed into a successful management company which looked after approximately 20 hotels in London, Amsterdam and the South of France. It had also made its first group acquisition, that of the George Washington chain.

Despite my own very limited expectations, it was beginning to look as though Tollman-Hundley was in fact becoming a successful business, and the potential for growth appeared huge. Bea and I began to feel that the United States might in fact represent somewhere more than just a place to enjoy our vacations.

Looking back now, it is possible to draw comparisons with the two catastrophic ventures in my life. The first – Court Hotels – I covered earlier in the book. The second – Tollman-Hundley – is about to be revealed. The Court Hotels transaction was born out of the ambition to establish a foothold in Britain. The political situation in South Africa was such, and the desire to relocate so strong, that my judgement was clouded. I allowed myself to be carried along with the enthusiasm of others, and of the moment, and I failed to look at the deal as carefully as I should. On this occasion, my luck clearly deserted me. Had it been a year later, with the Montcalm deal in place, we would not have needed even to consider Court Hotels. We would have been in London on our own terms.

Just as ambition played a fateful role with Court Hotels, it was also standing in the wings when it came to the creation of Tollman-Hundley. Ambition here was linked to the future of the family, and of the hope of creating a base in the United States. But this was an ambition which took hold only gradually. Originally considered as a platform from which Brett could develop his career, it became something more. After all, Tollman-Hundley became a business in 1979, but it was not until 1985 that Bea and I moved to the US.

Only after a good deal of thought, we had decided to say *au revoir* to Monte Carlo and to shift the centre of gravity of the family, putting down our roots instead in the States. Ironically, given the way in which this period of our lives would ultimately draw to a conclusion, the first thing we did was to file our first tax returns with the United

States Internal Revenue Service. This was, in 1983, in fact, two years before we moved there.

Before taking this step, I had taken detailed tax advice, having learned from others that it was crucial to get this right. I was introduced to a man called Bill Holt, an Englishman who was based in Arizona. We explained everything to him and he then worked very closely with our English accountant, Derek Evans. They then showed us what had to be done, and then went away to do it. Some complex corporate and financial structures needed to be put into correct order before they allowed us to make any move. Everything was laid out and carefully examined. No stone was left unturned.

As a result of Bill Holt's very detailed and extensive advice, fundamental changes were made. Amongst these were the transfer of ownership of the shares in the travel business to our daughter, Vicki. Ironically, this transfer, although to prove of great significance in later years, was not at the time viewed as being a major decision. Our travel businesses had yet to reach anything like their full potential.

In the mid-Eighties, Bea and I acquired Green Cards, enabling us to work in the United States, and we set about moving the base of our lives across the Atlantic. We bought a beautiful apartment occupying the whole of a floor of 485 Park Avenue, New York. And in 1987, we bought an exquisite mansion on the lake at Palm Beach, replacing our much smaller home there.

Southwood, in Via del Lago, is one of Palm Beach's greatest homes. It sits in four-and-a-half acres of land, a vast plot by Palm Beach standards. The renowned architect, Marion Sims Wyeth, designed the house in 1935 for the New York surgeon, Dr John Vietor, and his heiress wife, Eleanore Woodward Vietor. Mrs Vietor was the wealthy half of this partnership, her inheritance deriving from her father Orator Woodward's ownership of the Jell-O patent.[51]

For the interiors of what was to become their sub-tropical Georgian house, the Vietors retained Ruby Ross Wood, a leading New York interior designer who was the principal decorator for Wanamakers, at the time a famous department store.

---

[51] Jell-O is a US brand name famous for gelatine desserts such as fruit gels, puddings and no-bake cream pies. Jell-O is today owned by Kraft.

Immediately prior to our purchase of Southwood, the property had been owned by Percy Uris, a real estate owner from New York City. The house had come on to the market because both Mr Uris and his wife had died, and the property had been unoccupied for many months. It was thus in a poor state of repair and, as a result, we were able to buy it at a remarkable price.

Southwood is a property with 'wonderful bones'. It has extraordinary gardens, ponds filled with koi carp, a tennis court, a swimming pool and a dock. We restored it completely, making it into a very comfortable home. Over the New Year period – the peak season for Palm Beach – the whole of the family could be accommodated, including numerous grandchildren and their nannies. We now owned three beautiful properties in the United States.

Our three homes notwithstanding, we were still foreigners as far as the United States was concerned and being branded 'South African' was making life our lives increasingly difficult, whatever our own views of *apartheid* happened to be. Bea and I both remember vividly a flight from Hong Kong from London at around this time, which involved an extended layover in Bombay. As we stepped out of the aircraft, we saw a huge sign which said, "No dogs or South Africans allowed". We were forced to sit in a transit lounge for six long and very uncomfortable hours, banned from moving beyond it because of our South African passports.

In 1990, Bea became the first to acquire US citizenship. I joined her at the beginning of the following year, days before F W de Klerk announced that Nelson Mandela was to be released from prison. Looking back, there is nothing that Bea and I regret more than the decision we took to become US citizens. Ironically, had Mandela been released from prison just two years earlier than he was, Bea and I would never have given up hope for our home country, and we would never have embarked upon the path to become American citizens. Our lives would have been very different indeed.

MONTY HUNDLEY

I met Monty Hundley for the first time in Monte Carlo, just after we had moved there. This was at the time of the Montcalm deal, when he was still working for Bob Hausman at Loews.

I was told right from the beginning – a message which was to repeated to me endlessly over the years – that Monty Hundley was a brilliant accountant and that I was very lucky to be in partnership with him. His resumé was certainly impressive. At the age of 26, Monty had been appointed Manager of the Sahara Tahoe, a casino resort which had been built by the legendary Del Webb.

Delbert Eugene Webb was an outstanding real estate developer and construction magnate, best known for creating the retirement community of Sun City, Arizona. By all accounts, he was also quite a character – an associate of Howard Hughes, a golfing partner of both Bing Crosby and Bob Hope, and a part-owner of the New York Yankees baseball team.

The Sahara Tahoe was situated in Stateline, Nevada, and Monty Hundley's claim to fame was that he been the first person to put Elvis Presley in a showroom – or so he said. Certainly, Elvis played at the Sahara Tahoe regularly from 1971 to 1976, and his suite in the resort is still available to guests. But whether Monty was the first to put Elvis in a showroom, who knows?

Colleagues of Monty whilst he was with Del Webb were Tom Aro and Jim Cutler, both accountants and both subsequently part of the team which Monty would quickly assemble when he set up Tollman-Hundley. But Monty had been hired away from Del Webb in 1974 to become the Managing Director of Loews Paradise Island in the Bahamas. He was still only 29 years old.

Within Loews, it was soon adjudged that Monty was a man with a future. Although in some quarters viewed as brash, flamboyant and cocky, he was nevertheless generally liked and well-respected. During this time he began to work closely with Harvard-educated lawyer Sanford Freedman. Equally important, as far as my own story is concerned, he also caught the eye of Bob Hausman, who marked him down as a man to watch.

When I first met Monty, he was living with his wife and two children in a two-bedroomed rented apartment in New Jersey. As Tollman-Hundley developed, the company outgrew in every way its facilities at the Prince George and it moved to offices in Fifth Avenue, at the junction of West 57th Street. But change of address was not confined to the company itself. As Tollman-Hundley expanded, so, it seems, did Monty's needs. A brand new, chauffeur-driven Rolls Royce would take him home from work to a beautiful brownstone town house in Manhattan, complete with butler and other staff, and resplendent with fine antiques and expensive furnishings. I recall one rug which he told me set him back $80,000. I would be afraid to buy such a thing, let alone walk on it!

When I was in New York, which was not often, I shared a partner's desk with Monty in a corner office at the Fifth Avenue address. My journey home from the office to my apartment was a short walk, three long blocks east across Manhattan and one short block north to 58th Street. I often thought what my father would have said had he been around to see me. Here I was, a man whose childhood home had been a fishing village on the other side of the globe, living and working in the heart of New York, and doing so in the best way possible. In the summer months, Bea and I would leave the City on Thursday and take the two-hour drive up to the farm in Connecticut. Winters would be spent in Palm Beach until March or so. I would take *Concorde* twice a month back to London to deal with matters connected to the travel businesses. And if I was in Manhattan, I would arrive in the office around 11.00 in the morning, hear what was going on and then go for lunch. And lunch was, of course, always at the corner table in "21". What more could a man wish for? I really had made it.

However, the real estate crisis of 1990 had not yet hit and, like so many others, I was yet to realise that the merry-go-round was about to stop spinning. Throughout the 1980s, Tollman-Hundley had grown like Topsy, with almost every available mid-market hotel and management deal viewed as a potential addition to Monty's empire. This was very much in step with the mood of the time – a period of unprecedented confidence in the United States, with bankers and finance houses queuing up to lend us money. And Monty and his team were happy to borrow. All of this made me distinctly uncomfortable, and for two reasons.

I had said repeatedly to Monty that I had no interest in running bed factories. The Stanley Tollman formula for successful hotel management had been developed upon creating an experience for hotel guests which they found memorable, and which I had hoped that they might wish to repeat. This was not the philosophy of the team running Tollman-Hundley, which was not focused on the provision of service nor on the generation of genuine profit. Instead, its overwhelming objective appeared to be leveraged growth, whatever the cost. In terms of hotel management, I felt like a fish out of water.

The second, and more important, reason why I felt so uncomfortable with the way in which Tollman-Hundley was expanding stemmed from a deep-seated philosophical difference between Monty's view of business and my own. This centred, quite simply, on our attitude to debt.

I hate debt. I abhor it. I grew up in a household that lived in fear of the bank manager, and I have some stark and painful memories of the pressures which debt creates. Within days of my father's death, our banks had phoned not to offer sympathy, but to ask how my father's signature was going to be replaced in relation to the security of their loans.

And then there was the Court Hotels disaster, which had resulted entirely from us taking on a mountain of debt which I was to discover that we could not service. All my worst experiences have had debt at their roots. But my difficulty in dealing with Tollman-Hundley was that, as a nation, America itself appeared to run on debt. The actions of everyone around me told me that this was the case. I found myself to be a lone voice of caution surrounded by people who not only did not fear risk but did not even treat it with proper respect. Rather, they seemed completely to ignore it. "Things are different here," every over-qualified member of Monty's management team used to tell me. "Don't worry. It will be all right."

And it was clear to me that things were different in the United States, beginning with the extraordinary right a US taxpayer has to offset against tax all the interest they might pay on mortgages on their homes – irrespective of the number of homes and the scale of the borrowing. I was advised endlessly to borrow as much money as possible in this way, reduce my tax burden, and re-invest the borrowed money elsewhere. Every time I was told this, I explained that, in my view, one's home should be a secure refuge for the family, not a gaming chip. I depised the concept then and, thanks to the sub-prime fiasco, I despise it even more today.

What's more, in recent years, I have become more and more convinced that successful hotel businesses cannot be debt-funded. Repair and maintenance costs, and the need for near-constant refurbishment, mean that the additional burden which stems from the servicing of debt ultimately proves to be the last straw. The bodies of men and women who thought they could buck this fundamental rule litter the history of hotel management. It is no accident that many of the major trophy hotels around the world are today owned by cash-rich individuals and sovereign nation funds, for whom significant debt is simply not on the agenda.

To add to my worries, Tollman-Hundley was making deals at a speed which was frightening. The corporate machinery was constantly at work, spending millions on lawyers' and accountants' fees and closing dozens and dozens of transactions. I found myself constantly raising questions, almost always about the amount of debt which was involved and how we were going to service it. My concern was simple. I was fearful of Tollman-Hundley getting into financial difficulty. All of my own experiences were telling me that we should watch out. But I was repeatedly being told not to worry.

Invariably, I was concerned about how all these acquisitions were being funded, each time using negligible equity. In common with the US Treasury, everything in Tollman-Hundley was financed by borrowings. Equity was very difficult to find in any deal we did. This made me deeply uncomfortable.

At lunch with Monty (the occasions when all our serious business discussions took place), I would often raise my fears about debt, citing my experience with Court Hotels and how it had destroyed my South African business. But I was always assured that what happened in South Africa would never happen in America. I was regularly reminded that I was in business with a group of highly experienced professionals who had worked for major corporations and who brought a broad spectrum of top quality corporate financial, legal and accounting expertise to the table. These people endlessly assured me that every fear that I expressed would ultimately prove to be groundless.

Looking back, none of these people had ever built a business from scratch or had the anxiety of meeting weekly and monthly payrolls, an experience which all entrepreneurs go through when building their businesses. And I had also experienced the failure of Court Hotels, which had brought me to my knees in both England and South Africa. I had lots of experience both in building successful businesses and in knowing what can go wrong. Somehow, though, being in a foreign country I did not follow my natural instincts, which are always to confront problems and deal with them. Instead, I allowed myself to accept what later proved to be groundless reassurances. Meanwhile, blissfully indifferent to my concerns, 'the band played on'.

In my brain, red lights were flashing. Foolishly, I took more notice of the advice of Tollman-Hundley accountants and Harvard-educated lawyers than I did of my own instincts. The accountants and lawyers were of course wrong and the voice inside my head was right but, when the reckoning came, I took very little pleasure from knowing that I had told them so. What good would that have been? As I tried to swim against the tide of opinion, my feelings of being 'out-of-step' were heightened by the fact that I was surrounded by a team of people who had all worked for Monty for many years, and who were completely loyal to him. That loyalty did not extend to me. It was not uncommon for one of them to come into the office which I shared with Monty and whisper something into his ear. I was treated very much as an outsider, and an outsider is what I felt.

Against my better judgement, I tolerated this behaviour. Much worse, I allowed myself to be cajoled into signing personal guarantees. There was, however, a very important difference between personal guarantees given to Tollman-Hundley lenders and personal guarantees given in the context of the Court Hotels disaster. After we left South Africa, I had not only rebuilt my business interests, I had also reorganised my life. The first deal which had taken place under the new arrangements was the acquisition of the Montcalm. This was based upon Bea's inheritance and was structured accordingly. From that moment onwards, I owned almost nothing on my own account, the principal exception being the investment which I had in Tollman-Hundley. By agreeing to sign personal guarantees, I was not therefore putting other members of my family at risk. I was only betting what I had acquired through the Tollman-Hundley investment itself.

As Tollman-Hundley's debt soared to hundreds of millions of dollars, the banks and financial institutions continued to line up to shovel money in our direction. I remember two meetings at around this time, one of which demonstrates this point very firmly. The other meeting, looking back, is perhaps the earliest memory I have of thinking that the market was turning.

The first was with some senior bankers from the Chemical Bank one Tuesday morning in July 1989 in our offices in Fifth Avenue. Remembering a meeting with Tollman-Hundley's bankers is less difficult that one might imagine. In all the years I was involved in the business, I only attended two, or possibly three, meetings with the company's banks and, in every case, these were with the Chemical Bank. But this particular meeting was memorable for personal as well as business reasons.

The three Chemical Bank executives with whom we met that day in 1989 had heard that Tollman-Hundley was considering financing an important deal, but that we were using another bank to provide it. Although the Chemical Bank had not been asked for a proposal, they had nevertheless come to see whether they could provide the finance for us instead. During the middle of this conversation, I was called out of the meeting to take a telephone call. I was told that my mother-in-law had just died, and that Bea was leaving for South Africa that evening. I left the office and went home to be with her. I learned the following day that the meeting had concluded with the Chemical Bank telling us that they would be very upset indeed if we decided ultimately to take finance from somewhere else.

The second meeting was more social. I had befriended a senior figure in Barclays' operation in New York. In December 1989, he had financed for us the acquisition of the Palm Court Hotel in Palm Beach from Carteret Savings Bank for $4.16 million. We re-christened it the Chesterfield Hotel. Shortly after that deal closed, I took him and Monty Hundley for lunch one day at La Caravelle in West 55th Street.

As we ate, I said to him that acquisitions like the one which he had just financed might in the future become less common, and that we were in fact thinking of disposing of some hotel properties. I added that I was a little concerned about the state of the hotel market. He responded by saying, "Are you fellows in trouble?" Not realising that I was already sensing the first distant rumblings of trouble, I answered truthfully, if a little naively, "No. But I don't like the look of things, and we should lighten up on our debt." When we got back to the office afterwards, Monty rebuked me for having said that we were thinking of disposals. "That guy will think we have a problem." "Well, we do have a problem," was my response.

HE MARCHED THEM UP TO THE TOP OF THE HILL...

The expansion of Tollman-Hundley had taken place against a backdrop of extraordinarily high levels of merger and acquisition activity. One of the key engines of this activity was high-yield debt, the principal architect of which was the Wall Street investment bank Drexel Burnham Lambert, a major firm with an outstanding reputation as an advisor to both start-up companies and fallen angels. Drexel Burnham had a very big part to play in the next chapter in my story, the debacle otherwise known as Days Inn of America Inc.

Despite its august history, Drexel Burnham will be best remembered for a brilliant, if maverick, banker called Michael Milken. Milken almost single-handedly created a market in the financial instrument which came to be known as 'junk bonds'. As an undergraduate at the University of California at Berkeley in the 1960s, Michael Milken was seen by fellow students as a nerd. By the time he graduated in 1968, Berkeley had become a centre for student anti-war and counter-culture sentiment, but Milken had shown little interest in student politics. He didn't drink or take drugs, and had elected to study business administration rather than more fashionable subjects like sociology.

In 1969, he joined Drexel Harriman Ripley, an old-style investment bank. Following a merger with Burnham & Company in 1973, Milken found his metier working in the research department of the now re-branded Drexel Burnham. It was here that he cultivated his interest in the low-rated and unrated securities for which he would become famous. Although he was described at the time as being a genius, many now believe that his true brilliance was limited to seeing the profit potential of junk bonds, and then in his ability to sell them.

The financial markets had taken little interest in poor quality debt, even though it was high yielding. Milken put an end to that. By the end of the 1970s, his operation at Drexel spoke for more than a third of the US market in high yield securities and Milken became the most powerful man in American finance, with earnings in a single year alone of $550 million.

The unlikely link between Tollman-Hundley and Michael Milken was a chain of 1,200 moderately-priced motels which stretched across the United States and Canada. Days Inn of America was a franchise operation, and Tollman-Hundley had grown into its largest franchisee.

The Days Inn brand was a familiar sight on the highways of the United States, with rooms costing around $40 a night. The company had been founded in 1970 in Savannah Beach, Georgia by a real estate developer called Cecil B Day. Day was the son of a Baptist preacher, and was deeply religious. He ran bi-weekly devotionals at the corporate headquarters and was a leading financial supporter of Christian charities. Hotel guests were encouraged to take home a free paperback Bible when they checked out.

Days Inn was the first entry in the high end of the budget hotel market, with many of their hotels boasting restaurants and swimming pools, which the pure cut-rate chains lacked. Days Inn also became one of the very first successful hotel franchises.

From as early as 1986, not satisfied with Tollman-Hundley merely being a franchisee – however large a franchisee – Monty Hundley had become interested in acquiring Days Inn of America itself. But he was not the first to have this idea, the company having been acquired in 1984 from the Day family by Saul Steinberg, a financier, insurance executive and corporate raider. Cecil Day had died of cancer in December 1978, aged just 44, leaving his widow with instructions to sell the company within five years.

Almost 20 years earlier, Saul Steinberg had gained something of an international reputation by becoming interested in the strategic acquisition of Pergamon Press, Robert Maxwell's company. But Steinberg had claimed that Maxwell had falsely stated that a subsidiary responsible for publishing encyclopaedias was extremely profitable, when it was not. This allegation, subsequently proven to be true, led to a formal Inquiry by Inspectors appointed by the UK's

Department of Trade and Industry. The DTI Inspectors found that Robert Maxwell had contrived to maximise Pergamon's share price through transactions between his private family companies, and famously reported: "We regret having to conclude that, notwithstanding Mr Maxwell's acknowledged abilities and energy, he is not in our opinion a person who can be relied on to exercise proper stewardship of a publicly-quoted company."

Saul Steinberg also tried unsuccessfully to take over both the Chemical Bank and Walt Disney Productions. But in 1968, before he was 30, he had carried out an audacious and successful takeover of the Reliance Insurance Company. Reliance became Saul Steinberg's operating base and, in 1984, in a friendly LBO structured through a subsidiary called Reliance Capital, he had bought Days Inn from Cecil Day's family for what appeared at the time to be a very full price indeed – $570 million, if one included the assumption of Days Inn's existing debt.

Days Inn of America Inc is headquartered in Atlanta, Georgia, and since 1985 the fortunes of the company have been followed by *Georgia Trend*, *"The Magazine of Georgia Business & Politics"*. In December 1986, *Georgia Trend* reported:

> *"Had Saul Steinberg lost his touch? The other directors at Days Inn's first board meeting since Steinberg acquired the hotel chain cast worried glances around the room. Days Inn's new CEO, Henry R Silverman, was announcing the first six months' figures, and the numbers looked grim. The corporate staff had been slashed by more than half, nearly all of the chain's real estate holdings were up for sale and the company was staggering under a $535 million debt."*

What Steinberg and his colleague Henry Silverman had seen by the time of that meeting in April 1985, but others had not, was that the hotel chain was worth more without its hotels than with them. Reliance Group Holdings had raised the $285 million needed to buy Days Inn by issuing junk bonds. Reliance Capital and friends, who included Michael Milken and Ivan Boesky, contributed in fact just

$30 million, with the bulk of the funding being raised by Drexel Burnham. Steinberg then rapidly sold off nearly all of the chain's hotels to franchise holders and investors for $423 million in order to pay down the acquisition debt and other existing debt within the business. (He sold a number of them to Tollman-Hundley.) Finally, he took the company public in September 1985, raising $25 million. Steinberg and friends recovered their entire investment, and they still owned a controlling interest in Days Inn. Nice work.

The purchase of Days Inn had been masterminded by Henry Silverman, a man who had only recently joined Reliance but who was rapidly gaining a reputation for his skilful manipulation of transactions of this kind. Silverman had begun his career through an introduction which his father had made to Steve Ross, the CEO, President and Chairman of Warner Communications. He became an assistant to Ross, who was busy working on the transformation of Warner from a troubled movie studio into a huge entertainment business. This was a big and exciting job for a young man, but Silverman was keen to succeed on his own account. He joined the small investment banking firm of White Weld & Company, and then in 1984 he went to work for Saul Steinberg. He said of his decision to leave Steve Ross, "You want to be recognised for what you achieve rather than what your parents achieved."[52]

In 1986, Ivan Boesky, a prominent American stock trader and a close associate of Michael Milken, was investigated by the Securities & Exchange Commission (SEC) in connection with allegations of insider trading. In November of that year, he pleaded guilty to one felony count, paid a $100 million fine and went to prison for two years. As part of his plea bargain, he informed against various others, including those in the UK who were involved in the Guinness takeover of Distillers. One of those in the United States against whom he informed was Michael Milken. Within a week, Drexel Burnham was reported to be under 'formal order of investigation' by both the SEC and the US Attorney for the Southern District of New York.

---

[52] *Business Week*, 28 February 2000.

For the firm, this meant two expensive and difficult years. In late 1988, the US Attorney for the Southern District, Rudy Giuliani, threatened to indict the firm under the Racketeer Influenced and Corrupt Organizations Act, otherwise known as RICO. This was a decisive development. If Drexel Burnham had been indicted, it would have had to post a performance bond of up to $1 billion to avoid having its assets frozen. This would have taken precedence over all of the firm's other obligations – including the loans that provided 96 per cent of its capital. Since banks will not extend credit to a firm indicted under RICO, an indictment would almost certainly have put Drexel out of business. Faced with the prospect of the firm's meltdown, Drexel pleaded guilty to six counts of stock parking, and accepted a fine of $650 million. But Michael Milken himself was not out of the woods.

Meanwhile, less than three years after Reliance had taken Days Inn of America public, in 1988 the company was taken private again, and Henry Silverman embarked on a piece of financial engineering which many others would subsequently copy. He transformed Days Inn for a second time, turning it this time into an operating company. Having sold off its tangible assets, Henry then set out to sell off its income stream, in what is known as a securitisation. This was to become known as a blueprint for operating company securitisations, in which the parent company becomes an operating company managing, but not actually owning, its assets.

Once again, Drexel Burnham Lambert were the co-architects of the deal, which created $167 million of investment-grade debt from the revenue stream of a company whose corporate rating was significantly below investment grade. This sleight of hand involved Drexel Burnham putting the revenue stream from Days Inn's franchisees into a special purpose entity, which represented nearly all of Days Inn's remaining assets. Henry securitised the Days Inn income stream, taking the proceeds directly into Reliance Capital, even though the responsibility for the servicing of the resulting debt remained within Days Inn of America Inc itself. The securitisation was completed in 1989, and was one of the last that Drexel Burnham Lambert ever wrote.

Since the acquisition by Reliance in 1984, Days Inn had maintained between $400 million and $600 million of long-term debt, which was a constant and recurring theme at the company. Between 1984 and 1989, Drexel issued almost $1 billion in junk bonds for Days Inn. The debt load was so heavy that Silverman joked to one interviewer in 1986 that Days Inn was, "like Mexico. We don't pay down debt. We just reschedule it."

Monty Hundley's desire to acquire Days Inn of America Inc took many months to reach fruition. He too was backed by Drexel Burnham Lambert, who raised the finance necessary to fund the initial purchase. But throughout the sale negotiations, I expressed profound concern as to our ability to service the debt with which such a transaction would burden us. Drexel Burnham's response was always reassuring, saying that, once Days Inn was acquired, they would organise a restructuring of all the debt, and thus make the acquisition attractive. With this guarantee from Drexel Burnham, and with unanimous support from the rest of his team, Monty was able to push the deal through, against my wishes.

In November 1989, Henry Silverman and his backers sold us Days Inn of America Inc. This acquisition made Tollman-Hundley the largest privately-owned hotel group in the world.

The deal was a typical piece of Drexel Burnham leveraged financing. Reliance and its backers sold their interest in Days Inn to us for $87 million. Tollman-Hundley put in just $8 million and guaranteed two years' interest on a single loan to finance the $765 million deal, if one includes the assumption of the existing $675 million Days Inn debt. The balance of the deal was completed in junk bonds.

In order to raise the finance to complete the Days Inn transaction, we presented a 'dog-and-pony show' to potential investors. Monty Hundley would reel off the facts and figures of the transaction and I filled in the gaps. I suspect I was there to add a little gravitas. As part of this exercise, we flew out to California to meet investors on the West Coast. California was especially important because Drexel's junk bond operation was based there. Michael Milken's X-shaped trading desk in Beverly Hills was the centre of an empire which, by 1986, was responsible for $120 billion in new issues. Whilst we were waiting for the presentations to begin, and despite the criminal investigation hanging over him, Michael Milken dropped in for a few minutes to see us. As was to be expected, he told us that the acquisition of Days Inn was a great deal for us.

As I had suspected would happen, in raising the finance to acquire Days Inn, Tollman-Hundley experienced a little difficulty. This was the first time since the company's formation that funding had in any way been a problem. This experience represented the initial smell of tighter finance. I didn't like the feel of it. Credit across America was beginning to dry up. The only reason I had agreed to press ahead with the acquisition of Days Inn was the assurance from Drexel Burnham that they would re-finance the whole thing once we had completed the deal. Although Days Inn was profitable, I realised that, within a year or so, Tollman-Hundley would not be able to service the bonds which were held by third parties.

Looking back, it is difficult to explain how I allowed the Days Inn acquisition ever to go ahead, given that not only did it not smell good to me before the deal was closed, but that the assumption of this amount of debt was complete anathema to me. It was unquestionably a mistake.

Henry Silverman resigned as Chairman and CEO of Days Inn and I became Chairman of the company. Michael Leven, the man who ran the business day-to-day, stayed on as President of the Company. I was quoted in the press at the time as saying, "We expect the company under Mike Leven to continue the growth that Days Inn began in 1985, and which has resulted in Days Inn becoming the third fastest-growing hotel brand in the world."

Henry Silverman made the public comment about the deal, "We are confident that the growth will continue under the experienced and highly-regarded management of Tollman-Hundley." But I think that Henry may have had his fingers crossed behind his back when he said this. When he subsequently joined what was then the fledgling Blackstone, in private he said something very different. According to

Blackstone's Stephen Schwarzman, "When Henry joined us, he told us that one thing that we'd probably be able to do is to buy Days Inn. He said, 'I do not know why somebody paid 14 times cash flow for it, but they'll never be able to meet their debt costs, because these businesses don't grow fast enough to outrun them.'"[53]

We closed the Days Inn deal at the beginning of December 1989, and Drexels wanted to buy a celebratory lunch for all concerned. I was staying in Palm Beach at the time, and was not keen to come to New York for what was after all a purely social matter. The lunch was therefore deferred until February. I should have realised, though, that these were not celebratory times. Drexel Burnham was having problems of its own, and public confidence in leveraged buyouts was waning. Default rates on high-yield debt had increased dramatically. The liquidity of the junk bond market was drying up.

On 13 February 1990, we all gathered at "21", which Drexel had chosen as the venue for the lunch because they knew how fond I was of the establishment. They had booked an elegant private room at the club for the occasion. This was the Remington Room, the walls of which were decorated with a collection of gouache paintings by the well-known American artist Frederic Remington. These portrayed the artist's speciality – the Wild West. Surrounded by images of cowboys, indians, the US Cavalry and buffalo hunting, we made polite conversation for an hour or so, punctuated every so often by assurances from our hosts that the debt we had assumed would soon be refinanced by Drexel Burnham into a form which we could actually afford.

The lunch was interrupted when one of the Drexel Burnham team was called urgently to the telephone. He was away for a while and when he returned, he was ashen-faced. He said, "I'm sorry, but I do not know whether we are going to be able to pay for lunch. Drexel Burnham has just filed for bankruptcy."

This was a devastating blow for every person in the room. We had all assumed that the plea bargain which the firm had reached with Giuliani, and the rationalisation of the business which had followed, meant that Drexel Burnham would continue to trade. Here we were,

[53] *King of Capital*, David Carey and John E. Norris, Crown Business 2010.

owners of a business which we could not in reality have afforded to have bought, and which we certainly could not afford to run. And the firm which we were relying upon to make the unworkable work had disappeared in what felt like a puff of smoke. I knew that there was no-one else to replace them. We were on our own, up the proverbial creek and without a paddle.

If it were possible for things to get worse, they did. Within days, we lost the President of the company, Mike Leven. This was an avoidable disaster.

Mike Leven was one of the hotel industry's most recognisable executives, having for some years starred in all of Days Inn's television commercials. His resignation resulted from a telephone call which Tollman-Hundley's Jim Cutler had made to Linda Kyles, the Treasurer of Days Inn in Atlanta. Cutler had ordered her to transfer $11.3 million from Days Inn into a Tollman-Hundley account but not, it was later alleged, to tell anyone about it. Mike Leven had nevertheless discovered that the transfer had taken place and confronted his Treasurer, who promptly broke down in tears. Leven resigned in disgust. (Michael Leven is these days president and chief operating officer of Las Vegas Sands Corporation, the Macau casino giant headed by billionaire Sheldon Adelson, prominent financial backer of Republican Mitt Romney.)

My telephone rang at 8.00am the next morning. It was Monty, who told me what had happened and said that we would be in trouble if the money was not replaced. Surprise, surprise, this could not be made good within the company's own resources. The company needed $13 million urgently.

I called Arnold and talked the problem through with him. Eventually, we reached the conclusion that although none of this was our fault, if it became a problem, I would be blamed along with the others. In order to prevent my own reputation being sullied along with those responsible, we should lend Tollman-Hundley the $13 million. Nevertheless, as a guarantee for this loan, I took over the security of the Chesterfield Hotel in London. But the Chesterfield was the subject of a mortgage with Citibank, New York for approximately $8 million. In order to take our security, we had first to pay off this mortgage too, thus laying out twice as much in cash as the Chesterfield was at that time worth.

At around this time, Michael Milken found himself in a Federal Courthouse in Manhattan, pleading guilty to six counts of securities and tax violations, three of them involving dealings with Ivan Boesky. Also threatened with a RICO indictment, Milken had at first planned to fight the charges against him but, like so many before him, he eventually concluded that the odds were too heavily stacked against him. As part of his plea, Milken agreed to pay $200 million in fines and, in a separate agreement with the SEC, a further $400 million to investors who had been hurt by his actions. Finally, he settled a civil suit by agreeing to pay $500 million to Drexel's investors. Even before his legal fees were taken into account, he had paid out $1.1 billion.

One aspect of the US Attorney's prosecution of Milken received widespread criticism. That was the decision to indict Michael Milken's brother, Lowell, in order to put pressure on Milken to settle. The *New York Times* reported:[54]

> *The recent plea bargain of Michael R. Milken, the former head of the junk bond department of Drexel Burnham Lambert Inc. and the target of much of the Government's efforts over the last few years, has raised questions of propriety among some legal experts. In exchange for his plea, Mr. Milken won an agreement from the Government that it would not pursue any charges against his brother, Lowell, who was named in the original indictment. Defense lawyers and supporters of the former Drexel executive said that his brother was brought into the case to put pressure on the financier to settle. "I am troubled by – and other scholars are troubled by – the notion of putting relatives on the bargaining table," said Vivian Berger, a professor at Columbia University Law School.*
>
> *The settlement with Drexel Burnham has also raised questions about the Government's tactics, even among lawyers who generally support the agreement. The settlement, which was completed in early 1989, required that the company dismiss Mr. Milken and not pay him compensation for 1988, even though he had not yet been charged with*

---

[54] 'Tactics in Wall Street Cases Troubling Some Lawyers', *New York Times*, May 6 1990.

a crime. "The fact that the Government imposed on Drexel the condition that they had to get rid of Milken and keep his money before he was ever charged and before he was sanctioned by the Securities and Exchange Commission is disturbing," said Ira Lee Sorkin, a securities lawyer, former prosecutor and former head of the Manhattan office of the S.E.C.

As I read these reports at the time, I could not begin to imagine that, 15 years later, I would experience similar intimidation – and worse – at the hands of the US Attorney's Office for the Southern District of New York. But then, why should I at that time have feared such an outcome? After all, I had done nothing wrong. What I did not know was that doing nothing wrong is no guarantee of staying out of trouble with the law. At that point, I continued to believe that the system of justice in the United States was fair.

THE TIDE BEGINS TO GO OUT

Business Travel News reported in 1988 that Tollman-Hundley was the fastest-growing hotel company in the 5,000 to 15,000-room range. But all that was about to come to an abrupt stop. The boom years of the 1980s were drawing to a close, and the company found itself being asked to meet various banks and other institutions which had lent money. Project by project, hotel by hotel, each of those lenders wanted to review their exposure. It was clear that prices in both real estate and the stock market were beginning to fall, and they were all taking stock.

They were right to do so. Declining revenues meant that we found it increasingly difficult to service interest on a lot of our loans, and unloading property was far from easy. We found ourselves attempting disposals against a backdrop of falling values and receding business activity. Warren Buffett could well have been speaking about Tollman-Hundley when he said, "It's only when the tide goes out that you learn who's been swimming naked."

Around this time, I was able to play an important role in removing a substantial element of Tollman-Hundley's debt burden. As recently as 1989, Tollman-Hundley had spent $91 million in buying the Regal 8 group, a chain of 53 motels in 21 US states. This acquisition had almost doubled the number of Tollman-Hundley hotels to 122, and increased its bedrooms to more than 18,000. But just two years later, what had looked like an attractive asset in 1989 – if one ignored the debt which went with it – in 1991 looked like a burden which Tollman-Hundley could well do without. Through the travel business, I had had a strong personal relationship for many years with Accor, the giant French hotel company, which had just bought Motel 6, another US motel group. Through our travel business we were one of Accor's biggest customers. I approached them, and we managed to sell them Regal 8, recovering all of the money we had spent on the acquisition. A major chunk of debt thus disappeared overnight. If only the rest had gone the same way.

We found ourselves under pressure from the banks to find an overall workout solution, a realistic plan through which we could manage our debt, and ultimately repay or discharge it. In response to this pressure, in 1991 Monty found Policano & Manzo, a firm of workout specialists, a profession which, in all my 60 years of business, I had never before encountered.

Policano & Manzo was, I learned, a highly respected firm which specialised in providing financial advisory services to troubled companies, their creditors and other parties in workouts and bankruptcies. I had imagined, in my own naive way, that companies in trouble were bad news for all those involved. However, in keeping with the old saying that it is an ill wind indeed which blows nobody any good, I discovered that I was quite wrong to think this.

Michael Policano had co-authored an article in Morgan Stanley's *Journal of Applied Corporate Finance* in Summer 1990 in which he had observed that, *"in today's highly leveraged companies, operating and profitability problems will surface much earlier than in companies financed primarily with equity."*[55] The article went on (I have added the emboldening):

> *During the 1990s, debtor-in-possession lending will become an increasingly important source of funding for troubled (as well as not so troubled) companies.* ***As such, it will also represent a major profit opportunity for commercial banks and other lending institutions. The principal source of the expected growth in this market is, of course, the large number of highly-leveraged transactions during the 1980s. Many of these recapitalized companies are likely to default on their debt obligations in future years; and a good number will end up choosing to file for bankruptcy.***
>
> *One impetus to debtor-in-possession (DIP) financing has been the 1978 Federal Bankruptcy Code, which codified and standardized the*

procedures for companies in Chapter 11 to borrow new funds. As the business and lending community arrives at a better understanding of the rights afforded debtors and potential lenders to bankrupt companies under the Code, debtors will increasingly find Chapter 11 to be the most effective setting for reorganising the claims of creditors and getting their operating strategies back on track. In some cases, even debtors not confronted with immediate default may choose to file Chapter 11 and secure the appropriate DIP financing as a way of preserving their flexibility to fund future growth. **In this sense, Chapter 11 with the appropriate DIP financing may come to be regarded as a 'pro-active' financing strategy rather than simply as the last resort of dying companies.**

Monty invited the two partners, Michael Policano and Bob Manzo, to the Tollman-Hundley offices where he and I received a presentation from them. The two of them explained the manner in which they would go about sorting out the financing issues which we were suffering, just like so many other American corporations at the time. We were impressed, and we clearly had to do something radical. We decided to appoint Policano & Manzo, with Bob Manzo handling the account. We took this decision because of Bob Manzo's closeness to the Chemical Bank, which was one of our most important creditors.

Bob Manzo was given 60 days to develop a restructuring plan for Tollman-Hundley, after which his job was then to negotiate a workout arrangement for each and every one of the banks. These were to be covered by an umbrella arrangement called the Creditor Repayment Agreement, otherwise known as the CRA. Through this mechanism, all the banks were kept fully abreast of the overall strategy, either through communications from Tollman-Hundley, or by each of the banks keeping all the others completely informed. Indeed, there was an express obligation on all the banks to pass information between themselves.

There were nine banks in total – First Chicago Bank, Chemical Bank, Marine Midland Bank, Eurobrokers, United Jersey Bank, New

Street, Morgens Waterfall, Wells Fargo and National Westminster. For the next couple of years, and working hand-in-hand with Policano & Manzo, millions were spent on lawyers, consultants and accountants in coming up with settlement plans. During those years, unless my memory has failed me, I only attended meetings with one bank – certainly twice with the same bank, and possibly three times. These meetings were with the Chemical Bank. On the first occasion, in addition to the executive team, they had asked to see me as well in order to press us into taking their finance. And for the second and, I suspect, third meeting they asked for the same cast of characters.

The second meeting was most unlike the one which had taken place on the day when I was told that my mother-in-law had died. The reason the Chemical Bank had asked for all of us to be present on this occasion soon became clear. Having almost forced us to take money from them a year or so ago, they now laid out a set of rules against which they expected us to conclude matters. They did not anticipate my response, which was simple and direct, "I don't need this. I am going back to London in order to work on our family business." At this point, their attitude towards me changed. The Chemical Bank never again took me for granted. Although, through others, they subsequently made other unreasonable requests, they always took 'no' for an answer.

The reason I am unclear as to whether I attended two or three meetings with the Chemical Bank is that, after all this time and after thousands of other business meetings, recalling each meeting with precision is difficult. Learning of my mother-in-law's death during the first meeting with the Chemical Bank means that I have clarity about that particular gathering but the other, or others, I am unsure about. I recall only one subsequent meeting, but the events I recall come from two somewhat different stages of the process, so logic would suggest that there were a further two meetings. I am assuming that this was the case. Having now told you of the events of the second, I will return to the third a little later in in the story.

Over the next few years, one-by-one, the Tollman-Hundley properties were sorted out. Each case was different. Some were resolved simply by the mortgagor assuming ownership of the asset. This meant that any equity we had in the investment was completely lost. In other cases, loans were renegotiated, sometimes with the lender sharing in the loss in value by writing off some of the debt, more often by an amendment to the terms of the loan.

Reflecting the decline in the fortunes of Tollman-Hundley, Monty moved the business out of the comfortable – and for me convenient – offices in Fifth Avenue, which we could no longer afford, if, indeed, we ever could. He relocated the business to Valhalla, 30 miles to the north of Manhattan and 15 minutes from his home in Bedford, NY. Until then, my visits to the offices of Tollman-Hundley could at best be described as infrequent. Now, they became very exceptional indeed. I only ever remember going there twice.

It is perhaps worth reflecting briefly on my working arrangements with Tollman-Hundley, such as they were. I was to hear the following description more than once during various court hearings in the years ahead. I have to confess that it sounds remarkably like one of two things – either a callous attempt to deny accountability, or a catalogue of indolence and irresponsibility. Please believe me, it was neither of those two alternatives. From the beginning of the venture, my role at Tollman-Hundley was extremely limited. And Tollman-Hundley was never my principal business interest.

In truth, my working arrangements were these. Not only did I rarely visit the Tollman-Hundley offices, I did not arrive until after 11.00am, I did little work when I was there and I usually went for lunch at 12.30pm. Although I was asked to sign a great many things, I never read any of the documents which I signed, and was often provided with the signature page only. Before I signed anything, though, I had been assured of two things – that Monty had already signed, and that Tollman-Hundley's lawyers had approved the documents before signature.

I never took any Tollman-Hundley work home with me, even if I went straight home after lunch – which was a frequent event. My attention was always much more devoted to the affairs of the family's travel businesses. They, after all, preceded Tollman-Hundley, and were not only much more successful than Tollman-Hundley, they often had to be called upon to keep Tollman-Hundley afloat. Unsurprisingly, therefore, the travel businesses received more attention from me, not forgetting that those businesses also required extensive travel all over the globe by both Bea and me, taking us away from the United States.

My detachment from the day-to-day management of Tollman-Hundley was such that I remember finding out about the finalisation of the Creditor Repayment Agreement (CRA) by chance and in the street. I was walking along the sidewalk in Manhattan one morning when I bumped into Bob Manzo. He shook my hand firmly, slapped me on the back and congratulated me. He told me that he had just finalised settlement arrangements with the last remaining bank. In only one case, United Jersey Bank, had a lender refused to participate in the CRA and had chosen instead to go its own way.

Bob told me that Policano & Manzo's work for Tollman-Hundley was now complete. All had been resolved, and Tollman-Hundley was now able to move forward once more. He was really pleased for us. And I felt pleased too. When I got back to the apartment that evening, I told Bea that Bob Manzo had sorted out Tollman-Hundley's position with its banks. I wanted to send Bob a personal gesture of appreciation for what he had done. I found him a very nice piece of antique silver which cost me about $4,000 and I sent it over to him with a thank-you note. I was content that everything had been concluded properly and above board.

...AND HE MARCHED THEM DOWN AGAIN

During the two years in which we owned Days Inn, we increased the number of franchisees significantly and we reduced some debt. But, without the wizardry of Drexel Burnham, Tollman-Hundley simply could not refinance the company's mounting debt load and short amortization schedule.

These were in any case difficult times, made worse by the general drop in confidence, circumstances which translated almost immediately into a pronounced recession. Hotel revenues fell dramatically, and the value of commercial properties – especially hotels – collapsed. On 13 November 1990, we announced that Days Inn of America was in default on $352 million of long-term debt. The time to come clean with all concerned was long overdue.

We said that we were trying to restucture our debts but that, in the meantime, we did not anticipate making any principal or interest payments on the bonds and notes which were in default. Confirming that the Company had a total debt of $744 million, John Snodgrass, president and chief operating officer, said, "We have a fundamentally sound business. However, it is overburdened by a debt structure with high interest expense and rapid amortization, virtually all of which was put into place by the previous owners."

At the annual convention of Days Inn in February 1991, I addressed several hundred franchisees at the Marriott Marquis in downtown Atlanta's Peachtree Center. I did not beat around the bush. "The previous owners saddled the company with insurmountable debt. In order to correct what the 'whizz kids' of the 80s – now the 'was kids' of the 90s – have engineered, we need serious surgery." To lighten the mood, I added, "By the way, if any of you are hiring, we have found that these out-of-work investment bankers make pretty good desk clerks. They take a little more training than usual but they are generally well groomed and they smile a lot."

Georgia Trend reported the fact that when the franchisees had an opportunity to quiz me about the company's finances, not one of them said a word. They all knew that what I was saying was true. After all, they were well aware that we were also franchisees of Days Inn hotels, just like they were. A combination of recession and the Gulf War had been disastrous for all of us, not to mention the impact all of this was having on real estate values.

On a happier note, later that day I was joined on the stage by one of Georgia's favourite sons, former US President Jimmy Carter. He and I delivered speeches to the convention, and entertainment that evening was provided by Dolly Parton and The Spinners. Thankfully, it was not all doom and gloom.

Henry Silverman's reaction to my public statements at the convention was predictable and disingenuous. He said, "I find it offensive to keep reading that the previous owners are responsible for Days Inn's present plight. Nobody with half a brain would believe that. No-one put a gun to their heads and said they had to buy it. It's inconceivable to me that two smart guys would look at a company for a year and buy it without knowing how much debt it had." He was of course right. We should never have done this deal. Not only did he know this, too, but he had already told his colleagues at Blackstone that he knew we could never service the deal which we had done. Had it not been for Drexel Burnham's assurances that they would sort this out, we would never have gone ahead. In every respect, our acquisition of Days Inn of America Inc was a bridge too far.

Part of the financing which Drexel Burnham had put in place for Tollman-Hundley was something called a PIK bond, one of the most iniquitous financial instruments ever created. This is a type of loan which, typically, does not require any interest payment until a maturity or refinancing date is reached. These loans are typically unsecured and carry a whacking arrangement fee, payable up front. Interest on PIK loans is very substantially higher than on other debts, especially secured debts. When eventually the bond is triggered upon maturity, the borrower's cashflow needs to be astronomical in order to meet their obligations. The only other high-profile use of PIKs of which I am aware was by Malcolm Glazer in the 2005 takeover of Manchester United Football Club. Glazer utilised PIK loans, sold to hedge funds, in order to fund the takeover, much to the displeasure of the club's supporters.

I had been agonising about the Days Inn of America investment for some time, and began to conclude that we had little choice other than to sell it, an exercise in relation to which I realised that we would take a bath – and a deep one at that. One weekend in mid-1991, I finally decided that something had to be done, and soon. Bea and I were entertaining the author Barbara Taylor Bradford at our Connecticut farm. I stole away for a couple of minutes in order to make a telephone call to Henry Silverman, who had in so many ways been the architect of our misery. I was aware that Henry had left Reliance and was now with Blackstone, but I thought it was worth a try. I called him, knowing too that Henry had a weekend place in Bedford, NY. I asked him whether I might call in for a drink that evening on my way back into Manhattan.

Henry welcomed me into his home, and showed me through to the library. I did not beat about the bush. "You are going to have to buy Days Inn back from us," I said. "Because of the debt structure which you put in place and which we inherited, there is no way that Tollman-Hundley can service the interest payments which are now falling due. You got me into this mess. You are going to have to get me out of it."

I knew that Henry's interest in hotel franchising had not disappeared, although I knew, too, that he was also struggling with a couple of acquisitions that Blackstone had already made in this sector. Despite this, I felt sure he would be interested. My suspicions were proved correct when our informal meeting led a few days later to a meeting in the Blackstone boardroom with Henry and with the founders of Blackstone, Steve Schwarzman and Pete Peterson. After these initial soundings, detailed conversations took place to work out a deal. Having started the ball rolling, I handed the reins to Monty Hundley, who finalised the negotiations.

Blackstone had created an entity called Hospitality Franchise Systems (HFS), which was very much Henry's baby. HFS had been set up to take advantage of the financial ills of Prime Motor Inns, one of the world's largest operators and franchisors of mid-priced hotels and motels. In 1990, Prime ran into trouble and needed to pay down debt. Henry Silverman had jumped at the chance to get control of two of Prime's most treasured possessions, the Howard Johnson franchise operation and an exclusive licence to run the Ramada franchise. While the hotel business is cyclical, ebbing and spiking with the season and the economy, franchise fees are only partly tied to hotel earnings and are relatively steady, so it looked like a safe bet for a leveraged buyout. Moreover, Blackstone was buying in at a reasonable price: $195 million, or six times cashflow.

However, one month to the day after the buyout of Prime Motor Inns closed, on 2 August 1990, Iraq invaded Kuwait, an event which unsurprisingly was not factored in as part of Blackstone's forward planning. Almost immediately, it became clear that the United States would press for a war in the Gulf to drive back Saddam Hussein. Oil prices shot up and hotel bookings plummeted as people were deterred by the cost and the risks of travel. "Our reservation volume fell off a cliff," Silverman said later about this period. "It was down 30-40% in one day."[56]

The huge downturn in trade threatened to undermine fatally the investment which Blackstone had made. The underlying problem was that HFS had not actually bought the Ramada name. This was merely licensed from New World Development, a Hong Kong-based property conglomerate. New World had the right to rescind the Ramada licence should HFS fall behind on its royalty payments, which HFS had done. Losing the Ramada name would have rendered HFS largely worthless. This in turn would have been a disaster for Blackstone at that early stage of the fund's development. Steve Schwarzman and Henry Silverman flew to Hong Kong to persuade New World not to pull the plug. This was a crucial visit. Thankfully, it was also a successful one. I always say to my children and to those who work for me, "Never shirk a journey."

---

[56] *King of Capital*, David Carey and John E. Norris, Crown Business 2010.

Tollman-Hundley struggled on with the appalling acquisition it had made, but it was eventually concluded that there was little choice other than to take Days Inn of America Inc into bankruptcy. The timing of the filing was critical, and the last act of this bankrupt company involved Monty Hundley paying for a helicopter to fly the signed documents the 200 miles to Delaware, where they were needed before close of play. The company thus filed for Chapter 11 protection in September 1991, allowing Blackstone, through HFS, to pick up Days Inn for just $259 million – one third the price which Silverman had sold it for in 1989. Since HFS already had its franchising infrastructure set, there were huge savings in costs to be gleaned from the merger. Henry Silverman was quoted as saying, "Because of the people we already had in place, I thought we would be adding $50 million of revenue at virtually no cost."[57]

The deal with Hospitality Franchise Systems required both Monty and me to stick around and carry on working. In exchange for that commitment, we participated from an earnout agreement and received consultancy fees. Although at the time we expected the earnout to have only a relatively modest upside, it would later prove to be much more valuable. But there was no way of knowing that at the time. The earnout simply gave us the chance to recover something after a disastrous episode. This small 'something' would go some way towards helping Tollman-Hundley to get out of the mess into which we were certain the business was descending.

Under the terms of the earnout agreement, we were given a five-year period within which to purchase HFS stock at a fixed price, provided that the Tollman-Hundley-owned franchises met certain franchise fee payment goals. At the same time, Monty and I were to provide advice, knowledge and know-how with respect to franchise relations. In return, we were each to be paid $500,000 per annum.

It was originally envisaged under the earnout that Monty and I would receive a tranche of shares annually, subject of course to meeting revenue targets. Monty and I assigned all our rights in the earnout to Bryanston Group Inc, the original corporate vehicle through which Days Inn had been acquired.

[57] *King of Capital,* David Carey and John E. Norris, Crown Business 2010.

In the Spring of 1994, HFS declared a stock dividend of one new share for every share of stock outstanding. This two-for-one arrangement meant that, whereas originally we had a right to acquire 500,000 shares at each annual vesting, in years 3, 4 and 5, Monty and I now had the right to acquire one million HFS shares.

All of this depended, however, upon Tollman-Hundley making all of its franchise payments. Managing the cash flow against the backdrop of very difficult trading conditions was a huge task, and one that could not be fulfilled without assistance. Trafalgar and members of the Tollman family were regularly called upon to provide multi-million dollar loans to Tollman-Hundley. These loans often created cashflow difficulties for those lending. And, in a pattern oft-repeated as far as both Monty and Tollman-Hundley were concerned, a substantial proportion of the lending was never repaid.

With a huge amount of effort, all of the available shares reserved under the scheme – stock worth something in excess of $100 million – was able to be taken up, and was taken up. I had hoped that the payout would, as a minimum, repay in full the additional personal lending which had been provided to Tollman-Hundley. That lending was eventually repaid and, in addition, I received just 5% of the earnout, money which was immediately reinvested in other businesses. Unlike Monty, I declared the income from the earnout on my tax return, and paid tax on the whole amount.

Knowledge of the existence of the HFS Earnout and of its likely expected value were to become important factors during the troubles ahead. Looking back now, and based upon the research which I have undertaken, I am able to say with absolute confidence that the existence of the Earnout was known to the banks which were lending to Tollman-Hundley.

Although I had initiated the conversation with Henry Silverman which led to the Blackstone deal, it was Monty who had tied down the detail, including the consultancy fees and HFS share options. He had mentioned to me one day that Henry had demanded a personal share of our deal. But it was not until the ink was long dry on the contract that I realised that Monty had agreed to give him 10% of our potential earnings. Quite how Henry squared this arrangement with his employers, goodness only knows. I was just very glad not to have been a part of it.

During Monty's subsequent trial, about which I write later, the personal arrangement between Henry Silverman and Monty Hundley was raised in court. Not, I hasten to add, in terms which might have elicited the truth. But one journalist at least managed to see right through the answers which were extracted from Henry in exchange, so it would appear, for his being less-than-thoroughly examined in relation to the facts. The *New York Times'* Pulitzer Prize-winning business correspondent, Gretchen Morgenson, wrote in 2004:

Late last year, Mr. Silverman took the stand at another criminal trial. That case involved Monty D. Hundley, a former owner of Days Inn of America and a principal at Tollman-Hundley Hotels, who along with his partner Stanley S. Tollman, sold their company to HFS in the early 1990s.

Under the terms of the sale of their hotel company to HFS, the executives were to receive more than one million HFS shares in total, if the hotels did well. At the trial, prosecutors showed that Mr. Hundley and Mr. Tollman had sold more than $100 million worth of HFS stock from 1993 to 1995.

Around 1994, Mr. Silverman testified, Mr. Tollman offered to share some of those gains with him because the deal had been such a success. Over time, he told the court, he received more than $3.5 million from Mr. Tollman. Mr. Silverman testified that he gave some of this money to Martin L. Edelman, a Cendant director and a lawyer at Paul, Hastings, Janofsky & Walker in New York, for help he had provided in the arrangement with Tollman-Hundley. The Cendant chief also donated $1 million of it to charity, according to his testimony. In 1994, Mr. Silverman, who was then the chief executive of HFS, earned a salary of $1.4 million.[58]

Suffice to say that I never paid Henry Silverman anything. If he received monies from the HFS Earnout, as I believe he did, they came from Monty Hundley, not from me. But this fact, it seems, did not fit someone else's script.

It is worth mentioning, in a final postscript to the Days Inn episode, that John Snodgrass, the Sales Director of Days Inn, a man who had been earning about $200,000 a year, was appointed President and COO to replace Mike Leven. Here was a man who was most definitely in the right place at the right time. When Days Inn was bought by Hospitality Franchise Systems, John Snodgrass was given a stake in the business. In December 1992, with the Gulf War over and travel and hotel bookings recovered, HFS went public at $16 a share. The shares jumped 17% on the first day of trading and soared to $50 within a year. Snodgrass became a wealthy man overnight.

POLITICS AND HOUSEKEEPING

In having said goodbye to Days Inn, I had few regrets. But I did, however, retain one or two happy memories, including the fact that I had addressed two annual Days Inn Conventions alongside two former US Presidents. I mentioned earlier that Jimmy Carter had addressed the 1990 Convention. A year before that, the keynote speaker had been Ronald Reagan, just 12 months after he had left office.

My claim to fame is that on both occasions I sat alongside the President and we each addressed the 1500 delegates – the President first, and me second. Each was a hard act to follow, but having Ronald Reagan as my 'warm-up' was especially difficult. Delivering a speech after addresses from Presidents was almost as challenging, I fear, as Presidents having to listen afterwards to Stanley Tollman, notwithstanding the fact that I was the 1948 winner of the Marist Brothers Observatory Debating Cup.

I met Ronald Reagan on a number of occasions, originally as a result of my Monaco contacts, and I had huge respect for him. During the time we had spent in Monte Carlo, I had become friendly with an American called Francis Cresci, known universally as Frank. He was an extraordinary man who spoke both French and Italian fluently. As a lieutenant in the US Army, he had been one of the first soldiers to arrive in the South of France towards the end of the War. Frank had met Prince Rainier, who was impressed with his charm as well as with his linguistic abilities.

After the War, Frank went back to the United States, and became a New York police detective. During a visit of Prince Rainier to New York in the mid-Fifties, Frank provided security for the Prince who, by now, was a firm friend. So friendly had they become that Frank was invited to the wedding of the Prince and Grace Kelly. This fact was reported in the *New York Times*[59] at the time:

59 *New York Times*, 8 April 1956.

Prince Asks Detective to Wedding as Friend

Detective Frank W Cresci, the New York policeman who kept a friendly eye on Prince Rainier III of Monaco during his recent visit here, will attend the wedding of the Prince and Grace Kelly.

The carefully tailored and well-spoken 34-year-old detective acted as the Prince's bodyguard. Mr Cresci, a debonair man who speaks French and Italian fluently, and the Prince became good friends.

The policeman, who received a 10-day leave of absence for the occasion, said that he would be the Prince's house-guest in Monte Carlo.

The friendship between Prince Rainier and Frank became such that Frank was later appointed Consul General of Monaco in New York. During the period when Ken Bates and I were spending time in Monte Carlo, Frank would often visit Monaco and, during one of these visits, Ken and I appointed him as a director of Trafalgar America.

Frank introduced Bea and me to both Prince Rainier and Princess Grace, and on one occasion he took me to lunch at the Palace with the Prince. Frank later officiated at Toni's wedding at La Vigie, and read out a letter from Prince Rainier wishing the young couple Bon Voyage. Sadly, that particular voyage did not last a lifetime, as Toni and Francis Raeymakers – her first husband – divorced some years later.

Frank Cresci was a remarkable person with breathtaking social connections. He seemed to know everyone in New York and, indeed, everywhere else for that matter. In our years in Monte Carlo, and in our early years in New York, we saw Frank regularly. He often came down to Palm Beach and saw us first at our little house and later at Southwood, which he visited often. He was a wonderful friend who, in his latter years, married Barbara Tuck. Sadly, he died of prostate cancer. I liked him a hell of a lot.

In February 1984, almost 18 months after Princess Grace died in an accident, Bea and I were invited to the White House in connection with a visit by Prince Rainier and his children to Washington. This was for a gala fundraiser for the newly-established Princess Grace

Foundation, of which Bob Hausman was the Chairman. It was on this occasion that I met Ronald and Nancy Reagan for the first time.

It was a very moving event, and President Reagan spoke touchingly about Grace Kelly, the Hollywood star. He later wrote, "The big gala fundraiser for the Princess Grace Foundation was a great success. There were some moments. When I returned to the table after proposing a toast to Grace I found Princess Caroline, her daughter, quietly crying."[60]

In October 1986, we were once more invited to the White House, this time to an official banquet, again with Prince Rainier and his daughters, although Prince Albert was not there this time. We had been invited because of our connections with Frank and with Monte Carlo, but when we got there we discovered a number of friends were also there by virtue of their relationship with Ronald Reagan. Notable amongst these was Lew Wasserman, who had been Ronald Reagan's agent for many years.

Although in theory the banquet was a formal occasion, Ronald Reagan made it highly informal by virtue of his behaviour. There were only a few of us there and the conversation was relaxing and hugely enjoyable. It was clear that Ronald Reagan could be a handful for his minders, and that he really wanted to be one of the lads. He spent the whole evening in an endless telling of jokes. Two jokes which he told me that evening, but which diplomacy prevents from repeating here, I will remember for the rest of my days. But how he was able to remember quite so many jokes, and to deliver them with such rapidity, I will never know. Someone once told me that this behaviour was the first indication that he was slipping into Alzheimers. If that was Alzheimers, then I am a monkey's uncle.

After my visits to the White House, I started to get regular approaches from the Republican Party, writing to me in the hope that I would support the cause. Although we had left South Africa because we were deeply unhappy with the political situation there, I was not a natural liberal. My inherently conservative leanings led me to conclude that the Republicans stood for most of the things in which I believed. The Party invited a hundred prominent Americans to join something called the 100 Club, whose supporters would give $100,000 to the Party and $25,000 a year thereafter. And I was happy to join.

At about this time, I was at a Republican fundraiser in New York when I met Ambassador Charles Gargano. Charlie, a prominent member of the Italian-American community, was well-known around New York. Cutting a suave figure in expensively tailored suits and shirts with French cuffs, Charlie, it seemed, knew everyone.

Through Charlie, I went on to meet many prominent members of the Republican Party, including Alfonse D'Amato who became a close friend, and who lunched with me at "21" on a regular basis over the years. I helped Senator D'Amato enormously with his fundraising and, at the time of the George H W Bush inauguration in 1988, Bea and I hosted a fundraiser for him at Loews Hotel which was attended by hundreds of people, including such luminaries as Donald Trump. Such was the involvement of the Tollmans at this event that it merited a front page photograph in the *New York Times* of the two of us at the gathering.

And it was not just in relation to political fundraising where Senator D'Amato asked for help. One day in 1996, he told me that he was keen to see his new book feature in the *New York Times'* list of top ten best-selling titles. He asked me to help make that happen by buying a mere 500 copies. As I write, knowing that my own book is soon to be published, I am extremely nervous about appearing to comment on the literary work of others. I will say merely that ownership of even a single copy of *Power, Pasta & Politics: The World According to Senator Al D'Amato*[61] is enough for any man. Becoming steward of 500 copies of this work – and, more importantly, of their disposal – was a major responsibility. Attendees at our annual global conference were each able to fly home with the wisdom of Senator D'Amato accounting for a significant element of their baggage allowance. All our friends and every single member of the family received copies, as did everyone with whom I came into contact for several months, even if it was just the window cleaner. Yet still the pile of books never seemed to diminish. Eventually, when I had exhausted

---

[61] *Power, Pasta & Politics: The World According to Senator Al D'Amato*, Hyperion Books, 1996.

every available channel of distribution, I had to admit defeat. Even today, I suspect I am still the owner of multiple copies of *Power, Pasta & Politics.*

Given everything that this family did for Senator D'Amato, imagine the disgust which we all felt when, once I had been indicted, the Senator claimed never even to have met me. But then, Senator D'Amato is, of course, a politician. Perhaps I should have expected nothing more.

During the Reagan years, and subsequently during the George H W Bush years, we attended a number of conferences in Washington and quite a few dinners at the White House. During this time, I became well-known as a Republican donor either through Charlie Gargano or the 100 Club, or through various senators. I found myself involved in organising or supporting dinners in Washington sponsored by senators and congressmen raising money for their own pet causes. And having an office on Fifth Avenue in New York meant that political figures would drop by for a cup of tea when they were in town.

At a Republican dinner for the 100 Club in Washington around this time, I met the legendary Max Fisher. Max was born in Pittsburgh in 1908 to immigrants from Russia. He grew up in Salem, Ohio, and attended Ohio State University on a football scholarship. He moved to Detroit in 1933 to join his father's oil reclamation business as a $15-a-week salesman. Shortly afterwards, he formed his own gasoline company with two partners. That company, Aurora Gasoline, became one of the largest independent oil companies in the Midwest, with nearly 700 Speedway gas stations. He served as chairman until 1959, when he was bought out by the Marathon Oil Company. In 1963, aged 55, he retired, devoting his time, his energy and his money to a wide variety of causes.

Max served as an adviser or board member of more than a dozen corporations, including Comerica and the auction house Sotheby's. He headed several Jewish-American organisations including the United Jewish Appeal, the Council of Jewish Federations and the American Jewish Committee. Additionally, he founded the National

Jewish Coalition, an organisation of Jewish Republicans, and was one of the top donors to the Foundation for Florida's Future, created in 1995 by Governor Jeb Bush to promote conservative ideas.

But Max's interests extended far beyond Jewish and Republican causes. He was committed to the city of Detroit, where he worked to rebuild the urban core and mend race relations in the wake of the 1967 riots. He was a major benefactor of the Detroit Symphony Orchestra, whose new home, the Max M Fisher Music Center, is known affectionately as the 'Max'. And his name is on the business school at Ohio State, to which he contributed $20 million.

But Max is perhaps best known for his tireless work in Jewish affairs, notably orchestrating an international campaign of support for Israel after the 1967 Arab-Israeli war. Republican Presidents sought his advice on Middle Eastern affairs and on Jewish issues. In *Quiet Diplomat: A Biography of Max M. Fisher*[62] Peter Golden described how President Gerald Ford and his secretary of state, Henry Kissinger, asked Max in 1975 to help heal a diplomatic rift between the United States and Israel over relations with Egypt. "My fundamental responsibility was as an American," Max said. "Then as an American Jewish leader. And finally, I had my love for Israel."

Max lived between Detroit and Florida. Following that meeting in Washington, Bea and I began seeing Max and his delightful wife Marjorie at various dinners in Palm Beach. In the early Nineties, we acquired the Beach House at the end of our road in Palm Beach, which was right on the sands, alongside the Mar-a-Lago Club. Bea redecorated the Beach House and it became our daily lunch place. Over the years which followed, we entertained the occasional celebrity, numerous friends, and visiting dignitaries from all over the world. Our lunches became famous, and an invitation to lunch at the Beach House was much sought after.

Whenever we were in residence in Palm Beach, which was from just before New Year until the end of February, Max Fisher would come over for lunch two or three times a week, occasionally bringing friends from the worlds of politics or business. I spent some of my most enjoyable times there, listening to his endless stories. Max, who

62 Cornwall Books, 1992.

has known every Republican President of the United States since Dwight Eisenhower, was extremely well-connected, something which was clear when, in 1998, we were invited to his 90th birthday part in Dearborn, Michigan, a suburb of Detroit. The social pages of *WWD*[63] said of that evening:

> *Through the portals of the Ritz Carlton swept two United States' Presidents (Ford and Bush); a former Canadian Prime Minster (Brian Mulroney); a former United States Secretary of State (Henry Kissinger); the Speaker of the House (Newt Gingrich); the Governor of Michigan; the Mayor of Detroit; various business tycoons, diplomats, politicos and zillionaires. It was more a feast than a dinner: endless kilos of caviar – and I am here to tell you that George Bush loves caviar – served with potato pancakes and chilled vodka.*

Immodesty requires me to report that Bea and I also merited a mention in the same article. Max spent the evening sitting at the head table on a golden throne with a red velvet seat. His daughter had heard of this throne, which had been made for an official visit by the Pope to New York City. She had asked whether its owner would consider renting the throne for one night for her father's 90th birthday. She was asked who her father was. "Max Fisher," she replied. "*The* Max Fisher of Detroit?" "Yes," said Max's daughter, "how do you know of my father?" "I am a French Jew," was the response, "and I know all about your father and all the thousands of lives he has saved. I will happily ship the throne to Detroit with the greatest pleasure as my birthday gift to your father."

Max was an extraordinary man. Even though he was then in his 90s, his brain remained sharp as a razor. Through our darkest times, he would phone me every week or so. He did this right up until the time he died, in March 2005, aged 96.

Another regular visitor to Southwood was Congressman Mark Foley who was accompanied, as he was at every Palm Beach social event, by his friend Ray Floyd, a local golf pro. It was very difficult for us to understand Mark's 'outing' in 2006. Like most of his friends, we were never in any doubt that Mark was gay. It was no secret. Mark is a wonderful man and a great friend, and I find it very sad that his political career should have ended the way it did.

A further Palm Beach friend was Ambassador Nancy Brinker, a wonderful lady, and one of the true stars of the Palm Beach firmament. Nancy was United States Ambassador for Hungary from 2001 to 2003, and then Head of Protocol of the United States from 2007 until the end of the George W Bush administration. She is an impressive lady, but not merely for her record in public office. Her only sister, Susan Komen, died from breast cancer in 1980 at the age of 36. Nancy, a breast cancer survivor herself, founded the charity 'Susan G Komen for the Cure' after a promise she made to her dying sister that she would do everything in her power to end breast cancer. Since its inception, Nancy's charity has raised an extraordinary $1.5 billion-plus for research, education and health services, making it the largest breast cancer awareness charity in the world.

One of our guests in Palm Beach was Margaret Thatcher, who stayed in the Chesterfield on two occasions in 1992 and 1997, and who came to the house at Via del Lago in 1992 to see us. We got on very well together. In much the same way that I admired Ronald Reagan's political philosophy, it was clear that Margaret Thatcher was not only one of the world's great political figures, but someone whose ideals and objectives chimed with my own. Bea and I were eating recently at Heston Blumenthal's restaurant Dinner in the Mandarin Oriental Hyde Park and, as we entered, we noticed Baroness Thatcher, who was dining with Lord Powell. She waved at me as I walked in and I made my way over to her table to say hello. Given what I had read in the press of her state of health, I was taken aback when, without prompting, she started talking about Palm Beach and of the times we had spent there together. A remarkable woman.

Bea and I have always tried to support communities of which we have been part. In Connecticut, for instance, where it was public knowledge that we paid the highest property taxes in Litchfield County, and were therefore fair game for every fundraiser in sight, we supported a myriad of charities, notably New Milford Hospital and the building of a new village hall in Preston. We have always adopted a similar approach in New York, in South Africa, in Britain, and indeed anywhere where we had a role to play in the community. But being a good citizen is no protection, we were to discover, from the immediate damage to one's repuation caused by the smear tactics of the US Attorney's Office. We soon discovered that the presumption of innocence is a completely alien concept where gossip is concerned.

Take Palm Beach as an example. As the owners of an important residence in Palm Beach, Bea and I would in any case have been expected to have done our bit, and do our bit we certainly did. We were supporters of countless charities such as the Palm Beach Preservation Society and the Norton Museum of Art, and even the Palm Beach County Law Enforcement Fund, which looked after the families of policemen. But we went far beyond this. Hospitality is, after all, ingrained in both of us. Bea and I started to throw parties each year during the 'Season' which rapidly became *the* parties to which everyone hoped to be invited. It is no exaggeration to say that our New Year's Eve parties became legendary. Each had an individual theme. One year the theme was *Circus*, complete with trapeze artists. Another was *Cuba*, which featured cigar-rolling as part of the party. And on another occasion, ice skaters skated on the ornamental pool at the front of the house – a challenging spectacle given that this was Palm Beach and not the North Pole. Perhaps the greatest of our parties was our last, the one which we held on New Year's Eve 1999, heralding the arrival of the new Millennium. This was themed *Black & White* and featured, amongst other things, live zebra and black and white swans swimming in our pool. And although our parties were very different from each other, they had one thing in common. They were always private. This was something which we had learned many years earlier from "21" in New York. The press were never invited, and our parties were therefore not reported.

Perhaps the closest our parties came to being 'on the record' was in the run-up to New Year's Eve 1999. The London newspaper, the *Evening Standard*, asked well-known people where they planned to be as they saw in the new Millennium. Amongst the responses was:

New York-based best-selling author Barbara Taylor Bradford is to stay with friends in Florida: "We always visit the Tollmans, a British couple who have four hotels in London. They live at Palm Beach and they are doing a gala New Year's party this year."

A little over two years later Barbara appeared, sadly, to have difficulty in remembering that she had ever even met us. Bea in particular considered her a good friend, and her behaviour was very hurtful. But Barbara Taylor Bradford was not alone. Palm Beach holds some very happy memories for me, but also some that are not so happy.

I remember a wonderful surprise birthday party to celebrate Brian Mulroney's 60th birthday in March 1999. The guest speaker that evening was John Major, and the hundred or so guests included a number of people whom we considered to be our closest friends. Some of them, like Max Fisher, genuinely were our closest friends. But when I look at that guest list now, I also see the names of Senator Al D'Amato, Barbara Taylor Bradford and Jill and David Gilmour[64]. When I was later indicted, we were obliged to re-evaluate some of our friendships. But I will return to that subject much later.

Returning, meanwhile, to the autumn of 1991, I believe that this was in some ways a watershed for Tollman-Hundley. The filing for bankruptcy protection by Days Inn of America in September was followed the same month by Hospitality Franchise Systems agreeing to buy Days Inn out of the bankrupt business. The sale of Days Inn to HFS was completed almost six months later, in early 1992, whilst the Creditor Repayment Agreement was being negotiated. As mentioned earlier, as part of the Days Inn sale, Monty and I were to be given HFS stock, provided that we generated franchise fees which exceeded certain benchmarks. We therefore had the benefit, modest though I thought it was at the time, of a deal which would provide a small contribution to the task which I knew was ahead. We had bought some breathing space, but we were not yet out of the woods.

At the same time, Tollman-Hundley was talking to its lenders with a view to agreeing new, and affordable, arrangements looking

---

[64] Not the lead guitarist of Pink Floyd, but a Canadian-born entrepreneur, the founder of FIJI Water.

forward. With the disposal of Days Inn and the chance of an earnout if we delivered certain franchise targets, I felt that three or four years might yet enable us to clear up the mess. I had not, however, estimated either the extent of the decline in the economy nor the growth in value of shares in HFS.

In the meantime, Brett, who had risen under Tom Aro to be number two in Tollman-Hundley's Hotel Division, became less and less happy with the way in which the business was being run, and with the people who were running it. He came to me on a number of occasions voicing his concerns, and I consistently told him that he had to stick it out. I often wonder what might have happened had I listened more attentively to his warnings. Sadly, I never did.

Brett's response to being told to tough it out was to make a bid to become President of the Hotel Division. Monty was keen to move on to other challenges, and Brett had spotted this. Thankfully, in becoming President, Brett's concerns as to the management of the hotel division of Tollman-Hundley were essentially solved at a stroke. He was now able to make the changes which he knew were necessary, but which were not possible as long as Monty remained in charge.

Over time, my assessment of the people at Tollman-Hundley diminished, until I admitted to Brett that I had come to share his own view of them. I said that I had had my fill, and that I intended to go. I pointed out, however, that, for good or ill, we were part of the mess which had been created, and we owed it to all concerned to play our part in sorting things out. Tollmans, after all, do not run away. Besides, the HFS deal now provided a means by which the problems could be addressed. Not for the first time, we all had to knuckle down and work hard to get through it.

The Creditor Repayment Agreement (CRA) was negotiated between 1991 and 1992 and was finally signed at the end of September 1992. During negotiations, the banks had taken possession of various hotels, properties and collateral which secured the original loans. But because of the economic downturn in the US economy and the slump in property values, the collateral securing many of the loans did not satisfy all the payments which were due. As a condition of the CRA, the banks insisted that Monty and I should provide deficiency notes to cover the difference between the original loan notes and value of the hotels and other collateral which the banks had taken. These deficiency notes were personal obligations, replacing the original personal guarantees which Monty and I had provided, more of which later.

In the late spring of 1993, Monty and I assigned the benefit of the HFS stock to Bryanston, the company which managed the Days Inn franchised hotels, and which generated the franchise fees. These, in turn, triggered the stock distributions under the Earnout Agreement. This was a tidying-up exercise only, but Bryanston ends up with greater significance towards the end of this story.

Despite everyone's best intentions, when the time came for the first payment due under the CRA, the asset pool which was remaining had failed to generate enough money to meet the bill. From that point – June 1993 – onwards, the banks concluded that the co-operative effort which the CRA had represented was doomed to fail. They broke rank. Co-operation went out of the window, and it was every man for himself. From that moment, Tollman-Hundley's banks shamelessly competed against each other to get whatever they could for the delinquent deficiency notes. In every case, the notes became the responsibility of each bank's bad loan, or workout, department. They were written off as assets against the banks' balance sheets, and they were written off too against tax. Our deficiency notes were universally perceived to have about as much value as a used bus ticket.

ALPHA HOSPITALITY

With the sale of Days Inn completed and with a workout of Tollman-Hundley now at least theoretically possible, I should have got out and left them to it. That I failed to do so is a matter of everlasting regret to me. That was my moment to go, and I missed it. The decision to stay around cost me in every way possible. Looking back after all these years, what little comfort I take from my decision to see to it that the mess at Tollman-Hundley was sorted out comes from the fact that I acted through a sense of duty. This comfort, though, was modest, especially when viewed against the cost.

The commitment that I and other members of my family had to make in order to put things straight at Tollman-Hundley meant that, amongst other things, I missed countless business opportunities, especially in my homeland. In 1994, South Africa once again looked as though it had a future. Even though we were able to acquire part of the southern African-based Wilderness Safaris at around this time, the distractions of Tollman-Hundley had prevented me from devoting energy to many things, notably the process of reinvesting as fully in South Africa as I should have done.

In addition to addressing investment opportunities, at around this time I also gave more time to assisting in the development of the travel businesses. In 1992, for instance, I focused on the importance to our business of currencies, and of currency trading. Given the complex multi-national nature of our industry, and the significant fluctuations in exchange rates of major currency in recent years, this aspect of the business could well be disastrous or hugely beneficial. I am delighted to say that, consistently, it has proven to be the latter.

Although I saw the task ahead at Tollman-Hundley as essentially one of cleaning up and winding down what had become a messy and unfortunate business, others had different plans. These involved future investment in gaming, a means of making money with which I had very little sympathy indeed.

From my earliest days of work, I had loathed the idea of gaming as a source of income. I remembered only too clearly the race days which took place on Wednesdays and Saturdays in South Africa, and the scene in the Palace Hotel. Situated just around the corner from Tattersalls, the bars of the Palace would be occupied by the depressing sight of miserable-looking people, all of whom were contemplating their next bet; the one which was going to dig them out of the losses from earlier races. Dozens of people tried to borrow money from the bar simply in order to bet on that next race, often offering watches and jewellery by way of short-term security. This unhappy sight led to my conviction that I never, ever wanted to be involved in the gaming industry.

Although his involvement with Del Webb had given him stacks of experience of casinos, Monty always assured me that he never wanted Tollman-Hundley to enter the gaming business. I could not have been happier when he told me that. But, despite his reservations and mine, Monty came to see me one day to tell me that Tom Aro had found a casino that he felt the company should acquire.

Despite Monty's deep-seated reticence about getting involved in gaming, he had been persuaded by Tom that we should do this deal. It was only a small deal, it didn't involve too much money in that two-thirds of its cost could be financed, and by this time we were seeing money from the HFS deal. Everyone said that casinos were 'licences to print money' and the casino Tom had in mind was no exception, in that it offered the prospect of very good returns. I knew that the Tollman-Hundley mess still needed more sorting out, and the prospect of additional cash from a casino could be very useful in that process. This reason alone caused me to think more carefully. And, somehow, the idea took hold and before long the company had set up a separate operation called Alpha Hospitality which would be floated as a public company. Tollman-Hundley would remain a privately-owned hotel business, with Brett in charge, and Alpha would become a publicly-owned gaming business.

Despite my personal, and unequivocal, distaste for gaming as an investment, I allowed myself to be ensnared once again – and at the very time that I was labouring hard to free us from this mess. So it was that I became involved in the gaming business. I will never fully understand how or why. I should have walked away.

At the beginning of 1995, Alpha Hospitality acquired the Bayou Caddy Jubilee Casino, which operated from Clermont Harbor, Lakeshore. This was based on the Gulf coast, near Waveland, Mississippi, and about 25 miles from New Orleans. Six months later, we took over the Cotton Club Casino, which was situated at Greenville, Mississippi. Both of these were floating casinos, one of the advantages of which was that they were capable of being easily relocated.

In simple terms, Alpha negotiated an exchange of the two casinos, bringing the Bayou Caddy Jubilee Casino up the Mississippi to Greenville, where it was re-sited. This of course required the consent of the Mississippi Gaming Commission and the support of the local community. Alpha's plan was to achieve a better match of the two boats to the two markets. Our reopening in Greenville proved very popular, with almost 50,000 people visiting the Bayou Caddy during the first weekend of opening. This had far surpassed anything in any equivalent period when the Bayou Caddy had been based at Waveland.

Alpha then took the Cotton Club Riverboat Casino down the Mississippi, completely refurbished it and renamed it the Jubilation. This was reopened at the Lakeshore, Waveland location.

Greenville is a small and unremarkable Mississippi town, sitting alongside Old Man River, and about 300 miles inland. In doing business there, I found that a local man with whom I had been in negotiation was also one of the most remarkable men in American politics. I discovered that Clarke Reed was one of the fathers of the modern Republican Party in Mississippi, wielding significant influence in state, regional and national Republican politics. Clarke was a man with whom I was to develop a close friendship.

Although born in Missouri, Clarke had moved to Greenville as a young man – and a young man with an interest in politics. In the early 1950s, the South was solidly Democrat. Southern Democrats held powerful positions on Congressional committees, but the region played a negligible part in choosing presidential nominees. To all intents and purposes, Republicans were invisible south of the Mason-Dixon line, and moderates from the Northeast controlled the Party.

But the mood of the time was changing. Lyndon Johnson backed the civil rights movement and the Great Society, the aims of which were the elimination of poverty and racial injustice. Clarke Reed predicted that there would be an exodus of Southern white voters from the party of their ancestors. Interviewed later about this period, he said, "We were out of step. With desegregation coming, I knew that we would need friends in both places, so I came to the conclusion I was a Republican."

In 1969, Clarke Reed invited right-leaning Southern Democrats to the Jung Hotel in New Orleans. He told them, in no uncertain terms, that the GOP[65], which had been despised in the South since the days of Abraham Lincoln, was in fact the future of the South and that, in turn, the South was the future of the GOP.

Clarke's New Orleans initiative was to herald Richard Nixon's 'Southern Strategy' in the very early 1970s. Later, Ronald Reagan and George H W Bush were to shift the South towards the Republicans in presidential elections. Finally, the Newt Gingrich-led Congressional election gains of 1994 included many of the last Blue Dog Democrats' seats. For a generation, the South has been the anchor of the national Republican Party. And much of that is down to Clarke Reed, who played pivotal roles in the nominations of Richard Nixon and Gerald Ford, and who watched his protégé Haley Barbour rise first to National Party Chairman and then to Governor of Mississippi. As you will soon discover, Clarke Reed also played a small but important part in my own story. But that is a little later.

One day in 1995, I got a telephone call from Charlie Gargano, who was well-known to me through his Republican fundraising. On this occasion, Charlie was not, however, calling to ask for political

---

[65] Short for 'Grand Old Party', the nickname of the Republican Party.

donations, but in his capacity as a member of the recently-appointed administration of New York Governor, George Pataki. He asked me to come and meet him at his new office in the World Trade Center, and to bring Monty with me.

During the 1980s and 90s, Charlie Gargano was widely perceived as one of the most influential Republicans in America. He studied civil engineering at college, and then went on to work in Brooklyn in New York City's Highways and Sewers Department. But he had not given up on education, nor on his civil engineering degree. He continued to study, obtaining an MBA in his spare time and, in his late 20s, joined J D Posillico, a Long Island construction company, of which he was to become a partner within three years.

Charlie, though, was a man with close political ties and great connections. He was appointed by Ronald Reagan to become Deputy Administrator at what was then known as the Federal Transportation Administration. And in 1988, he was made US Ambassador to Trinidad and Tobago. Five years later, he met Senator George Pataki, who was then contemplating a challenge to New York Governor Mario Cuomo.

George Pataki was a first-term State Senator from Westchester County when he launched his bid for the Republican nomination for Governor in 1994. Considered an underdog at the start of the campaign, Pataki was running against three-term Cuomo. Charlie Gargano became his Campaign Finance Chairman, a job at which he was immensely successful. He said afterwards, "Perhaps I brought stature to the campaign – particularly because I was known in the private sector. I felt that through our fundraising, we were able to accomplish whatever we needed to do to get George Pataki's message across."

Pataki ran neck-and-neck with Cuomo in the polls, focusing largely on tax cuts and the death penalty during his campaign. In the end, he narrowly defeated Cuomo, becoming the first Governor since Franklin D Roosevelt to have come from outside the five boroughs of New York City. George Pataki took office on 1 January 1995. The following month, he asked Charlie Gargano to become part of his administration. Charlie's unwieldy job title was – Chairman of Empire State Development Corporation of New York State, Commissioner of the Department of Economic Development and Vice-Chairman of the Port Authority of New York and New Jersey.

Charlie was a third-generation American citizen. His grandfather was an Italian immigrant and Italy was firmly in Charlie's blood. By chance, he had actually himself been born in Italy, even though his father had been born in New York. Having served as US Ambassador in Trinidad and Tobago, Charlie's lifelong ambition was to become US Ambassador to Italy, but this was never to be. In November 2007, George W Bush did nominate Charlie to become US Ambassador to Austria, but by then rumours concerning Charlie's business dealings had surfaced, and his name was quietly withdrawn.

But back in 1995, Monty and I went to see Charlie as he had requested, at his office in the World Trade Center. This was a building of which he was immensely proud. Five years later, and only six weeks before 9/11, the Port Authority was to put out a press release claiming that the World Trade Center was then the most desirable commercial property in New York. Charlie himself was quoted as saying, "The World Trade Center and its Twin Towers are among the handful of instantly recognizable structures on the entire planet, like the Pyramids at Giza or the Great Wall of China."[66] But in 2006, Charlie, as Port Commander, was to play himself in Oliver Stone's *World Trade Center*, a film based upon the events of 11 September 2001.

Charlie was aware that, through Alpha Hospitality, we had recently entered into a joint venture agreement with the Mohawk people. This concerned the operation and development of a gaming facility located on the reservation of the St Regis Mohawk Indian Tribe at Hogansburg, New York, close to the Canadian border and almost 400 miles from New York City.

He told us that Governor Pataki wanted to encourage gaming in New York State but specifically in the Catskill Mountains. If we were able to alter our deal with the Mohawk Nation, the Governor would support any attempts we might wish to make to get a gaming licence

---

[66] Press release: The Port Authority of New York and New Jersey Press Center, 24 July 2001.

in the Catskills instead. Unlike the Waveland Casino which was decidedly small beer, the prospect of gaming barely an hour away from Manhattan had the prospect of being extremely valuable. Charlie was so enthusiastic about this project that he wanted to invest in it himself.

I will not recount the chequered history of events since the meeting which Monty and I had with Charlie Gargano in 1995. Suffice to say that the idea remains a good one but, 18 years later, the casino has yet to be built. The concept has undergone various metamorphoses during the intervening period, and more than a little intrigue. As I write, I am involved in multi-million dollar litigation about the project – as the plaintiff!

Monty and I responded with enthusiasm to Charlie's idea and we struck up a partnership with a local wheeler-dealer called Robert Berman, a man who had grown up in the Catskills. With Robert, we made a new deal with the St Regis Mohawks, and later with the Cayuga Nation. We acquired the 225-acre Monticello Raceway, located off route 17 in Sullivan County, just 90 miles from Manhattan and with no fewer than 20 million people living within 100 miles. We offered to donate 30 acres of the Monticello site to the Indians for the construction of the casino, which we would then build and operate under a management contract. A number of backers were interested in this proposal, one of whom was Charlie Gargano himself, who bought shares. But his shareholding in the project was criticised during his confirmation hearings, and Charlie ended up selling his stock. The timing of his disposal was not good, and he took a bath on the investment. This is how the local newspaper reported it[67]:

> *That Pataki's chief 1994 campaign fund-raiser, Charles Gargano, who now heads the state's business development agency, was formerly on the board of directors of a casino management company hardly suggests unbiased policy making. Gargano reportedly still owns stock in the company, Alpha Hospitality, although his spokesperson says the stock is in a blind trust.*

---

[67] *Albany Times,* 10 August 1996.

Charlie Gargano was indeed a member of the Board of Alpha Hospitality, but decided to resign at the time of his confirmation hearings. At around the same time, Robert Morgenthau, as District Attorney, subpoenaed him.

In the context of those hearings, I was told that I was to be called as a witness. At a personal level, this did not bother me one little bit. But I felt nervous about answering questions honestly – as far as I am concerned my only option – if honest answers from me made it difficult for others. I was sufficiently nervous about this point to ask one of our in-house lawyers, a good man called Herb Koslov, to hire a strong external counsel to advise me. Thus it was that I came into contact with stellar New York defence attorney Ben Brafman, who has a bigger role to play later in my story. As it happened, however, I was thankfully never called as a witness.

In 2001, Robert Morgenthau announced that he was not proceeding with an investigation into Charlie, rumours of the existence of which had stained his reputation for some time. This is how the *New York Times* reported it[68]:

No Charges After Inquiry Of Pataki Ally

The Manhattan district attorney yesterday closed a long-running investigation into whether Charles A. Gargano, the state's top economic development official, had done favors for political contributors, and said that he would file no charges against Mr. Gargano.

District Attorney Robert M. Morgenthau had never formally announced the inquiry of Mr. Gargano, who oversaw billions of dollars in economic development deals as chairman of the Empire State Development Corporation. But its existence was widely known and hung like a dark cloud over Mr. Gargano for the last two years.

Although Mr. Gargano was never charged with anything, the investigation appeared to cost him a top post in George W. Bush's presidential campaign, just as he was packing the photographs on the walls of his office on Third Avenue in preparation for that job.

The inquiry began with an examination of spending by one part of Mr. Gargano's agency, and later broadened to focus on Mr. Gargano's role in nearly every aspect of its work. Mr. Gargano, a former construction industry executive who had risen to prominence in Republican circles because of his prowess as a fund-raiser, had consistently maintained that the investigation would not turn up any wrongdoing.

Yesterday, the district attorney's office released a terse statement saying, "No criminal charges will be filed in connection with the two-year investigation." Prosecutors would not elaborate on their decision to end the inquiry. "Chairman Gargano is gratified by District Attorney Morgenthau's decision," said Maura Gallucci, his spokeswoman. "He has always been confident that there was no basis for any action to be taken."

With the investigation now behind him, Mr. Gargano seems poised to return to the prominence he once enjoyed as a close aide to Mr. Pataki and a leading Republican fund-raiser.

The district's attorney's investigation of Mr. Gargano began in 1999 as an inquiry into whether agency officials misspent funds from annual receptions to honor Italian-Americans. It initially revolved around Paolo Palumbo, an old friend of Mr. Gargano's, whom he had appointed to be deputy commissioner for international business. A former baker and professor of Italian literature at Fordham University, Mr. Palumbo arranged the Italian affairs and sometimes wrote Mr. Gargano's speeches. Mr. Palumbo subsequently resigned from his $91,877-a-year state job in July, 1999, and agreed to plead guilty to a bribery charge. At the same time, Mr. Palumbo was also working with investigators.

Mr. Gargano told friends at the time that he felt that his old friend had betrayed his trust. But within months, the inquiry had grown into a wide-ranging exploration of Mr. Gargano's role in a variety of economic development projects in Westchester, his involvement in the sale of state land to Republican contributors and the construction of his new home in the Hamptons.

Investigators interviewed a dozen current and former staff members of the state agency and deluged the Empire State Development Corporation with subpoenas demanding cartons of documents, memos and e-mail messages.

While Mr. Gargano never went to work for the Bush campaign, he has remained head of the state development agency during the inquiry, and in recent months, he has resumed his high-profile role in state affairs.

There is little doubt that these rumours had a major impact on Charlie's aspiration to become US Ambassador to Rome. Within a matter of weeks, the *Albany Times* carried the following story[69]:

WASHINGTON – Charles Gargano, New York State's economic development czar, has arranged for an array of backers, including Governor George Pataki, to plug his name with the White House as the perfect U.S. ambassador in Rome.

But Gargano, a major Republican fund-raiser, has also seen to it that another letter found its way to Washington: one from the Manhattan district attorney, Robert M. Morgenthau, clearing him of criminal charges after a two-year probe of the Empire State Development Corp., which Gargano heads.

White House aides chuckled over the Morgenthau letter, which they considered one of the more unconventional recommendations they had received during what has become a mad scramble for ambassadorships by friends and political allies of President Bush.

Gargano is just one of 1,700 people who applied or were recommended to the White House for top jobs at U.S. embassies, according to White House aides. Two hundred made the first cut. In the end, 49 lucky political appointees will receive the keys to an ambassador's residence.

Gargano, who like others seeking ambassadorships declined to be interviewed, was ambassador to Trinidad and Tobago during the administration of the elder George Bush. With plenty of competition for the Rome posting, Gargano brought up the Morgenthau investigation for a reason: It already cost him one job with Bush. He had been in line to become chairman of the Bush New York campaign effort just about the time the inquiry surfaced.

---

[69] *Albany Times*, 21 March 2001.

Charlie's dreams were soon to be dashed[70]:

Floridian, not a New Yorker, will be Ambassador to Rome

President Bush has decided to appoint a Florida developer and major Republican Party fund-raiser as ambassador to Italy, New York State and Republican officials said yesterday.

The ambassadorship in Rome, one of the government's plum patronage appointments, will go to Mel Sembler, who was finance chairman of the Republican National Committee during Mr. Bush's run for the presidency.

Mr. Sembler, who became rich building shopping centers, has raised money for the Republicans for many years and was especially helpful in soliciting contributions for the two gubernatorial races of Jeb Bush of Florida.

Through all of this and more, Charlie and I were to stay the very best of friends – until, that is, I was indicted. But more of that later.

At the end of March 1995, Bea and I were on holiday in Europe when I received a telephone call from the office in Valhalla to tell me that Monty Hundley was resigning immediately from Alpha Hospitality. When I asked why, I was told he had some sort of tax problem. The press statement announcing Monty's departure merely said that "his resignation was solely for personal reasons". The same release also informed the world that I had been elected as Chairman and CEO of Alpha Hospitality. I had not even wanted to get into gaming in the first place at all, and yet here I was in charge of the whole damn business.

The office also reminded me that, in six weeks' time, Alpha was making a very important submission to the Indiana Gaming Commission. Monty could not, of course, play the lead role in that presentation given that he was now out of the picture, and I would have to stand in for him. If I didn't, the gaming licence which we had spent the last two years and millions of dollars trying to secure would be lost. I had little choice.

Realising that there was no alternative, when the time came, Bea and I took the *Concorde* to JFK where a private plane was waiting to take us on to Indianapolis. This was 15 May 1995, a watershed day in terms of my relationship with Monty. Looking back, it was arguably the day when my problems with the United States kicked off. I should have realised that the gods were not smiling that day when the car which picked us up from Indianapolis airport was rammed in the back by another car as we were en route to the Gaming Commission presentation. Bea was thrown into the seats in front but, as she always does, she picked herself up and said she was OK.

Somewhat shaken, we arrived at the Indiana Government Center in West Washington Street, where we were greeted by Sanford Freedman. I had been given some words in advance which I had been asked to present, and Sanford added that the Commission might also want to ask me a few questions. I walked into the hall where the presentation was about to take place and realised for the first time that it was a public meeting, and that there were hundreds of people present. I realised, too, that not only would Alpha Hospitality be presenting its proposals, but that there would also be a presentation by our competitors from Hyatt. Across the room I spotted Nick Pritzker, although it was somewhat difficult to recognise him with a beard. Sitting next to him was Jay Pritzker's son, Tom. They had both grown more than a little since the time when Bea and I went to stay with Jay Pritzker at his home in Chicago, when Nick and Tom were just boys.

We were all welcomed by the chairman of the Commission, Alan Klineman, who sat with four other Commission members and was supported by various officers of the Commission. David Frick, our local attorney, introduced the Alpha team, explaining that we had been working for two years as Alpha Rising Sun to create something called the Fulton's Landing Resort at the small town of Rising Sun, Indiana, at a point on the Ohio River where there were no boundary issues concerning next-door Kentucky. He explained that we were a team of people of good character and reputation with decades of experience in the gaming, travel and leisure industries. Having set the scene, he then introduced me as Chairman of both Alpha Rising Sun and its parent, Alpha Hospitality Corporation.

I stood up and explained why we had been attracted to Rising Sun, and how we had invited a group of Rising Sun officials to visit Old Town in Kissimmee, Florida, to witness a development which was already managed by us. I told the meeting that we had hosted a job fair and voter registration day at which we had received 600 applications and registered 115 new voters – the largest single day's registration of voters in the history of Ohio County. I went on to remind the meeting of the history of our application and the fact that in the face of strong competition from other people, Alpha had been reconfirmed on two occasions as not only the preferred applicant but the very strongly preferred applicant. All good stuff.

I then handed over to Sanford Freedman who, along with other members of the team, explained the detail of what we had planned for Fulton's Landing Resort.

Questions started to come from the Commission, initially connected with the financing of the project. As far as finance was concerned, we had signed a partnership deal with Bally Entertainment Corporation, and we were therefore as strong as the competition on the only point where I thought we might otherwise have a weakness. However, once the issue of financing was resolved to everyone's apparent satisfaction, one of the commissioners, Donald Vowels, stood up and asked the question, "What is the status of Mr Hundley? My understanding is that he has resigned." Tom Aro, who was the President of Alpha Rising Sun Inc confirmed that Monty had indeed resigned. There was then an exchange between Mr Vowels, Tom Aro and Sanford Freedman concerning the disposition of the shares which Monty had held in Alpha. These Monty had distributed to other members of his family in order to ensure that Monty himself no longer had involvement of any kind in the business. The commissioners were puzzled about all of this. I sat there listening, equally as bemused as to what all of this meant.

Donald Vowels then followed up with a more aggressive line of questioning. Referring once again to Monty, he said, "Is this guy shamming us or not? He wouldn't provide Federal and State tax return information to us. And from what I understand, he also did not provide the necessary information to the Commission in Mississippi. I am trying to figure out what is going on. Do you have any idea why he wouldn't submit the information to the Mississippi authorities when they requested it from him?" Sanford Freedman had to admit that he had no idea. The Chairman stepped up to demand, "What's going on here with Mr Hundley? Do you want to tell us?" Once again, Sanford Freedman was forced to admit, "I wish I knew, Mr Chairman. He has resigned from all his positions. He told us it was for personal reasons, and he withdrew from the company. I cannot answer for his personal reasons."

At this point, the Executive Director of the Commission, John Thar, added that the Commission had also been seeking information from Joan Hundley, Monty's wife, but that she too had refused to respond to the same inquiry of the Commission. "She refused to provide us with any information. Do you understand how this looks?" Mr Vowels stepped back into the questioning. "It's strange, to say the least. It seems that in Mississippi they have the same problem. If we give somebody a license, we have a responsibility. I am feeling really uneasy about what I am hearing. Is this a slippery eel that we have given ourselves?"

I had been sitting listening to this extraordinary exchange and I, too, was wondering what the hell was going on. Initially, I had been stunned by the aggressive tone of the questioning from the Commission, but it was clear that something was seriously wrong. I asked myself the question, "Would I give a politically-sensitive licence to an organisation which had been headed up by a man who, it seemed, had something to hide?"

Long after the event, I discovered what the references to Mississippi meant. These related to an event at which I was close at hand, albeit in the next room, and after which I had not been told the truth. Alpha had been seeking a licence in Mississippi but, at the time in question, the Mississippi Gaming Commission had been overwhelmed with work. The Mississippi Commission had therefore asked the Colorado Gaming Commission to conduct some investigations for them. Gaming licences are always held in the name of individuals, and so four of us – myself, Monty, Tom Aro and our CFO, Jim Cutler – had each submitted applications.

The arrangement for handling the applications was that the four of us would fly to an airport somewhere in Colorado where we would each be interviewed by the Colorado Gaming Commission. We all arrived, and each of us was taken to a separate room to be interviewed, at the conclusion of which I asked Monty how it had gone. He assured me that everything had gone well. But I discovered only many years later that Monty's account of the interview was completely untrue. Not only had it not gone well, it had not gone at all. Monty had quite simply refused to answer any question concerning his tax affairs. For this reason, if for none other, he had been refused a licence.

Back in Indianapolis, the Indiana Gaming Commission went through the motions of allowing us to complete our presentation. They then took a presentation from our competitors, Rising Sun Riverboat Casino.

The day after the meeting, Sanford Freedman issued a press statement, which included the words:

> *Alpha Hospitality's Indiana subsidiary appeared Monday before the Indiana Gaming Commission to make its presentation in support of its application to operate riverboat gaming on the Ohio River at the Ohio County City of Rising Sun. The company is one of only two applicants for a license in Ohio County, and believes that, in light of the management skills and strong financial support of Bally Entertainment Corp. which has joined with the company for this project, it is a strong contender for a license.*

Had I not seen him there with my own eyes, I would have imagined that Sanford Freeman had not been at the meeting. Only a fool would have thought that we were any longer a strong contender.

To cut a long story short, the other team got the licence and we did not. Given what they had heard, or to be more accurate what they had not heard, I could not blame the Commission for having reached the conclusion it had. I would have done the same.

This was the defining moment in my relationship with Monty Hundley. I decided that this was the last time that this man was going to let me down. When I looked back at the 16 years since Tollman-Hundley had been created, I found myself able to remember countless examples of when Monty had disappointed, and almost none when I had been pleasantly surprised. Brett had told me that, sooner or later, these guys would get us into trouble and I should have listened to him. But what I did not appreciate was that that day in May 1995 in Indianapolis was the beginning of the end.

With Monty resigning from Alpha, Brett having become President of the hotel division, and me becoming more involved with Alpha and its pursuit of a licence in the Catskills, this was a very busy time. It was also a time of responsibilities between which we were all torn. The family business was going from strength to strength, but in the United States Brett and I were fighting a rearguard action. We had to continue to clean up the mess of the hotel division but we knew that, if we were able to secure a gaming licence in the Catskills, it might represent a salvation of the remaining pieces of our empire there. Tollman-Hundley, and Alpha beyond it, had represented a bottomless pit, requiring constant loans over the years to keep it afloat. During the 1990s in particular, the family was called upon endlessly for money to keep things going. Funding and yet more funding, with the endless reliance upon Tollman family resources. And all of these resources came from outside the USA. In overall terms, we never, ever made money in the United States. Sure, there were fees and dividends, but these did not come close to covering the losses we made on our investments and our loans.

This was a time of reassessment and change. Monty Hundley, who some years earlier had given up his Manhattan brownstone townhouse in exchange for a huge mansion in Bedford, New York State, now sold up and moved himself down to Orlando, Florida. Brett and I were left holding the crying, hungry baby.

GETTING OUR LIVES BACK
PART IV

Keeping out of sight of the camera was now becoming tedious. What were those guys in New York playing at? Simmons & Simmons was of course looking after me but why, oh why, was it taking so long to get ready? I saw on the screen that people were still moving around in the courtroom at the other end, and I presumed they knew what they were doing. Whatever it was, they appeared to be doing it purposefully. I had little choice other than to keep on waiting.

I thought of other set-piece events over the years at which I had been present. And I thought of that dreadful experience before the Indiana Gaming Commission. That day in 1995 was really the start of all of this. I had to admit to myself that this was the day when I had sensed a 'nasty smell' for the first time. Although Tollman-Hundley was in almost every way a less than wonderful experience, at no time had I suspected that anything had been done which was other than completely proper. The management team was professionally qualified and we had, after all, used top-drawer advisers in everything we had done. God knows, we had spent enough money on them.

But Indianapolis had made me suspect for the first time that Monty might not have been as straightforward as I had assumed. After all, what possible explanation could there have been for his bizarre behaviour which had cost us the Indiana licence? From that moment onwards, I had begun to lose trust in Monty. In fact, I began to realise that so far as Monty was concerned, truth and fiction appeared to be readily interchangeable.

Recognising the imperfections of memory and the passage of many years, as we waited for the courtroom to be ready I tried to remember when it was that the penny finally dropped. When was it that I decided that Monty was not a man with whom I should be in business? After several minutes' thought, all I could conclude with confidence was that there had been a slowly dawning realisation rather than an epiphany. There was never a revelation. It was not like that. I just thought less and less of Monty as time moved on, and as I learned more about the man.

I recalled that, shortly after Indianapolis, the United States' Internal Revenue Service – the IRS – had opened an investigation into Monty's affairs. Precisely what had triggered this I do not know for certain, but Monty's refusal to answer questions about his tax affairs from two Gaming Commissions probably didn't help.

I remembered too that day in Palm Beach when I had received a copy of a letter which had been sent to Monty Hundley. This was the letter notifying him that he was under formal investigation by the IRS. I had telephoned and asked Monty what this was all about. He said that it was a personal rather than a business matter, and that it was "some tax bullshit". He was, of course, "sorting it out". I took him at his word and thought little more about it.

I then recalled the second letter, received about a year later, in July 1997. This one was written to me direct. This time, the IRS was informing me that I was under investigation too. Understandably, I was now far less prepared to be fobbed off, and I asked some serious questions. Gradually, the extent of Monty's transgressions emerged. I became aware that he had failed to file tax returns. This was undoubtedly bad news for Monty but, for my own part, I breathed a sigh of relief. This had nothing to do with Tollman-Hundley, and even less to do with me. Let the IRS poke around. There was nothing to find.

When I discovered that Monty had been ignoring the US taxman for almost two decades, I, as a taxpayer, was deeply shocked, but I wasn't troubled. This was indeed a personal matter. And my affairs were very much in order.

But the IRS investigations were, of course, not the end of these matters, as this morning's proceedings at Simmons & Simmons were proof. My advisers may have told me that all was well, but that counted for very little.

The IRS investigation had taken a couple of years, after which the file was passed to the Office of the US Attorney for the Southern

District of New York. And it was allocated to a man who is the antithesis of reason, a man who is known even by his colleagues for having 'Drunk the Kool-Aid'[71].

My heart sank when I reminded myself of that man, Stanley Okula, Assistant US Attorney. The man whom *The Times* of London had described as my nemesis, and who had been branded a liar by senior judges in two continents.

What was worse, I remembered that I was about to see that person for the first time, because he was one of the players in the drama which was about to unfold on the screen before my eyes in London. Thankfully, the man of whom I was thinking was 3,000 miles away. But as far as I was concerned, even that distance was a little too close.

---

[71] 'Drinking the Kool-Aid' is an expression used in the United States and Canada to denote an unquestioning believer: someone who believes blindly without critical examination. The metaphor owes its origins to the Jonestown Massacre in 1978, where almost a thousand members of the Peoples Temple were persuaded to commit suicide by drinking a Kool-Aid-like drink laced with cyanide.

PROSECUTORS ARE
'SHEPHERDS OF JUSTICE'.

WHEN A
GOVERNMENT LAWYER,
WITH ENORMOUS RESOURCES
AT HIS OR HER DISPOSAL,
ABUSES POWER AND IGNORES
ETHICAL STANDARDS,
HE OR SHE NOT ONLY
UNDERMINES PUBLIC TRUST,
BUT INFLICTS DAMAGE
BEYOND CALCULATION
TO THE SYSTEM OF JUSTICE.

UNITED STATES FEDERAL JUDGE
JUAN GUERRERO BURCIAGA (1929–95)

THE SEEDS OF THE NIGHTMARE GERMINATE

The Internal Revenue Service (IRS) had begun the investigation into Monty Hundley's tax affairs around about August 1996. Given that this investigation related, in part at least, to his dealings with Tollman-Hundley, the IRS had decided to seek information from Howard Zukerman, who was the Senior Vice President of Finance for the company. Despite this seemingly important title, Howard Zukerman is someone with whom I had almost no dealings, and hardly knew. I am keen to point this out because, when Zukerman thought it might work to his advantage in respect of his own personal issues with the Department of Justice, he claimed that he reported directly to me. It appears that Mr Zukerman has only a fleeting relationship with reality.

As a preparation for the meeting, the IRS decided to do a little homework on Zukerman's personal tax affairs. When they did so, it was discovered that he too had not filed personal income tax returns for each of the preceding four years. An intrigued IRS investigator visited Zukerman's home. Upon discovering that he was out, he left a card with Zukerman's wife asking that he call him.

When the call came, it was not, though, from Zukerman, but from his accountant. He 'informed' the IRS agent that his client had indeed not filed returns from 1992 to 1996, but that he was in the process of preparing those returns now.

Howard Zukerman later claimed that he agreed after these conversations to talk to the IRS – but only after he had been assured that he, Zukerman, was not currently under investigation. Within a few months, he had filed personal tax returns for the four years in question which showed that he had an obligation to pay tax of $130,000. Zukerman argued that he was eligible for immunity under the IRS's Voluntary Disclosure Policy, and would shortly be presenting an offer-in-compromise regarding his outstanding tax liability.

This approach did not, however, have the desired effect. The IRS continued with an investigation of Howard Zukerman's own tax affairs, and on 8 September 1999, long before any Tollman-Hundley indictment, Zukerman was indicted on eight counts of tax evasion and tax fraud.

Zukerman continued to argue that he was eligible for consideration under the IRS's Voluntary Disclosure Policy. Under this policy, the IRS can choose not to recommend criminal prosecution where an individual makes a timely, voluntary disclosure of his failure to file a return. But all of this fell on deaf ears and Howard Zukerman then tried to claim trickery by the Government. Eventually, though, he realised that the game was up and he pleaded guilty. He was sentenced to a year and a day in a federal prison.

The Zukerman story is in very many ways unrelated to my own, but his actions in evading tax, and the actions of Monty Hundley in evading tax, served to colour both the investigation and the subsequent indictments and trial. These were both demonstrably guilty men. Others sharing a dock with these men in an alleged conspiracy were severely compromised by their behaviour.

I was aware that a tax investigation had been commenced, but was in the dark as to the manner in which it was developing. In reality, I hardly gave it a moment's thought for several years. And, looking back over events in preparation for this book, I found little fresh or re-considered evidence to persuade me that I was either wrong or misguided to take the view I did at the time.

In January 1999, my lawyer, Jack Tigue of Morvillo & Abramovitz, met the Department of Justice's Tax Division, in the hope of gaining information as to the status of the IRS investigation. (The investigation had recently been referred to the Department of Justice.) Two weeks later, Tigue wrote to me, reporting on what had been said at the meeting.

He told me that the IRS had a theory of the case against a number of individuals. This was based on the selling of debts to Paternoster Holdings at a discount. The debts in question had been owed to nine banks[72]. He pointed out that, whilst the facts differed in

---

[72] First Chicago Bank, Chemical Bank, Marine Midland Bank, Eurobrokers, United Jersey Bank, New Street, Morgens Waterfall, Wells Fargo and National Westminster.

relation to each individual lender, the notes in question were mostly deficiency notes which resulted from old guarantees which had been signed by me and by Monty Hundley.

When the original loans were defaulted upon, the lenders either foreclosed or took a deed to the hotel property in lieu of foreclosure. In one or two cases, there was a bankruptcy. In almost all cases, Monty and I had signed a deficiency note for the shortfall on the originally guaranteed loans. It was those deficiency notes which were sold or assigned to Paternoster Holdings. According to the IRS theory, each sale or assignment to Paternoster (and in one case to Chelsea Acquisitions), resulted in the cancellation of debt income to me, to Monty, and in three transactions, to Sanford Freedman.

The IRS had claimed that these transactions were 'shams' and that Paternoster Holdings was a sham corporation. They claimed that, by using Paternoster as a conduit or tool, Monty, Freedman and I had in reality acquired our own debt. But these transactions, they reasoned, in fact cancelled our debts. (Paternoster Holdings and Chelsea Acquisitions will be explained shortly.)

The resulting 'income' from the debt cancellation should have been reported on our income tax returns for the years in question (1992-1995). The IRS then calculated that Bea and I owed a further $14 million tax on the theoretical 'income' from the cancellation of debt. This theory was little short of madness.

Having set out the IRS position, Jack Tigue then made three telling observations.

First:
"Forming Paternoster for the purpose of having outstanding debt in the hands of a friendly creditor is a perfectly proper business plan even if it has the added benefit of avoiding income tax."

Second:
"Even if the IRS theory were correct, no income would need to be reported by you on your income tax returns because you were legally 'insolvent' at the time of each of the Paternoster transactions. As of 1991, the

Tollman-Hundley entities were about $800m in debt. You and Monty guaranteed most of that debt. In March 1991, more than $120m of debt was in default. It is clear at that point both you and Monty were legally insolvent. This is a legal defense to any tax evasion which would seem to me to be insurmountable."

Finally:

"The third line of defense is also powerful. Almost all of the notes were deficiency notes. A mere guarantor who signs a deficiency note realises no cancellation of debt income when his liability is extinguished. The Government ought not to try out novel tax theories in the criminal area. The Department of Justice declines to prosecute about 10% of the cases referred to it by the IRS. I believe that this should be one of those cases."

Having said all of that, Tigue was also convinced that Monty's failure to file tax returns, Jim Cutler's failure to report the value of his apartment, and Howard Zukerman's failure to file tax returns would mean that this matter would be sent to the US Attorney's Office in New York. He was right. The file was handed on to the Southern District of New York three months later, in April 1999.

Tigue's analysis was very much in line with my own assessment. Monty Hundley, Jim Cutler and Howard Zukerman may all have had problems, but these were of a personal nature. For my own part, it seemed that there was not much to be genuinely concerned about. It was as I expected, but I had not appreciated the implications of the matter being *"sent to the US Attorney's Office in New York"*. And it would be many months before I did.

I will now introduce a figure who is unquestionably the villain of the whole piece. He is a man who, by virtue of the office he holds, wields enormous power, and who regularly abuses that power and his own office. The man of whom I am talking is Stanley J Okula, Assistant US Attorney for the Southern District of New York.

In 1990, Okula had been appointed to a similar position for the Eastern District of New York, the Southern District's far-less-glamorous neighbour. But in 1995, he joined Southern District, where he was appointed to serve as Tax Coordinator. When Okula was handed the Hundley investigation by the IRS, he had been in his job for a matter of months only. But the allocation of the Hundley file to the desk of Stanley J Okula was one of the cruellest hands which fate has ever dealt me.

Okula has few redeeming features, but I guess that his determination is one of them. He has a fearsome reputation for getting what he wants, irrespective of what that entails. When I first heard his name, I thought little of it. But in the years that followed I was obliged to hear the word 'Okula' so frequently and in such distasteful circumstances that I came to view him as the devil incarnate.

Before I became entangled in the mesh which I am about to describe, as a law-abiding taxpayer, I would have viewed the actions of a tough prosecutor supportively, possibly even with enthusiasm. But being at the receiving end of the attentions of a zealot is not good. And when that zealot is able to claim that he is acting with the authority of the most powerful nation on earth, one is required to take a different view. A very different view.

GUERNSEY

The island of Guernsey is a British Crown Dependency situated in the English Channel, only a handful of miles from the French coast. Like many island jurisdictions, Guernsey's tax-friendly environment means that around a third of its income is accounted for by financial services.

Around 1976, Tom Proctor, who worked for Ken Bates at Trafalgar, moved to Guernsey and became resident there, in anticipation of some corporate restructuring of the business. At about the same time, London accountants Saffery Champness also decided to establish an office for the firm in the Channel Islands. Guernsey was chosen because Saffery Champness was too small to compete with the larger firms which operated out of neighbouring Jersey. The Saffery Champness Guernsey office 'came of age' the following year, when a charming man called Clive Nicholson arrived to become its Managing Partner. Clive, a liveryman of the Merchants Taylors' Company and a lifelong rugby referee, is today a partner in Saffery Champness' London office. As anyone who has done business with him will tell you, Clive is the archetypal English gentleman, and a very polished operator.

Shortly after his arrival in Guernsey, Clive Nicholson was speaking at an investment seminar at which one of the other speakers was Ken Bates. The two already had a passing acquaintance with each other. Clive approached Ken at the end of the seminar and invited him to visit the new facility in Guernsey, an invitation which Ken accepted.

This would prove to be an important step in the relocation of both business and, later, of family arrangements. It began with Ken's appointment of Saffery Champness Guernsey to manage a substantial proportion of his own affairs. And as part of this, Trafalgar became a Guernsey company. And, at around the same time, he also bought the Guernsey Bus Company, and brought in his old friend, Barrie Spears, from Hong Kong to run it.

A year or so later, Trafalgar also established a base in Monte Carlo, which was around the time we all moved down there in 1978. At about the same time, a bank account was opened for Bea and me at the Royal Bank of Canada in Guernsey, even though neither of us had ever set foot on the island. Over the years, we were to become two of the most important clients of Royal Bank of Canada in Guernsey, even though our visits to the island were few and very far between. When our Guernsey-based advisors needed to see us, they would most often come to London rather than us going there. When Bea and I eventually went to the island, we did so together with Ken and his then wife, Pam. We all stayed in a hotel called Old Government House which, many years later, we decided to buy and completely refurbish. It is now Guernsey's first and only 5-star hotel, and is proudly part of Red Carnation.

Guernsey only really became important to us when Bea and I won our extradition battle in London, and we discovered that we could travel safely to Guernsey without fear of being apprehended. Having being trapped in London for six years, Guernsey was almost 'going abroad', and without fear of underhand tricks from the office of the US Attorney.

After a little while, Bea and I decided to follow Ken Bates' example and relocate to Guernsey ourselves. I had met Clive Nicholson on a handful of occasions, and we decided to appoint Safferys too. But a move of this kind is complex, and we were assisted in this by a man called Derek Evans, an accountant who was working for Ken at Trafalgar. I believe it was Derek who opened bank accounts for the family with the Royal Bank of Canada.

Derek Evans was an FCA with 30 years of post-qualification experience, and was one of the principals of Hargreaves Brown Benson, a firm of accountants based in Colne in Lancashire. Derek had in fact been introduced to me by Ken Bates many years before, and he now became the man responsible for the organisation of all the family's financial affairs.

At the beginning of the assignment, he came to Guernsey regularly in order to establish our accounts and, once they were established, he visited as and when necessary to oversee their management. From the moment that he was appointed, Derek sat at the centre of my tax arrangements, and I depended upon him absolutely to make sure that everything was done properly. Even though Ken and I parted ways, Derek continued to work for us and for the travel companies, which the family then owned outright. At the same time, he developed close relationships with our other enterprises. He was the man with a finger on every pulse.

I discovered only recently that the Tollmans were in fact a very unusual client for Saffery Champness, the reason being that our requirements were quite different from those of others. The business of Saffery Champness Guernsey was almost entirely about the tax-efficient management of trusts, many of which had been established to look after the affairs of UK-based landed estates. These trusts had been established in Guernsey for tax reasons, with Saffery Champness acting as trustees. Our accounts, uniquely, were not designed with tax efficiency as an overriding consideration, nor were they trusts. This meant that there was a fundamental difference between the handling of all other clients and the handling of our affairs.

Unlike the trust business, where Saffery Champness were in fact acting as *principal*, in respect of the firm's work for the Tollmans, Saffery Champness was acting merely as *servant*. In respect of trust business, money was being looked after by trustees who had the authority to take decisions in much the same way as if it were their own. But when it came to us, it was clearly the family's money and not theirs. In relation to our business, Saffery Champness did not therefore have authority to act at its own discretion.

This required all those at Saffery Champness who looked after us not only to seek proper instructions, but also to create a record of instructions. Sadly, these instructions were often 'over recorded' to the point where they were of questionable accuracy, let alone of comprehensibility, especially by third parties. And I was to learn to my cost that Saffery Champness Guernsey was very much a risk-averse, CYA environment.

Our business also differed from the day-to-day trust activity by virtue of the size and the number of transactions. Our payments were much smaller than average, but there were many, many more of them.

Although Saffery Champness Guernsey account managers changed regularly, the first and most influential in terms of the structure of the account was a woman called Debbie Mollett, a short-tempered and generally difficult woman. Mollett was not easy to work with. She insisted – unreasonably as far as many of her colleagues were concerned – on creating excessive documentation and unwarranted procedures simply in order to safeguard her own position and her personal anonymity.

Saffery Champness' standard confidentiality procedure meant that each account was identified first by the initials of the manager's name, and then numbered sequentially. Mollett, however, insisted that nothing which identified her must be created.

In regard to our own business, she instead devised two accounts – the 'X' account and the 'Y' account. (She used similar procedures for other clients' accounts.) The firm's requirement to protect the privacy of its clients, combined with Mollett's paranoia about her own identity, meant that the accounts on which she worked were thus mystifyingly anonymous. Others were to allege later, however, that 'mystifyingly anonymous' really meant 'suspiciously secretive'.

She was also greatly assisted in her need for voluminous paperwork by the procedures of the Royal Bank of Canada. These meant that every time a transaction on any account took place, however small, no fewer than two separate records of that transaction would be sent separately in the post to Debbie Mollett. This meant that each and every morning, the Saffery Champness postal delivery would include large numbers of envelopes from the Royal Bank of Canada – sometimes several hundred – each addressed to the X account or the Y account.

Every so often, account managers would change or introduce new procedures in order to preserve security. Changes to code names, for instance, for the authorisation of telephone instructions, became important at times like this. In respect of our business, Saffery Champness staff were not of course acting as trustees, but as administrators. The account manager's overriding concern was to ensure that instructions were coming from the correct people. Identification procedures and code words were an essential part of this process. The Saffery Champness point of contact was always Bea, and never me, and passwords and procedures would always be agreed with Bea.

A combination of unidentified accounts coupled with passwords, none of which were of our own invention, would later be held out as evidence that we had things to hide. Nothing could be further from the truth. Equally damning, as far as Okula was concerned, were regular demands which were made for large amounts of cash.

It is true that Bea and I regularly use cash, but there is a very simple reason for that, as those who travel extensively will confirm. As everyone knows, travelling is expensive. For many years, Bea and I were almost constantly on the move. Keeping abreast of the payment of credit card bills when one is on the move is a source of major anxiety. Like most people, I have suffered the embarrassment more than once of having my credit card declined. In my experience, this always happens at *the* most embarrassing times. Cash is always the safest option, not forgetting of course the importance of tipping properly for good service, and invariably doing so in cash.

Nevertheless, asking for large amounts of cash was never something which Bea did without ensuring that she was observing the rules. With no hint of irony, she often used to tell Saffery Champness that she did not want to get into trouble with the IRS. Bea always wanted everything to be done properly.

When Ken and I decided to close our partnership, we had to go to Guernsey to sign the documents. That act represented the turning of the page as far as Ken was concerned, although Bea and I held on to the Monte Carlo apartment for a little while. But in 1985, Bea and

I also chose to leave Monte Carlo, having decided that we wanted to shift our base to the United States.

In 1997, when I knew that the IRS investigation into Monty was widening, I telephoned Derek Evans. "Derek," I said, "I need you to reassure me that all my arrangements are in good order. Bea and I want to come and see you to make sure that all is well."

Bea and I flew to Manchester airport where Derek met us, together with his son, Michael, who was also a Hargreaves Brown Benson accountant and who had just been made a partner. Michael had become more than an assistant to Derek, because Derek had been diagnosed with cancer and knew that he did not have long to live. Sadly, he died about a year later. In the meantime, Michael was shadowing everything to make sure that his father's business would be managed properly after his death.

Derek told us that he had reviewed everything and that, structurally at least, everything was in perfect order. He could not immediately speak for the day-to-day operations in Guernsey, but he would make a trip there the following week to audit everything which was happening. He wanted simply to make sure that nothing was falling between the cracks. A couple of weeks later, he reconfirmed that everything was in order.

Bea and I declared our Guernsey bank accounts to the US Internal Revenue Service (IRS) as long ago as 1983. Since then, we have spent fortunes with Rothstein Kass New York in having our tax returns filed properly. Over time, these returns became ever more complicated. Bea and her secretaries handled the administration of income, expenditure and assets, at all times working under the direction of the accountants. Every piece of information was supplied by the secretaries to the accountants, who would then complete our tax returns.

Eventually, instructions would arrive from the accountants, telling me exactly how much tax to pay, to which office, and when. I always did as I was told, even though it was a source of everlasting wonder that I should be required to pay all this tax even though I was employing legions of advisors to ensure that it was minimised.

I was told by the IRS in 1997 that my tax affairs were being investigated. But it was not until 2001 that Okula and the IRS decided to ask Guernsey for documents: a request which ultimately uncovered a tax issue. There were almost five full years intervening. At any time during those five years, I could easily have removed, destroyed or tampered with the files. But I did nothing.

I mention this now because, as you will learn, I was soon presented by the US Attorney in the role of master criminal. Odd isn't it? Here I am, a successful businessman. Yet, even though I have five years in which to cover my tracks, I fail to get rid of incriminating evidence which is sitting all together in one office, the address of which the IRS has known about for more than 10 years. Am I at one and the same time brilliant and stupid?

The truth is that I was blissfully unconcerned to hear that there was an IRS investigation. I had paid the IRS millions of dollars each year in taxes. And I had also paid millions to three leading accountancy firms – Rothstein Kass, Saffery Champness and Hargreaves Brown Benson – to make sure that everything was in order and to prepare and file my tax returns fully and openly. As an example of their diligence, my 1992 return contained no fewer than 150 schedules. No-one could ever accuse *me* of not filing returns.

In fact, when Okula applied to Guernsey to get access to our records, we could have challenged his applications, and I was told that we would have won such a challenge. I nevertheless decided not to resist the applications. Why should we? After all, we were certain that we had absolutely nothing to hide.

Throughout a long career, I have always relied heavily upon advisors in respect of everything which I have done. Almost all the business structures and procedures which I have operated over the years have been designed by people who knew about these things and who were paid to make sure that we were at all times the right side of the law.

All my life I have used the finest professionals, never nickel and diming their bills, always imagining that I would get the best service and the correct advice if I treated them well. Every lawyer, accountant, and investment banker with whom I have dealt has always been treated in this way. And I have always trusted them. In turn, I have assumed that they would always protect me. Something I have discovered, though, is that, in the end, you are on your own. It is your neck which is on the line. It is rarely theirs. You are responsible and you must look after yourself because no-one is going to do it for you. Sadly, I have come to the conclusion that, over many years, I have been very poorly served by the vast majority of advisors with whom I have come into contact.

THE SILENCE OF THE FRIENDS

Between 1999 and the summer of 2001, I had heard very little more about the tax investigation. I was aware, of course, that the file had been passed to the US Attorney's Office in New York, but I was expecting little to come out of that which would affect me directly. In the meantime, Bea and I had established a home in Switzerland.

In August 2001, Bea and I were on safari together in Botswana, and were so far in the bush that we were almost entirely out of contact with the world. Being incommunicado was a happy state of affairs, one which seems to be less and less achievable these days. Just before the start of the safari, Bea had received a message asking her to contact Saffery Champness. Bea assumed it was some sort of administrative query only, and decided it could safely be dealt with at the end of the trip. When we got back, however, she discovered that the person who was trying to get hold of her was the compliance officer at Saffery Champness.

Bea learned that a request for assistance had been received by the Guernsey authorities from the US Department of Justice. As a result, the Guernsey Law Offices had issued a notice requiring Saffery Champness to produce documents relating to a single financial transaction involving Bank of America. These documents had been provided to the authorities although, unhelpfully, Saffery Champness appeared not to have taken a copy of whatever it was they had disclosed.

It was later claimed by Okula and the IRS that the disclosure in relation to Bank of America had *revealed* that Bea and I had assets in Guernsey. This was a remarkable claim, given that we had been reporting the fact that we had disclosed Guernsey assets on our tax returns to the IRS each and every year since 1983. In other words, for almost 20 years.

At the beginning of December 2001, Bea and I arrived in Palm Beach for the beginning of the 'Holidays', the extended period running up to, and including, New Year's Eve. On 4 December, two days after we arrived in the United States, Okula again met Jack Tigue of Morvillo Abramowitz. This time, Tigue was accompanied by two colleagues – Robert Morvillo and John Chun. The meeting had been called at Okula's instigation in order to consider his request for an extension of the statute of limitations in relation to certain tax matters. My 1994 tax returns were on the point of passing into a position where action against them would soon be time-barred.

Okula told those present that the "precise contours of the charges against Stanley Tollman" have "not yet been determined". He said that he was seeking the extension because he wanted "to exhaust possible areas of investigations", emphasising that he was not asking for more time simply in order to secure an indictment. He pointed out that I was in fact not "at the forefront" of the alleged fraudulent activities.

A week later, I signed a stipulation in which I voluntarily extended the time in respect of my 1994 tax liability. Bea and I then spent the rest of the month enjoying life in Palm Beach, still unconcerned about the interest of both Okula and the IRS. On 2 January 2002, we left the United States together and travelled to Europe, and to our home in Switzerland. This was the last time that Bea and I were to spend any extended time in the United States.

Meanwhile, excited by the 'discovery' that we had money in Guernsey, Okula then made a much more substantial request for documents, and this time directives were sought from us whereby Bea and I would give consent for the disclosure. We were advised that we could challenge these directives, and that we would succeed, but we chose not to obstruct what seemed to us to be a perfectly straightforward exercise. Little did we appreciate the manner in which Saffery Champness would respond to the request.

In early 2002, a vast amount of material was sent over to the US Attorney's Office. The disclosure of documents went way beyond the scope and legitimacy of the consent directives. Saffery

Champness acted without any apparent concern for our own confidential material which fell outside of the directives, nor for the confidential material of others in whose business no interest had even been expressed by the US Attorney's Office. Saffery Champness simply sent everything to Okula. And it was to be Okula's interpretation of some of this material, much of which had been created by Saffery Champness personnel, which ultimately placed in peril various members of the family.

Just three months after leaving the United States, on Wednesday 3 April 2002 – the timing is important – Bea and I flew back into New York from South Africa. I was on a mission, providing assistance by way of a deposition in court in a piece of civil litigation in which Alpha Hospitality was involved.

Following Alpha Hospitality's agreement with the St Regis Mohawk Tribe in 1996, a great deal of work had been undertaken in preparation for the casino at Monticello Raceway. But three years or so later, a fly had landed in the ointment in the shape of Park Place Entertainment Corporation. Park Place may only have been incorporated in 1998 but, from its inception, it had become the biggest gaming company in the world. This is because it had been spun out of the Hilton Group, taking with it, amongst other things, Caesar's Palace and Bally's casinos.

With 29 casinos worldwide, Park Place had manoeuvred an introduction to the Mohawks through a small, already-existing casino at Akwesasne. Park Place, having eased its way in front of the Mohawks through various minor inducements, persuaded the tribe to adopt Park Place as an alternative partner to Alpha Hospitality at Monticello. They provided a little cash to the tribal government in the form of a loan. More importantly, however, they also worked with the owners of the casino at Akwesasne to accentuate an apparent decline in the casino's fortunes.

The Mohawks depended upon the casino for both income and employment. Arthur Goldberg, the President of Park Place, had suggested that payroll cheques at the existing casino should be artificially delayed in order to create the belief that cashflow was a real problem. The calculation had been made that the Mohawks would then be forced to seek financial support from Park Place, thus reinforcing their relationship, and doing so at our expense.

In truth, Park Place was never really interested in developing the Catskills themselves. They viewed Monticello as a potential threat to their existing operations in Atlantic City, and they saw this as an inexpensive way to neutralise the opposition. This was a spoiling operation. Interestingly, Arthur Goldberg's adviser in all of this was none other than former Senator Al D'Amato, a close friend of Charlie Gargano, whose brainchild he was endeavouring to kill at birth. With friends like that...

In much the same way, Donald Trump objected to our proposal when it was first mooted. He was one of the first to realise the significance of the fact that whilst Atlantic City – the location of his own casino – was 140 miles from New York, the Catskills were a mere 75 miles away.

I was, of course, now Chairman and Chief Executive Officer of Alpha Hospitality. When I got wind of what was happening, I demanded a meeting with Park Place, and I took a helicopter to New Jersey to confront Goldberg. When I saw him, in fairness to the man, he had the good grace to admit that Park Place's tactics were wrong. He agreed that the company should instead do the decent thing and buy out our interest at a proper price. During the following few days, negotiations between Park Place and Robert Berman, President of Catskill Developments, which represented all our various interests in the Catskills, concluded with agreement to buy out our interest in Monticello for $300 million. Goldberg agreed to sell this deal to the board of Park Place.

The following Monday, 17 October 2000, I had flown to Beijing for the annual sales conference of the Travel Corporation. I was about to deliver my speech to the conference when I was asked to come to the telephone urgently. It was Tom Aro, the director of Alpha Hospitality who was the man in charge of gaming. He told me that the 58-year-old Arthur Goldberg had just died. Not only had the proposal to buy out Alpha's stake never got to the board, Arthur

Goldberg's death meant an immediate and comprehensive management reorganisation at Park Place. Negotiations were over and Alpha had little choice other than to sue.

As I had been a major player in the events leading up to Monticello, 18 months later I was asked to make a deposition in Court in New York, even though Bea and I had by now moved to Switzerland.

Thus it was that Bea and I flew in on *Concorde* on Wednesday 3 April 2002, the day before the hearings, in order to make my deposition in the matter of Catskill Development LLC et al v Park Place Entertainment Corporation. I was represented in that hearing, which lasted two days, by Jack Tigue. During the hearing, Jack mentioned to me that Bob Morvillo had discovered that I was in New York, and had asked to see me. Jack said that he thought it was important.

I duly gave my deposition and after court on Friday 5 April (once again, I am being precise for reasons which will become clear) I went to see Bob Morvillo, having made an appointment with his office beforehand. Although it was the end of the day, I was then kept waiting by Morvillo for over two hours. I abhor lateness in much the same way as I abhor rudeness, but I stuck it out because I had been told that it was important that we met. Besides, I knew I was leaving New York in the morning. Eventually, Bob Morvillo turned up – two hours 15 minutes late.

Without any apology whatsoever for keeping me waiting, he sat on the edge of his desk and began a conversation with me which was as casual as any I had ever experienced in a Manhattan office. His manner was not only rude, it was almost contemptuous. Had it not been for the fact that he continued to take telephone calls from others whilst he spoke to me, I suspect that the conversation itself would have lasted barely five minutes.

In essence, he said the following, without notes or preamble, and producing the words as though he were pulling them from the ether: "This is the deal. $100 million. Wife walks. Brett serves one year. You serve two. Best deal I can do." Completely stunned, I asked him what all this meant and what would happen next. "You will be indicted this month, next month. Who knows?" And that was it. He did not ask me to respond to his bombshell in any way and I left, not knowing what to think.

For the best part of five years, I had been told by Jack Tigue that there was little to worry about. I knew I had done nothing wrong. I had been told that an indictment was only a very remote possibility. And I had also been told that I could successfully defend any charge which might be laid at my door. If all of this was true, how could this possibly be reconciled with the end-of-the-world scenario which had just been described to me?

As I left Morvillo's office I was deep in thought. I slept little that night, not knowing what any of this meant. And the same thoughts were still troubling me as *Concorde* touched down at Heathrow the next day.

Little did I know at the time that a significant meeting had taken place one week earlier. In doing research for this book, I discovered for the first time a note which had been taken of a meeting which took place on 29 March 2002, and about which I had not been told.

Jack Tigue, Bob Morvillo and John Chun had once again seen Okula and a number of IRS/FBI officials at White Plains, in a meeting lasting 45 minutes. John Chun had made an internal note to the file of this meeting. For some reason, this had not been sent to me. Without the research undertaken for this book, I could well not have seen it to this day.

At the outset of the meeting, Okula announced that over the last four months and in relation to the Channel Islands investigation, "things had changed" as a result of the discovery of what he described as damning documents from Saffery Champness. He talked of "nearly verbatim records" of telephone calls and of meetings with the "Tollmans", including meetings with me.

He then talked about the "bank fraud allegations" and other Tollman-Hundley matters, predicting that I would be indicted in a two-phase process. He said that I, Hundley, Freedman, Cutler and

Zukerman would be indicted, but that charges would not be brought against Brett.

In relation to 'perks' he said that I, Hundley and Cutler would be charged. There is no mention of Brett. The final paragraph of Chun's note says:

> At the conclusion of the meeting, we asked about the potential global resolution of this matter. While Okula was not specific, he did state that 'accommodations' could be made for SST's[73] family members, like BNT[74], given their age. Okula emphasized, however, that this was not a typical case where the head of a family directed the criminal activity of other family members who could receive leniency as a result of the head of the family's plea. In this case, Okula views BNT as bearing significant responsibility for the alleged crimes and therefore would expect that she pays a significant penalty.

In what he had told me in his office that evening, I have little doubt that Bob Morvillo was relying in some way upon what he had heard at the 29 March meeting. But there was no way I could have known this. Nor could the short and shocking meeting with him be represented truthfully as a component of even a plea, let alone a plea negotiation.

In 2006, however, Okula was to swear a witness statement for Westminster Magistrates' Court which included the following:

> … representatives from my office met with attorneys for Stanley Tollman in New York in or about early 2002, prior to the return of the 2002 indictment. This meeting, customarily given to counsel in cases of this sort, was consented to by our office as a result of a request for such a meeting made by Mr. Tigue. During the meeting, Tigue and his partner, Robert Morvillo, made an attempt to persuade us not to ask for an indictment, but we told them of the nature and extent of the Guernsey evidence, and that we would proceed with criminal charges
>
> The conversation with them turned to the question of sentence. We specified – based on our then-current analysis of the evidence, which has

---

[73] SST: Initials of Stanley Stephen Tollman.
[74] BNT: Initials of Beatrice Nina Tollman.

*since been subject to a more exacting analysis, particularly as it
relates to the Guernsey evidence – how many years Stanley, Beatrice,
and Brett Tollman would likely be required to serve (as dictated by the
then-governing United States Sentencing Guidelines), on the basis of the
evidence then available to us, if the judge agreed with the agreement
reached by prosecution and defence.*

*Stanley Tollman, we proposed, could plead guilty, and we could
present a factual basis that, if accepted by the judge, would be in the
approximate range of between six to seven years in prison. Beatrice and
Brett Tollman would face lower sentences, but we maintained that,
consistent with the Sentencing Guidelines, they would be required to serve
sentences of imprisonment. Mr Morvillo, present with Tigue and an
assistant, said (either at that point or a later point, when delivering
Stanley Tollman s response to the offer), that he thought the sentence
estimate was what he expected and not unfair. A day or two later, Mr
Morvillo telephoned to say that his client would not accept it.*

Establishing what actually went on behind closed doors is no
longer possible. We know that Okula's witness statement is not a
document upon which to rely, and his account therefore of his
conversations with Bob Morvillo cannot be taken at face value. But
what I am able to say without equivocation is that Bob Morvillo did
not ask me to express acceptance or otherwise of any plea 'package'
and, unsurprisingly, I did not volunteer an answer to a question I had
not been asked. Furthermore, I did not instruct Bob Morvillo or
anyone else to inform the US Attorney's Office of my preparedness –
or lack of it – to accept anything at all.

Barely a week after Bea and I got back to London, as Morvillo
had intimated, a grand jury handed down indictments against me and
against Monty Hundley, Sanford Freedman, Jim Cutler and Howard
Zukerman. This is how the *New York Times* reported it[75]:

---

[75] *New York Times*, 18 April 2002.

5 Men, One With Political Connections, Are Indicted in $42 Million Bank and Tax Fraud

Federal prosecutors announced charges yesterday against a politically connected Manhattan businessman and his partner, accusing them and three of their hotel business associates of defrauding five banks of more than $42 million.

The Manhattan businessman, Stanley S. Tollman, and his partner, Monty D. Hundley, are accused of running a complex scheme with the help of an employee, an accountant and a lawyer to avoid repaying tens of millions of dollars they had borrowed from banks to build their hotel business.

The two men also avoided taxes on millions of dollars in income, according to an indictment unsealed late Tuesday in United States District Court in Manhattan. They did so by not filing tax returns, concealing offshore bank accounts from tax advisers and the Internal Revenue Service, and having their businesses pay for personal items like the insurance on Mr. Tollman's fleet of luxury cars, including Rolls-Royces, Bentleys and an Aston Martin, prosecutors said.

John J. Tigue Jr., a lawyer for Mr. Tollman, said, "Mr. Tollman intends to plead not guilty and defend himself in court." A lawyer for Mr. Hundley did not return a call seeking comment yesterday.

They will be arraigned on Wednesday, said a spokesman for the United States attorney's office. Four of the five men charged Tuesday were also connected with Alpha Hospitality Corporation, a gambling company that has been involved in efforts to build a casino in the Catskills with the St. Regis Mohawk tribe. Until February, Mr. Tollman was the chairman and chief executive of Alpha.

The company had been a contender to become the casino's chief developer, but two years ago Alpha lost that opportunity to Park Place Entertainment. Alpha is now a party to a suit against Park Place, and is likely to own slot machines at the casino regardless of the suit's outcome. Mr. Hundley was a longtime officer of Alpha, resigning in 1995.

Until 1995, Alpha included on its board of directors Charles A. Gargano, a prominent Republican fund-raiser and friend of Mr. Tollman's who is now chairman of the Empire State Development

Corporation, the state's chief economic development agency. Mr. Gargano's role in the company led to criticism in the Legislature during his confirmation hearings, and as a result he promised to resign from Alpha's board of directors and sell his stock.

According to the indictment released yesterday, Mr. Tollman and Mr. Hundley, of Bedford, N.Y., began building a hotel business in 1979, borrowing money from banks that ran within a decade into the hundreds of millions. In 1989 they bought the Days Inn hotel chain's corporate parent for $765 million, using mostly borrowed money. A year later they declared bankruptcy and sold the parent company, while retaining their substantial ownership of Days Inn franchises, which they had bought separately.

They then told their creditors, including Chemical Bank, National Westminster Bank, First National Bank of Chicago, Marine Midland and Security Pacific, now Bank of America, that they could not repay their debt, according to the indictment. But they lied to the banks about their assets, concealing about $100 million worth of stock they had gained in the sale of the Days Inn parent company, prosecutors said.

Both men also concealed private properties, including homes belonging to Mr. Tollman in Manhattan, Florida, Connecticut and London worth more than $13.5 million, according to the indictment. In addition, the two men enlisted a New York businessman to pose as the representative of European investors who were hoping to buy the banks' debt at a steep discount, prosecutors said.

In fact, those investors were straw firms controlled by Mr. Tollman and Mr. Hundley, who used them to repurchase surreptitiously more than $50 million of their own debt for less than $7.6 million, prosecutors said. According to the indictment, relatives of Mr. Tollman who did not share his last name served as officers of the two companies, Paternoster Holdings and Chelsea Acquisitions.

The government also charged both men with evading taxes on the income they had effectively gained by reducing their debt through the fake European investors.[76]

---

76 *5 Men, One With Political Connections, Are Indicted in $42 Million Bank and Tax Fraud,*
    New York Times, 18 April 2002.

An arraignment hearing was set for Wednesday 24 April, just ten days after the indictment was handed down. Bea and I bought tickets and booked seats on British Airways flight BA001 for the day of the arraignment. Now a piece of history, BA001 was the early morning *Concorde* flight which used to leave London Heathrow at 9.30am, and which landed at John F Kennedy airport, New York at about 8.15am. In effect, one arrived in the United States over an hour *before* having left England. This meant that one could be in Manhattan for the start of business the very same day one had left London.

Whilst we were making preparations for the trip, Jack Tigue was engaged in bail discussions with Okula. For obvious reasons, I was advised of the importance of agreeing a formula for bail before I again set foot in the United States. But this proved difficult. I discovered only the day before we were due to fly to New York that Okula was demanding as security every one of the three US properties – the Park Avenue apartment, the Connecticut farm and the mansion in Palm Beach. These were not only three extremely valuable properties, more importantly, they were owned by Bea – not me.

To place Okula's demand into context, these properties were together valued at many tens of millions of dollars. Monty Hundley, I discovered, was being required to put up only 650,000 dollars worth of security. How could this possibly be right? If there was a central figure in all of this – whatever that meant – it was of course Monty Hundley. It was most certainly not me.

A very close friend of mine pointed out to me what the disparity in the bail demands signified. "*You,*" he pointed out, "are the real target of all of this, not Monty Hundley. You need to be very careful." I am not going to name my friend, for his own sake, but this was just the first instalment of professional advice – and very good advice it was too – which we were to receive from him as the dreadful story unfolded during the years which followed. He knows who he is, and I am sure that he appreciates the extent of our gratitude to him for helping us get through.

Jack Tigue went back to Okula, and told him why it was impossible to accede to his demand for the security of the three homes. Okula's alternative was to demand just one of the properties. He was once again told by Tigue that this was not possible. "Mrs Tollman's own lawyer will not allow it."

Okula then described our US homes as only "nominally held in Beatrice's name". But there was nothing 'nominal' about her ownership of these properties. In many ways, they represented the physical manifestation of her family inheritance – of the monies which she had brought to our marriage, enhanced by 50 years of hard and unswerving labour. They were very much her properties, and could never have been 'agreed in principle' without her even knowing about it, as Okula had wanted. The whole idea was preposterous.

Given that the negotiations were far from concluded, I was advised that I should not return to the United States until the matter of bail had been resolved, which was in any case expected to take no longer than a day or two.

The arraignment hearing took place at White Plains, as planned, on 24 April 2002, but I was not present. Jack Tigue did, however, represent me there. The transcript of those proceedings includes the following exchanges:

Jack Tigue: *"Your Honor, I expected Mr Tollman to be here as well today. I spoke to him this morning and he is still in London where he lives. I had thought we had pretty much negotiated a bail agreement with Mr Okula and the property that was to be posted was Mrs Tollman's real estate here in New York. Her lawyer raised a last minute objection to the posting of that property as bail. I hoped to resolve it today. I have not been able to resolve it with her lawyers because I don't represent her and it's my hope and expectation that Mr Tollman will be here shortly and I would ask your Honor to hold off for one week and to adjourn the arraignment of Mr Tollman until I can work out the details for the bail package with Mr Okula.*

Okula: *"Your Honor, we vigorously oppose that. We have no understanding or any facts that we can really grab on to that demonstrate that Mr Tollman is going to come and face the charges. He's a fugitive... "*

The *New York Times* reported on the arraignment hearing the following morning:

An arrest warrant was issued yesterday for Stanley S. Tollman, a hotel executive, after he failed to appear in United States District Court to face charges that he and his partner, Monty D. Hundley, and three of their business associates defrauded five banks of more than $42 million. John J. Tigue Jr., a lawyer for Mr. Tollman, said that his client still intended to fight the charges, but had decided to remain at his home in London until a bail agreement could be worked out. Mr. Tigue said that Mr. Tollman's wife, Beatrice, had been expected to put up her $7.5 million Park Avenue apartment on behalf of her husband, until her lawyer raised objections.[77]

The sequence of events in April 2002 and, most significantly, my being wrongly branded a fugitive, not only had enormous ramifications for me, but for the rest of my family as well, not to mention our relationships in business and with friends. As you will later see, it was to be five years before conversations of any kind were once again possible with the US Attorney's Office.

In insisting that I not be allowed a further week or so to resolve the negotiations over bail conditions – something which I am absolutely certain could have been concluded satisfactorily – Okula had set everything on a course to disaster. I should have been allowed to come back. I would have come back. As it was, not only was I branded fugitive without good cause, Bea too was dramatically misrepresented as to what she had done during this period. In the now-discredited witness statement which Okula swore for Westminster Magistrates' Court he made the following comment:

"the course taken by Beatrice Tollman – who, although in the United States when Stanley Tollman was charged in April 2002, fled the United States and all of her properties here in May 2002 and joined her husband in London".

This statement was untrue in every respect. Bea accompanied me on my last trip to the USA in April 2002, entering and leaving with me on the same aircraft. We have the tickets and the passport entries to prove it. She was not in the United States at the time of my indictment. And neither was I. I did not flee, and nor did she.

Within weeks, Okula followed up the document disclosures by visiting Guernsey in person, accompanied by officers from both the IRS and the FBI. He wanted to interview a number of people who had worked at Saffery Champness, and also a man called Mick Holland, one of our own employees who, since his recruitment in 1995, had been based in Guernsey, working for us.

Saffery Champness readily agreed to be interviewed, but Mick Holland, an old hand at such matters, having worked for almost ten years for Guernsey's own tax authority, properly insisted that he would not disclose confidential information unless compelled to do so by order of the Court. A court order was issued and, thus compelled, Mick made his way to Saffery Champness' offices, where the interviews were being conducted.

Mick, for whom Bea and I have the greatest respect, is a man who is not easily intimidated, and it is clear that he gave his inquisitors as good as he got. As Okula and the others got into their stride, Mick told them exactly what he thought of the whole exercise. He pointed out that the family's businesses employed thousands of people, many of whom had families to support. Although Okula may not himself have been concerned about the damage he was causing, nor of the livelihoods of ordinary people which he was placing at risk, he jolly well should have been. Mick Holland could see nothing at all in the lines of enquiry which were being pursued, and the sooner that Okula realised this, the better.

Okula nevertheless pressed on with his questions, none of which appeared to bother Mick at all, much to Okula's disappointment. Disappointment turned to anger, however, when Okula attempted to deploy what he had obviously considered to be his coup de théâtre. Thinking that his researches had revealed a suspiciously close relationship between Mick Holland and our bank – a relationship which was so close as (in his mind) to suggest impropriety – Okula asked solemnly, "Mr Holland, all the staff at the Royal Bank of Canada here in Guernsey say that they know you very well indeed. Why is that?" Mick answered swiftly, "Because I worked there for 16 years, that's why!" Okula's research had been so superficial that it had failed to discover that, immediately prior to joining us, Mick had in fact been General Manager of the Royal Bank of Canada, Guernsey. Not surprising that all the staff at the bank knew him very well indeed.

With that, the interviews were over, and the delegation from the United States left the building. As they did so, the television screen in the Saffery Champness reception which was linked to the camera over the entrance to the building displayed the sight of Stanley Okula kicking the wall outside. A moment to savour. Mick is a great man.

We learned later that when Okula had interviewed those who had worked at Saffery Champness, his approach had been aggressive to the point of intimidation. He had without doubt seriously frightened a number of those to whom he spoke. Even senior managers admitted that they had been unsettled by this experience – so unsettled, in fact, that they were extremely reluctant to say anything which they thought likely to provoke an adverse reaction against them personally.

One senior manager, who owned a small property in the United States, was fearful that Okula would seek to have it forfeited if he did or said anything that was likely to be perceived as helpful to Bea and me. And another admitted that he had been so disturbed by Okula's behaviour that, heading for vacation on a flight to Salt Lake City, he had imagined that Okula had taken steps to secure his apprehension when he landed. This fear developed into a full-blown anxiety attack in the air, such that he had to be sedated. When the plane landed, he was admitted to hospital, where he spent the next two weeks. Some vacation!

Okula's intimidatory tactics, and his delusions, were not reserved for Guernsey. In 2005, having imagined that an over-arching international tax evasion scheme was at work, he came to London to interview three Trafalgar employees, who happened to have overseas bank accounts. The London solicitor who oversaw the process reported that Okula had begun each interview by saying, "I am fighting a global tax conspiracy on behalf of the nations of the world." He then conducted the interviews with all the rudeness, aggression and intimidation which had become his hallmark.

The solicitor, a partner of a major City law firm, expressed the view that it was clear to him that Okula would do whatever he needed to secure a prosecution, and that that Okula was really after Mike Ness, to whom all three reported. "He is gunning for Mike Ness!" Mike's connections with the United States were, to say the least, remote. Even so, as one of the interviewees was leaving the room, Okula stood in their way and said, "Give my regards to Mike Ness." I later discovered that Okula had tried to meet Mike Ness himself and to ask him some questions direct. Understandably, Mike had asked what the questions concerned. But Okula refused to tell him and, equally understandably, Mike had declined to meet. Okula was furious, telling Mike, "I will follow you all over the world to get you."

Once indicted, the news of my predicament spread quickly amongst everyone who knew us and especially within the communities to which we had been closest. Bea and I began to experience what is perhaps the most unsettling feature of this kind of trouble. We discovered that our telephone began to ring rather less frequently, and that certain close friends were surprisingly unavailable. Calls were simply not being returned. An eerie froideur settled over some of what we had considered to be our closest friendships. Bea had cause to remind me of Martin Luther King's famous words, "In the end, we will remember not the words of our enemies, but the silence of our friends"[78]. Nothing more apposite

---

[78] *The Trumpet of Conscience*, Canadian Broadcasting Corporation (CBC), Massey Lectures 1967, Martin Luther King Jr (1929-1968).

could have been written to describe what we were to discover from this awful experience.

It was not all terrible. In the weeks and months which followed my indictment, we we able to discover who our real friends were. Some of those whom we had felt were amongst our closest simply disappeared over the horizon in a cloud of dust. Worse, some felt the need not only to deny that they had ever known us, but became openly critical – of me especially. Some of these people had been regular visitors to our home and in some cases we had even shared holidays together. But our friendship and the acceptance of our hospitality appeared now to be something of which they were ashamed. Bea especially was hurt by this behaviour, and she continues to this day to be hurt. I was disappointed. In truth, I suspect this episode reinforced my doubts concerning my judgement of people to whom I have become close.

Although some decided to forget or to deny that they ever knew us, there were those who were to stick with us through thick and thin, thus demonstrating that they were indeed true friends. In identifying only some of these wonderful people, there is a danger that I will offend those whom I have failed to mention. I feel, though, that I would like to mention a few of those for whom open friendship with the Tollmans, post-indictment, was not without social or commercial risk as far as they were concerned.

In this context, Palm Beach deserves a special mention. Looking back, the jewel of Southern Florida simultaneously displayed both the best and the worst of human nature. We had indeed some extraordinary friendships there, and many of these people continued to support us, even though other so-called friends and the local media couldn't wait to stab us in the back.

The reaction from our fair-weather 'friends' was remarkable. But the true friends from Palm Beach who deserve a special mention include Max Fisher, Kate Ford, Brian and Mila Mulroney and Frank Chopin. All of these were to stay loyal to us during our exile years. They were a constant source of comfort and inspiration to us. To a man and a woman, these were stand-up guys.

Another stand-up guy was Isadore Rosenfeld, who has been my doctor for the best part of 40 years. During that time he and his delightful wife, Camilla, have become very close friends indeed. Some years ago, Isadore nominated me for membership of the Board of Cornell University, Weill Medical College, New York, a voluntary position which I was honoured to hold as a volunteer, and which was immensely rewarding.

Isadore is perhaps the best-known doctor in the United States, which arguably makes him the best-known doctor in the world. He is a practicising cardiologist in New York City, as well as being the Ida & Theo Rossi Professor of Clinical Medicine at the New York Presbyterian Hospital/Weill Cornell Medical Center. Over the years, his consulting rooms in East 72nd St have been graced by movie stars and magnates, Presidents and Pontiffs. But they have also welcomed many ordinary New Yorkers for whom Isadore is generous with both his time and his billing.

When a tsunami hit Indonesia in 2004, Isadore, then 78 years old, joined the humanitarian team aboard the US Naval Ship *Mercy* which had treated more than 10,000 patients both ashore and afloat. Isadore spent one week on board, reporting on the work which was being undertaken. It was clearly a moving experience. He said at the time, "I had never in my entire life seen so much rampant, unrecognised, undiagnosed and untreated disease."

Amongst Isadore's better-known patients have been Aristotle Onassis, Sophia Loren, Danny Kaye and the Duke of Windsor. Until recently, he appeared every Sunday morning on *Sunday Housecall* on the FOX News Network. And he has had a few walk-on parts in major motion pictures, notably Ron Howard's *A Beautiful Mind*. Isadore is a fine doctor, and an even finer human being. He spoke at my 60th birthday party, telling those present that he had known me since I was 40. "When Stanley Tollman first consulted me, he drank too much and smoked cigars. Since then, things have changed. I too now smoke cigars."

BRETT

27

I have now reached what I know will be the most difficult chapter for me to write. I have experienced many challenging and painful events over the years, but nothing which came even close to the anguish which I suffered during the following episode. To this day, it continues to give me nightmares. Even after the passage of many years, I shudder at the thought of what happened to my son Brett and of my helplessness to come to his aid. I pray this never happens to another father. Nor to another father's son.

In writing this chapter, I am conscious that I might be accused of telling someone else's story, and one which they themselves might not choose to tell. But it is very important to point out that others, notably Brett, have paid a big price simply for being part of my family. And in every case, this price has been exacted entirely without good reason. They were targeted only because they were viewed by Okula as leverage in order to get to me – his real target. Without my involvement as explanation, their stories are at best misleading; at worst, utterly inexplicable.

When the grand jury handed down its first indictments against Monty Hundley, my name was there too, as were the names of Monty Hundley's closest lieutenants – Sanford Freedman, Jim Cutler and Howard Zukerman. No-one else was involved. Hundley and Zukerman's undeniable cheating of the taxman was the entrée of which Okula took advantage. This opening enabled Freedman, Cutler and Zukerman then to be cast as co-conspirators with Monty in an alleged fraud, into which conspiracy Okula considered he could successfully rope me as well. But my role in all of this, according to Okula's script, was not as spear-carrier, but as leading man. As had been pointed out by others, it was always about me. I was the prospective prize: the one with – as the *New York Times* had suggested – *"political connections"*.

On advice, I had not, however, allowed myself to be bulldozed at the beginning of the process, and I was now in London, whence I intended to exercise my constitutional right to defend myself. Sadly, owing to the iniquity of plea bargaining, most US citizens are unable properly to defend themselves. In nine cases out of ten, a guilty plea reflects nothing more than pragmatism, and has little to do with either guilt or innocence. As far as I am concerned, being able to defend oneself properly is a pretty fundamental human right.

Teddy Roosevelt used to refer, with pride, to the Office of the President of the United States as 'the bully pulpit'. By that, he meant that it was of such importance that its holder could speak out on any subject, and be listened to. He saw it simply as a wonderful platform. A hundred years later, bullying by the Executive of the United States is no longer restricted to the pulpit, nor is it exercised in pursuit of the high-minded objectives and ideals contemplated by Roosevelt.

In the case of the United States Department of Justice, bullyboy actions mean that 96% of all those indicted by a Federal court decide to plead guilty rather than stand trial. But this says nothing about the skill of American investigators to find the guilty, nor of the effectiveness of the grand jury system. In reality, the extraordinarily high percentage of pre-trial convictions is testimony to the persuasive power of institutionalised coercion. In any civilised society, plea bargaining would be viewed as blackmail.

In the United States, sentences are severe, often running into 20 or 30 years' jail time for offences which would carry a sentence of five to ten years in other developed nations, and in which countries the time actually spent behind bars would be even less. In the United States, where parole has been abolished, most defendants, whatever their guilt or innocence, simply capitulate, with the objective of removing the risk of an excessive term in prison. Under pressure, completely innocent people often choose to accept a short jail sentence as a guaranteed outcome, rather than run the risk of long-term incarceration which is inherent in pleading not guilty at trial, and failing to persuade a jury of one's innocence.

The numbers are chilling. The United States has the highest rate of incarceration of any developed country in the world. According to a Department of Justice report[79] published in 2006, more than 7.2 million US citizens were at that time in prison, on probation, or on parole. That means roughly one in every 32 of all American citizens was held by the justice system. Ignoring children, the elderly and the infirm for the purposes of the calculation, this means that at least one in 20 able-bodied adults is held by the US justice system. According to the International Centre for Prison Studies at King's College, London, of that 7.2 million, 2.3 million were actually behind bars. That compares with the People's Republic of China, which is in second place with 1.6 million in prison, despite the fact that its population is over four times that of the United States.

In July 2002, Chris Todd and Jim Webster of Kellogg, Huber, Hansen & Todd became my US counsel. One of their first duties was to visit Stanley Okula in order to recover documents which had been seized unlawfully from our Park Avenue apartment. The two of them visited the White Plains office of the US Attorney Southern District of New York, where Okula is based, and where they were allowed to look through one or two boxes of documents from the many which had been seized. Afterwards, Okula and other prosecutors decided which documents could be returned. A few dozen only were handed over.

After this exercise was completed, Chris and Jim's first and, as it proved to be, only meeting with Okula took place. This was on 11 July 2002. Towards the end of this brief meeting, Okula told them both that he intended to make my life "as miserable as possible" unless I chose to return to the United States to stand trial. These words would later prove to be of great importance, as was the fact that he had said this in the presence of two people.

Okula knew full well that an indicted 70-year-old who was within his grasp was a man who might be coerced. Let's face it, innocent or guilty, there are few successful businessmen who, standing accused of tax evasion, would wish to take their chances against a New York jury. Given the non-discretionary sentencing guidelines which were then in

---

79 *Probation and Parole in the United States 2006*, Glaze and Bonczar, US Department of Justice, Bureau of Justice Statistics.

place, a guilty verdict could likely mean spending the rest of one's life inside a Federal prison. Men in this situation were men from whom a plea bargain could easily be extracted. And Okula recognised this.

But I was having none of it. The idea of pleading guilty to something which I had not done was anathema to me. Moreover, given the quantum of bail which had been demanded from me by comparison with that demanded of others, it was clear that I was viewed as the mastermind. The big fish. I knew by then that I had, for the time being at least and as far as I was able, to defend myself from the United Kingdom.

Bea and I had travelled almost constantly for several decades, rarely staying in one place for more than a couple of weeks at a time. But once the indictments were laid, I knew that I would have to respond to the charges from a familiar and reliable base. Bea and I once again took residence in London, a city in which we had had a home for 40 years. I may have been in a terrible position, but at least I was able to take comfort in the fact that Britain has a criminal justice system which is the envy of the world – and with good cause.

Although the July 2002 meeting would prove to be the only time that Chris and Jim ever met Okula, this was not because they did not try. From that moment onwards, Okula simply refused to deal in any way with my attorneys. The reason? Because I was now considered to be a fugitive, and the United States has something called the Fugitive Disentitlement Doctrine. This means that a fugitive is to be denied access to all of the procedural processes of US Courts.

The Fugitive Disentitlement Doctrine dates from the 1800s, and holds that defendants who flout the law by fleeing a jurisdiction cannot then call upon the court for help. I am no lawyer (although I have spent so much time in the company of lawyers during the last ten years that I suspect that something must have rubbed off on me), but I always considered that it was both wrong and counter-productive to deny me access in this way. The sides should have been talking, but weren't. We tried, and we tried again. The other side repeatedly refused.

I read recently that attention was given to the Fugitive Disentitlement Doctrine in Los Angeles in 2009 when lawyers acting for film director Roman Polanski argued that there was misconduct by the judge (now dead) who had originally overseen charges against their client. Superior Court Judge Peter Espinoza agreed with Polanski's attorneys that there was evidence of 'substantial' misconduct in the original handling of the case. However, he also said that the principle of fugitive disentitlement barred him from convening a formal hearing or otherwise taking action.

Polanski may indeed have fled the United States, and the judge may have been right to take that view. But I most certainly had not fled. Even though I had been in Europe at the time of the indictment and had simply stayed there, I was nevertheless branded a fugitive by Okula at the arraignment hearing, and that was the end of it. The 'fugitive' tag was pinned to me permanently from that moment onwards, and was repeated endlessly every time someone wrote about me in the press. I can say with complete honesty that I have never fled from anything. It is not in my make-up to do so. As long ago as the Boy Scouts' camp in Margate, when I was the only 12-year-old Jewish boy in a troop of 14-year-old Irish Catholics, I learned that the only way out of a problem was to stand and fight. Fleeing was never on my mind. But standing and fighting most certainly was.

But I viewed this fight as mine alone. Having now seen the charges which Okula was levelling against me, I saw them as little more than – please forgive my language – bullshit. I knew I had done nothing wrong, and I was confident that, in time, the truth would out. I had not, though, fully assessed the impact all of this would have on other members of the family, especially Brett who, by coincidence, was in London on business at around this time.

Bea and I had never wanted Brett to get involved in the hotel industry. When he said that he intended to do so, it was almost like history repeating itself. The resistance I had experienced from my father when I said I wanted to become a hotelier I, in turn, displayed when Brett told me all those years ago of his chosen path. It took a while for Bea and me to come to terms with this news, but we began to adjust, imagining that he would study at the Ecole hôtelière de Lausanne, the oldest hotel school in the world. But Brett had other thoughts. He had made his mind up to go to EHL's great competitor, Cornell. And this choice would in turn prove to influence the family's decision to become more involved in the United States, and indeed with Tollman-Hundley.

Brett had moved to the United States in 1979, aged 18, in order to attend Cornell. After graduation, he had gone to work at Tollman-Hundley, where he eventually worked his way up to become President of the Hotels Division. He reached the top of the business during a time when the company was entirely focused on hotel management, rather than hotel ownership. Before then, he had experienced at first hand the difficulties which Tollman-Hundley had faced with its banks, and with the challenge of insufficient cashflow to pay creditors. Brett had risen to be in charge of the operation under very trying circumstances. And these were conditions created not by himself but by managers whom he viewed as being highly incompetent.

I often think what it must have been like for Brett to have found himself working alongside a group of people at Tollman-Hundley with whom he had so little in common. Brett had a highly developed sense of duty, and was someone of modest tastes and high personal standards – in complete contrast to the team at Tollman-Hundley. The family often talk of Brett's legendary 21st birthday party at Xenon in New York in 1982, which was memorable mostly for Brett's absence from proceedings. At the time, Brett hardly drank, but he was persuaded to loosen up before he went to the club, and to start the evening with a drink. Two vodkas finished him off completely, and he never actually made it to the party. Everyone at Xenon kept asking where Brett was, and many people believed that they had seen him "just a few minutes ago". But no-one had in fact seen Brett, who was out for the count.

Brett was ill-prepared for the challenge which was Tollman-Hundley, but he had nevertheless faced it decisively. He was doing a fantastic job, despite the people, the banks, and the shortage of cashflow, and despite the subsequent distractions of the IRS investigation. Under his stewardship, Tollman-Hundley had become one of the largest management companies in the United States and, latterly, Brett had in addition become a director of Alpha Hospitality.

Like both Bea and me before him, in 1993 Brett had become a naturalised US citizen. And in 1995, he had married a California girl, Miranda Rich, whose parents were in the movie and television business. Miranda's mother, Pippa Scott, is a former Hollywood actress who, amongst other roles, played Lucy Edwards in John Ford's classic, *The Searchers*, which starred John Wayne. Miranda's father Lee Rich's television career began at the advertising agency Benton & Bowles. During the early days of television, advertising agencies enjoyed almost total control over programming. Lee's job was to package and sell, amongst other things, *The Dick Van Dyke Show*. He left Benton & Bowles in 1965 to form his own production company, moving on subsequently to co-found Lorimar Productions. Lorimar was the largest supplier of programming to network television for two decades, and its television hits included *The Waltons* and *Dallas*. Lee went on to become Chairman and Chief Executive Officer of MGM-UA. Sadly, just before I finished this book, Lee died, a fact recorded in newspapers and magazines across the United States. The following is extracted from the *New York Times'* obituary of Lee[80]:

Lee Rich Dies at 93:
Helped Create Both JR and John-Boy

Lee Rich, the creative force behind Lorimar Productions, an independent studio that spawned two of television's most enduring (and archetypally opposite) fictional American families — the poor but happy kinfolk of "The Waltons" and the rich but tortured Ewing clan of "Dallas" — died on Thursday in Los Angeles. He was 93.

Lee Rich was born on Dec. 10, 1918, in Cleveland and raised in the suburb of Shaker Heights, Ohio, the older of two children. His father worked for a bank. He left for New York shortly after graduating from Ohio University with a degree in marketing. He sold handbags for a year, traveling up and down the East Coast, before talking his way into his first job in advertising.

Mr. Rich was an executive with the ad agency Benton & Bowles in the 1950s and '60s, a time when sponsors often became involved in the financing and even casting of shows, a business model carried over from the golden age of radio. In that quasi-producer's role, Mr. Rich represented major advertisers like Procter & Gamble and Philip Morris in bringing a raft of prime-time shows to the air.

When advertisers became less involved in television production, he decided to start a company of his own that would allow him to "do something pertinent and meaningful" in television and film. Between 1969 and 1986, Lorimar placed more than 30 shows on the air and produced a dozen feature-length films.

Lorimar's most successful television productions included "Dallas," which ran for 13 seasons, and "The Waltons," which was on the air from 1971 to 1981 and won 29 Emmy Awards.

He had a hunch about "Dallas": "I just felt that, if daytime serials could work, why couldn't a nighttime serial work?" he said. And "The Waltons," he said, was clearly destined for success — "like God was looking down on us" — even after network executives first tried to convince him that it needed a star like Henry Fonda as the father. "So we showed the pilot to Henry Fonda," he said, "and afterward he turned around to me and said: 'What do you want me for? The family is the star. You don't need me.' "

Brett and Lee developed a very close relationship over the years. They shared a common interest in reading, and the two would swap notes on the latest titles.

By the time of the Millennium, Brett was well aware of the investigations at Tollman-Hundley. He had found himself answering endless enquiries from both the IRS and the Department of Justice, and he knew too of the failure of both Hundley and Zukerman to file personal tax returns. And whilst I was being represented by Morvillo & Abramovitz, Brett had been receiving guidance from a former partner of Bob Morvillo called Thomas Fitzpatrick, now a sole practioner. An ex-federal prosecutor himself, Thomas had been Chief of the Criminal Division for the Southern District of New York. But he was a one-man band. Once Brett knew that I had been indicted, he needed to reassess everything. What ramifications were there for the rest of the family, and for him in particular, given that Tollman-Hundley had been very much part of his life?

Brett knew that Frank Chopin had been assisting me in the recruitment of lawyers in London and, unbeknownst to me, he now sought advice from those lawyers to find out what all of this meant, and what he should now do. It would be several years before I found out what Brett had done, and the nature of the advice which he had received.

I have been told by the barristers whom Brett consulted that they had expressed concern as to his position. Thomas Fitzpatrick had apparently warned Brett that he was likely to be indicted too, and the British barristers had cautioned him against returning to New York. However good such advice may have been, it was severely impractical. Brett was married to a US citizen, and his home was in Park Avenue, New York. (He and Miranda were living with their then two children in an apartment at 485 Park Avenue, two floors below the apartment which Okula wanted to use as security for my bail.) Brett was running a US business, and he was also a director of a public company which was listed on the New York Stock Exchange. Realistically, sitting it out in London was simply not an option. Brett, who had done absolutely nothing wrong, instead returned of his own volition to New York, informing the Office of the US Attorney that he would present himself for questioning, should that be needed.

Although Brett had been receiving guidance from Thomas Fitzpatrick, the view was taken that he now needed access to lawyers who were fully equipped to handle what was clearly becoming a serious and complex matter, and which could well involve Brett himself. Once again, Herb Koslov, the in-house lawyer, was asked to recommend the best counsel. He recommended two attorneys to work as co-counsel, both leading members of the New York criminal bar. First, he hired Robert 'Bob' Fink, a partner of Kostelanetz &

Fink, a highly respected New York trial lawyer specialising in civil and criminal tax controversies and white-collar criminal defence.

The second co-counsel, hired because we were aware that any action against Brett was likely to involve complex corporate allegations, was veteran attorney John (Rusty) Wing, one of the most respected criminal defence attorneys in New York. For twelve years, Rusty had himself been an Assistant United States Attorney in the US Attorney's office for the Southern District of New York, and the Chief of the Fraud Unit for six of those years. He then spent over 25 years as a partner of Weil, Gotshal & Manges. A former President of the New York Council of Defense Lawyers, Rusty had written extensively and taught at the Law Schools of both Harvard and Columbia.

Despite his willingness to co-operate, in the late afternoon of Thursday 6 June 2002, Brett was instead arrested without warning, and in public. I got a call from Miranda. She told me that Brett had been apprehended on the street in Manhattan whilst he was walking with her to a meeting of the board of 485 Park Avenue, of which Brett was the President. He had been arrested by Special Agent Christine Mazzella of the Internal Revenue Service, who had been accompanied by FBI officers. Brett was being held overnight in remand facilities in Manhattan.

Sadly, there was nothing which could be done that day to ensure Brett's immediate release. The arrest had been timed to guarantee that. The following day, Friday, Brett appeared in court in Manhattan, where Assistant US Attorney Peter Neiman demanded an extraordinary level of bail. Miranda called me to explain that, to secure Brett's freedom, we needed to post no less than $25 million in cash, at the time the highest bail ever required in any jurisdiction anywhere in the world, irrespective of the crime alleged. An unindicted man, who had chosen of his own free will to come back to New York, and to tell the US Attorney where he was if he was needed, was now apparently a flight risk demanding world record security. I discovered later that $25 million was in fact much less that Neiman had originally demanded. The initial call was for $50 million!

This outrageous demand confirmed beyond doubt the bias which Okula clearly held against the Tollman family. Producing $25 million in cash at the drop of a hat would, I suggest, pose problems even for the wealthiest families. Keen to ensure that Brett was saved from a weekend in the hell of a holding facility, I not only swiftly established sources of cash that were immediately available, but I also reached out for assistance to those people who had expressed a preparedness to help.

One of these was George Kaufman who, upon hearing earlier in the year that I had been indicted, picked up the telephone to offer to do anything that he could to help. I managed to get George on his cellphone and he told me he was on his way to the Hamptons. I explained that I needed help for Brett. It was now Friday afternoon, and I had to move swiftly in order to save him from being kept in the holding facility.

I was, of course, making a big ask of George, especially as it was a Friday afternoon. I was nevertheless hoping that he would be prepared to do something significant to help, and at very short notice indeed. But it was clear that this was a telephone call which George was uncomfortable to receive. Instead of behaving as I had expected and pulling out the stops to assist, all he said was that he would have to call his lawyer. It was obvious that this approach was not going to produce anything within the time available. I thanked him, but told him not to bother. I cannot pretend that I was not disappointed. But George's reaction that day did not alter my assessment of him as a thoroughly decent man. However, I was obliged to reconsider whether he was a stand-up sort of guy.

I compared George's reaction that day to that of Steve O'Hana, Vicki's ex-husband. Despite being hounded himself at the time by the French authorities over unfounded but nevertheless major allegations, Steve dropped everything in order to help his ex-brother-in-law. Steve is a stand-up guy by any measure, and I say a big thank-you to him. In fairness to George Kaufman, though, as you will read a little later on in this chapter, when he was asked two years later to write a letter in support of Brett, he was of enormous help.

Ironically, although we began the search for funds that Friday in the belief that only cash would meet the needs of the Court, later that day guarantees were accepted too. These were swiftly put in place and Brett was released.

Brett had been held at the Metropolitan Correctional Center, a high-rise pre-trial detention centre in lower Manhattan, across the street from the Federal courthouse. Typically home, however temporary, to terrorists, gangsters and drug dealers, the MCC, as it is known, houses 700-plus inmates, who include both minimum and maximum security prisoners. In the past, the facility had held Ramzi Yousef, the mastermind of the 1993 World Trade Center bombings, and John Gotti, the boss of the Gambino crime family. Its 7½ft by 8ft cells contained two bunk beds and a shared sink within white-washed cinder block walls.

Remarkably, the first thing Brett did after he was released was to order some books for the stranger with whom he had shared a cell. Although the man concerned was allegedly a dangerous offender, Brett had discovered they had a common interest in reading. I suspect that few people would behave in this way, but this is Brett and, as you will soon discover, kindness to others is Brett's hallmark. He was now in trouble because Okula was trying to get to me and, ironically, it would be Brett's own thoughtfulness for the plight of others which Okula would ultimately succeed in using against him.

Within a couple of weeks, a Federal Complaint alleging tax violations was filed against Brett. He had little choice other than to resign as a Director and Vice-President of Alpha Hospitality. Alpha made clear in its announcement to the market that Brett had submitted his resignation but that he considered the allegations entirely unwarranted. Nevertheless, and even though the allegations against him were unrelated to the business of the company, Brett felt that his resignation was in the best interest of Alpha Hospitality.

There is little doubt that this was the beginning of a very difficult period for Brett, and for Miranda. Having gone through the humiliation of a public arrest, the implications for Brett's business dealings and for his personal life were profound. And it would get worse.

At this point, I would like to quote from a letter which Miranda wrote to Brett's attorneys three months after he had been arrested. Miranda is a remarkable young lady, who has been a tower of strength for Brett throughout their marriage:

> *"We came back last May from London with our baby in our arms, knowing that we would be facing the storm. We had the option of staying there, if that was the way we wanted to fight it. But we knew that would be wrong. To Brett it was not an option. Even though he knew that it may potentially be a very long time before he could be reunited with his family and the work life that was so promising for him, he decided that the only thing to do would be to fight this head on. Within weeks of our return, he was arrested. And so here we are. We stand by our decision firmly, to be here and to fight this. We are moving forward in our personal lives. Our second child will be born in April, our two-year-old starts school next fall."*

Brett's future was now in the hands of attorneys, and they reported back to him exchanges with Stanley Okula which were deeply troubling. It became clear that they were not dealing with a reasonable man. Bob Fink, who was in regular but unhappy contact with Okula, revealed the undercurrent of intimidation which characterised many of those conversations. On one occasion over the Christmas period in 2002, Bob Fink had bumped into Okula at a drinks party, and the conversation had got around to the Tollman family, at which point Okula became highly agitated. Fink felt that Okula was over-reacting, and accused him of being hysterical. Okula's response was to poke Fink vigorously in the chest whilst saying forcefully, "I'm not hysterical!"

Okula made his objective clear to anyone prepared to listen, "I am going to get to Stanley Tollman through his family!" He would later explain the reason for his animus toward me. In later conversations with Elliot Sagor, Travel Corporation's New York Attorney, he said that he felt that he had been 'burned' by me because I had declined to return to the United States to stand trial.

And on another – now infamous – occasion, Okula, referring to Bea, said to Bob Fink during a telephone conversation one day, "I should have nailed that woman, and I would have perp-walked her from 485 Park Avenue, right down to the Court House."

Some readers may be unfamiliar with this expression, but these are unlikely to be American citizens. The 'perp walk' has become a regular, if infrequent, element of the criminal justice system in the United States. The expression perp walk (perp meaning perpetrator) refers to the choreographed parading of suspects in full view of the media (who have been tipped off in advance). The suspect is often restrained by handcuffs and leg irons, and has the ink from fingerprinting still evident on their hands.

In recent times, this procedure has been used in the public humiliation of Dominique Strauss-Kahn, the head of the International Monetary Fund. This was described by Elisabeth Guigou, a former French Justice Minister, as "a brutality, a violence of an incredible cruelty". In France, where the presumption of innocence still matters, it is in fact a criminal offence to publish photographs of an identifiable person in handcuffs who is not yet convicted. But in the United States, things are very different indeed.

Dominique Strauss-Kahn joined an illustrious list of individuals who have faced the barrage of press photographers who accompany the perp walk. This list includes 'Son of Sam' serial-killer David Berkowitz; badly-behaved actor Russell Crowe; John Gotti, the head of the Gambino family; and Lee Harvey Oswald, whose perp walk ended with his death at the hands of Jack Ruby.

Although relatively commonplace against men, especially famous men, it is exceptional for the perp walk to be used against women. One case involving a woman which I remember was that of Susan McDougal, who refused to answer questions about Bill Clinton, her former business partner in the Whitewater venture. She was led from an Arkansas courthouse in chains and leg irons, an undignified and appalling sight, even for a younger woman. But at the time Okula told Bob Fink that he was looking forward to doing a perp walk with Bea, she was very nearly 70 years old.

Bob Fink had been both shocked and appalled when Okula had told him that he wanted to parade Bea down Madison Avenue in this way. Giving evidence to Westminster Magistrates some years later, Bob admitted that he had been taken aback by the comment.

Notwithstanding the shock Bob Fink may have felt, in January 2003, Okula had initiated the process which he hoped would lead to him to getting his hands on Bea, when a Complaint was filed against her. In the United States, prosecutors have a choice between seeking an indictment from a grand jury and filing a charging document directly with the court. Such a document is usually called a Complaint, to distinguish it from a grand jury indictment. In Bea's case, the Complaint was also sealed by the Court, meaning that no-one learned of its existence.

Much later, Bea would discover that the seven-count Complaint alleged that she and I had received in excess of $35 million in income from the Travel Corporation through "secret" Channel Islands bank accounts, which we failed to report to the IRS. It went on to allege that Bea herself had had extensive dealings with the accountants and bankers in order "to further the tax fraud scheme". These extensive dealings included telephoning the accountants and bankers from home using "phony" names such as "Toni," "Vicki" and "Chantelle", and of using coded language when speaking with the Channel Islands accountants and bankers.

For reasons about which we can only speculate, it would be more than a year before the Complaint was unsealed. Even when it was, and we were able to learn of its contents, we would be little wiser, other than knowing the certainty that Okula now had Bea in his sights as well.

Two months before the sealing of the Complaint against Bea, on 22 November 2002, a further indictment was handed up in relation to the Tollman-Hundley matter. This represented the second superseding indictment (there would be a third in April 2003), and this time those accused included Brett as well as me. This is how the *New York Times* reported it [81]:

Fugitive Hotelier's Son Indicted in Tax Case

A federal grand jury has indicted the son of Stanley S. Tollman, a prominent Manhattan hotelier who is a fugitive on tax evasion charges, **in a growing tax evasion case against the Tollman family and their associates.**

Brett G. Tollman, 41, was accused of tax fraud and conspiracy in **a 49-count indictment handed up on Friday** *by a federal grand jury in White Plains. He is free on $25 million bail. The unusually high bail for Brett Tollman was set after his father refused to return from Britain for arraignment in April.*

The indictment is the third in an investigation that has been expanding since the initial grand jury action on April 18. The Tollman family, which at one time controlled the Days Inn hotel chain and owned 50 Days Inns, owns Trafalgar Tours International and Red Carnation Hotels, a group of luxury hotels in Florida, Switzerland and South Africa. It also owns the Chesterfield, the Milestone and the 41 in London.

Stanley Tollman, 71, and four other men were indicted in April on tax fraud and conspiracy charges growing out of a suspected plan to defraud banks of $42.6 million. That indictment accused Mr. Tollman and his partner, Monty D. Hundley, 59, of making false statements, hiding $100 million in profits from sale of the Days Inn company and creating straw businesses in Europe to trick six banks into settling $50 million of overdue loans for $7.6 million.

The new indictment says taxes were evaded on at least $32 million of income that was run through secret bank accounts in the Channel Islands, tax havens under British rule. The indictment cites numerous acts by Stanley Tollman's wife, Bea, advancing the fraud, including creating accounts and moving money without paying the banks or taxes to the United States. **Bea Tollman was involved so deeply that, according to the indictment, she arranged to send $3,000 from one of the secret bank accounts to**

**"a London shoemaker to pay for two pair of shoes" for
her son Brett.**

*Bea Tollman was not indicted, however. Stanley Tollman and
Mr. Hundley told Bank of America, which was trying to collect the
Security Pacific loan, that they had not filed tax returns for several years
because their incomes were so low that they were not required to do so,
according to the indictment.*

*In fact, Mr. Hundley had not filed a tax return since 1981, and
each man had "more than sufficient income" to require filing tax returns,
the indictment contends.*

As you can see, I have emboldened three sections of the article.
But before I comment on those, I just want to make clear that the
suggestion that I had not filed tax returns was a complete lie. I *always*
filed tax returns.

The first emboldened section is the reference to the *"growing tax
evasion case against the Tollman family and their associates"*. Taking their lead
from the US Attorney, the Tollman name was now central to this
matter, even though we were barely bystanders.

The second, is the reference to a *"49-count indictment handed up on
Friday"*. Not every defendant was accused of every charge. Far from it.
The allegations against Brett were not only not central to the case, but
were barely related. He had been squeezed in with a great deal of
effort, as is obvious from the third reference: *"Bea Tollman was involved
so deeply that, according to the indictment, she arranged to send $3,000 from one
of the secret bank accounts to 'a London shoemaker to pay for two pair of shoes'
for her son Brett."*

As a result of this indictment, Brett found himself a co-accused
with Hundley, Freedman, Cutler and Zukerman, a bunch of people
for whom he had little respect and about whose behaviour he had
complained to me in private on a number of occasions.

Over the months ahead, and in common with all litigation, there
followed a series of applications to the Court. Almost without
exception, the applications made by Hundley, Freedman, Cutler and
Zukerman failed dismally. Brett lost faith especially in Zukerman's

defence team. There were frequent outbursts in Court, and it was clear that this was annoying the judge. There is little doubt that, in private at least, Brett was becoming increasingly despondent about his fate. This, he felt certain, would now be decided by the actions of a group of no-goods and losers.

He and I spoke often during this period – always, of course, on the telephone. He would consistently reassure me that his mental state was in good order. The truth was that he was terrified about his prospects, and of standing in the dock alongside the others. With this in mind, and given the discrete nature of the charges laid at Brett's own door, Bob Fink and Rusty Wing endeavoured to separate Brett from the other actions and argued for him to be tried separately. When this attempt failed, Brett was in a very susceptible state.

Brett has a highly developed sense of duty and of the need to fulfil his role in the family. When Wynn chose to tread an independent path, Brett decided that it was now his duty to take over as the 'elder' son. I have little doubt that the actions which Brett took during the late summer of 2003 were only in part intended to draw a line under matters and to be able to get on with life. In equal, if not in greater, part, I suspect that Brett believed that he could sacrifice himself and in some way save me.

Had I known that he was thinking in this way, I would never have allowed him to do what he did. Brett realised this and decided that I should not find out until it was too late. Even before this event, I had every reason to be proud of my son, but what happened in September 2003 served to remind me what an exceptional human being he truly is.

Just as in so many things in life, something was needed to trigger the sequence of events which took place. A catalyst. This was an order from Judge Preska to Bob Fink and Okula to review the allegations against Brett, which were a combination of Tollman-Hundley-related charges, and others of a non-business nature. So it was that a conversation ensued between Bob Fink and Okula on Thursday 4 September 2003.

Bob Fink began by berating Okula for the catalogue of charges which Brett was facing. "This is ridiculous. Brett is a good guy. He had nothing to do with all this stuff, and he shouldn't be standing alongside these people." Okula's response was direct and to the point, "If so, why doesn't he plead guilty and get on with his life?" Bob replied that he had nothing to plead on – there was nothing on the table. Okula replied that something should, perhaps, be done about that. And he went off to work out a proposal.

There then began a rapid, perhaps hasty, exchange during the ensuing 24 hours, during which time a plea bargain was constructed. The first draft emerged at about 7.15pm that evening, which suggested that Brett should plead guilty to three counts – count 22, the perks charge; count 35, a conspiracy charge; and count 49, the so-called 'Maxie' charge, which resulted from some household bills being settled for Brett by the people in Guernsey who did so using monies from the wrong bank account.

In presenting the draft plea bargain to Bob Fink, Okula made clear that the matter had to be concluded by noon the following day. He said this was because he was booked to fly to Guernsey on Friday evening and that, once he set foot on the aircraft, it would be too late to do a deal. But with a guilty plea in the bag, he would cancel his trip. Once he had set out, though, Brett's inclusion in the trial would be unavoidable.

Brett and Miranda agonised over the pros and cons of a guilty plea with Bob for some time. Bob warned that a conviction alongside Monty and the others might mean 20 years in jail, but that it was up to Brett and Miranda to choose whether or not to go along with a deal. At about 8.30pm they decided together that Brett should 'take the deal'.

Rusty Wing had not been involved until now but Brett was keen to ensure that he too approved of what was being contemplated. Brett and Miranda went to see Rusty at 10.00pm well after the close of business, and sought his approval. Rusty, who had been hired to cover the corporate allegations, admitted that Bob had much greater knowledge of the other aspects of the investigation which were troubling him. If Bob, Brett and Miranda all thought that this was the right thing to do, Rusty would go along with it.

At 8.00am the next morning, Okula was on the phone to Bob Fink to see whether his client had decided to plead. Bob confirmed that Brett had decided in principle, but that some work was needed on the formulation of the deal. Brett was prepared to plead guilty in repect of the 'perks' matter and in relation to the Maxie charge, but would not plead guilty to any conspiracy charge.

There were then a number of further drafts of the agreement, designed by Okula and approved by a female colleague called Shirah Neiman, the Chief Counsel to the US Attorney for the Southern District of New York. Okula and Shirah Neiman represented a diabolical double act, the Southern District of New York's equivalent of Burke & Hare. In the months ahead, I would hear the name Shirah Neiman mentioned frequently by those in the know, and it was usually accompanied by an audible groan and a reference to, "the US Attorney's attack dog".

Throughout the brief but intensive process of formulating the structure of the plea agreement, one thing remained fixed, and that was its bottom line. Even though the various elements of the plea changed, their mathematical summation never did. They were designed always to reach the same conclusion. In each case, the calculation ended up with a 'Guidelines offense' level of 20. This was the number of points under the non-discretionary Sentencing Guidelines then in force which would convert to a jail sentence of between 33 and 41 months.

Eventually, Okula, Neiman and Bob Fink were content, and it was over to Brett to decide. Count 22 remained, and the other two counts had been replaced with a brand new indictment. Bob set off for the Courthouse to meet another Assistant US Attorney called Peter Neiman to finalise the drafting of the agreement, whilst Okula headed into Manhattan from his White Plains office to join them. Judge Preska was asked to be on hand from 3.00pm, a somewhat unusual request for a Friday afternoon.

Brett's legal team also assembled outside the court at 3.00 to finalise the details of the agreement, and this took a further hour. It was not until 4.15 that everyone went into the courtroom, where two surprises were in store. The first was the presence in the courtroom of four journalists, about whom nothing had been said. The second was a short statement or allocution which Brett was given, and was asked to read out when the time came. This had been drafted by the US Attorney's office, and was edited as they sat down in court.

So it was, that in the afternoon of Friday 5 September 2003, Brett appeared before Judge Preska and pleaded guilty to two offences. Brett's allocution went as follows:

> *"From about the year 1991 through about the year 2000, I was a senior officer of Tollman-Hundley Hotels, T-H Administration and Bryanston Group Inc. As such, I was in charge of determining salaries and pay rises of various employees of these entities. I conspired with employees of these entities to defraud the United States by concealing certain sums paid to these employees, which sums were not reported on forms W-2 or 1099.*
>
>   *"During the period from about the year 1993 through about the year 2000, I had signatory and withdrawal authority over a bank account in the name of Maxie Group Limited in Guernsey in the Channel Islands. I failed to report on my income tax returns over $2.7 million in consultancy fee payments made by or through the Travel Corporation or its affiliates which were paid into this account and which I knew was income to me. In addition, I knew of approximately $6 million of income in other Channel Islands accounts and, although that money was not mine, it was reasonably foreseeable to me that the income belonged to others involved in the evasion scheme and was not being reported by them to the Internal Revenue Service."*

Brett had pleaded guilty to two charges, in relation to only one of which had he been indicted. The other 'Tollman-Hundley' charges were simply dropped, never to be heard of again. These had been replaced by a new charge, one created out of the blue for Brett. As for his allocution, the requirement to admit to having signatory and withdrawal authority over the Maxie bank account was preposterous. Brett had no such authority, a fact which had been conveniently overlooked by those who had constructed his 'admission'.

The single Tollman-Hundley charge was known universally as 'the matter of the perks'. This was from the third superseding indictment. From time to time, Tollman-Hundley would make payments to various members of its staff which went above and beyond normal remuneration for the individual in question. In relation to the charge to which Brett had just pleaded guilty, the perks in question benefited other people, not Brett, and had been made in order to help people with particular needs.

I will not embarrass the beneficiaries by naming them, even though I should. By way of example, I will simply say that they included an accountant who received money to cover rent on a New York apartment which she failed to report. And they also included an administrative assistant who received payment to cover additional commuting expenses following the office move from Fifth Avenue to Valhalla, which likewise she failed to report. These two, and others, took the money and did not, as they should have done, tell the IRS. Now, their misbehaviour was being held at Brett's door, and he was having to pay the price. And a very big price at that.

As a caring manager, and a caring human being, Brett would of course be at the forefront of assistance, helping staff members with particular problems. This meant that Brett's name was attached to a number of the perks payments which had been made. There would have been nothing at all wrong with these payments had their recipients accounted for them properly to the IRS. But this lot didn't. Ironically, one Tollman-Hundley employee whom I know did account for his 'perk' was none other than Brett himself, who entered it incorrectly on his income tax return and as a result ended up paying more tax than he should have done.

The other offence to which Brett pleaded guilty was, and remains, mystifying. At the heart of the allegation there was evidence of a small but significant administrative error, when a payment for some of

Brett's clothes had been made by Saffery Champness from the wrong account. However, Brett now pleaded guilty to failing to report money that in reality was never his, and of being aware of unknown individuals who were involved in some non-specific tax evasion scheme. In fact, it was agreed explicitly between all parties before the agreement was concluded that this admission did not relate to me, nor to Bea. What's more, Brett was held accountable for something of which he might reasonably have been aware, but was in fact unaware. If you can make any sense of that, then you are a better man than I.

Nevertheless, Brett went ahead with the agreement and pleaded guilty to these offences. As he left the court two photographers were waiting for him outside. This is how the *New York Times* reported it the following day[82]:

Tax Fugitive's Son Pleads Guilty to Evasion Charges

The son of Stanley S. Tollman, the fugitive New York hotel and travel executive, pleaded guilty yesterday in Manhattan to federal charges of tax evasion. It was a significant break in the government's case against the Tollman family and employees of their businesses who have been indicted on charges of cheating the government.

Brett G. Tollman, 42, admitted that he failed to pay taxes on $2.7 million of income from 1993 through 1999 and that he took part in a plan to funnel untaxed money to accounts in Guernsey in the British Channel Islands.

He agreed to pay $1 million on his tax bill within 60 days under a plea bargain with James B. Comey, the United States attorney for the Southern District of New York.

Brett Tollman admitted that he funneled unreported pay to the Guernsey bank account and that employees who helped out were paid with unreported money and lease payments on cars they drove. The other defendants in the tax evasion case are scheduled to go on trial next month in Manhattan.

You may remember that earlier in this book I admitted to being an eternal optimist. I claimed that I am never, ever, prepared to give up. I also suggested that there is no such thing as the inevitable. I even went so far as to say that on one occasion only have I ever found myself helpless, unable to change the course of events. I made clear that this particular story would come much later on in my book. The time has now come to tell it.

I was at home when I heard the news that Brett had agreed a guilty plea. He telephoned me, and asked me whether I was sitting down. He said that he wanted to tell me some bad news. He explained that he was bringing certainty to the situation, and that he would be able to serve his time in jail and return to the family when his children would still be young enough to be untroubled by what had happened to their father. He told me that he had discussed this in great detail with Miranda, and that they were both of the opinion that this was the best thing to do, given the impossible situation. Finally, he explained that he had not told me beforehand because he was certain that I would not want him to do it and that I would try to prevent him from doing it. More importantly, though, he had not wanted to give me the opportunity of returning to the United States and negotiating a substitution of me for him.

As one might expect, I was mortified by Brett's news. Despite nearly 75 years' experience of the trials and tribulations of life, I had absolutely nothing in my business or emotional armoury which would help me to deal with this. It was at once a tragedy, an ethical dilemma, a disaster and, I was to discover, an insoluble legal conundrum.

I am immensely proud of my son and want so much for him. And even though I could never be considered impartial, I can honestly say that he is one of the most decent, honourable and honest human beings I have ever met. But Brett had now found it necessary to do something which meant that he would spend almost three years in prison. How could this possibly have happened? I was lost.

Brett was of course right to say that I would have tried to stop him from doing what he had done. In fact, I would have moved heaven and earth to prevent it. It was difficult therefore to disagree with the logic of him keeping it to himself. But surely something could now be done to set things right? Surely, he would not have to live with the consequences of this decision?

At this point, I asked for advice from New York defence attorney Ben Brafman, whose services had been sought for me by Tom Aro some years before but who, in the end, I had not needed. Now, though, his advice most certainly was required.

At the time, Ben was well-known, although nothing like as famous as he has become since his successful defence of Dominique Strauss-Kahn. Ben is an extraordinary man. Impressive, immensely likeable and hugely principled, he is a great attorney and a thoroughly decent guy.

An orthodox Jew (his brother is a rabbi), Ben is faithful to Judaism, and observes its dietary laws strictly. He came to visit me in London on a number of occasions, and would barely eat anything in Britain which he had not brought with him from New York. This meant that trips to London were measured in hours rather than days.

Ben originally became well-known for his defence of Sean Combs, the rapper, singer, record producer and entrepreneur otherwise known as Puff Daddy. In December 1999, Combs and his then-girlfriend Jennifer Lopez were at Club New York, a midtown Manhattan nightclub, when gunfire broke out. Combs was arrested for weapons violations and other charges and was indicted after his driver claimed that Combs had tried to bribe him into taking the weapon after the shooting. Sean Combs' attorneys at trial were Johnnie L Cochran Jr and Ben Brafman.

Ben tells two stories about his opening address to the jury at the start of that trial. He began, "My name is Ben Brafman. My co-counsel is Johnnie Cochran. The way you can tell us apart is that I always wear a collar pin in my shirt. If you see someone wearing a collar pin, it's me." It is true that Ben wears a collar pin in his shirt, but he is also white. The late Johnnie Cochran was black. The humour was not lost on the jury, who were immediately at ease.

Ben went on, "Ladies and gentlemen, this is Sean 'Puff Daddy' Combs. You can call him Sean. You can call him Mr Combs. You can call him Puff Daddy. You can him just plain Puffy. But you cannot call him Guilty." At the conclusion of the trial, Combs was found not guilty on all charges.

Ben has attracted a great deal of press attention, especially in recent years. The New York Times in 2004 wrote:[83]

> *Mr. Brafman shines in a courtroom, wresting acquittals that the smart money bet against. He can deliver a perfectly modulated cross-examination, and is a savvy, gutsy tactician, an elegant manipulator, a jury charmer.*
>
> *As part of the package, though, he is unapologetic, aggressive and possessed of a boundless immodesty, in the grand tradition of self-made men who are long on success and short of stature. He has the defensive scrappiness of a Brooklyn guy raised without luxuries or Ivy League polish, but with a relentless work ethic.*
>
> *Home, for Mr. Brafman, an Orthodox Jew, means Long Island, where he lives with his wife, Lynda, and in walking distance from grandsons, in-laws, synagogue. There, far from the courtroom, he is known as a soft touch who has quietly, spontaneously paid for this one's chemotherapy, that one's tuition.*
>
> *His parents were Holocaust survivors who infused him with a potent sense of heritage, an awareness of how his public persona could reflect on his people.*
>
> *"The teachings of Judaism I respect most," he says, "are about sharing your blessings, giving people the benefit of the doubt and living your life with honesty. That's pretty much it. And that's pretty good stuff for a criminal defense lawyer, too."*

Ben reviewed Brett's plea, and told me that it was effectively beyond challenge. For Brett to attempt now to change his mind would almost certainly have disastrous effects. He advised me that the die was sadly cast. I was forced to recognise that any assistance which Ben might be able to give the family would have to come later, and in as yet undefined circumstances. More of that later. In the meantime, Ben put Brett in touch with a consultant to assist in preparing him for his inevitable incarceration.

---

[83] *New York Times*, 12 February 2004.

It took me some time to face up to the fact that Brett, of all people, had pleaded guilty, and even longer to accept that there was little or nothing which could be done about it. The iniquity of non-mandatory Sentencing Guidelines now preoccupied me. I discovered that I was not the only one to be concerned about them. The very judge who had originally been in charge of Brett's case had been sufficiently distressed about non-discretionary sentencing that he had resigned, and done so publicly, writing to the New York Times[84]:

Let Judges Do Their Jobs
By John S. Martin Jr., a federal district judge in Manhattan.

I have served as a federal judge for 13 years. Although I find my work to be interesting and challenging, I have decided to join the growing number of federal judges who retire to join the private sector.

When I became a federal judge, I accepted the fact that I would be paid much less than I could earn in private practice; judges make less than second-year associates at many law firms, and substantially less than a senior Major League umpire. I believed I would be compensated by the satisfaction of serving the public good -- the administration of justice. In recent years, however, this sense has been replaced by the distress I feel at being part of a sentencing system that is unnecessarily cruel and rigid.

For most of our history, our system of justice operated on the premise that justice in sentencing is best achieved by having a sentence imposed by a judge who, fully informed about the offense and the offender, has discretion to impose a sentence within the statutory limits. Although most judges and legal scholars recognize the need for discretion in sentencing, Congress has continually tried to limit it, initially through the adoption of mandatory-minimum sentencing laws.

Congress's distrust of judicial discretion led to the adoption in 1984 of the Sentencing Reform Act, which created the United States Sentencing Commission. The commission was created on the premise, not unreasonable, that uniformity in sentencing nationwide could be promoted if judges and other criminal law experts provided guidelines for federal judges to follow in imposing sentences. However, Congress has tried to micromanage the work of the commission and has undermined its efforts to provide judges with some discretion in sentencing or to ameliorate excessively harsh terms.

For example, when an extensive study demonstrated that there was no justification for treating crack cocaine as 100 times more dangerous than powdered cocaine, the ratio adopted by Congress in fixing mandatory minimum sentences, the commission proposed reducing the guideline ratios. However, the proposal was withdrawn when Congressional leaders made it clear that Congress would overrule it.

Congress's most recent assault on judicial independence is found in amendments that were tacked onto the Amber Alert bill, which President Bush signed into law on April 30. These amendments are an effort to intimidate judges to follow sentencing guidelines.

From the outset, the sentencing commission recognized the need to avoid too rigid an application of the guideline system and provided that judges would have the power to adjust sentences when circumstances in an individual case warranted. The recent amendments require the commission to amend the guidelines to reduce such adjustments and require that every one be reported to Congress. They also require that departures by district judges be reviewed by the appellate courts with little deference to the sentencing judge.

Congress's disdain for the judiciary is further manifested in a provision that changes the requirement that "at least three" of the seven members of the sentencing commission be federal judges to a restriction that "no more than" three judges may serve on it. Apparently Congress believes America's sentencing system will be jeopardized if more than three members of the commission have actual experience in imposing sentences.

Every sentence imposed affects a human life and, in most cases, the lives of several innocent family members who suffer as a result of a defendant's incarceration. For a judge to be deprived of the ability to consider all of the factors that go into formulating a just sentence is completely at odds with the sentencing philosophy that has been a hallmark of the American system of justice.

When I took my oath of office 13 years ago I never thought that I would leave the federal bench. While I might have stayed on despite the inadequate pay, I no longer want to be part of our unjust criminal justice system.

Brett's family, his attorneys and many friends now set about the task of ensuring that, having pleaded guilty, the judge in his case could be under no doubt at all as to the fact that she would be sentencing a decent human being. No-one felt that Brett deserved punishment of any kind, let alone to go to jail for almost three years, separated from his wife and two young children.

Brett's sentencing took place on 12 March 2004. Brett had pleaded guilty in September and, during the intervening six-month period, not only had the trial of Monty Hundley and the others commenced, it had actually concluded. Judge Loretta Preska had presided throughout, and had plenty of time to assess the four men whom Brett did not want to be tried alongside. I am about to come on to that trial, and am mindful that I am about to take the edge off that story by revealing that all four were found guilty by the New York jury. But it was not quite as simple as that, as I will explain in the next chapter. In the meantime, though, Brett had reason to be thankful that he had chosen not to run the risk of being judged guilty alongside men who were evidently tax cheats. But he also had reason to fear that Judge Loretta Preska would not look kindly on his team's hopes for a minimum sentence if she believed that Brett was as bad as they were.

Judge Preska's Courtroom 12A was packed with family and friends. Numerous letters had been sent to the Judge prior to the hearing. One of these was from Toni, who could not be present, even though she had been living and working in New York until relatively recently. Toni had built up a successful business there from scratch, but Okula had accused her, without justification, of being present illegally in the United States, and of working there unlawfully. He told her that she should leave the US, otherwise she too would be arrested. Okula frightened her into leaving. I know that Toni was deeply disappointed not to be there to support Brett, as was clear from her very moving letter, in which she talked about her brother over the years.

She mentioned Brett's conscientious nature and the fact that he was deeply upset as a youngster because Wynn would always make the pair of them late for school. Brett's remedy for this was to go to bed wearing his school uniform so that he would be ready the next morning. Toni went on, "Wynn failed out of choice to step up to the plate as the eldest. Brett at the young age of twenty-two stepped in and took his place. He did this out of a sense of responsibility and in an attempt to ease the pain and disappointment of our parents."

Toni continued by talking of Brett's many acts of kindness. "Our parents taught us to live by a simple philosophy: Those who bring sunshine to the lives of others cannot keep it from themselves." She mentioned that at 485 Park Avenue there was an elderly doorman called Marvin. Marvin had worked in the building for 30 years, and his work was his life. He was well past retirement age, but had no wish to retire. Despite pressure from other tenants, who wanted to 'let Marvin go', Brett had made certain that he kept his job. Marvin had died, aged 81, when it was discovered that he had no relations and few friends. His only family and friends were his colleagues and the residents of 485 Park Avenue. Brett arranged Marvin's funeral, and underwrote its cost.

Toni then pointed out that Tollman-Hundley had been through one of the most turbulent times within the hospitality industry as well as one of the most financially-strapped periods for the Company. Brett had asked the entire executive team to take a 5% pay cut, so that they could save the jobs of a number of employees. Meanwhile, he had cut his own pay by 10%.

Finally, Toni wrote of a very sad incident in May 1995 when Tom Wilson, Tollman-Hundley's Executive Vice President of Sales & Marketing, had died in a road traffic accident in Orlando, Florida. Brett had travelled personally to Pennsylvania to break the news to Tom's wife and children and to help make the funeral arrangements.

Another moving letter to the Court was from Brett's father-in-law, Lee Rich, who said:

I have known Brett now for almost ten years. I can honestly say that he is the single most honorable human being that I have ever known. His values are sound and generous. He is thoughtful and cares for people. He is good, kind and loving to everyone within his close circle as well as to others.

Brett is and always has been the perfect son-in-law. He cares for and protects my daughter and my grandchildren in just the way every father-in-law would wish. To describe his family unit as close is not to do justice to the relationships which bond them. He is the cornerstone of the household, and his family is everything to him.

My second observation relates to his concern for the needy and the homeless, a concern of which I was made aware shortly after we met. Brett was driving me out of the City one chilly winter's afternoon when he unexpectedly pulled over and got out of the car. He negotiated his way through the traffic to the centre of the highway where an old lady was huddled. This was no easy task! I had barely noticed the woman, but Brett had spotted that she was squatting there in hope of some change from the passing motorists. Brett checked that she was capable of fending for herself, gave her some money, and made his way back to the car.

I have to confess that I was amazed at what Brett had done. The lady had picked the only place available on this route, but it was very, very difficult to stop a car there. I told Brett that I could not think of another person that would have gone out of his way as he had done. I said that I thought he was mad to have done so.

In the months that followed, I discovered that giving to the homeless was not an exceptional business for Brett, but that he did it all the time. A conversation with Brett whilst walking down 5th Avenue was constantly interrupted by his going out of his way to give a dollar or two to numerous of the homeless. Eventually, I tackled him about this behaviour. 'Are you crazy?', I said to him. 'How do you know these people aren't going to spend that money on alcohol or drugs?' 'I don't.' Brett replied. 'All I know is that some of them desperately need help,' and of course he was right. I had cause to reconsider my approach to the poor and homeless, and to admire his approach to helping others. In the years that followed, I have been given countless opportunities to reinforce that admiration. I am so proud to have him in my life.

Bob Fink and Rusty Wing presented the case in mitigation of the offences to which Brett had pleaded guilty. Bob went through the technical detail, and Rusty made the case for leniency. He called upon the Court to take Brett's character into account in order to mitigate the sentence:

> *Since character matters in sentencing, as it does in life, I would like to just say a few words about the character of Brett Tollman.*
>
> *Although his participation in these offences was a serious mistake, he has conducted other aspects of his life with honour, integrity and a remarkable, if not unique, concern for the wellbeing of other people. For the better part of his life, Brett Tollman has personally reached out and extended himself to help other people from all walks of life, whether it is family or friends or employees or strangers. If they crossed Brett Tollman's path and they were in need, they got help.*
>
> *Someone once said, 'Only a life lived for others is a life worth living.' Someone must have whispered that in Brett Tollman's ear at an early age because he began living that life long before this case was ever a gleam in a prosecutor's eye, and there is no doubt that he will continue to live that life long after this case has been forgotten. But I won't forget. Because I never met anyone quite like Brett Tollman, and I doubt I will again.*
>
> *Proof that Brett Tollman is a good man, proof beyond any reasonable doubt, has been laid out for the Court in the many letters that have been submitted to Your Honour by people who know this man. People who, from their different vantage points, have witnessed what he has done, how he has lived his life watching out for and taking care of other people. That, in effect, has been his guiding principle. As Bob Fink has indicated, he and I have both come to know Brett quite well during the two years we have been representing him. And we can say without equivocation that the description of the man in the many letters you*

received is consistent with the man we saw and the man we came to know during one of the most difficult times of his life.

I wish I could have been the father that Brett has been, or the humanitarian that Brett has been, but I can't say that. He is an extraordinary man whose concern and compassion for others reflects a sensitive, if not a saintly soul. Sure, he came from a well-to-do family and has financial resources that others don't. But how many wealthy people will stop the car in the middle of traffic and get out to give a homeless woman some money?

Judge Preska thanked Rusty and Bob, and then reviewed the material which the professionals had produced in helping to guide her sentence. One was from the probation office in New York, to which Brett had apparently reported that he had always enjoyed a close relationship with me. He also said, though, that I had gone through a period of heavy drinking in the early 1970s when I was having financial difficulties and that I was often loud and boisterous in the home, though never violent. When Brett had made those comments he was of course thinking of the Court Hotels episode 30 years earlier, when he was barely a teenager. But the young are impressionable, and it was clearly something which he had long remembered.

Judge Preska then concluded proceedings by saying, "Counsel, this was probably the best pre-sentence presentation I have ever seen. It is very clear that Mr Tollman is, in fact, an exceptional human being." She then went on to sentence Brett for the minimum prison time for which we could have hoped – 33 months. This was the lowest envisaged under the Sentencing Guidelines given the 20 points 'score' of the plea, but also given Brett's previous record, which was without blemish of any kind.

The US Attorney's Office issued a press release later that day, reporting on the sentencing, but which also announced the unsealing of the complaint against Bea. This said:

HOTEL EXECUTIVE SENTENCED TO 33 MONTHS IN JAIL FOR PARTICIPATION IN MULTI MILLION-DOLLAR FEDERAL TAX EVASION SCHEME CHARGES UNSEALED AGAINST HIS MOTHER, BEATRICE TOLLMAN, FOR INVOLVEMENT IN SAME SCHEME

David N. Kelley, the United States Attorney for the Southern District of New York, announced that hotel executive Brett G. Tollman was sentenced in Manhattan federal court to 33 months in prison today based on his involvement in two tax schemes involving millions in unreported income through the use of secret foreign bank accounts.

Mr. Kelley also announced the unsealing of tax fraud charges against Beatrice Nina Tollman, Brett Tollman's mother and wife of indicted defendant Stanley Tollman, based on her involvement in the tax fraud scheme involving foreign bank accounts.

Brett Tollman pled guilty to two tax fraud conspiracy charges on September 5, 2003. According to court records and his guilty pleas to the two charges, Tollman served as an executive at Tollman-Hundley Hotels, a private company based in New York, which owned and managed various Days Inn hotels throughout the United States. Also according to court records and the Information, Tollman had various positions with The Travel Corporation, a British Virgin Island company that was and is the parent company to various travel and tourism companies, including Trafalgar Tours International and the Red Carnation Group of hotels. Brett Tollman admitted as part of his guilty plea that from 1993 to 1999, he received from The Travel Corporation more than $2.7 million in compensation through a secret Channel Islands bank account maintained in the name Maxie Group, which amounts he knowingly failed to report to the IRS. According to court records and the Information, Brett Tollman and others had signatory authority over that account, which was opened in order to receive the secret compensation from The Travel

Corporation and its subsidiaries and affiliated companies, including Trafalgar Tours International and Red Carnation.

Tollman also admitted that he was aware of an additional $6 million that was paid to others by The Travel Corporation as part of the tax evasion scheme, which amounts were also not reported to the IRS. According to Tollman's plea agreement, the unreported income from the Channel Islands scheme resulted in a tax loss to the United States of more than $3,150,000.

Tollman further admitted during his guilty plea that he conspired with employees of the Tollman-Hundley companies to pay those employees various forms of compensation that was not reported to the IRS by the Tollman-Hundley companies or by the employees. According to the tax conspiracy charge to which Tollman pled guilty and other court documents, the unreported compensation included rental payments for the employees' residences, off-the-books overtime payments, car lease payments, and insurance for employee vehicles. According to Tollman's plea agreement, the unreported compensation to Tollman-Hundley employees involved the payment of almost $900,000, and a tax loss to the United States of over $350,000, bringing the total tax loss to $3,500,000.

In addition to the prison term, Brett Tollman was sentenced by United States District Judge Loretta A. Preska to pay $3.5 million in restitution to the IRS based on his involvement in the schemes. Judge Preska also ordered Tollman to pay a fine of $50,000, and the costs of prosecution in the amount of $27,500.

As the press release correctly suggested, in addition to serving time in a federal prison, Brett was also ordered to pay restitution to the IRS. This included paying the tax of the Tollman-Hundley employees who had failed to report the extra income they had received.

Two months then passed, during which time Brett worked from home in Manhattan, preparing for the time he was to be away. He surrendered himself on 6 May 2004 to the minimum security Federal Prison Camp at Eglin, Florida, in the grounds of

Eglin Air Force Base, in the Florida Panhandle, and close to the city of Pensacola.

I struggle to comprehend just how difficult it would have been for Brett to drag himself away from his young family and to enter a world so completely alien to him. I was pleased that Brett's cousin, Gavin, travelled with him to Eglin in order to give him support on what must have been the most difficult journey imaginable.

Settling into life at Eglin was not without great emotional pain. But Brett learned quickly that his life was likely to become easier once he had been allocated a regular job there, especially if the job itself was something with which he would be content. On 25 May, three weeks after arriving at Eglin, Brett was assigned that permanent job. Someone was needed to help cut the many acres of grass at the base. This was of course an outdoor assignment, and to Brett was as attractive an opportunity as was ever likely to be available. This was something with which he could live and into which he could settle. But settling was not something which he was allowed to do. Okula had not finished with him yet.

Just one day after Brett had been allocated a permanent job and started work, the Eglin authorities received a writ obtained by Assistant US Attorney Stanley Okula. This required the Bureau of Prisons to return Brett to New York, 1,200 miles away, in order that he could appear before a grand jury. Okula wanted to ask Brett some more questions.

Brett had only recently arrived at Eglin, and had been in Manhattan for months before that. Okula's decision to wait until Brett had just settled in to Eglin before "yanking him back out" (to use Rusty Wing's words) was questionable to say the least. But what happened next was little short of disgraceful.

The first effect of Brett's untimely removal was the loss forever of the attractive job to which he had been allocated. His absence meant that these duties would now be fulfilled by someone else. Much worse, Brett then discovered with horror that Okula expected him to be transported to New York not by air, a journey which would have taken a few hours, but by road.

Okula had ensured that Brett would be transported by the Bureau of Prisons in a paddywagon, within which he was chained to other prisoners – and to prisoners of all levels of security classification at that. This was not only arduous, it was potentially dangerous. Brett was hauled in this way first to Tallahassee, Florida, and then on to Atlanta, Georgia. These were long and exhausting journeys, during which he was subjected to extreme discomfort. During one of the many stop-overs, he was forced to sleep lying on the floor of a cell in Atlanta with neither mattress nor blanket, and chained to another prisoner. During the night, that prisoner was bitten by a venomous spider, and became very seriously ill.

Brett's attorneys requested a furlough from Okula, which would have allowed him to fly back to New York, meeting all the costs of air transport himself – a normal procedure in such cases. But Okula refused this.

When Brett eventually arrived in New York, he was taken back to the Metropolitan Correctional Center. However, unlike his first brief stay at the MCC, which was in the general population area of the facility, this time Brett was installed in Unit Nine South, the special housing unit. Unit Nine South is the highest security area of the jail, where Zacarias Moussaoui, the so-called 9/11 '20th hijacker', and mobster Sammy 'The Bull' Gravano were held. Yet Brett, a minimum security prisoner, spent more than two weeks there. He was under lock-up for almost the entire time, was allowed only two showers a week and was handcuffed every time he was moved anywhere, including to the shower.

Okula's actions were unquestionably deliberate and calculated. Rusty Wing and Bob Fink felt so strongly about his behaviour that they wrote jointly to David Kelley, the then US Attorney for the Southern District of New York. Their letter included the following words:

> *"It became apparent during the prosecution of this matter that Mr Okula had developed an unprofessional animus towards the Tollman family; his comments to counsel about Mr Tollman and Mr Tollman's parents were*

venomous. We believe that Mr Okula's present conduct does not properly serve a prosecutorial function…"

United States Attorney General Robert H Jackson, who was also the chief United States prosecutor at the Nuremberg Trials, addressed the conference of United States Attorneys in 1940. In a speech entitled 'The Federal Prosecutor' it is recognised that he set the standard by which Federal prosecutors have since been judged[85]. Amongst other things, he said the following:

"The prosecutor has more control over life, liberty, and reputation, than any other person in America.

    "Nothing better can come out of this meeting of law enforcement officers than a rededication to the spirit of fair play and decency that should animate the federal prosecutor. Your positions are of such independence and importance that while you are being diligent, strict, and vigorous in law enforcement you can also afford to be just. Although the government technically loses its case, it has really won if justice has been done.

    "The qualities of a good prosecutor are as elusive and as impossible to define as those which mark a gentleman. And those who need to be told would not understand it anyway. A sensitiveness to fair play and sportsmanship is perhaps the best protection against the abuse of power, and the citizen's safety lies in the prosecutor who tempers zeal with human kindness, who seeks truth and not victims, who serves the law and not factional purposes, and who approaches his task with humility."

Stanley J Okula is without doubt the antithesis of everything for which Robert Jackson stood. And his abuse of authority in his dealings with Brett was not the last to be suffered by my family. But I will come to that.

Brett returned from New York to Eglin. Thankfully, David Kelley, the US Attorney at the time, overruled Okula and allowed Brett to return by air, rather than paddywagon. This cost us $5,000 dollars, including the seat for the Marshal. Sadly, though, Brett was prevented

---

[85] The Federal Prosecutor: Address delivered to the Second Annual Conference of United States Attorneys, April 1940.

from serving out his sentence at Eglin. This time, Okula was not to blame but Mother Nature, an authority truly deserving of respect. The 2004 hurricane season was one of the most deadly for Florida, the only one on record when no fewer than four hurricanes were to affect the state. In fact, five named storms made landfall in Florida that year – hurricanes Charley, Frances, Ivan and Jeanne, and tropical storm Bonnie. Experiencing winds of well over 100 miles per hour, the Federal Prison Camp at Eglin was largely destroyed, and its inmates relocated.

Brett was moved to Federal Prison Camp, Talladega, in Alabama, a minimum security facility alongside a Federal Correction Institution, and approximately 50 miles from Birmingham and 100 miles from Atlanta, Georgia. Whilst Brett was there, Okula attempted once again to bring him back to New York in a repeat of the same dreadful process in order to appear before another grand jury and answer yet more questions. At this time, Brett was preparing to move from the Federal Prison Camp to a halfway house in Florida. Okula's request was challenged, and this time Okula did not get his way.

By all accounts, Brett was a model prisoner, nothing less than I would have expected, given what I know about my son. He became a mentor to many of his fellow prisoners, passing on to them a variety of life skills. Thanks to his behaviour and various concessions, Brett served just 11 months in prison, and his transition through the halfway house and to complete freedom was flawless. At a personal level, he sustained his family and professional relationships and was able to close this chapter of his life in a highly creditworthy manner.

Brett's incarceration was exceptionally difficult for me, made worse by the demand of the US Prison Service that he never spoke to me on the telephone, even during his time at the halfway house. Thus it was that the two of us were separated in almost every sense of the word for several years. He was of course able to speak to other members of the family, but the isolation which both Brett and I experienced during this time was palpable.

These days, Brett is the CEO and President of the Travel Corporation, which has grown into a global enterprise. The Travel Corporation comprises a number of niche businesses including, amongst many other things escorted touring, boutique hotels and river cruises. It has nearly 50 major brands such as Trafalgar Tours, Insight Vacations, Contiki Holidays, AAT Kings, Uniworld Boutique River Cruises, African Travel, Red Carnation Hotels and Evans Evans.

Brett's life may now be back to normal, but throughout the whole period of his maltreatment at the hands of Okula, Bea and I lived a daily nightmare. This was not helped when we heard that the word going around in certain circles, notably Palm Beach, was that Brett had gone to jail instead of me.

It is difficult to describe just how hurtful it was to hear that this was being said. Especially distressing was my inability at that time to explain to other people what had happened, and why. The relationship between any father and son is often complex. Brett, in taking over the reins of the family business, finds himself following the path which his father trod before him. However, in much the same way that I resisted the path which my father had chosen for me, even from his days as a teenager Brett has shown a wish to do things differently – to be his own man. I respect that wish for independence, and I admire it. He and I are, after all, very different people. Notwithstanding that we are different, I admire his wish to build on the traditions of a family which has now been in this business for four generations.

In preparing to write this book, I came across a letter which Miranda wrote almost ten years ago, in which, even then, she was able to sum up Brett's character perfectly. She wrote:

"He doesn't shirk a journey or cut corners. He remembers everything, into which he puts great effort. At night, when he empties his pockets, piles of small notes spill out – reminders of everything – birthdays, a book to send to my father, a phone call to be made to a hotel manager regarding a guest, a new recipe to try out. He never takes a break from his expectations of

Stanley Baker as Lieutenant John Chard in *Zulu*

Diamond Films/The Kobal Collection

Arnold, displaying his
beauty contest good looks

With Arnold (right) in
Trafalgar Square, London, 1956

With Brett

Brett and Miranda

With our good friends Isadore and Camilla Rosenfeld

Seeing in the 21st Century at our 'Black-and-White' party in Palm Beach
From the left, Bea, Max Fisher and Alexandra (Mrs Arnaud) de Borchgrave

Brett, at an event for Days Inn

With Monty Hundley

Lew and Edie Wasserman

Ron Wolfson/LFI/Photoshot

Monaco days

Meeting Ronald Reagan for the first time

With Margaret Thatcher at our home in Palm Beach

With Bea and the children
From the left: me, Toni, Wynn, Brett, Bea and Vicki

With Bea and Wynn at the farm in Connecticut

With Ken Bates

Jerry Berns and members of the "21" 'family'
(Jerry is wearing glasses)

"21" Club/Alfred Eisenstaedt

At *'Li Galli'*, Italian hotelier Giovanni Russo's private islands off the Amalfi coast, near Positano, 2001: (from the left) Frank Chopin, Charlie Gargano, me, Ronnie Hersov and Brian Mulroney,

With John Schlesinger

With Max Fisher

My brother Ivan and his wife, Lillian

Nicky Kerman

Receiving my Honorary Doctorate
from Schiller International University, London

My girls on safari
Toni (behind), Vicki (left) and Bea (right)

The generation now running the family's businesses
(with a little help from the girls and me)
From the left Gavin, me, Brett and Michael

Left: Leaving an extradition hearing in February 2007, supported by Vicki
Westminster Magistrates' Court, London

Steve Parsons/PA Archive/Press Association Images

I am a lucky man indeed to have met this lady

Peter Strongwater

himself, and of others whom he respects and admires. He has time for everyone and never ceases to ask after that person's loved ones. None of this is done without true intent and genuine concern."

Although I love and care for all of my family, besides Bea the most important person in my life is without doubt Brett. For many years, I have wanted him one day to take over everything and, during that time, I suspect that everything I have done has been with Brett in mind. Indeed, in recent years, I have built the business in such a way that one day Brett would be able to take over from me. Three years ago, I handed over to him, confident in the knowledge that he would be ably supported by his cousins and sisters. Make no mistake, though, I have not forgotten my other children. I most definitely have not. But I have seen Brett as the one individual who would pick up the baton of the family enterprise and take it forward.

Brett was 50 in August 2011 and, in celebration of his life thus far, ninety people were invited to Marseille. Members of the family and Brett's friends and business associates boarded the Uniworld cruise ship *River Royale,* and together we travelled northwards up the Rhône to Lyon. This was a unique celebration. It felt in so many ways that things had come full circle and each evening was marked with unique and very special occasions during the course of which many people spoke about Brett.

Inevitably, my turn came to say something about my son. I was able to say something that I suspect most sons would like to hear their fathers say during their life. I got the opportunity to say many things about Brett but the most important was how proud I am of him. I am incredibly proud to call Brett my son. He is as fine a man as one could wish to have as a son.

I would just like to say a few words to Brett himself. My son, I think about you often – about your dreams, your ideas and your ambitions. Remember: wherever you are, and wherever I am, my thoughts are always with you. I haven't always been perfect, but I have always tried.

The extracts which conclude this chapter are from the letter which George Kaufman wrote when Brett was about to be sentenced, and to which I referred earlier. In 2004, these words were written for Judge Preska. Today, reader, you are the judge:

Although Brett was born into a loving and caring family, it is difficult to imagine a more challenging or competitive environment for any child. He has great parents. Loving parents. But as is so often the case with high achievers, Brett has very unreasonable parents. They had the highest expectations of their children. And Brett has struggled for years, often against all the odds, to be a credit to his father and mother.

Brett is a good man. He is a kind and generous man. A complex man who gives freely of himself. Perhaps too freely. Wanting to please and wanting to be loved are major elements of Brett's character. Nothing is too much trouble if it is to help others, regardless of the personal cost.

It baffles me that Brett, of all people, should have committed an offence. It is so fundamentally out of character. But if he has pleaded guilty, then guilty he must surely be. He is normally so scrupulously straightforward and honest, there can be other explanation.

George Kaufman

ARNOLD

Arnold and I were extremely close for almost all of his life, and it is a matter of enduring regret that I was unable to see him during the two years which preceded his death.

He was the younger brother whom every older brother would wish for. He was always the Tonto to my Lone Ranger, the Sancho Panza to my Don Quixote. Consistently and unwaveringly loyal, he was always there to offer help, guidance and support. To say we were very close is to understate how unique the bond was between us. I miss him hugely.

From the time shortly after my father died, until illness overtook him, Arnold was at my side in business as well as in family matters. We went through many trials and tribulations together, as well as sharing the enjoyment of the good times. But illness was to take a great deal of joy out of Arnold's life.

Arnold followed us to the USA in 1978, where I made him head of Trafalgar America, a job at which he became a great success. Before he retired, 20 years later, he had built Trafalgar into one of the two biggest escorted tour companies in the United States.

In the 20 years prior to his retirement, I only went to Arnold's office three times, such is the measure of the trust I had in him. Throughout the whole of his life, I always knew he was there to cover my back. And, in the same way that I knew that he would always support me, I always supported him.

Arnold was a wonderful guy, although not perhaps the world's best father. When he left his wife to raise four young children, she went out to work selling shoes, which cannot have been easy. But I know that he always cared deeply for his children.

I remember that Gavin, his elder son, telephoned him from South Africa one day in December 1981 to say that he was two weeks away from his final exams. This meant that he could be required to do military service. Under the *apartheid* system, white men were at the time called to compulsory military service for two years. These meant being part of an unpaid militia which propped up the regime. Gavin, who was a strong-willed and liberal-minded young man, was very uncomfortable with sustaining a regime[86] which he did not support. Arnold said to him, "Come to New York." And so it was that before the end of that month, as soon as he graduated from high school, Gavin, aged 18, came to the United States to be with his father and enrolled later that year at the American University, Washington, DC.

In his early years Arnold was very much mummy's boy; and my mother adored him. Until my father died, Arnold was in fact much closer to my mother than I was. After my father had passed on, my mother and I got to know each other much better.

Arnold retired to Monaco, where he died on 19 August 2004, aged 72. The late Joel Abels, the New York-based editor and publisher of *Travel Trade*, said at the time, "I met Arnold almost immediately after his arrival in New York from South Africa. Over the years, he and I developed a strong business and personal relationship that lasted for the past quarter century. We shared a love for travel agents and the travel industry and I especially remember his generous spirit and great sense of humour. The entire travel industry benefited significantly from the lifelong contributions made by Arnold."

There were the first indications of kidney disease when Arnold was in his early 30s, but he dealt with this quietly and privately, beginning regular dialysis many years ago. But during the last 20 years of his life, ill health became a serious concern for him. He had a dialysis room built in his New York apartment, and in many ways became a prisoner of the regime which he had to follow religiously. In 1990, we celebrated my 60th birthday in Paris with all our family and friends. The logistics which Arnold, then aged 58, had to deploy in order to be present were extreme. He flew direct to Paris on the Air France *Concorde*, which allowed him to be at L'Ami Louis for my birthday dinner, before flying back to New York on *Concorde* the following morning in time to get back for his dialysis.

---

[86] Compulsory military service was abolished in South Africa in 1994.

Shortly after that event, Arnold received a kidney transplant. This improved the quality of his life for some time, but in time his health gradually deteriorated once more. Renal disease is usually accompanied by extensive cardiovascular and other damage. During the last two years of his life, Arnold was barely capable of any form of physical activity or communication. He developed a very serious heart condition, and his eyesight and hearing had all but deserted him. He was also severely diabetic.

The last time I saw Arnold was in July 2001. He had moved to Monaco two years earlier. Bea and I had chartered a boat out of Cap Ferrat to spend a vacation with Kate Ford, Frank Chopin and Brian and Mila Mulroney. Arnold came over from Monaco and joined us for dinner one evening. Even at that time, he was already incredibly fragile. He and I had a talk before dinner, during which conversation he told me that Okula was looking for me. I simply didn't believe him. I couldn't understand at that time that anyone could come after you for something you had not done. It was not long before I had to change my understanding.

When Arnold retired, he asked me for a payment to reward his contribution to Trafalgar. Without hesitation I agreed and a substantial amount was paid to him. Arnold's duty to account to the tax authorities was, of course, his business and it was only years later that I discovered that he might not have declared everything he should have done. But it was not I who made the discovery but the IRS. Okula calculated that this made him an easy target for a little coercion, and that he would readily 'spill the beans' on others. Okula was of course thinking of me. Arnold was granted immunity from prosecution, and was then interviewed by Okula in the US Embassy in London. Arnold was at that point suffering from a 90% loss of hearing. Even so, he allowed himself to be interviewed without representation. I have little doubt that the exchanges which took place were not only confused and worthless, but probably misleading.

Around 1991/92, Monty Hundley approached me one day and asked me whether Arnold would like to make some money. It is important to realise that Monty and Arnold had very little to do with each other. They had met a few times through me, but Arnold was working full-time for Trafalgar and had nothing whatsoever to do with Tollman-Hundley. In response to Monty's question, I replied, "Everybody likes to make money. Why are you asking?" Monty replied that, in the context of some of the financial restructuring, he needed to seek assistance from third parties and he had thought of Arnold. I suggested that he should pick up the telephone to Arnold. That was the last I heard of it until, some years later, I discovered the link between Arnold and Paternoster Holdings which had purchased some of the Tollman-Hundley bank indebtedness. In much the same way, I was aware in the most vague terms of a conversation which Monty had had with Ken Bates about Chelsea Acquisitions.

The idea that I was largely unaware of my own brother and my former business partner having been intimately involved with financial transactions which were important, if not central, to Tollman-Hundley may seem difficult to understand. But it is true. Remember, during this period I was rarely in the same part of the world for more than a few days. The constant travelling, and my propensity to get much more involved with the big picture rather than the detail meant that I never spoke to anyone about this.

Indeed, it was only much later that I learned that Arnold was the sole shareholder of Paternoster Holdings and the 90% shareholder of Chelsea Acquisitions. I never talked to Arnold about that, and I never knew what was entailed. Did he view these as investment opportunities, or did he agree to cancel or to forgive the debt which the businesses had bought? He can't tell me, and there is no-one alive whose word I would believe. I am resigned to never finding out.

Okula's view of Arnold seemed to change over time and, long after he had offered him immunity from prosecution, he appeared to have regretted this tactic, suggesting that he was now of the view that Arnold was "at the center of the web". There was a period when he considered that Arnold was 'Mr Big', the criminal mastermind at the heart of everything. Perhaps this explains why, during the summer of 2003, about a year before Arnold died, Okula sought to interview him as part of a grand jury investigation.

Arnold, who was in Monaco and was very ill, was examined locally by his doctor, Nabil Sharara, who was asked to assess Arnold's ability to travel to the United States. Having completed his examination, Dr Sharara issued a medical certificate declaring that his patient was incapable of travelling or even moving and, on medical grounds alone, could not be heard in any criminal proceedings whatsoever.

This report enraged Okula, who then proceeded to harangue and to intimidate Dr Sharara with numerous telephone calls, in a vain attempt to get him to change his mind, and to allow Arnold to travel. Dr Sharara refused to budge, despite accusations of obstruction of justice and threats from Okula to have him blacklisted. Dr Sharara later testified that "after several unacceptable remarks impugning my dignity and my honesty" he had refused to have any further contact with Okula.

On 12 December 2003, Arnold was advised by his US lawyer that a doctor designated by the Government of the United States intended to appear at his home three days later, in order to conduct a medical examination. Donald Manasse, Arnold's Monaco-based lawyer, replied immediately, saying that Arnold did not wish to be subjected to the examination. He also pointed out that the US Government's intention to require a resident of Monaco to submit themselves to a medical examination in the Principality by a US Government-designated physician was questionable to say the least. Without the consent of the Monaco government, and unless the physician concerned was authorised to practise medicine in Monaco, this would represent a violation of Monaco sovereignty. In simple terms, Donald Manasse told Okula that what he was intending to do was illegal.

Okula's response to being told that he was trying to commit an illegal act was to apply instead to the US District Court in New York for Arnold to be adjudged in contempt, and for massive financial penalties to apply. On 16 December 2003 such an order was granted, holding Arnold in contempt of Court for refusing to testify. Arnold, a man who was by this stage gravely ill, was now faced with a fine for contempt running into millions of dollars, which was escalating every day he failed to come to New York, something which he was simply not capable of doing. Of the lengthy catalogue of Stanley Okula's heinous abuses, this action ranked amongst the worst.

Dr Sharara, who learned this news on Boxing Day, generously stood aside in the face of this outrage, and asked Professor Saoudi, Head of Cardiology at the Princess Grace Hospital in Monaco, to replace him. This was agreeable to Okula.

The second examination was conducted on New Year's Eve 2003. Professor Saoudi first examined the extensive dossier of Arnold's medical history. Following this, he conducted a brief and – as Professor Saoudi immediately realised – entirely unnecessary examination of Arnold himself. Within ten minutes, Professor Saoudi had no hesitation in reconfirming Dr Sharara's original assessment. There was no question whatsoever of Arnold being fit enough even to travel, let alone to be subjected to the kind of examination which Okula had in mind. Professor Saoudi reported his findings, and the contempt order in New York was lifted immediately.

Towards the end of the saga, it was necessary for Dr Sharara's experience at Okula's hands to be presented to Westminster Magistrates. But Okula's legacy of intimidation meant that Dr Sharara was too frightened to attend in person and give evidence. Appearing for him instead, Arnold's Monaco-based lawyer, Donald Manasse, explained his absence. "He was concerned that there would be retribution against him if he did. He felt he might be excluded from travelling to the United States and that his children might be excluded from doing the same."

During the final months of his life, whilst at the receiving end of cruel and inhuman behaviour from Okula, Arnold was admitted to hospital on numerous occasions. On three of those admissions his lungs needed to be drained of blood. He was a very, very sick man. But this appeared to be of little concern to Okula. Arnold spent the last few weeks of his life being pressured. And this pressure not only diminished severely the quality of Arnold's final days on earth but, in the view of his medical team, actually shortened them.

Throughout his life, Arnold displayed the most wonderful qualities, including excellent judgement. He did, though, have one significant blind spot, and that was the choice of his second wife.

You may remember that Sandi Philip first came into Arnold's life as the blonde cocktail waitress in the short skirt at the Hyde Park Hotel in Johannesburg. The woman for whom Arnold left his wife and four young children. For many years, Bea and I were completely open-minded about Arnold's choice of Sandi. Until, that is, the time came when Arnold decided to marry her. And it was not the decision to marry, but the way they went about it, which forced us to judge Sandi.

Bea and I were in Miami when Arnold called from New York to say that he and Sandi were going to get married, and that the ceremony was to take place in Manhattan. "Wonderful news!" was our reaction. "Many congratulations. We will fly up to New York to be there." "No. Don't do that," said Arnold. "Sandi says that none of her family can make it to the wedding, so we have decided that none of my family should be there either."

Not only were we not invited, nor was anyone else from the family, including Arnold's three surviving children. In fact, the children were not even told about the wedding until after it was all over. Our view of Sandi altered from that moment – if I am honest, irretrievably so. And, sadly, all our doubts about the woman whom Arnold had chosen as his life partner were borne out after Arnold's death. Her behaviour, especially towards Arnold's children, has been disappointing to say the least.

As to her character, I think the following short extract from a recent column in *The Spectator* speaks volumes about the woman who used to be my sister-in-law:

> *I met a wealthy widow in Monaco the other day who was so pressed for space to keep her designer frocks she paid $1.5 million to buy the apartment below her penthouse as a walk-in wardrobe. Sandi Tollman is an attractive blonde whose late husband made his fortune in smart boutique hotels like The Milestone overlooking Kensington Palace. Sandi*

today has a new partner, Emile, a handsome, youngish, Lebanese gentleman. Emile used to be Sandi's chauffeur. "We knew something was up when Sandi moved from the back of the Rolls to sit beside Emile in the front seat," one observer told me.

Sandi is a friend of Prince Albert, Monaco's ruler. She is also very generous. When she heard two leopards from his private zoo were being flown to a game reserve in South Africa she offered to pay the £50,000 transportation costs.

Sandi and Emile made the long trip to Shamwari. Their Louis Vuitton luggage was lost at Johannesburg airport, but it eventually turned up, allowing Sandi and Emile to be the best-dressed safari tourists ever seen on the savannah.

Sandi said the insurance bill for her case would have been $100,000. "Well, I did have to buy some new dresses," she explained. Emile was wearing blue velvet slip-on shoes with a faux royal crest stitched in gold thread on the toe.[87]

Arnold will not be forgotten by his true family, nor by his many friends. The problems which stemmed from his kidney disease meant that, during his later years especially, he suffered enormous deprivation. The family is acutely aware that many others also suffer with kidney disease. As a contribution towards a better life for some of those people, and as a lasting memorial to Arnold in the city where he was born, in July 2011 Arnold's surviving son, Gavin, and I jointly made a donation to the renal unit of Groote Schuur Hospital, Cape Town. We wanted to support South African healthcare, and we thought the best way we could do that was by providing essential medical equipment for the treatment of patients with kidney failure.

Gavin said at the time we made our commitment, "This is deeply personal for our entire family. We are all acutely aware – from our own personal experience in supporting my father through his many battles with kidney disease – just how critical equipment is to the provision not just of healthcare, but of hope, for patients with acute and chronic renal failure, and indeed for their families."

[87] *The Spectator*, 29 March 2008.

Bea and I have also made a commitment in London to support the treatment of kidney disease, this time as it affects children. For some years, we have been members of the Tick Tock Club at the world-famous Great Ormond Street Children's Hospital. Amongst other things, we have been supporting the development of a new children's kidney centre. Great Ormond Street is already a major centre for kidney transplant and for renal treatment of all kinds. The hospital cares for one in five of those children in the UK who suffer from life-limiting kidney conditions and treats premature babies as well as children in their late teens. The centre is extending the Hospital's wonderful and pioneering research into severe kidney conditions, and is developing new and better ways of treating such problems – even of preventing them in the first place. Arnold would have been proud to be associated with this work.

MONTY HUNDLEY'S TRIAL

Brett had elected to plead guilty, and had thus de-coupled himself from the fate which was awaiting Monty Hundley, Sanford Freedman, Jim Cutler and Howard Zukerman, whose trial date was approaching apace. I had been advised to take a close interest in those court proceedings. For good or ill, there could well be implications for me.

I knew that it was in my best interests for the four men to be defended properly, but I was at the same time forced to recognise that none of the four, despite their lifestyles, was capable of affording decent criminal defence attorneys for a trial set to last for many weeks. Reluctantly, the family picked up the tab for all of them, taking the view that it was ultimately in my best interests for them to be properly defended. Thus it was that, including my own team, the family ended up paying for no fewer than five very expensive legal teams. Even a major corporation might wince at such a thought. To a family, it was painful in the extreme.

The trial of Monty Hundley, Sanford Freedman, Jim Cutler and Howard Zukerman began on 4 November 2003 and ran for three months. Three months might make this sound as though it was a long trial. Given the complexity of the allegations, however, and given just how many charges there were against the four of them, my own view is that the trial was nothing like as long as it should have been. Many of the central issues were barely considered at all. There was a great deal which should have been examined, but very little actually was.

Monty's abject failure to file tax returns over many years had been the very reason there had been any sort of investigation in the first place. With justification, I could have screamed at Monty for his stupidity, and for his total disregard for others, whom he had succeeded in putting in harm's way with him. But I made just one observation about the charges of personal tax evasion which had been laid against him and other defendants. Given the cavalier attitude that they had displayed towards filing returns and paying tax, it was clear to me that they could expect little sympathy from a jury of New York tax-payers. It soon became evident that I was not alone in that view. The defendants and their attorneys had clearly formed a similar assessment of the challenge ahead. Together they ran an extraordinarily faint-hearted defence, notwithstanding the flimsy nature of many of the allegations which they were facing.

My own attorneys, Chris Todd and Jim Webster, attended much of the trial, and they talked extensively to the defence teams outside court. Their detailed reports of events, taken together with the transcripts of each day's proceedings, gave me a very clear picture as to what was going on. Within days, it became obvious that the strategy of the defence teams was to offer no substantive rebuttal of the allegations.

When the time came, not one of the defendants elected themselves to give evidence, and none of the central allegations concerning the handling of bank debt was ever examined with help from expert witnesses. This was a conscious and deliberate choice on the part of the attorneys acting for Hundley, Freedman, Cutler and Zukerman. Experts had been identified, and a vast amount of preparatory work had been done, but they and their work were never deployed. The jury ended up hearing what was, in effect, one side of the argument only. In my view, this was madness, not to mention an enormous waste of money.

It would be wrong to attempt to explain in any sort of detail what happened at the trial. Not only would it make uninteresting reading, any attempt at an abridgement of the transcripts would run the risk of misrepresenting what the jury actually heard. In a nutshell, the trial proved to have very little directly to do with me. Stanley Tollman was barely mentioned, as an analysis of the transcripts shows. But, despite the fact that I was not only not there, nor barely even mentioned during the trial, I was once again roundly and publicly condemned at the close of the trial, as you will soon see. For this reason alone, and to allow readers to judge for themselves, I would like to take the opportunity to say a few words about what

was *not* said at Monty's trial, and of the implications of all of this
for yours truly.

Bear in mind that it was now late 2003. The US Attorney claimed
that, over a period of nine years between 1988 and 1997, I had
committed a number of offences. (By 2003, some of the alleged
offences were purported to have taken place fifteen years earlier.)
Specifically:

> – it was alleged that I had conspired to conceal my assets
> from the banks [88];
> – it was alleged that I had benefited from the cancellation
> of debt, and that I had failed to disclose to the IRS the
> 'gain' I had received from the cancellation of debt;
> – and it was alleged that I had misrepresented the
> relationship between Tollman-Hundley and certain third-
> party entities, and which were in reality 'sham' entities.

Let's begin by looking at the allegation that I had conspired to
conceal my assets from the banks. It is true that information was
provided to certain banks, and that this clearly purported to represent
a statement of my assets. This is undeniable. But remember, I had no
day-to-day responsibilities at Tollman-Hundley, and no-one at the
company reported to me. My role was merely as non-executive
financier and strategic advisor. I was unaware that anyone was
producing 'statements of my assets'. Unsurprisingly therefore, I
made no contribution to this process. I never reviewed what was
being submitted, much less approved it. Notwithstanding my
remoteness, I understand that these statements were in some cases
signed with my name, but by other people.

It is important to remember, however, that at this time the only
significant assets which I owned were Tollman-Hundley assets. After
the Court Hotels disaster, the only assets which I held in my own
name were those which stemmed from Tollman-Hundley, and the
records for those were held by the company. The idea, therefore, that
the management of Tollman-Hundley would produce a statement of
my own assets was not so unlikely.

---

[88] Bank of America, Marine Midland Bank, First National Bank of Chicago,
National Westminster Bank and Chemical Bank.

With the benefit of hindsight, it did not, though, help matters that I had allowed a pattern of working to develop at Tollman-Hundley which was less thorough than perhaps it should have been. I explained earlier in the book that I was only an infrequent visitor to the Tollman-Hundley offices. But although I myself may not have been in the offices often, the business was nevertheless continuously engaged in countless transactions and procedures which generated vast amounts of paperwork.

I, of course, did not have time to read these documents in detail, and I routinely signed things without being able to read them properly, or at all. Others became aware of this and, for convenience, often sent me only the signature pages of contracts. These I was asked to sign, even though I never saw any of the other pages of the contracts. Shocking though I suspect that this admission will be to some people, I defy anyone to confirm with honesty that they have always read every word of every contract they have ever put their name to. For instance, have you ever met anybody who has *truthfully* ticked the box to confirm that they had read all the 'Terms & Conditions'? Of course you haven't. At Tollman-Hundley, however, I accept that things went too far, especially when that involved other people signing in my name.

I can imagine how the statements of personal assets were produced. And I can also understand how and why the authors of those statements believed that they were merely going through the motions. As far as they were concerned, they were responding to yet more requests from the banks for information upon which few people, if indeed anyone, would ever rely.

And I can see why, after the event, others could look at such statements and say that they were fundamentally untruthful. I say this because not everyone understood that I had restructured my financial arrangements long ago. Many of the assets which others believed were mine, and which they felt therefore should have been disclosed, in reality belonged to other family members and to trusts. As I have explained, my principal asset was my investment in Tollman-Hundley, and this was now worth very little indeed. A true statement of the affairs of Stanley Stephen Tollman around this time would have included some near-worthless assets and a whole load of liabilities. For long periods, I was unquestionably insolvent.

But what was being said to the banks at the time, and what the banks had understood by what they had heard, was a complete mystery to me. The only possible exemption to this general rule – and a partial exemption at that – was the Chemical Bank, and that was because I had met them, unlike all the others. The meetings with the Chemical Bank were unique, in that I do not believe I attended any other meeting with Tollman-Hundley's lenders. I didn't have a clue as to whether others thought I was as rich as Croesus or as poor as a church mouse. I didn't even know what these people looked like.

All I knew was that no-one appeared to be asking me to cough up personally for anything. I took comfort in this. It was clear to me that all the banks had taken a view. They had recognised that all concerned, lender and borrower alike, were in the same mess. In many ways this was different from the Court Hotels fiasco, and we were certainly not being treated with similar contempt by our bankers. Tough they may have been, but they were also realistic. A chill had descended over corporate America. We were all in it together.

At the centre of the trial of Monty and the others was the Earnout which had been negotiated as part of the sale to HFS of Days Inn of America. Something which had been negotiated in 1991 was now being examined in a Manhattan courthouse after the passage of 12 years, and with all the distortion which hindsight guarantees. When the Earnout had been signed, it was thought by everyone to be of very little value. The deal had required both Monty and me to stick around and carry on working, but it had given us a modest hope of recovering something after a completely disastrous episode. Most commentators had made the correct assessment that the targets enshrined within the Earnout could only be attained through a great deal of effort. And, even if we did work hard, the reward was expected to be small beer. But modest though that reward may have been, it made all the difference between my staying and my going.

When the Chemical Bank had tried to lay out a set of rules for me they got my immediate response – simple and direct. "I don't need this. I am going back to London in order to work on our family business." Once I had made my position clear, as I explained earlier, the Bank's attitude towards me had changed, and they never again took me for granted. One of the Chemical Bank's managers, Dwight Arnesen, who – unlike his colleagues – was a thoroughly unpleasant man, admitted in the witness box that he had known about the Earnout Agreement in December 1991. He went on to say that he had discussed it with his colleague Thomas Kozlark and had recommended that the Earnout be included in the asset pool. He had, however, been overruled by his superiors at Chemical Bank, and it had been accepted that the Earnout would not be included in the asset pool for the Creditor Repayment Agreement (CRA).

Arnesen's admission proved that the banks had not only known of the existence of the HFS stock, but had accepted that the Earnout was going to be excluded from the CRA. The Government argued that the Earnout had been excluded fraudulently, and that we had gone as far as to keep its existence hidden from the banks. Both points were demonstrably untrue. The detail of the Earnout was fully documented, and properly reported at the time of the bankruptcy of Days Inn. It was also extensively publicised in the press.

The bankruptcy filing of Days Inn of America, and its eventual sale to HFS, took place during the very period within which the banks were negotiating the CRA with Bob Manzo. Tollman-Hundley was under the magnifying glass, and every single one of the company's banks was certain to have known about the sale of Days Inn. The Earnout Agreement was part of the public record for the Days Inn bankruptcy proceeding. And even if the banks had not read the bankruptcy filings themselves, under the CRA, Chemical Bank had a fiduciary obligation to share information about the Earnout Agreement's existence with every single member of the syndicate.

Besides, the Earnout was widely reported in the financial press. *The Wall Street Journal, Washington Post* and *Forbes Magazine* were amongst those papers to record it. For example, the report in the Washington Post included the following:[89]

Hospitality Franchise's Days Inn Package Is No Suite Deal

...Tollman and Hundley, the people who put the chain on the road to a bankruptcy court filing, do nicely too. Their agreement with Hospitality releases them from personal guarantees of $19.2 million of past-due franchise fees if all goes well, and they can get almost 1.8 million Hospitality shares, worth $28 million if this offer flies. Creditors have blessed all this, but I don't know why. To keep Tollman and Hundley off the bread lines, Hospitality also pays them each $375,000 a year for part-time consulting, an hourly rate of more than $500.

A substantial article, covering two pages and illustrated with three photographs, appeared in *Forbes Magazine*.[90] Under the headline Triple Dipper, it said:

Wonder why junk bonds have such a bad name? Just look at how Henry Silverman and his friends got rich while the bondholders of Days Inn lost their shirts. Too much debt and a weak economy drove the 1,200-unit motel chain into bankruptcy.

HENRY SILVERMAN has played Days Inn of America, an Atlanta franchisor of a chain of 1,200 moderately priced ($40 a night) motels, about as shrewdly as it could be played. A familiar sight on the highways of America, Days Inn has been a gold mine for Henry Silverman, 51, a fast-moving buyer and seller of companies, and his investors.

Twice in less than a decade, Silverman has bought Days Inn and twice he has sold it. By, in effect, arbitraging between the debt markets and the equity markets, between private markets and public markets, Silverman has already made a tidy profit of $126 million for his backers and for himself out of this humdrum motel company. Now Silverman is trying to buy Days Inn again...

89 *Washington Post*, 15 September 1992. Author: Allan Sloan.
90 *Forbes Magazine*, 25 November 1991. Author: Howard Rudnitsky.

... *In November 1989, Silverman and his backers turned around and sold the company to one of its biggest franchisees, Tollman-Hundley Lodging's Stanley Tollman and Monty Hundley. Boasts Silverman: "We acquired our shares at $2 and sold them [to Tollman-Hundley] at $11.78." All told, the Reliance Capital partnership investors made almost $60 million. Silverman personally made about $5 million.*

The deal was a typical Drexel Burnham leveraged financing – done with thin equity, with the junk holders taking most of the risk. Tollman and Hundley put in $8 million cash and guaranteed two years' interest on one loan to finance a $765 million deal, including assumption of the existing Days Inn debt. Good timing, because Drexel's ability to hawk product was fast eroding. "If the sale had been the following year," admits Silverman, "we'd have been in deep yogurt." As it turned out, the junk holders and the new buyers landed in the soup. The junk bond market and Drexel Burnham collapsed, blocking a badly needed refinancing. Then the hotel business slumped as the economy weakened. The overleveraged deal collapsed, and by September 1991 the company filed for Chapter 11.

Back in January 1990 Silverman had moved on to become a partner in Peter Peterson's Blackstone Capital Partners. Blackstone was flush with $850 million raised to restructure busted buyouts and do other deals. Aha! Busted hotel chains. Through Blackstone's Hospitality Franchise Systems, Silverman bought Ramada and Howard Johnson from ailing Prime Motor Inns in June 1990 for $169 million. About a year later Silverman formally offered to buy Days Inn out of bankruptcy for $250 million – less than half what Tollman-Hundley paid for it two years ago. If approved by the bankruptcy court and if no higher bid comes forth, creditors with $280 million of unsecured claims against the company would get 25 cents on the dollar, in cash and convertible preferred shares. The deal would also give some hapless Tollman-Hundley Lodging's bondholders about 15 cents on the dollar.

The unlucky buyers, Tollman and Hundley, don't fare as badly as one might expect. They still own 41 Days Inn motels, which are not tied up in the bankruptcy, and they stand to get $1.85 million each in consulting fees over the next five years. The two partners would also *receive stock worth about $17 million in five years, if they can deliver $27.5 million in franchise fees to the chain's new owners over the same period.*

And, of course, Henry Silverman and Reliance came out fine. Just fine.

At the trial, evidence relating to the Earnout was also given by Martin Edelman, an attorney at Battle Fowler, the firm which had advised Tollman-Hundley throughout the negotiation of the Earnout. In testimony, Edelman confirmed that it had not been possible to know with any degree of certainty what the Earnout would eventually be worth. He testified that there had been discussions of a 'ballpark figure' at the time of the deal, but that the highest estimated future value of which he had been aware was $15-20 million. He also said that this figure had been considered as a remote possibility only. Moreover, if the economy had not improved in the early 90s, the Earnout would have been worth nothing at all. In 1990/92, nobody could have been certain that the Earnout Agreement would ultimately have *any* value at all. In the end, there proved to be significant value in the HFS stock, against all predictions. More importantly, though, the banks had all known precisely what was going on throughout.

Perhaps the most telling piece of evidence, though, was that Chemical Bank, Tollman-Hundley's most significant lender, did not just *know* about the HFS deal, Chemical Bank had themselves formulated the HFS deal. Of course they knew about the deal. They had created it!

In December 1997 – after the Earnout had concluded – Henry Silverman had merged HFS with CUC International and had created the Cendant Corporation. It was with a Cendant title that former HFS executive James Buckman, now Senior Vice President and General Counsel, Cendant Corporation, gave evidence at the trial. As part of his testimony, he acknowledged that an amendment to the HFS registration statement dated 19 June 1993 represented a general disclosure of the Earnout Agreement. Everyone would have known all about it. And he also confirmed that the final prospectus disclosed both the Earnout Agreement and specifically the number of shares that Bryanston was selling at the time of that offering. And from the time it went public, HFS made quarterly as well as annual filings, in which there was complete disclosure.

The product of a $14 billion 'merger of equals', Henry Silverman had combined a franchising powerhouse in HFS with a membership-club giant in CUC International. In this way, Cendant Corporation was created. Henry was to find though that things at CUC were not as he had imagined. As a commentator later said, Henry had bought 'a pig in a poke'. False accounting at CUC International had inflated revenues over three years by a staggering half billion dollars. Henry said at the time, "The premium success story of the 1990s was HFS. We blew it up with this transaction. I feel like a schmuck." Cendant was broken up and sold and, since 2009, Henry has been Chief Operating Officer of Apollo Global Management, a New York-based private equity firm. Apollo's Chief Executive is none other than Leon Black, a long-time friend of Henry's and one of the key figures in Drexel Burnham Lambert, where he had been the co-head of Corporate Finance.

The second charge which had been laid at my door was the allegation that I had benefited from Cancellation of Debt (COD), and that I had failed to disclose to the IRS the 'gain' which I had received from that cancellation. I am not going to attempt to rehearse tax law within this book. Not only am I not qualified to do so, I can think of few things likely to be more boring. I will, though, explain the circumstances which led up to this allegation. And I will also pass on the views of others, not to mention the views of the jury which decided the outcome of Monty's trial.

Readers of this book who live outside the United States need to understand that in the US, when a loan liability is cancelled, the borrower is deemed to have received a taxable benefit. That borrower should then file an IRS Form called a 1099, disclosing this taxable benefit, and treating it as though it were part of their gross income.

I recognise that if one borrows money, and the lender of that money chooses to cancel or forgive that debt, one should include the value of a cancelled debt as though it were income. But the deficiency notes which Monty and I had signed did not reflect borrowings which had been extended to the two of us. We had merely provided personal guarantees which stood behind some of the corporate borrowings of Tollman-Hundley. As a final port of call, the lenders might have been able to come to us for monies. But things had never got to that stage and, personally, I was never asked by the banks for so much as a nickel. This was not an unexpected outcome.

Neither directly nor indirectly had I received so much as a brass farthing from the loans which had supported Tollman-Hundley. When the debts were cancelled and my guarantees released, my personal receipts were not affected in the slightest – positively or negatively. I had received no benefit from these cancellations, and there was nothing for me to disclose to the IRS. To allege that I had somehow received a gain was an inventive concept, to say the least. It didn't persuade the tax advisors, nor any of the lawyers. And it was clear that the jury thought little of it too. In relation to the Cancellation of Debt charges, the jury acquitted every defendant.

It had also been alleged that I had been guilty of misrepresenting the relationship between Tollman-Hundley and the third parties which bought the deficiency notes at a discount. These, the US Attorney alleged, were in fact 'sham' entities only, and the banks had thus been defrauded – conned into selling their debt at a fraction of its true worth.

It is true that the banks had agreed to sell certain elements of the outstanding Tollman-Hundley indebtedness to third parties. But these debts had, in their entirety, already been written off by the banks. Any payment at all therefore represented a real upside for the banks, however inadequate it may have looked to the outside world. Most of the deficiency notes were bought for something in the order of 15 cents on the dollar. But 15 cents was a great deal better than nothing. In reality, this was rather like a 'clearance sale' in which dead stock is disposed of swiftly, and cheaply, with the aim of realising a little cash.

At the time these deficiency notes were sold to third parties, Monty and I had been required to sign statements which recognised the terms of these sales – that the monies were coming from third parties, and not from Monty and me. This was required for a very simple reason. The banks had to be sure that, whatever happened, they would be able to hang on to the money that they were receiving for these notes. They were fearful that Monty would be made bankrupt, and they needed to protect themselves against having to return the money in such an event. If Monty had filed for bankruptcy protection, they were fearful of the bankruptcy trustee's ability to void what might be viewed as 'preference payments'. In other words, if Monty had chosen to file for bankruptcy, and if there was any suggestion that the monies had come from Monty himself, that could well have been followed by a demand on the banks to return the money, lest this repayment be in any way considered to have been preferential. The banks needed these statements for their own future protection, and for no other reason.

The truth was that the banks simply didn't care who had produced the funds for the discounted purchase of the deficiency notes. Prior to the sale of these notes, with the exception of the Bank of America, every bank had written off the deficiency notes and they were no longer carried on the banks' balance sheets as assets. These losses had, moreover, been offset against tax.

Any recovery, therefore, from any source whatsoever, was looked at as a victory for those in the banks' bad debt departments who were responsible for selling the deficiency notes. Not one of the banks has ever filed a civil complaint for bank fraud against me, nor against Monty, nor against any of the other defendants prosecuted alongside Monty. Indeed, a number of the banks freely admitted that they sold the deficiency notes knowing that the information with which they had been provided was unreliable. Let me explain.

It was always believed that I was the brains behind the entities which bought the deficiency notes. Not true. I had nothing to do with the establishment of either Paternoster Holdings or Chelsea Acquisitions. Having explored a number of possible alternatives with third party investors, Monty came up with the idea of the deficiency notes being acquired by vehicles created for that purpose. And, with this in mind, Monty had approached two people who were very well known to me – even though he did not consider it necessary to involve me in the process.

The two people to whom Monty had spoken were my brother, Arnold, and my former business partner, Ken Bates. Although, as I wrote earlier, I was aware that Monty intended to approach Arnold about something – although he never said what – I had absolutely no idea until long after the event that he had involved Ken too.

When Monty had called me one day and asked me whether Arnold would like to make some money, and I had replied, "Why don't you ask him yourself?" it seems he had done just that. In time, I discovered that this call had led to the formation of Paternoster Holdings, of which Arnold was a director, and which was one of the two key entities which acquired the Tollman-Hundley deficiency notes.

Unbeknownst to me, Monty had also phoned Ken Bates. Through me, Monty had developed something of a relationship with Ken, and had been invited by Ken on occasion to matches at Chelsea. Ken even viewed Monty as a key member of what Ken described as the New York Chapter of the Chelsea Supporters' Club. I remember Monty and me having lunch with Ken in 1984 at the wonderful Pierre Martin restaurant, La Croisette, in Ifield Road, before watching a football match at Fulham, who were playing host that day to Manchester City. Additionally, Ken, Monty and I had jointly owned a property in Orlando, Florida called the Caravan Hotel. Ken had paid $130,000 for 10% of this investment, and Monty and I had held the balance between us.

At some point in the past, Ken had felt sufficiently close to Monty to be able to ask a favour. He had approached him, asking him to sponsor a signing-on fee for a player at Chelsea. Although Monty had agreed to do this for Ken, for some reason the favour was ultimately not required. Nevertheless, Monty felt able in return to ask Ken for something. In much the same way as he had put it to Arnold, Monty asked Ken whether he would stand behind a new venture which would acquire some of the deficiency notes.

The two resulting ventures were hardly secretive in the manner in which they were named – Paternoster Holdings after Arnold's home town, and Chelsea Acquisitions after Ken's most famous football investment. The requisite paperwork for both entities was put together by Sanford Freeman and the share certificates, which I was later to see, reflected the involvement of both Arnold and Ken. It was something of a surprise to a number of people to hear that Ken felt able not only to claim in Monty's trial that he had *not* been involved with the establishment of Chelsea Acquisitions but that he had *never* had an investment in the United States.

I had never been aware at all of the negotiations with the banks leading up to the sale of their deficiency notes to Paternoster Holdings and Chelsea Acquisitions, with one exception. I was attending one of the very rare meetings with the Chemical Bank, and was surprised to find my brother Arnold standing outside the meeting room. Given that Arnold was not himself involved with Tollman-Hundley, but with the travel businesses, this was odd to say the least.

It was explained to me that the Chemical Bank had asked to meet the person behind Paternoster Holdings, and Arnold was there for that reason. But the bank had apparently lost interest in seeing him, and Arnold was never asked to join the meeting.

It was clear to everyone that the banks did not care about the source of the money which they were receiving in exchange for the deficiency notes. They were ready and willing to sell for cents on the dollar, and I suspect they would have dealt with the devil if they felt he was good for the money. The banks had written off the deficiency notes, no longer viewing them as assets on the banks' balance sheets. The written-off debt had then been assigned to each bank's bad debt department and these departments viewed any sort of recovery at all on the deficiency notes as a successful result.

The trial ended during the first week of February 2004. Despite the complexity of the allegations and the weeks of evidence to which they had listened, the New York jury was swift to reach verdicts in relation to each of the 34 counts facing the defendants. In simple terms, the jury acquitted on everything to do with cancellation of debt, the technical definition of which was 'Conspiracy to Commit Mail Fraud', and found guilty in relation to most of the rest.

The US Attorney's version of the convictions was set out in a press release:[91]

HOTELIER AND THREE EXECUTIVES CONVICTED IN U.S. COURT IN $100 MILLION-DOLLAR BANK FRAUD

David N. Kelley, the United States Attorney for the Southern District of New York, announced that Monty D. Hundley, a principal of a major United states hotel chain, was convicted yesterday in Manhattan federal court of masterminding a scheme that defrauded a dozen creditors out of nearly $100 million dollars, following a three-month trial before the United States District Court Judge Loretta A. Preska. Three former senior executives of the company were also convicted for their roles in the scheme.

Hundley was one of two principals of Tollman-Hundley Hotels, a group of companies that at its peak owned, managed, and operated more than 100 hotels throughout the United States and he was also one of the former owners of Days Inn of America, the parent company of the Days Inn hotel chain.

*The three former executives of Tollman-Hundley Hotels convicted were Executive Vice President and General Counsel Sanford Freedman, Chief Financial Officer James Cutler, and Vice President of Finance Howard Zukerman. Hundley's business partner and alleged co-conspirator, **Stanley Tollman**, is a fugitive.*

*According to the Indictment and the evidence presented at trial, throughout the 1980s and 1990s, Hundley and **Tollman** built a series of companies that owned and managed more than 100 hotels. The growth of those companies came about largely through borrowing of hundreds of millions of dollars from and through various financial institutions, including Chemical Bank, National Westminster Bank, First*

National Bank of Chicago, Marine Midland, and Security Pacific (now Bank of America)("the Defrauded Financial Institutions").

Hundley and **Tollman** *personally guaranteed many of these loans. In the early 1990s, many of their hotel properties failed to repay these loans, and, following a restructuring, Hundley and* **Tollman** *signed deficiency notes making themselves personally liable to their creditors, including the Defrauded Financial Institutions, for approximately $100 million. According to the evidence at trial, at around the same time, Hundley and* **Tollman** *sold Days Inn of America to Hospitality Franchise Systems ("HFS"), the predecessor of Cendant. In connection with that sale, Hundley and* **Tollman** *entered into an earnout agreement with HFS, entitling them personally to more than a million shares of HFS stock under certain circumstances. Pursuant to that agreement, between 1993 and 1995 Hundley and* **Tollman** *received and sold more than a hundred million dollars worth of HFS stock.*

Rather than use the proceeds of the HFS stock sale to repay their creditors in full, the evidence at trial showed that Hundley and **Tollman**, *with the assistance of Freedman, Cutler and Zukerman, instead pulled off a massive fraud. The conspirators (1) falsely represented to Hundley and* **Tollman***'s creditors that Hundley and* **Tollman** *were broke and lacked the means to repay their debts; and (2) duped the creditors into selling those debts, at a steep discount, to purportedly unrelated third parties who, the evidence showed, were in fact sham entities controlled and funded by Hundley and* **Tollman**.

To convince the banks that **Tollman** *and Hundley were broke, the evidence at trial showed that the defendants made various false oral and written statements to the banks, including providing the banks with financial statements and schedules which omitted numerous substantial assets of Hundley and* **Tollman**, *including:*

(1) the $100 million from the sale of HFS stock;

(2) **Tollman***'s multimillion dollar homes in* **Palm Beach***,* **Florida***,* **485 Park Avenue** *in Manhattan,* **New Preston***,* **Connecticut***, and* **London***,* **England***;*

(3) Hundley's multimillion dollar home in Bedford, New York; and

(4) **Tollman** *and Hundley's ownership interests in various*

businesses they controlled, including Alpha Hospitality, a publicly traded gaming company.

*To convince the banks that the purported third parties offering to purchase the debts were real, the evidence at trial showed, Hundley and **Tollman**, with the assistance of Freedman, Cutler and Zukerman, falsely represented to the Defrauded Financial Institutions that they had found a group of "European investors" willing to purchase the debt from the Defrauded Financial Institutions, at a steep discount (typically 10% of the face value of the debt). Hundley and **Tollman** thereafter identified two companies that they secretly controlled – Paternoster Holdings, and Chelsea Acquisitions Inc. – as the companies through which these unnamed European investors purportedly would purchase the debt. The evidence at trial showed there were no European investors; instead, Paternoster and Chelsea were straw entities controlled by Hundley and **Tollman**, and Paternoster and Chelsea purchased the debt largely with the proceeds of the sale of HFS stock that Hundley and **Tollman** had hidden from their creditors. In certain transactions, Hundley, **Tollman**, Freedman, Cutler and Zukerman enlisted a New York businessman, James Cohen, to pose as the representative of the "European investors" supposedly financing Paternoster and Chelsea, and pretend to negotiate with the Defrauded Financial Institutions on their behalf. In truth, Hundley and **Tollman**, directly and through Freedman and Zukerman, dictated to Cohen, their co-conspirator, his negotiating positions. The evidence also showed that Hundley, **Tollman**, and Freedman allegedly arranged for business associates of **Tollman** and family relations of **Tollman** who did not share **Tollman**'s last name to sign contracts and other documents for Paternoster and Chelsea. In many of the contracts, the family relations expressly represented, falsely, that Paternoster and Chelsea were truly separate entities, not controlled or beneficially owned by Hundley and **Tollman**. In certain transactions, Hundley and **Tollman** themselves also specifically represented, falsely, that they had no financial interest in Paternoster and Chelsea, or that they were not funding Paternoster's purchase of their debt.*

The evidence at trial established that between 1993 and 1996, the *conspirators persuaded the Defrauded Financial Institutions and certain other creditors to sell more than $100 million in **Tollman** and Hundley's personal debt to Paternoster and Chelsea for less than $10 million.*

*The jury also convicted defendant Freedman of perjury for giving false testimony in a deposition relating to a bankruptcy case. The evidence at trial showed that one of Hundley and **Tollman**'s creditors became suspicious of whether Paternoster was truly an independent entity from Hundley and **Tollman**, and attempted to investigate that subject during a bankruptcy proceeding by, among other things, questioning Freedman under oath at a deposition. The evidence at trial showed that during the deposition, Freedman lied in an effort to create the false impression that Paternoster was a legitimate third party, rather than a pawn, controlled by Hundley and **Tollman**.*

In addition to the bank fraud scheme described above, the jury also convicted defendants Hundley and Cutler of participating in a separate, decade-long conspiracy to defraud the IRS by causing the Tollman/Hundley companies to fail to report to the IRS more than $29 million in compensation paid to a dozen Tollman/Hundley employees during the 1990s. The evidence revealed that for certain senior executives at the Tollman/Hundley companies, the companies simply chose not to issue W2s or 1099s reporting their compensation to the IRS, and that for other executives and employees, the companies issued W2s or 1099s reflecting only a portion of their true income.

The jury also convicted Hundley of numerous personal tax charges: income tax evasion for the tax years 1994 and 1995, failure to file timely tax returns for the tax years 1994 and 1995, and filing false tax returns for the years 1995-1999.

The evidence at trial showed that Hundley – who received no W2s or 1099s from his companies – owed more than $2 million in taxes for 1994 and more than $1 million in taxes for 1995, but failed to file a timely return in either year. Indeed, the evidence at trial showed that Hundley failed to file any personal income tax returns from at least 1974 until the start of this investigation in 1996. The evidence further showed *that upon learning he was under criminal investigation, Hundley for the years 1995 through 1999 filed tax returns which falsely denied his ownership of a secret bank account in Guernsey, the Channel Islands.*

The jury also convicted defendant Cutler of two counts of tax evasion, for the tax years 1994 and 1995, for failing to report tens of thousands of dollars in "consulting fees" he received from the Tollman/Hundley companies for which no 1099s or W2s were issued.

Defendant Zukerman was previously prosecuted for his own tax crimes in the Eastern District of New York, where, in 2000, Zukerman pled guilty to failing to file tax returns at a time he was earning more than $150,000 per year for which no 1099s or W2s were issued by the Tollman/Hundley companies.

*Brett Tollman, the son of the fugitive **Stanley Tollman**, pled guilty on September 5, 2003, to participating in the conspiracy not to report to the IRS the true compensation paid to Tollman/Hundley executives and employees and to a separate tax evasion scheme involving millions of dollars in income not reported to the IRS earned from the Tollman family company Trafalgar Tours.*

Assistant United States Attorneys Peter G. Neiman, Justin S. Weddle, John P. Collins Jr. and Stanley J. Okula are in charge of the prosecution.

As you can see, I have emboldened all the references to my name in the US Attorney's press release. My name appeared no fewer than 32 times, exactly the same number of times that Monty Hundley's name was mentioned! Remember, Monty was a defendant in this trial. Monty was there. Much of the testimony was about him. And Monty was convicted. Stanley Tollman was not only not there, my name was hardly mentioned. It was difficult to see how a press release purporting to be fair account of proceedings could possibly be drafted in that way. It was yet another example of prejudicial behaviour by those responsible for the protection of justice. To add insult to injury, at the end of a 1,500-word press release from which any reader could only conclude that I was one of the guiltiest people on the planet, the US Attorney had simply added the following words:

The charges contained in the Indictment are merely accusations as to Stanley Tollman and he is presumed innocent unless and until proven guilty.

Sadly, it would seem that lip-service only is paid to the presumption of innocence in modern-day America. In the case of this press release, the concluding words, to extend the analogy, were merely lipstick for the gorilla.

With the trial now over, Okula then sought to portray me as the evil mastermind who had managed to slip the net. Notwithstanding this, even after the conclusion of Monty's trial, the guilty verdicts against the four defendants and the various press releases of the US Attorney, not one single bank ever attempted to recover the money which Okula always maintained had been stolen from them. That the banks did not attempt to do this speaks volumes – a much more powerful piece of evidence as far as I am concerned than anything which was presented to the jury.

I spoke at that time, and have spoken subsequently, to people with huge experience of dealing with the workout departments of banks. The universal assessment of these people has been that the banks knew full well what was happening. And, although they may not have been exactly delirious with joy, they were certainly content. This was not a group which considered it had been defrauded.

It was to be more than a year later before Monty was sentenced, Judge Preska seeing fit to send him to prison for eight years, and ordering him to pay $111.4 million in restitution. She also also entered a forfeiture order against him in the amount of $44 million, which allowed the Government to seize Monty's assets. In the short term, that seizure gave the family some serious headaches, because we found ourselves in a business partnership with, of all people, Stanley Okula. Joy. But when, some years later, it came to settlement of the whole exercise, that seizure provided us with a very useful opportunity. But that is later.

However angry I may have been with Monty, I never wished incarceration on him. As I write this, Monty has already served his time, and I know that he is getting on with rebuilding his life.

EXTRADITION BEGINS

Because I had been indicted by the US Department of Justice, my lawyers in Britain prepared for what was likely to arrive soon – a request from the United States for my extradition. Colin Passmore wrote to the authorities in London responsible for extradition matters, informing them that Simmons & Simmons were instructed to act for me. If any request were to be made for the extradition of Stanley Tollman, the authorities now knew whom to approach.

As expected, on 18 March 2003, Colin was informed that, by way of Diplomatic Notes, the United States had made an extradition request for me. He was also informed that a similar request had been made for Bea. Each request was in accordance with the 1972 Extradition Treaty between the United Kingdom and the United States of America. Although it was no surprise at all that a request had been made for me, given that I had been indicted almost a year earlier, why on earth had Bea been included? After all, she had not been indicted. And it was impossible to imagine how she ever could be.

Colin wrote immediately to the Crown Prosecution Service and to the Extradition Unit of the Metropolitan Police telling them that, although Bea and I would defend ourselves against any extradition request, we would nevertheless make ourselves available to be arrested at any specified time and place. The CPS replied by return, agreeing that no provisional arrest would take place. Everything would be civilised.

The Crown Prosecution Service (CPS) acts on behalf of requesting states in extradition matters. It liaises closely with those making the requests, but the CPS has day-to-day management of the cases itself. This includes the selection and day-to-day instruction of the British barristers who will act for the state which makes the request, in our case the United States. Some would say surprisingly –

I would go as far as to say shockingly – the enormous costs involved in such matters are borne not by the requesting state itself, but by the UK public purse. The British taxpayer pays. How fair is that?

It was to be a further five months before we heard any more about the extradition. On 5 August 2003, the CPS wrote to confirm that it had now received the extradition requests themselves, under the Extradition Act 1989. We then waited.

The following month, Brett negotiated a plea bargain and, understandably, the focus of our attention switched across the Atlantic. For a while, our extradition fight was no longer front of mind. Nor had there been much about it by way of news. All we had heard was that the CPS had appointed a QC and a junior barrister to act for the US Government, both of whom were extremely well known to our own legal team.

Frank Chopin had originally hired what he described as the 'dream team' for me, which comprised Clive Nicholls QC, supported by James Lewis (who very shortly afterwards became a QC himself). The two of them were instructed by Colin Passmore of Simmons & Simmons. As we now knew that Bea would also require representation, we split the two Leading Counsel – Clive Nicholls QC continuing to act for me, and the now-elevated James Lewis QC for Bea. And we supported each with junior barristers. Clive was backed up by James Hines, and James Lewis by Hugo Keith. Clive, James Lewis, Hugo and James Hines were all barristers in the same chambers – Three Raymond Buildings, Grays Inn. But the barristers for the United States Government were also at Three Raymond Buildings, Grays Inn. This was a concept which many failed to comprehend. How could both sides of this battle co-exist under the same roof?

The junior barrister whom the CPS had chosen to act for the United States against us was a thoroughly decent man called John Hardy. I found it very difficult during the years which followed to dislike him, even though he was employed to ruin my life. But his was a professional duty only, and it was clearly nothing personal. However, the man who led John Hardy was a very different kettle of fish. I had no difficulty whatsoever in disliking the CPS's choice of senior counsel for the United States. This was a thoroughly unpleasant man called Alun Jones QC. During the period of the attempted extradition, Mr Jones was to become the one barrister of the six to be based elsewhere than at Three Raymond Buildings. In 2005, he left to found his own chambers in Great James Street.

In March 2004, Brett was sentenced, and the US Attorney took advantage of Brett's incarceration to announce the unsealing (making public) of a Complaint against Bea. This sealed complaint was to explain the reason why extradition requests had been made against both of us. With Brett beginning his prison sentence and with Bea's name formally in the frame too, things were hotting up still further. Or so we thought. However, against all expectations, on 19 April 2004 the United States Embassy informed the Foreign and Commonwealth Office in London that it wished to withdraw the requests for our extradition.

The first we heard about it was five days later, when John Hardy approached his Head of Chambers, Clive Nicholls, to say that the extradition requests for us had been withdrawn. This news was not only a bolt from the blue, it seemed far too good to be true. After all, it was only a month since the Complaint against Bea had been unsealed. And now the US Government was giving up? I did not believe it for a moment. And I was right not to believe it. The United States had not given up at all.

EXTRADITION – UNDER NEW RULES

By mid-2004, having spent the whole of our lives criss-crossing the globe, Bea and I had been obliged to spend more than two years living almost constantly in London. Some people were born to put down permanent roots. Bea and I were not. Wanderlust is in our blood. We of course had access to a comfortable home in London, and we were able to escape for the occasional weekend in the country. But we needed to be able to spread our wings a little.

When South African friends approached us at about this time and said that Bea and I should consider coming home for a few months, we listened. They said that the change of air and scenery would do us the world of good. I said that I would love to, but I did not want to get arrested at Johannesburg airport and find myself having to fight extradition from a base in South Africa. It was better that I fought from London. If I were to go to South Africa, I absolutely had to be certain that I would be able to get back to the UK.

Unconcerned by my response, our friends told us that certainty could be arranged. They said that we should allow them to approach the South African authorities on our behalf, and that they would get the whole thing pre-approved. In this way, we would get guaranteed safe passage into and then back out of the country. This could all be done in a fairly straightforward manner, and without fuss. Or so they told us.

We took them at their word, thanked them, and asked them to try, even though we were never quite sure how they intended to make this happen. I merely insisted that the whole thing be done legally and above board. It is clear that they took my instructions to heart, for one of their actions resulted in a completely open approach by the South African Government to the US Consulate General in Johannesburg.

I am not quite sure what the South African Government expected to receive by way of response from the United States to a credentials check made in respect of a federal indictee. Uncle Sam would not have been my ideal choice for character referee. Nevertheless, whatever the South Africans were expecting, it was not, I am sure, the shockwave which ricocheted from Johannesburg to Washington, then on to New York, then back to Washington and, finally, onwards to London.

There was, of course, absolutely nothing wrong with what was being attempted by friends on my behalf. Although I had been indicted two years earlier, I had also been told that the US Department of Justice had withdrawn its extradition requests. Why, therefore, could I not travel to South Africa for a few weeks? I was, after all, an innocent man, and surely able to act as I chose. But Okula and his colleagues did not see it that way. They assumed that Bea and I were about to flee, and to flee for good. They imagined that the South African Government would protect us through thick and thin. We were trying, or so they thought, to slip away under the radar.

Without warning, on 11 August 2004, the Metropolitan Police, acting on behalf of the United States, applied for warrants of arrest for both Bea and me. The police, pre-warned that we had legal representation in London, picked up the telephone. The elegant circumstances of this perfectly proper communication proved to me what a truly civilised society Britain is. The officer in charge had James Lewis' details, and called James on his mobile. James, who was playing tennis at the time, broke off from his game, and thus the process began. Bea and I were informed, and an appointment was made for us to go to a police station formally to be arrested a week later. The eye of the storm appeared to have passed over. Bea and I were back in the maelstrom once more.

As far as I am concerned, visiting Savile Row is something which normally involves an appointment with my tailor. Our visit to West End Central Police Station on 17 August 2004 may have been for very different reasons, but it was every bit as friendly and charming as a trip to Huntsman[92] might have been. A New York perp walk this most definitely wasn't. Even Bea, for whom this was an especially difficult experience, was put firmly at ease. Formalities over, we then went over

---

[92] Founded in the 19th Century, Huntsman is arguably the greatest of the Savile Row tailors.

to Bow Street Magistrates' Court for the start of proceedings – proceedings which were to last for well over three years.

For many years, Bow Street was Britain's best-known Magistrates' Court. Directly across the street from the Royal Opera House, amongst other things it housed the office of the Senior District Judge, Britain's top magistrate. Over time, Bow Street's high profile defendants had included Dr Crippen, the Krays, Oscar Wilde, Giacomo Casanova and the Suffragettes.

As Bea and I trod a similar path that day to our more famous and infamous predecessors, we were welcomed by court staff with a most unusual sales pitch. Would Bea and I like to buy the building? Bow Street Magistrates Court was up for sale, possibly for conversion to a hotel. They had heard that we were hoteliers. What about it? "Why don't you make them an offer?"

Bea and I thanked them for the opportunity, but explained that our hands were a little too full at the moment. We were then ushered into a surprisingly small and rather grubby courtroom. It was clear that little money had been spent on these facilities for many years. Bow Street was evidently being allowed to run down.

This was to be the first of many hearings at Bow Street Magistrates' Court in the matter of *United States of America – v – Stanley Tollman*. The building was finally closed two years later and was indeed sold off for conversion to a hotel.

This was also to be the first of a great many appearances in London courtrooms by the legal team representing us. Many of those hearings involved me too. However, whilst I myself may have been required to appear on numerous occasions, I am relieved to say that this was Bea's first and only appearance in a London court, for reasons I will later explain. The hearing was also the first opportunity I had to glimpse the barristers for the United States, and to observe the Senior District Judge, Tim Workman, in action.

Supporting us in the public gallery, which was in fact simply a dozen seats in a tiny area screened off from the court by thick glass, were a number of family members and friends. This group included Toni and Vicki, Mike Ness, and Vicki's soon-to-be-ex-husband,

Steve O'Hana. The hearing that day had to deal, amongst other things, with the question of bail. But bail was never really in doubt. I think that the only person who risked imminent incarceration that day was Steve O'Hana. His persistent use of a mobile phone in the visitors' gallery, despite repeated warnings, culminated in a notice being placed ten centimetres from his face telling him that unless he desisted he was risking a night in the cells.

The issue of bail was dealt with swiftly and elegantly, with our old friend Nicky Kerman standing surety for both Bea and me in the sum of just £50,000. Had I ever been in any doubt, this fact alone reassured me that London was the right place from which to mount our defence. Contrast the £50,000 guarantee-only which Nicky was required to lodge with the $25,000,000 which had been demanded by the United States in order to secure Brett's liberty.

Bail agreed, the first action of Counsel for the US Government was to seek an immediate adjournment of proceedings for 60 days in order to allow the receipt of papers from the United States. The decision to apply for our arrest may have been prompted by the South African enquiry, but it was clear that the United States was not yet ready to recommence the extradition proceedings. This adjournment was to set a pattern of behaviour by the United States. This was merely the first of many, many delays caused by the other side.

The most important part of the proceedings was the challenge made by both Clive Nicholls and James Lewis to the way in which the extradition requests were being viewed. They pointed out to the court that the request to extradite, having been initiated the previous year, should properly be governed by the 1989 Act – not, as the Court had been led to believe, by the Extradition Act 2003. This was an absolutely fundamental issue, one which would become central to the early stages of the extradition proceedings.

On 1 January 2004, a new extradition regime had been enacted in the UK, the Extradition Act 1989 being replaced by the Extradition Act 2003. Under the older act, prima facie evidence of a case to answer was required to be presented to the court. Under the new extradition arrangements, only a summary of the allegation by the prosecutor became necessary. If the 2003 Act were to be used, resisting our extradition would be infinitely more difficult for us. This was of course very, very important. Crucially, the rules by which the new act was implemented – its Commencement Provisions – stated expressly that the new Act would only apply to requests which were received by the United Kingdom after 1 January 2004. All existing requests would continue to be dealt with under the former Extradition Act. This was confirmed by no less a figure than Baroness Scotland who, in her capacity as Minister of State at the Home Office, told the House of Lords in 2003 that no existing cases would be transferred to the new arrangements:[93]

> *"The Government's position is that the new legislation should apply to all requests received after the point when the new Act comes into force. Therefore, if, as we hope, the new Act comes into force on 1st January 2004, a request received on 30th December 2003 will be handled under the 1989 Act procedure. A request received, for example, on 5th January 2004 will be handled under the new procedure.*
>
> *"The Government have decided that no existing cases will be transferred to the new arrangements and that all cases already in the system when the new Act comes into force will continue to be dealt with under the 1989 procedures. I hope that that statement is unequivocal and unambiguous."*

All cases in the system when the new Act came into force would continue to be dealt with under the 1989 procedures. It was crystal clear. And, with this in mind, it is worth spelling out the precise sequence of events.

On 18 March 2003, Simmons & Simmons was informed, by way of Diplomatic Notes, that the United States had made extradition requests for both Bea and me. Then, on 5 August 2003, the CPS wrote to confirm that it had now received the extradition requests themselves under the Extradition Act 1989. In other words, the United States' extradition requests for Bea and for me were commenced in 2003 under the Extradition Act 1989 and should have

93 Baroness Scotland, *Hansard*, 30 Oct 2003: Column 416.

been considered against that Act. But that would have required Okula to have produced evidence against us, something which would have given him very great difficulty indeed.

On 19 April 2004, the United States Embassy had informed the Foreign and Commonwealth Office in London that it wished to withdraw the request for Bea's and my extradition. Now, it seemed, Okula was trying again. And it was clear that he was trying to do so under the much less taxing arrangements of the new Act.

Okula was attempting to take advantage of new, slimlined legislation which had been introduced after years of treaty negotiation in order to speed up the process of extradition, and principally to assist the war against terrorism.

It had been almost three years since the events of 9/11, and the damage caused that fateful day had not been restricted to loss of life and harm to property. The world had accepted changes which affected us all. Few quibbled at the inconvenience of enhanced airport security, or were upset by increased surveillance. But changes in other areas were more questionable.

Even back then, there had been calls from various quarters for Parliament to review the grounds for permitting extradition. This would in time grow into a clamour. Indeed, as I write, there is a clear wish on the part of many parliamentarians to re-establish the authority of British courts and to restore safeguards which protect against unfair extradition. The now commonly-held opinion is that, in order to justify extradition, a requesting state should be required to produce *'evidence of the commissioning by the individual of the offence which is alleged'*. It is also considered by many that this evidence must then be tested and evaluated – independently and judicially. Sadly, this is not currently the case with extradition requests from the United States, nor those covered by European Arrest Warrants.

Irrespective of the quality and independence of the judicial system within the country seeking extradition, summary extradition should simply never take place. As you are about to discover, I have been through this process, and it is clear to me that it offends the basic precepts of human rights. In every case, there must be independent judicial assessment of the evidence against the accused. As a result of the current extradition arrangements, Britain is operating against double standards, a fact which is wholly unsatisfactory. In other matters, UK prosecuting authorities are required not only to consider the evidence in weighing up charges, but also the public interest. In relation to extradition, there is also no public interest test.

What's more, under the old Act, the Home Secretary had responsibility for exercising discretion. And the Home Secretary's decision was itself subject to judicial review, a further guarantee of protection to the individual, and a reassurance to all concerned that justice was at work. In the pursuit of speed, and hiding under the banner of the 'War on Terror', crucial safeguards were abandoned.

Whether I held any view at all about extradition before the events which I am about to describe took place, I can no longer remember. But if I did, they would not have been fully informed. I am now able to speak from personal experience, and from the perspective of a very lucky man who was eventually able to mount a defence which supposedly was no longer available. I will explain shortly.

The Unites States is unique in its extensive extra-territorial reach. This has been enshrined within its domestic legislation, and asserts that the United States' jurisdiction to prosecute beyond its borders is without restriction. In other words, America considers that it can legitimately pursue anyone, anywhere. The United States takes pride in its assertion that there is no hiding place from Uncle Sam. At the time I write this chapter, the vast majority of extradition cases in Britain which are currently causing concern are requests from the United States.

The new extradition treaty had been entered into with great haste, and had been adopted without full parliamentary scrutiny. The Extradition Act 2003 which resulted from that treaty stripped away many of the traditional protections in Britain against summary and unfair extradition. Under the 2003 Act, those who live in Britain could now be extradited without any requirement for a British court to be persuaded that there was any evidence at all against the accused, let alone that the evidence was sufficient to merit prosecution. Since the introduction of the new Act, a consensus has formed around the view that Britain has gone too far, and that its extradition arrangements, especially in relation to the United States, should be re-examined. It now seems that the House of Commons is preparing to do just that.

Proceedings at Bow Street may have been adjourned until 14 October 2004, but my lawyers were not prepared to wait that long before challenging the manner under which the proceedings were being brought under the Extradition Act 2003. Were this procedure to be accepted, Okula would avoid the need to present evidence of a *prima facie* case against Bea and me. Simmons & Simmons wrote twice during September to the CPS, then to the Home Office and to the court, reiterating our contention that Okula was attempting this avoidance. These extradition proceedings, we contended, had been unlawfully brought under the Extradition Act 2003. Their re-submission amounted to a manipulation of the process – in other words, an abuse.

There then began a series of exchanges, initially by way of correspondence and latterly in court, whereby my lawyers attempted to find out precisely what had transpired. What was the history of this matter? How had the extradition been stopped and restarted? Under what circumstances? As a result of whose advice? And what was that advice?

It did not require the brain of Sherlock Holmes to work out that a convenient reason for the change of tack was in order for the US Government to have a much greater chance of success under the 2003 Act than under the 1989 Act. But Parliament had dictated that switching in this way was not to be allowed.

My legal team decided to seek disclosure of the history behind Okula's switch from one Act to the other. Thus began a fascinating, albeit laborious, series of exchanges. A book of this nature could not possibly report the minutiae of those exchanges. I will instead summarise.

It was clear from the beginning that the CPS was not itself a party to the deceit which was being attempted. Indeed, in replying to Simmons & Simmons, the CPS confirmed with candour that the new requests for extradition appeared "to relate to the same matters alleged in the requests of March 2003".

Given what was happening, the court was unsurprisingly sympathetic to my lawyers' application for disclosure, and ordered the United States to disclose documents. This should have required the complete disclosure of all correspondence between the Federal authorities and their British counterparts. This, so I am told, was the first time such an order against the United States had ever been made.

Senior District Judge Workman did of course recognise that some of the documents concerned were likely to be subject to both legal professional privilege and/or public interest immunity, and that the scope of the disclosure might thus be affected. The US Government was therefore required to produce a schedule of relevant documents which were subject to the disclosure order, but which might in part be covered by privilege and/or immunity.

The CPS and its counsel decided, however, to ignore the order of the Court, and failed to produce a schedule of documents, as had been required. It was clear that the Judge was very unhappy with this. Counsel for the United States claimed that the entirety of the correspondence file was subject not only to public interest immunity and legal professional privilege, but also something which no-one seemed ever to have heard of called diplomatic privilege. We did discover, nevertheless, that the file contained three categories of correspondence. Correspondence between the USA and the Home Office; between the CPS and the Home Office; and between the USA and the CPS.

The deployment of these multiple lines of defence – public interest immunity, legal professional privilege and diplomatic privilege – was designed to represent the ultimate slamming of the door on this information, which information we were certain contained a 'smoking gun'. But the United States appeared determined that we would never know what had transpired. Our legal team refused to take this lying down. They challenged each and every obstacle which had been placed in their way. And they were very critical of the overall approach of the US Government.

James Lewis, acting for Bea, was vocal in his condemnation of the behaviour of the United States. His comments were all the more telling because he himself is regularly retained by the Office of the US Attorney for the Southern District of New York – the very same office which was now attempting to extradite Bea and me. James said at one of the hearings before Bow Street Magistrates:

> *"We are concerned by the apparent disregard of the United States Government for the authority of this court and, it seems, for this jurisdiction. The approach of the United States is characterised by lack of respect and, as we have observed before, in the case of Assistant United States Attorney Stanley Okula, by a lack of honesty.*
>
> *"It is a serious matter and it has to be treated seriously. One only has to compare the breadth and depth of our submission, with over 57 authorities in support, with that of the United States Government, with none in support of the issue. Either the United States Government is supremely confident or they perhaps are supremely indifferent. To us it appears to be the latter."*

As the CPS and counsel representing the United States were pushed further and further towards disclosure, it became apparent to them that they were making no headway in persuading the Senior District Judge of their own position. They could see the writing on the wall. And it was equally clear that the United States would not allow disclosure under any circumstances. The decision was taken by the CPS instead, upon advice from counsel, to seek judicial review. This was requested in February 2006, but it was not before July of that year that it actually took place. In other words, thanks to the US Government and its legal team, two full years had slipped by since the whole process had commenced, during which time absolutely nothing had been achieved.

Whilst all this was going on, a request made under the Freedom of Information Act revealed that, as at 1 January 2004 – the 'watershed' moment between the two Acts – there were 32 existing extradition requests which had been received from the United States of America. It also showed that of those 32 requests only two – for Stanley Tollman and Beatrice Tollman – had been withdrawn and resubmitted under the new Extradition Act.

I will pause briefly, and possibly tangentially, for a comment on my physical wellbeing at the time of the extradition proceedings. For the first 70 years of my life, I had always considered my health to be excellent. Other than a cartilage operation following a rugby injury at school, and treatment over the years for hypertension, my relationship with doctors and hospitals had been fleeting. My polo-playing days may have been in the past, but I had kept myself fit by playing a lot of tennis. When in Palm Beach, I used to play four or five times a week, and I was in very good shape for a man of my age.

The Spring of 2002 marked the start of what I would later consider to be my period of exile, the time when I found myself stranded in Britain without any prospect of resolution in sight. Frank Chopin warned me from the beginning that it would be a very long time before things were settled. Seven years was his estimation, but at the time I took this comment with a pinch of salt. If I had known from the beginning that his prediction would be almost spot on, I am not sure I would have been able to stay the course. I and the rest of my family would have gone mad. But it was not simply the state of my mental health about which I had reason to be concerned. When I was indicted by the US Department of Justice, my lifestyle changed completely and with it, so it seemed, my health.

I know that when a man is tired of London, he is supposed to be tired of life. But Bea and I had become not so much bored with London, but keen to spread our wings and breathe a little fresh air. In September 2002, we chartered the *Fair Lady*, a beautiful 37-metre motor yacht which had been built in 1928, and which was now owned by the Sainsbury family. We took the *Fair Lady* for a cruise around the Scottish islands.

I am reliably informed that today the *Fair Lady* is equipped with every means of modern communication, including WiFi internet access. But in 2002, the Scottish islands were beyond the range of even the *Fair Lady's* mobile phone reception. We relied instead upon the occasional message via the ship's radio. One such message was marked urgent. It asked me to telephone Monty Hundley. I had no idea why Monty wanted to speak to me. The only thing he had said was that I needed to phone him urgently. My nephew, Gavin, and I prepared to take the yacht's tender into port to make the call. But boarding the tender was not a simple process. The sea was choppy, and the exercise was made more difficult by the fact that there was a little sea water in the bottom of the boat. I had to jump down into the tender and, as I did so, one of my legs went out from underneath me and I felt a searing pain in my groin. Although I was in agony, we nevertheless pressed on and made it to port. I found a telephone and called Monty.

The urgency of the call was, as always with Monty, his need for money. He told me that his house was being repossessed, meaning that his wife and son would be put out on the street. Could I help him? Once again, despite the fact that this clown had got me into a very serious mess indeed, we arranged to get the money to him that he needed. If you think we were mad to do so, Bea and the rest of the family would be the first to agree with you.

The pain in my groin did not go away. Whatever it was I had done, the injury was not healing, even with time. After two years of living with the pain I consulted a doctor. He told me what I already knew: I had a hernia and I needed an operation. He then sent me to a surgeon who managed to make a complete hash of the operation. The surgeon came to see me the morning after the operation and told me that I could go home. But when the sheets were pulled back, it was discovered that I had been haemorrhaging all night. The bed was covered with blood and, from my waist to my knees, my skin was black.

By this time, we were deeply involved in the extradition proceedings, and I was required to make regular court appearances, irrespective of my health. The wound from the operation seeped endlessly, and did not heal up for two months.

This was a miserable time, not helped by the fact that I was diagnosed with a prostate problem. And it was around this point that Arnold died. During the two years preceding his death, I had been unable to visit Arnold in hospital, and he was unable to communicate by telephone, as his hearing had deserted him completely. He and I had been the closest of brothers, and the best of friends, for 70 years. For long periods, we had also been colleagues. But in the end, our unique partnership had been broken by a combination of failing health and by the intervention of Assistant US Attorney Stanley Okula.

And Okula was still scheming. He was about to pull off yet another diabolical act, the repercussions of which would ultimately show to the world what we had realised long ago – that he was a liar and a cheat.

GAVIN

In his campaign to "get at me through the family", Okula had persecuted my brother, terrified my wife and imprisoned my son. The next to find himself in the firing line was my nephew, Gavin Tollman, the surviving son of my brother, Arnold, who also happens to be married to my daughter, Toni.

It was not until five days after she and Gavin got married that Toni summoned up the courage to tell Bea and me what they had done. When I asked her why she hadn't told us beforehand, she said that I would have tried to prevent it. She was probably right. In fact, for some years afterwards I refused to acknowledge the existence of their wedding anniversary. I have always been very close to Gavin, but there is little doubt that the family crisis created by the United States Department of Justice, and in particular the chapter which you are about to read, brought me even closer to him.

I am devoting just one chapter to Gavin, explaining as best I am able what happened to him and to his family. In reality, this episode alone would be sufficient to fill the pages of a whole book. In condensing the story, I hope that I have managed to retain its essential elements and preserve its accuracy.

At the time of this episode, Gavin and Toni were living together in London. This was not the first marriage for either of them. Each had two children from earlier partnerships. Toni's two children were living away from home. Alexandra, then 20, was studying at Bristol University and Andrew, then 17, was at boarding school. Gavin's children – daughter Deia, then aged 10, and son Jack, then aged eight – were living with their mother, but Gavin saw a great deal of both of his children, and was devoted to them.

One Sunday morning in January 2005, Gavin, then 42 years old, shut the door of the Battersea home which he shared with Toni and headed for the airport. Only two weeks or so earlier, over Christmas and the New Year, he and Toni had taken all four children to ski together in Whistler, in the Canadian Rockies. It had been a wonderful bonding time for the whole family. But it was now very much back to work. A year earlier, Gavin had been promoted to global CEO of one of our travel companies, and had moved from New York and begun to live and work in London.

Toni was in South Africa on business and Gavin was embarking on a four-day business trip to Bermuda and Toronto. He planned to meet Toni at Heathrow later that week when they both flew back to London. Little did Gavin know as he locked the door that day that it would be almost two years before he would again set foot in Britain.

Toni and Gavin knew already that they were members of a family which found itself at war, and was defending itself against an opponent of awesome power. Brett was in a federal prison camp. And Bea and I were fighting extradition. Family conversations had rarely been normal for several years. But for Toni and Gavin, the worst was yet to come.

Having concluded his meetings in Bermuda, on Tuesday 18 January Gavin took a flight onwards from Bermuda direct to Toronto. He was travelling on this part of the trip with Mike Ness, the then Global CEO of Travel Corporation, David Hosking, from the Geneva office, and John Weeks, the head of Travel Corporation's Australian operations. The four of them, having met initially in Bermuda for a board meeting, were travelling for follow-on meetings in Canada. In an increasingly electronic world, Toronto had acquired a particular importance for the Travel Corporation, the company's global IT structure having moved there from its previous base in Australia.

Gavin is a South African by birth, but had also become a naturalised US citizen. He had been educated first in South Africa and later at the American University in Washington, DC. Gavin had begun his career as a stockbroker at Drexel Burnham in New York. In 1988, he joined Tollman-Hundley hotels where he worked for ten years, before joining the family's travel businesses in 1999. It was envisaged from the outset that he would in time take over the position which Arnold had held in the enterprise, and by 2005 he had become a key figure within the Travel Corporation.

As Gavin leant back into his seat on the plane, his thoughts were interrupted by the announcement that the flight was now just 50 minutes out from Lester B Pearson International. Bermuda had made a pleasant change from the damp, grey skies of London, from where he had set out 48 hours earlier. However, the First Officer informed passengers that Toronto was shivering in sub-zero temperatures and biting wind. The overcoat Gavin had been wearing in London may have been unnecessary in Bermuda, but would certainly be needed in Ontario.

The wheels of the Airbus touched down a little after 3.00pm, and the plane taxied to the brand new Terminal 1. As it slowed to a halt, there was an unusual disembarkation announcement from the flight deck: "Would all passengers please carry their passports in their hands and present them as they leave the aircraft." Possibly some form of new security procedure, Gavin thought. Or perhaps a procedure introduced for the new terminal building? Who knows?

He pulled down his bag from the overhead locker and, with his three colleagues, filed out of the aircraft door, passport in hand. He was in the leading group to leave the plane, and quickly spotted the four officials checking passports. Not a typical immigration scene, however. With their flak jackets and weapons, these fellows looked more like a SWAT team, apparently on the look-out for a terrorist.

One by one, the passengers filed past the guard who was checking passports, the rest of the security team adding to the intimidation. However, the line was moving quickly and Gavin satisfied himself with the knowledge that he was not the terrorist they were looking for. After a couple of minutes, it was his turn at the front. He proffered his passport. The guard examined the photo-page and said simply, "Are you Gavin Tollman?" "Yes," Gavin replied. At this response, the guard pulled his earpiece microphone closer to his lips and announced to an unseen colleague, "We have him!"

Gavin had no idea what was going on. What did the guard mean when he had said, "We have him"? He felt that there must be a mistake. But he was nevertheless ushered by the four-man squad away from the remaining passengers and from the direction of regular passport control. He was taken instead to a holding area which dealt with 'immigration problems'. Mike Ness and the others were firmly directed towards the regular route, in a state of bewilderment that one of their group should have been the reason for the special checks.

Gavin concluded that it was clearly a case of mistaken identity. He had read only recently that there was a 'watch list' of suspected terrorists which contained well over 100,000 names. What's more, many of the names of those suspected were often the same or similar to the names of completely innocent passengers. This was a recipe for great confusion, and hold-ups at airports were commonplace. There had, for instance, been reports of a US Senator, the late Ted Stevens, complaining to the authorities that his wife, Catherine, was often delayed whilst security or immigration staff worked out whether she was in fact the 'Cat Stevens' they had on their list.

The 'Stevens' for whom the authorities were in fact keeping a look-out was a British musician of Greek-Cypriot origin who was well-known in the 1960s and 1970s under the stage name Cat Stevens. In 1977, he had converted to Islam, changing his name to Yusuf Islam, and was now on a 'no fly list'.

The holding area for 'immigration problems' at Lester Pearson airport is little different from similar facilities all over the world. Suffice to say that it was not the welcoming environment to which a traveller might look forward. Having been ushered to a cold, windowless and featureless room, Gavin was told to take a seat. After waiting patiently in that seat for almost an hour, he went looking for someone in order to find out what was going on.

He was informed that his associates had been told to leave, but that he should continue waiting. As an experienced traveller, Gavin knew full well that there was only one way to deal with immigration officers – politely, calmly and, on this very unusual occasion, patiently. He felt sure that the mix-up would be sorted out soon, and that he could catch up with the others.

After a further lengthy wait, a female officer came into the room carrying a file which she handed to him, allowing him to read what it contained. Gavin first read her name badge: "Officer Contenta: Canadian Border Service Agency". Little did Gavin know then, but the words Canadian Border Service Agency or, more simply, its acronym CBSA, were to feature prominently in his life for many months to come.

As he turned the cover of the file which he had been handed, the first thing that he saw was a photocopy of his own United States driving licence. And it really was *his* licence. Thoughts of mistaken identity swiftly ebbed away. It was indeed him in whom these people were interested. But why?

The second document in the file hit him in the pit of his stomach. This was a warrant for his arrest, issued by a Judge in the District Court for the Southern District of New York. This had been granted, so the file showed, in response to a series of accusations which had been laid before the Court to justify the application for the warrant. Gavin read through the extraordinary catalogue of allegations with a growing sense of disbelief and anger. How could anyone possibly say all this? And why had he not heard about it before? The warrant showed that it had been issued on 8 November 2004 – more than two months earlier. Why had no-one told him about this? But far worse, the allegations against him, as well as being untrue, were chilling in their extent and magnitude.

As he turned the final page, everything became clear. For there was the signature of the man who had laid all these lies before the Court and, in type, his name and title – Stanley Okula, Assistant United States Attorney, Southern District of New York. A year before, Okula had terrorised Gavin's father – my brother Arnold – whilst he was in the final weeks of his life. In the opinion of his doctors, this had shortened Arnold's life. Having driven his father into an early grave, the same man, it seemed, was now picking on Gavin.

The female agent had been observing Gavin's reaction to the file. The relaxation in her body language indicated that she had already decided that he was not a threat. Politely and unemotionally she asked him a number of simple questions. These concluded with the most important. "Are you guilty?"

Gavin had no need to collect his thoughts. He answered instantly. "No. Absolutely not. What this man is saying is totally wrong." Although this was a spontaneous answer, given without a moment's hesitation, Gavin's assessment of the document he had just read would not change in any way from that day to this. Despite the passage of many years, mountains of paperwork and hour upon hour of analysis, Gavin's position would not change by one iota. This contrasted dramatically with the case against him brought by the US Government, which was to change comprehensively on at least six occasions before being abandoned altogether.

Immediately prior to his relocation to London, Gavin had been President of Travel Corporation North America, where he was responsible for all tour sales. Even making allowance for the 'creativity' of Stanley Okula, there had never been any serious prospect of Gavin being indicted alongside Brett and me. He had, though, received a subpoena from the grand jury shortly after the first indictment in the Tollman-Hundley matter was returned in April 2002. And Trafalgar Tours USA had also received a number of subpoenas relating to various business and financial records.

In June 2002, Trafalgar Tours USA and Gavin had each retained Elliot Sagor of Hogan & Hartson in New York to respond to the subpoenas. A former federal prosecutor and respected member of the New York criminal bar, Elliot struck up a line of communication with Okula, always providing him with what he had requested. On a number of occasions, he produced documents voluntarily, thus avoiding the need for additional subpoenas. Nevertheless, in the face of active co-operation, there had still in total been 12 subpoenas, the last of which was served on Friday 23 April 2004. By this time, all concerned had become used to the timing. Subpoenas were invariably served on a Friday afternoon, and were increasingly in relation to matters about which Okula had already asked precisely the same questions. It became clear that this tactic was designed to be worrying and distracting. Notwithstanding everyone's view of what was going on, in each and every case Elliot Sagor's office complied fully with the subpoenas. Between June 2002 and May 2004, even after he had moved his home to London, when needed, Gavin would go to Elliot Sagor's office in New York to assist in the process of responding to the subpoenas.

Now, in January 2005, Gavin observed that the warrant for his arrest had been obtained six months after the last subpoena had been answered. But that warrant was now more than two months old, and had been kept hidden until the time that Okula could spring his trap. Notice of that warrant should either have been sent to the appropriate authorities in Gavin's country of residence, the United Kingdom, or to Elliot Sagor in New York, requesting that Gavin surrender voluntarily. Either course would have been entirely proper.

But the warrant had been sealed and Okula had then bided his time. Not to mince words, he waited for a chance to kidnap Gavin. There was absolutely no legitimate reason to get Gavin arrested in Canada. He could have been arrested easily at any time in the United Kingdom. And although Gavin did not of course know this as he sat in immigration at Toronto airport, documents from the Offfice of International Affairs in Washington would later show that Okula knew full well that Gavin had moved his home from New York to London.

Three years later, in the context of court proceedings in London in the extradition battle over Bea and me, the truth about the United States' attitude to kidnap was openly divulged. This revelation came from a most unlikely source – in the form of an admission from Counsel acting for the United States, and in a hearing about me. The *Sunday Times* reported this development as follows[94]:

US says it has right to kidnap British citizens
David Leppard

AMERICA has told Britain that it can 'kidnap' British citizens if they are wanted for crimes in the United States.

A senior lawyer for the American government has told the Court of Appeal in London that kidnapping foreign citizens is permissible under

---

[94] US says it has right to kidnap British citizens, *Sunday Times*, 2 December 2007.

American law because the US Supreme Court has sanctioned it.

Until now it was commonly assumed that US law permitted kidnapping only in the 'extraordinary rendition' of terrorist suspects.

The American government has for the first time made it clear in a British court that the law applies to anyone, British or otherwise, suspected of a crime by Washington.

Legal experts confirmed this weekend that America viewed extradition as just one way of getting foreign suspects back to face trial. Rendition, or kidnapping, dates back to 19th-century bounty hunting and Washington believes it is still legitimate.

During a hearing last month Lord Justice Moses, one of the Court of Appeal judges, asked Alun Jones QC, representing the US government, about its treatment of Gavin, [Stanley] Tollman's nephew. Gavin Tollman was the subject of an attempted abduction during a visit to Canada in 2005.

Jones replied that it was acceptable under American law to kidnap people if they were wanted for offences in America. "The United States does have a view about procuring people to its own shores which is not shared," he said.

He said that if a person was kidnapped by the US authorities in another country and was brought back to face charges in America, no US court could rule that the abduction was illegal and free him: "If you kidnap a person outside the United States and you bring him there, the court has no jurisdiction to refuse – it goes back to bounty hunting days in the 1860s."

Okula had originally drafted documents for an arrest in Australia, but Gavin had been forced to cancel that particular trip. Okula then learned that Gavin was about to arrive in Toronto for a two-day business trip, and would be returning home to London on 20 January. Okula communicated directly with Canadian immigration officials, sending them a copy of the now ten-week-old sealed arrest warrant, plus the other documents which Gavin had now been shown. But there had been no communication at this stage with the Department of Justice in Canada and no request for a provisional arrest warrant under the extradition treaty between the US and Canada.

Okula planned to have Gavin deported whilst in Canadian custody, and have him handed over to United States IRS agents at Buffalo, which is on the border between the USA and Canada, a little over an hour's drive from Toronto. In this way, Okula intended to avoid the inconvenience and delay of extradition.

To aid his plans, Okula had grossly inflated the gravity of the allegations against Gavin, telling the Canadian immigration case officer that it involved a breathtaking $480 *million* tax fraud. The truth was that Gavin was alleged to have under-reported income of $258,000, and thus to have evaded $103,000 in personal income taxes over a four-year period – about $25,000 a year.

Importantly, Okula had also failed to disclose the fact to the Canadian authorities that Gavin had been aware of an investigation for the past two and a half years. Nor did he tell the Canadians that throughout this period Gavin had been represented by Hogan & Hartson, and that, through the offices of Hogan & Hartson, Gavin had been co-operating fully with the investigation. Gavin had continued to live and travel openly throughout the time that the investigation had been progressing. And why not? Gavin had no inkling that Okula had put his name in the frame.

In the days which followed his apprehension, Okula and his cohorts would repeatedly characterise Gavin as a serious flight risk. But the truth was that Okula knew exactly where Gavin lived and where he worked. And he also knew that Gavin was completely unaware of the charges, and could have been arrested at any time on a provisional warrant in the UK.

Mike Ness and the others, suspecting that Okula might well be behind all of this, had got a message through to Elliot Sagor to tell him that his client had been apprehended at immigration. Sagor was horrified, and immediately called Okula asking him if he knew what the hell was going on. Okula replied that he had obtained an arrest in conjunction with a sealed complaint. From what Okula had just said, Elliot assumed that Gavin was being held on an extradition warrant issued in Canada. Having made this assumption, he then offered to travel to Canada, accompany Gavin back to the United States and have him surrender. Okula refused this offer, saying that "it was too late for that" and that he had already been "burned" by Stanley Tollman for my having resisted extradition in the UK. Recognising the challenge which Gavin was now facing, Elliot raised the possibility of waiving extradition altogether. But Okula did not correct Elliot's obvious misbelief that an extradition warrant had been issued. Okula finished the conversation knowing that he had misled Gavin's attorney.

This was a seriously unprofessional act. Elliot Sagor is a highly respected member of the New York Bar, as is his partner, Ira Feinberg. Both Elliot and Ira were themselves formerly Assistant US Attorneys for the Southern District of New York. A year later, Elliot and Ira wrote a letter of complaint to the Chief of the Criminal Division, Southern District New York. Speaking of Okula, the letter said:

> *"We believe that he has allowed himself to get too caught up in this case, that it has become something of an obsession for him, and that he is too close to the case to exercise proper independent judgment."*

As Gavin continued to shake his head in disbelief at the documents in front of him, he and Officer Contenta were joined by a man who was not wearing uniform, but whom Officer Contenta clearly recognised. Gavin did not know that he was entering a very dark period of his life, during which he would be at the receiving end of actions which were fundamentally hostile to him and to the rest of his family. He did not yet know that he would not see his home again for two years, nor that hostile acts would be perpetrated not simply by Okula himself, but by Okula's representatives in Canada. Nevertheless, among the many whom he would come to consider as enemies, the unknown man who had just joined them was to play an important part in Gavin's ultimate salvation. Enemy he wasn't. Gavin would learn in time that the unknown man was called Russ Dagg, a supervisor with the CBSA. He would learn too that it was Dagg's insistence upon correct procedure which eventually foiled Okula's attempt to kidnap him.

Aware that Gavin had been allowed to read at least part of the file, the man asked the question, "Would you like to make a call to the US Embassy?" The answer was swift and certain. "No. Thank you." Gavin had no way of appreciating the importance of what he had just done. Intuition had told him that this was the correct thing to do. And his intuition was completely correct. But it would be some time before he was to appreciate what might have happened had he answered, "Yes".

A trap had been set for Gavin, into the jaws of which he had thankfully now elected not to step. Okula is a man who regularly bends or ignores the rules, and he was was attempting, with the Canadian Authorities acting as his unwitting accomplices, to bundle Gavin over the border. Had he succeeded, the ending of the book which you are reading could well have been very different.

Despite fate's helpful guiding hand, Gavin's immediate prospects were far from being a bed of roses. But this was not yet apparent. As the short interview with the Canadian officials proceeded, the exchange was civil and the people cordial. Gavin was told by the female official that he was going to be held, but that she would recommend that he be transferred to a holding facility suitable for low-risk detainees. She then politely wished him well and departed. Once more, he was left on his own.

It would be more than a year before Gavin was able to discover the sequence of events which had led to him being arrested. This came with the disclosure of documents to which Gavin's lawyers had successfully sought access. Thus it was that on 3 March 2006, the CBSA was required by an Order of the Court to disclose a revelatory and damning series of email exchanges. From this point on, my account is able to quote from those emails.

Four days prior to Gavin leaving London, Okula, who knew where Gavin was living and the outline of his travel plans, forwarded a draft "provisional arrest request" to a lady called Naydene Baca, at US Homeland Security in Washington, DC.

Later that day, Naydene Baca acknowledged receipt of Okula's email, and said that she would be communicating with a man called Gord Morris, who was Removal Enforcement Supervisor at the CBSA. She described him as someone who had in the past been extremely helpful. The following day, Okula asked Officer Paradis, of the Royal Canadian Mounted Police (RCMP), a liaison officer based in Washington, to provide him with Gavin's flight itinerary from Bermuda to Toronto.

Meanwhile, Naydene Baca advised Okula that Gord Morris had confirmed that when Gavin arrived in Toronto, he would be taken into custody. The Canadians would then notify the United States authorities, and would begin the process of escorting Gavin to the US Port of Entry and onwards into US custody.

The day before Gavin left Bermuda, Officer Paradis provided Gavin's travel itinerary. "Gavin Tollman will arrive in Toronto at 3.20 pm on 18 January 2005." Okula then informed Naydene Baca that he had heard from the RCMP, described Gavin's travel itinerary, and concluded: "Based on the strength of our arrest warrant; *we seek to have him refused entry into Canada and turned over to United States law enforcement.*" (My emphasis.)

On the morning that Gavin was due to arrive, Naydene Baca wrote again to the CBSA's Removal Enforcement Supervisor Gord Morris: *"Okay, Gord let's do it! You've got the info, please call me as soon as you have him and hopefully we can get him back no later than the end of the week."* (Once again, my emphasis, which continues ahead as appropriate.)

At around the same time, Okula wrote to Naydene Baca, asking, *"Assuming everything works as planned, into whose custody do you anticipate Gavin Tollman being placed?* I ask because I have to plan to have him presented in US Federal Court before the 'nearest' Magistrate Judge in the US, as required by Rule 5 of the Federal Rules of Criminal Procedure. *Would IRS-CI agents take him through Buffalo? Detroit? Fly him to NYC? Please advise."*

This email exposes the double standards of the US Department of Justice, in the marked contrast of its respect for its own jurisdiction, as compared to its respect for the jurisdiction of others – even near neighbours such as Canada. The plan which Okula was hatching was a clear breach of the Canada-US Extradition Treaty, and of the Canadian Extradition Act, but Okula clearly didn't give a fig about that. He was, however, concerned to have receiving agents in position at the right port of entry so that he could comply with United States domestic law. Just over an hour later Naydene Baca advised Okula that Gavin would *"likely be turned over in Buffalo"*.

So it was that, two hours before Gavin was due to land at Toronto, still blissfully ignorant of the storm into which he was heading, Okula wrote once again to Naydene Baca about a "troubling" telephone call he had just had with Russ Dagg. Okula told her that Dagg had suggested that, after Gavin was detained on immigration hold, the US Attorney would have to go through formal extradition proceedings to get him back to New York. As far as Okula was concerned, this was not part of the script, as he spelt out to Naydene Baca: *"Based on my communications with you, I did not think that was the case; rather I thought that because he was being denied entry, he could be summarily turned over to US."*

This email was a clear admission by Okula of the true nature of his scheme – to avoid the inconvenience of proper extradition processes in favour of a summary handing over of Gavin at Buffalo. In other words, a kidnap.

In the waiting area at Immigration Control, time ticked by. Gavin had much to think and worry about. Toni was in South Africa on business. Had she yet heard that he had been detained? Had his colleagues let others know that there seemed to be a major problem? He had been here since three o'clock. It was now six.

Once again, he tried to find out what was going on. This time he was told it was now a matter for the supervisor. He returned to the agonising wait, unable even to make a telephone call to find out what was going on in the outside world or to tell anybody what was happening to him. After close to a further four hours he was told he would be taken to the facility where he would be detained overnight.

Earlier, Naydene Baca had sent an email to Okula (and others) confirming that Gavin had been "intercepted and will be detained overnight. *It appears that we may be able to get him escorted to the POE[95] tomorrow and have our agents take custody. We will have to work quickly tomorrow after I touch base with Gord Morris.*"

But at about the same time in Toronto, Officer Contenta wrote to Russ Dagg: "*I wrote the guy up – A 36(1)(a) – see FOS. U.S. Embassy called from Ottawa asking about the status of the PC . They apparently want PC[96] deported (at POE). Told her that is not an option at POE - PC is currently at the review stage.*"

Okula, however, had not given up. Notwithstanding that he had been told by Russ Dagg that extradition was required, he still planned to go ahead with his attempt to seize Gavin unlawfully. The emails which the CBSA were obliged to disclose demonstrated beyond doubt that at no time through this process was Okula acting in 'good faith'.

Although, as was later admitted in a London Court, the US Department of Justice permits 'Deportations, Expulsions or other Extraordinary Renditions', these must always be undertaken by the Office of International Affairs in Washington. But the OIA was never involved in this process. Okula was acting as a rogue. Even when Okula was put on explicit notice by Russ Dagg that "formal" extradition proceedings would be required, Okula and others still resolved to give "summary" deportation a try, albeit they would have to "work quickly".

Lester B Pearson International Airport is situated to the west of Toronto. A journey into the city normally takes about 45 minutes by car. But Gavin's journey that evening was barely a few minutes long. Despite the earlier assurances he had received, a comfortable, low-security detention centre was not to be his destination. With a slowly-dawning horror, Gavin realised that he was being taken to a maximum-security facility.

The Toronto West Detention Centre, known previously as the Metro West Detention Centre and now often referred to simply as 'The West', is Ontario's maximum-security remand facility, located in Rexdale, on the western fringes of Toronto. Designed to hold 630

---

[95] Port of Entry.
[96] Prisoner in Custody.

prisoners, it houses men who have been remanded in custody or are serving short sentences.

Just before 10.00pm, the RCMP car carrying Gavin drew up to the sprawling, low-rise, brick-faced edifice, just off the Macdonald-Cartier Freeway. The thermometer in the police car indicated that the air temperature outside was minus 21°C, and ice crystals were cutting through the air in the stiff breeze. These dug into Gavin's face like sand as he was manhandled the short distance to the entrance.

Had he been aware of the fearsome reputation of 'The West', his despair would no doubt have sunk even lower. As it was, he was only too aware of the indignity of the full strip search to which he was subjected, and the removal of all his possessions, to be replaced by bright-orange regulation overalls.

As Gavin was escorted along the corridors and through the locked gates and bars of the centre, he quickly became aware that he had already been nicknamed the '25 Million Dollar Man'. This sobriquet was shouted, in some cases with admiration, by detainees and guards alike. "Boy, *you* certainly pissed off the wrong people!" Gavin did not understand initially what they were saying or why they were saying it, but the 25 million dollar tag lasted for the duration of his detention in the Centre. He would soon discover that it stemmed from the widely-held belief that he stood accused of stealing $25 million from the US Government.

Gavin learned that in the section of Metro West where he was to be held there were 12 cells, each holding two detainees. He was allocated a cell sharing with a man accused of second degree murder. Another detainee of that very section was a former head of the Tamil Tigers, a man who bravely displayed the evidence of more than 30 bullet wounds.

Fitness is important to Gavin. His regular daily routine for years has begun with a visit to the gym to work out. At a time when others are still sleeping, he is looking after himself. As he entered Metro West that evening, he was as fit a 42-year-old as one could reasonably expect to meet.

One might also have thought that he was tougher than most, as Gavin is a man to whom life has dealt some cruel blows. On Christmas Day 1987, his younger brother was killed in a car accident in South Africa. And a little over a year later, on Valentine's Day 1989, his mother was murdered when her home in South Africa was invaded by a gang intent on robbery. Gavin has certainly been at the receiving end of more than his fair share of knocks. But none of his life experiences had prepared him for being incarcerated in Metro West with violent criminals and terrorists.

The concept of a maximum-security facility may well enable the population to sleep more easily in their beds at night. But it is not difficult to imagine that the reverse is true for a 'civilian' who finds himself locked up inside such a facility with people whom society considers to be dangerous. Thanks to the picture of him which Okula had presented to the Canadian authorities, Gavin found himself lying in an uncomfortable bunk, with neither pillow nor blanket, in precisely those circumstances.

Gavin tried hard to get some sleep, but his brain continued to go over everything he had seen and heard. He thought, as he had done many times that evening, of Toni, herself away from home in South Africa. He was certain that by now she was frantic with concern as to his fate. He thought of his two children in London, who may have lived with his first wife, but whom he saw as often as he possibly could and to whom he was extremely close. He endlessly re-examined the lies he had read that afternoon in those court documents, and he tried to work out what precisely was going on. And he thought of that bastard Okula, who was no doubt lying snugly, and no doubt smugly, in his own bed somewhere in New York.

With unanswerable questions going around and around in his head, he eventually dropped off to sleep, to be awakened, he thought minutes later, as a new day at Metro West dawned.

Gavin was informed that his colleagues had secured the services of a local immigration counsel called Lorne Waldman, who would be representing him at something called an Immigration Review Board hearing the following morning. This would be held at Metro West. He was told that his counsel was coming to see him later that day.

At around the same time, Russ Dagg wrote to Gord Morris, who was a more senior official within the Agency. "Subject detained for an admissibility hearing. US Officials informed and will no doubt be seeking extradition. *My brief conversation with US Attorney indicates he spoke to client's lawyer in USA and looks like subject may 'voluntarily' surrender to US Officials.*"

When Gavin's lawyer, Lorne Waldman arrived to see Gavin, their conversation represented the first dizzying step on a learning curve for Gavin, which he later discovered was to stretch steeply upwards for months ahead.

Waldman told him that CBSA immigration hearings were unusual, in that the judge who handled the hearing attended the premises where the detainee was being held. Ontario had a panel of three judges available for such hearings and, as luck would have it, the nominated judge tomorrow was a lady before whom Mr Waldman had appeared on numerous occasions. Depressingly, he admitted that he had never won a case in front of her.

So it was that, in the extraordinary setting of Metro West, Gavin contested his alleged inadmissibility to Canada under immigration law. (Bear in mind that he had been happily skiing in Canada just three weeks earlier.) The CBSA introduced Gavin to the judge as being the ruthless mastermind behind a staggering, but of course preposterous, $450 million fraud, whose release on bail should be resisted at all costs. "No amount of money could hold him. He is an indescribable flight risk," the hearing was told. "He will get out of Canada as soon and as swiftly as possible. He must be detained in custody pending a later admissibility hearing."

Lorne Waldman fought hard and ultimately successfully against these patently absurd claims, and in so doing broke his duck with this particular judge, who found for Gavin, and against the CBSA. She granted bail pending his immigration hearing but, given what she had just heard about him, she felt obliged to set the most onerous bail conditions imaginable. In fact, she set the bar at a record height. Not only were the financial conditions of bail higher than they had ever been in an immigration hearing, Gavin was required to report every day, seven days a week. The CBSA were less than pleased with this requirement. "But your honour, we're only open five days a week." To which the judge replied dryly, "I believe I am right in saying – am I not – that there are flights at the weekend?"

The hearing finished at about noon, and Gavin was taken back to his cell whilst the formalities of bail were dealt with. Once again, he sat and waited patiently. At about four o'clock, he felt he had waited long enough and he asked to be able to make a telephone call to Lorne Waldman, from whom he received some bad news. "I am sorry, Gavin. There's been a hiccup. You're not getting out tonight."

Waldman explained that he had gone to the appropriate office with the sureties required, and had handed over all the requisite documents. But for some inexplicable reason, Officer Missio, the immigration official on duty, said that the Immigration Review Board order had been made without jurisdiction. He refused Gavin's release. Waldman was perplexed and, as he walked away, he made a note of the time – 2.50pm.

Just ten minutes later, at 3.00pm, Missio left the office for the day, meaning that nothing could be done about the injustice he had just perpetrated. And just ten further minutes later, Jason Carter of the US Department of Justice sent an urgent email to Christopher Mainella of the Canadian Public Prosecutor's Office. In this, he sought Gavin's urgent arrest under the Extradition Act, arguing that Gavin "could make at any time bail in connection with the pending immigration case again him". The US Department of Justice had been tipped off and, with the help of a friend or two, was now desperate to ensure that Gavin was not released. They had at last turned to the extradition treaty between Canada and the United States and had contacted the International Assistance Group in Ottawa, seeking a provisional warrant for Gavin's arrest.

In the meantime, Waldman had tried to go over Missio's head by applying to a more senior immigration officer. They both agreed that the Immigration Review Board order was correct in all respects, and that Gavin should have been released. But it was now too late to do anything that day. Waldman was told that if he attended the office in the morning, Gavin would be released.

As Lorne Waldman explained all this to Gavin, he mentioned that there were two quite separate issues. One was immigration, with which he was dealing. But there would also be something called extradition, where a lawyer called Michael Code would be helping. Immigration? Extradition? And why different lawyers for each? Gavin found it all very confusing.

As soon as I had heard from Mike Ness that Gavin had been stopped by the Canadian authorities, and before any of us really knew what was going on, I got cracking on finding Gavin the best possible legal representation in Toronto. Lorne Waldman was the first into the fray, but Michael Code was to play a much bigger part in protecting Gavin, along with a third Canadian lawyer, whom I will introduce shortly.

Once I was satisfied that I had got things moving, and that Gavin was at least going to get proper representation, I reflected on the man who appeared relentless in his pursuit of me and my family. I can't remember exactly when the comparison set root in my mind, but my best recollection is that it was around this time. Okula became for me the modern-day equivalent of Victor Hugo's Inspector Javert, the evil and obsessed policeman in *Les Miserables,* who doggedly pursued Hugo's hero, Jean Valjean.

I stopped short of comparing myself with Jean Valjean, the man who was sent to prison for 19 years for stealing a loaf of bread, and whose recapture became Javert's fixation. I had no role in my own comparison beyond being the target of Okula's zealous and fixated pursuit. Just like Javert, Okula appeared to be omnipresent, attempting his worst in Bermuda, in Guernsey, in Australia, in London, in New York, and now in Toronto. During the months and years which followed, I found that I was not the only one to be using the Javert analogy – almost the whole of my legal team was as well.

When Gavin climbed onto his bunk that night he was exhausted, but in a way he was also light-hearted, in the knowledge that he would be getting out the next day. It was time for lights-out, and peace gradually settled over the detention centre, broken only by the sound of the increasing wind outside. A major storm was starting to blow across Ontario, and with it blizzards.

He had been asleep for about an hour when he became aware of a disturbance somewhere in the centre. Raised voices were asking in concert, "What the fuck is going on?"

Gavin had learned quickly that the unspoken rule within a facility of this kind is that YOU (the detainees) are up against THEM (the guards). When the source of the night-time disturbance reached his cell, the two guards whose behaviour had challenged the peace of Metro West were by now universally hated, and the victim of this extraordinary intervention was to be defended. But who were these guards? They were not normal detention centre staff.

The cell door opened and two Royal Canadian Mounted Police officers asked Gavin to go with them. It was clear that questions were not even to be asked, much less answers expected. They placed him in handcuffs and escorted him along the corridor past the other cells. "Who the fuck are you?" "This has never happened before!"

Dressed only in a T-shirt and orange overalls, Gavin was escorted through the building and out into the freezing night air. The temperature was now minus 40°C and there was a stiff wind. By the time he got to the car, two long and agonising minutes had passed. He hurt from cold.

It was only a short drive to the police station, but Gavin wondered whether they were ever going to make it. Snow which had been falling for several days was now being blown into vast drifts. Road conditions were by now near impassable, even for a country that takes the worst that winter can offer in its stride. When they eventually made it to the station, it was not to the protection of an underground car park. Gavin was told to get out of the car and wait whilst the policemen went and parked the vehicle. An unchallenging request, one might think, until you remember the weather conditions and the fact that Gavin was dressed only in a set of thin overalls.

The policemen took four or five minutes to return, by which time Gavin was shaking uncontrollably. He was far colder than he had ever been in his life. So cold that when they eventually got back to him and took him inside the police station he could not speak.

When he had managed to regain his composure a little, he asked what was going on. Their response was as mystifying then as it is today. "We're arresting you," they said calmly. "What?" Gavin responded. "But I was in jail!"

What Gavin did not at this stage realise was that Okula, who had been trying to kidnap him without the inconvenience of due process, had now been obliged to recognise two things. First, that his prey was about to get bail. Second, that he was obliged to do things properly. This could well mean a long and complicated process, which he had thought that he could side-step, but he had concluded that extradition proceedings were inevitable if he was going to secure his prize.

Okula's underlying strategy against me was one of coercion. By his own admission, he was "going to get Stanley Tollman through his family." Okula calculated that pressure on any member of my family ultimately represented pressure on me. Okula's original plan for Gavin was to have him incarcerated in the most inhospitable conditions imaginable, before one of two things happened. Either Gavin was successfully bundled across the border at Buffalo or, failing that, Gavin would be forced to recognise the hopelessness of his situation, and would agree to cross voluntarily into the US. In either case, Okula calculated that he would have gained substantial leverage over me.

The reason why Gavin was being dragged out of bed at midnight in a snow storm was that Okula was desperately attempting to prevent his release from detention. He was now about to be arrested not on an immigration matter, but under Canada's Extradition Act. Yesterday's immigration hearing was rendered meaningless, as were the bail conditions.

At this point, the horror story turned momentarily into farce, because the two policemen, who had been called upon to run a very unusual errand in the middle of the night, realised that neither of

424
CHAPTER THIRTY TWO

them was capable of operating the computer which they needed to complete the formalities of the arrest. After struggling ineptly for almost half an hour, they resorted to asking Gavin whether he knew how to fix a computer. Thus it was that Gavin re-booted the police computer, enabling the completion of the formalities of his own arrest. What had begun as a chilling episode in every way imaginable, ended in a spirit of bizarre bonhomie.

The following morning, Lorne Waldman returned to the immigration office. Once again, he handed over the documents. Once again, he was refused. "These are no good. Your client is now being held under the Extradition Act. You need now to apply for bail to Ontario's Superior Court of Justice."

Still recovering from the extraordinary events of the previous night, Gavin found that he had another visitor. This was Michael Code, the counsel whom Lorne Waldman had told him about yesterday. Gavin did not, nor could not, appreciate quite how important this man would become over the months ahead. And his uncertainty was heightened significantly when he discovered that his new lawyer did not even possess a mobile phone.

Gavin's concerns about Michael Code's failure to embrace the modern world may have been justified. But he would have been quite wrong to assume that Code was a man who was not up to the job, as Gavin would soon discover.

A remarkable lawyer, educated in Toronto and at the Sorbonne in Paris, Michael Code is today a Judge of the Superior Court of Justice in and for the Province of Ontario. When Gavin met him for the first time in 2005, Michael, then aged 54, was in private practice with the firm of Sack Goldblatt Mitchell. His previous career had included not only extensive private practice, but both teaching and legal journalism. He had even been Ontario's Assistant Deputy Attorney General (Criminal Law) – the equivalent of the Director of Public Prosecutions in other jurisdictions. He is probably best known for his work as an appellate lawyer, arguing many leading cases before the Supreme Court of Canada and the Court of Appeal for Ontario.

Before becoming a judge he was an assistant professor at the Faculty of Law in the University of Toronto. A very serious lawyer indeed.

Michael explained to Gavin what was happening, and what the next steps were. A hearing before the Superior Court of Justice was scheduled for the following day, Saturday. Having just received the brief, Michael Code explained that he had a great deal of reading to catch up on in order to be able to help his new client. He promised to do this in good time for the next day's hearing.

Whilst Michael was reading into the case, the third Canadian lawyer was being brought into the team by Clive Nicholls, my English QC. Clive, whose experience of life is almost as lengthy as mine, has worked with some of the best criminal lawyers in the English-speaking world. And within his address book was the name of an exceptional Canadian criminal lawyer called David Martin. David was based not in Ontario, but in Vancouver, British Columbia. David would shortly join Michael Code in defending Gavin in Toronto.

It is important to remember that the immigration proceedings, in relation to which Gavin had been granted bail, may have been overtaken by the extradition request, but immigration remained an important and additional issue for the whole of the period that Gavin was to spend in Canada. The CBSA had been provided with bogus and damning information by Okula and, as a result, had arrested Gavin. But now, Gavin had been arrested on the provisional extradition warrant whilst still being held illegally in immigration custody. In fact, CBSA continued to refuse to comply with the IRB release order until 28 January, when Gavin was released from immigration custody.

In the meantime, there had been an extradition bail hearing on 26 January. Counsel for the United States had vigorously opposed it, but Mr Justice Nordheimer ordered Gavin's release on extradition bail that very day. Nordheimer's ruling in relation to findings of fact in those proceedings, even though delivered barely a week after Gavin had been held at Toronto Airport, contained some remarkably apposite comments, some of which I will repeat. And bear in mind that when he wrote this Mr Justice Nordheimer had not seen the emails which would later emerge.

Nordheimer said that there was "a complete absence of any explanation" as to why Gavin had not been arrested in his country of residence in the period between 8 November 2004, when the Complaint was filed in New York, and 18 January 2005 when the US authorities caused him to be detained by immigration upon arrival in Toronto. He said that the Court was "troubled" by the fact that "US authorities did not at any point advise Mr Tollman's attorney of these charges and provide the opportunity for Mr Tollman to voluntarily surrender during the same two and a half month period".

Mr Justice Nordheimer went on to say that the American authorities "appear to have orchestrated a situation where Mr Tollman would be apprehended in Canada which might have been achieved without the need for an extradition request or, failing success on that score, require him to be held in custody with all of the attendant consequences". He added that it was "disconcerting" that the United States had used that situation, namely Gavin's arrest in Canada, and away from his home, in order "to assert that Mr Tollman is a flight risk and therefore ought to be held in custody".

Finally, he pointed out that the materials filed in support of the request for a provisional warrant "omitted some quite material facts" and, as a result, the normal rule relating to full, frank and fair disclosure on ex parte applications "was not met by the requesting State in this case". He added: "The almost covert approach of the United States in this proceeding is simply inexplicable. The manner in which this matter has begun is unsatisfactory."

With these statements, Gavin was released from detention. He had arrived at Metro West on 18 January, and he finally left on 28 January. He had spent ten whole days locked up a high-security facility, and all thanks to Okula. But if Gavin imagined that the end of his nightmare was at hand, he was in for a rude awakening. And although Mr Justice Nordheimer had got the measure of what was happening, Gavin was to discover that many of the Canadians who should have been overseeing this process fairly and independently were in fact happy to do the bidding of the United States, whatever that entailed. Uncle Sam cracked the whip, and they fell in line. Gavin soon discovered that it was not only the manner in which the matter had begun which was unsatisfactory. The manner in which it had then continued was little better.

Gavin may have been released back into the real world, but freedom was not yet within his grasp, nor anything which even remotely resembled freedom. One early condition of Gavin's bail was that he would live with his attorney, Michael Code. Nice people though Gavin and Michael both are, I have little doubt that this arrangement was not exactly what either had planned.

Thus began an especially difficult period for the family and for our businesses. Brett had been incarcerated and Gavin had been effectively trapped in Canada. Even Mike Ness felt unable to travel to the United States, or even close to it, for fear of what Okula might attempt to do to him too. There was no doubt that this was a dark time from which the family's prospects of recovery looked gloomy indeed, but it was against this backdrop that Gavin somehow blossomed in his own adversity.

Toni had by now made her way to Canada and she and Gavin were able to give each other some mutual support. But the weeks, and then months, became increasingly difficult. Eventually Gavin was allowed to live with Toni in a rented apartment and they were able to do some work at our offices in Toronto. But life in Toronto is, I understand, something of an acquired taste. The unrelenting winter was soon replaced by an unforgiving summer, during which time, both being separated from their children, Gavin and Toni found life very difficult indeed.

Toni was able on occasion to come back to London and to see Alexandra and Andrew, but Gavin had to rely on the occasional visit in the school holidays from Deia and Jack. Problems which Gavin and Toni might have been able to resolve quite simply had they been home in London became almost impossible at a distance. Differences with his first wife became an increasing problem for Gavin who, through no fault of his own, was unable to respond as effectively as he might have done had he been in London. He was then, of course, to blame. There was little 'milk of human kindness' coming from that quarter. Unsurprisingly, Toni then became ill, and she soon discovered that Canadian healthcare leaves much to be desired by comparison with either New York or London.

Gavin and Toni had each other of course, but they missed the contact with the rest of the family and with their friends. Although they were able to go for a walk or a run, they were in many ways just as imprisoned as Brett.

The family was as dispersed as I had ever known it. Wynn was in New York, Brett was serving his sentence in Alabama, Gavin and Toni were in Toronto, Bea and I were in London, and Vicki, our younger daughter, was in Geneva.

At this point it is perhaps the right time in my narrative to reflect on the place in my life of my daughters. People always speak of the relationship between fathers and daughters, and there is no doubt that this can be very special indeed. And I am no exception. Indeed, in my case I have been doubly blessed, in that I have two extraordinary daughters with whom I have very special relationships. Although very different in overall character from each other, they do share a large number of common characteristics. Each wears her emotions on her sleeve. Each is dynamic and also intelligent. But they both laugh and cry, and each requires a great deal of love. Sadly, the love which they both require proved to be lacking in their young marriages. Thankfully, Toni has now found love with Gavin, and I retain the hope that Vicki will also find lasting love one day.

Whilst Gavin and Toni were stuck in Canada, Vicki was going through troubles of her own. She suffers from severe tinnitus, something which makes life very difficult for her, even at the best of times. But she was also dealing with other traumas. Apart from the problems affecting her parents and her siblings, she was also coming to terms with the break-up of her marriage. And through all of this she was raising three teenage girls, bringing them through a very difficult stage of their own lives. Together with her ex-husband, Steve O'Hana, Vicki has brought up three wonderful children – three clever and attractive young ladies who are now getting ready to make their impact on the world.

Notwithstanding everything, Vicki continued to support the family at every stage, coming to London to see us, and travelling regularly to South Africa to work during a period when our business there was growing strongly. And, in the context of South Africa, I must also mention Toni too who, even though she found herself based against her will in Toronto, regularly flew to South Africa from either Canada or London to help wherever she could.

But returning to Gavin's plight in Toronto, I will conclude this chapter with what must necessarily be an abbreviated version of what transpired over a period of almost two years. Believe me, there is a very great deal more to be said, but what you are about to read are the essential elements.

On 21 April 2005, the Canadian Minister of Justice issued an Authority to Proceed (ATP) after receiving an official request from the United States for Gavin's extradition. Crucial to the success of that request was an allegation that Gavin had failed to report employment income paid to the credit of certain Guernsey-based accounts. Importantly, Okula certified as part of the request that a man called Philip Blows, who was the manager of the Guernsey accounts, would be prepared to testify that Gavin owned and controlled these accounts. But Okula was lying. He was already in possession of information provided by Blows to the effect that the accounts in question were established and funded not by Gavin but by Arnold, his father. Despite this, Okula maintained the pretence that Gavin 'controlled' and 'effectively owned' the accounts, even though he had read a signed witness statement from Blows to the contrary.

Okula's disingenuous assertions about Philip Blows were part of a series of filings which were made to the court. These began with a filing made by the United States on 17 March 2005 entitled 'Record of the Case', which was referred to by everyone by the acronym ROC. This was followed a month later by a 'Supplementary Record of the Case' or SROC. And, 20 months later, the United States made a further filing – a 'Second Supplementary Record of the Case (SSROC)'.

Conversations about Gavin's case during this time may have been peppered with acronym upon acronym, but what shone through were two things. First, that there was absolutely no truth in the underlying allegations and, second, our firm belief that Okula had planned Gavin's arrest at Toronto airport in order to circumvent extradition – in other words, to kidnap him.

As far as the allegations were concerned, although it required a good deal of work, the team was confident that Gavin could be proved innocent. But Gavin was having to defend himself against possible extradition to the United States where he would come under exactly the same kind of pressures to enter into a plea bargain as Brett had experienced. The team knew that they had to defeat the extradition request, and they recognised, too, that the key to success lay in the record of exchanges between Okula and the Canadian officials around the time of Gavin's arrival in Toronto.

Gavin's lawyers – Michael Code and David Martin – knew that they had to persuade the Canadian court that there had been an abuse of process by the Government of the United States of America. They had asked the United States and the Canadian Border Service Agency to provide the underlying records of what had taken place, but their requests had been refused. So it was that, in January 2006, a year after Gavin's seizure, they applied to the court to order the disclosure of any relevant documents.

The issue underlying Gavin's application for disclosure, and the essential element which had to be proven, was whether there was an 'air of reality' to the allegations of abuse of process. If there was, the court might be persuaded to make the exceptional order that documents should be disclosed.

Two weeks later, Gavin's lawyers' determination was rewarded when the 'key' which would unlock the whole of the problem was delivered to the court by none other than Counsel for the Canadian Border Service Agency. On Valentine's Day 2006, Counsel for the CBSA informed the judge, Mrs Justice Molloy, that the Agency had in fact received the document from the United States requesting extradition on 18 January 2005 only. This was the document that should have formed the basis for Gavin's detention and interrogation at the airport. But 18 January was also the date on which Gavin had been apprehended. Was it really possible that the arrival of the extradition request document was the first thing that happened, as should have been the case?

Counsel for the CBSA conceded, in light of this admission, that there really was an 'air of reality' to the allegations of abuse of process and agreed that a disclosure order should be made relating to the CBSA documents. Mrs Justice Molloy concurred and an order was drawn up. This stated that the Court was "satisfied that the Applicant has demonstrated an air of reality with respect to the allegations against the CBSA".

And so it was that the CBSA delivered a batch of documents, mostly emails, which revealed the shocking truth of what had really happened. I have described the sequence of events earlier in the chapter, and do not propose to go over the same ground again in detail. But it is worth remembering that the first move in all of this was, as the emails revealed, the delivery from Okula on 13 January of a draft "provisional arrest request. Precise flight arrangements to follow." This was dated four days prior to Gavin's departure from the UK and notes "Believed to be in the United Kingdom."

The emails, as you already know, exposed the detail of Okula's machinations to avoid extradition and instead to bundle Gavin over the border at Buffalo. When this proved impossible to achieve, Okula switched plans, instead relying on the compliance of Canadian border officials to ensure that Gavin was held in the worst conditions imaginable, and for as long as possible.

The disclosure of the email exchanges was decisive, and Mrs Justice Molloy's judgment, in September 2006, was excoriating of Okula. Referring rather confusingly to Gavin both as 'the applicant' and by name, Mrs Justice Molloy's judgment includes the following findings:

> *The theory of the applicant is that United States authorities attempted to engineer a situation in which Mr Tollman would either be delivered directly to the United States for prosecution or detained in custody*

away from his home, work and family where he would be under considerable pressure to abandon his rights and surrender to the jurisdiction of the United States to face trial. **There is substantial, indeed overwhelming, evidence to support that theory.**

The applicant submits that the conduct of the United States constitutes an abuse of process that caused personal harm to Mr Tollman and undermined the integrity of the Canadian judicial system.

Gavin Tollman was easy to find. A ten-year-old with internet access could find him. There is no question that he could have been easily located using the resources of the United States justice system. I find as a fact that the United States authorities knew Mr Tollman was living in London and that, if they did not have his precise address, it would have been easy for them to obtain it. Mr Okula was determined, for whatever reason, to seek Mr Tollman's arrest outside his home jurisdiction.

The paper trail begins with an email from Mr Okula to Naydene Baca. Only those emails that eventually were forwarded to Canadian officials have been disclosed.[97]

The US authorities took no steps to commence extradition proceedings on January 20, 2005. It would appear that US efforts on January 20, 2005 were directed towards ensuring that Mr Tollman remained in custody rather than obtaining bail. According to Gord Morris's notes of his conversation that day with Mr Okula, he was told that two members of Mr Tollman's family were fighting extradition (which was true, this would be Stanley and Beatrice Tollman who took the position that the extradition proceedings against them were an abuse of process) and that two other family members were also fugitives (which was not true). Mr Okula also told Mr Morris that Mr Tollman might try to flee to Switzerland, as the United States did not have an extradition treaty with Switzerland that covered tax fraud and that he could skip out on any amount of bail, as he had access to a South African passport (which was not true, as Mr. Tollman's South African passport was in his luggage and had been seized by the authorities at the time of his detention). Mr Okula recommended that Mr Tollman not be released on any amount of bail.

---

[97] The United States could not have been ordered to disclose its own internal exchanges, nor were they volunteered.

I conclude, based on the unrebutted evidence before me, that the intention of the American authorities was to ensure Gavin Tollman was kept in custody in difficult conditions for as long as possible, in the hopes that he would abandon his rights under Canadian law and surrender to the American authorities in Buffalo. Their objective from the outset was to get Mr. Tollman into American custody without extradition proceedings anywhere. I find that the US authorities deliberately set out to avoid extradition proceedings in the UK or elsewhere, or alternatively, to have Mr Tollman extradited from a jurisdiction where he would be under significant pressure to abandon his rights to resist extradition.

It is often said that actions speak louder than words. The actions taken by the United States against Gavin Tollman in this country speak loudly of a deliberate plan to engineer the return of Mr Tollman to the United States to face tax fraud charges without having to go through the nuisance of an extradition proceeding. The fall-back plan was that if extradition had to be resorted to at all, it would be pursued in this country where Mr Tollman had no ties to the community, away from his wife, his children, his friends and his work; a place where he was more likely to be held in custody or to have his freedom severely curtailed, and therefore more likely to waive his rights and simply surrender to the United States. When the actions taken are coupled with the words found in the exchange of emails between US and Canadian authorities, the nefarious nature of the plan is all too clear. There have been no words of explanation in the face of the serious allegations now made; the actions taken and words said at the time of the events speak all the more clearly.

This is not simply a case of disguised extradition. The US authorities did not simply discover that a fugitive from their justice system was living in Canada and attempt to persuade Canada to turn him over, rather than commence extradition proceedings. The entire process in this case was engineered by the United States. US authorities deliberately laid in wait to trap Mr Tollman in a jurisdiction where he would be without any kind of support system, where it would be relatively easy to effect his removal and where they expected to have the cooperation of local authorities. The United States hoped that once arrested in a foreign country Mr Tollman would be held in custody or under restrictions that were sufficiently onerous that he would waive his rights and surrender. Against this engineered backdrop the actual steps taken by way of disguised extradition take on an even more sinister character.

It is odd that Mr Tollman was detained at the Metro West Detention Centre, the most restrictive facility in which he could be imprisoned. There is good reason to believe that the US authorities influenced the decision as to where Mr Tollman would be detained, and further that their purpose in doing so was to ensure that his detention was as unpleasant as possible so as to pressure him into abandoning his rights and surrendering to the United States. This is a contributing factor to the abuse of process.

The actions of the United States against Mr Tollman in this country, whether with the willing or unsuspecting cooperation of the Canadian authorities, are abusive. Canadian legal processes were manipulated in an attempt to get Mr Tollman into US custody to face charges without the safeguards of an extradition proceeding. Efforts were made to keep Mr Tollman in a harsh prison setting, away from his family, friends and community, in order to pressure him into abandoning his rights. Those attempts failed, but that is no answer to the allegations of abuse. Indeed, but for the egregious conduct against him, Mr Tollman might well have simply surrendered into US custody, as his counsel in New York was negotiating at the outset.

I do not propose to detail all of the ways in which Mr Tollman has suffered personally. The first, and most obvious, is that he spent 10 days in custody in harsh circumstances at the Metro West Detention Centre. Since his arrival here for a two-day business trip on January 18, 2005, he has been unable to leave the jurisdiction. Quite simply, he does not want to be here. He has been able to work, but not efficiently and without the ability to travel that is vital to his ability to do his job well. His wife has joined him here, but had to abandon her own job to do so. She has had health problems while she was here that were difficult for the Tollmans to deal with as outsiders to our medical system.

Most importantly to Mr Tollman, he has missed his children terribly. He is a devoted father. His children live in London in the custody of their mother. Mr Tollman has been able to arrange for them to travel to Canada a few times to spend vacation with him here, but that is hardly a substitute for the almost daily contact he had with them in London. He sees this loss of contact as a personal tragedy of huge proportion. I found his evidence on this point to be genuine and moving. There is no doubt that he has suffered personally as a result of the actions taken against him.

In addition to the personal impact on Mr Tollman, the conduct here must be condemned as contrary to the fundamental principles upon which our justice system is based. The justice system must be fair for all who become enmeshed in it, regardless of intellect, wealth or station in life. Mr Tollman was able to insist on his rights, albeit at considerable personal and financial cost. However, he was armed with intelligence, stamina, a social position of power and prestige, and enormous personal wealth. Very few people would have been able to do what he has done. If the system went awry for him, what hope is there for the weak, the poor and those less powerful? The answer must be in the vigilance of the justice system itself. Misconduct of this sort cannot ever be tolerated, for to do so is to condone, perhaps even to invite, similar conduct in the future. This is the kind of conduct that offends this community's sense of fair play and decency. Having conducted itself in this manner, the requesting state is disentitled to any relief from this court. Accordingly, this extradition proceeding is permanently stayed.

Gavin had won.

Mrs Justice Molloy's judgment is now more that five years old, and I have read it many times since it was handed down. It remains as fresh today as the first time that I read it. It is a devastating indictment of the actions of a man determined to abuse the authority of his office in order to pursue what had clearly become a personal vendetta against the family.

But what was especially shocking was what happened to Okula as a result of this judgment – or, more accurately, what didn't happen. But more of that later.

Gavin no longer had extradition from Canada to the United States to worry about, but the matter of his immigration was still an issue, and his return to the UK was something which needed to be managed safely. He was not yet out of the woods. I will return to that a little later in the book. In the meantime, I will allow the *Ottawa Citizen* to close the chapter with a report it published upon Gavin's return to the UK[98]:

Gavin Tollman's extradition ordeal offers a behind the scenes glimpse of the relationship between Canadian and U.S. authorities

Abuse of process findings happen only in exceptional circumstances, and are often difficult to prove, lawyers say.

About six years ago, U.S. authorities lost an attempt to extradite four Canadian men who allegedly defrauded Pennsylvania residents in a telemarketing scheme.

A judge ruled that U.S. officials tried to intimidate the Canadians into giving up their rights, after a trial judge said the people who resisted extradition would ultimately receive the maximum jail sentence possible. The prosecutor in the case also said in a television interview with the CBC's Fifth Estate that by fighting extradition, the men could face longer sentences under stringent conditions.

Asked to explain further, the prosecutor said: "You're going to be the boyfriend of a very bad man if you wait out your extradition."

Criminal lawyer Brian Greenspan, who represented one of the men in the case, said if not for the "absurdity" of the prosecutor's interview, "that position could never have been revealed". Proving abuse in such cases is as much about luck as anything else, he said. "There's not a science to it, and there's not a formal investigative procedure that would yield the results. You usually have to be lucky and ask the right question at the right time".

Mr. Tollman's lawyers were lucky to find a trail of messages that made the plot clear. Judge Molloy didn't accept arguments from U.S. lawyers that authorities misunderstood proper processes to take.

Their actions, "whether with the willing or unsuspecting co-operation of the Canadian authorities, are abusive," she wrote in her reasons for judgment, which were released in September.

---

[98] Abuse of Process, *Ottawa Citizen*, Neco Cockburn, 6 January 2007.

Only e-mails that were eventually forwarded to Canadian officials were disclosed during the case, but Judge Molloy wrote that the U.S. didn't provide any evidence to refute Mr. Tollman's suggestions of abuse, "despite ample opportunity to do so and ample warning as to the likely consequences of remaining silent".

Canadian authorities, meanwhile, didn't appear to have any concerns of their own about Mr. Tollman's presence in the country, but acted "at all times solely at the request of the U.S. authorities and on the strength of the U.S. warrant for his arrest," she wrote.

Mr. Tollman, "armed with intelligence, stamina, a social position of power and prestige, and enormous personal wealth", was able to insist on his rights, Judge Molloy wrote.

"Very few people would have been able to do what he has done."

THE LORD CHIEF JUSTICE

I explained earlier that Uncle Sam, my father's younger brother, had based himself in Cape Town when he arrived in South Africa, where he became a pillar of the local community. One of his grandsons, Michael Tollman, was born about two months after Brett, and Bea and I would always see Michael during our regular trips to Cape Town when we went to visit his family. We have always been very fond of him, and we both remember him clearly as the little blond boy who always smiled. And I think it is fair to say that, even from the time that he was a little boy, Michael always had something of an affinity towards us too.

In 1975, Michael's parents decided to emigrate from South Africa, and went to live in Toronto. At the time of the move, Michael was 14 years old. On my annual business trip to Canada, I would also visit Michael's parents, and I would always meet the children too – Michael, his older brother Lawrence, and his sister Gail. At the age of 19, Michael, together with Lawrence, travelled around Europe. We were living in Monte Carlo at the time and the two of them came to visit us.

Michael had just finished school, but he did not yet know what to do with his life. It is fair to say that his family's Canadian immigration was not a complete success, and Michael still felt an outsider in Toronto. I encouraged him to consider returning to South Africa, and to go to university in Cape Town. I felt that having a successful grandfather would give him an identity and a sense of belonging, which seemed to be missing for him in Toronto. Uncle Sam had become wealthy and was extremely well-known in the Cape Town area – a leading figure within the community. This contrasted firmly with Michael's experience in Toronto, where he felt that the family really didn't belong.

Michael took my advice and returned to Cape Town where he stayed with his grandparents whilst he completed an accounting degree at university, from which he went on to qualify as an accountant. After Uncle Sam died, Michael decided to move to London, where he undertook a number of temporary assignments, first with British Telecom and then with Forex Trading, the currency brokers' association based in the City. He was then offered a job in our travel businesses, reporting to Mike Ness.

His arrival, in the Spring of 1989, was a very interesting time for our travel businesses. Within three months, we made the major acquisition of Contiki, the market leader in tours for younger adults. Michael was asked to become European financial controller, a job which he carried out for about a year. He was then invited to become CFO of Contiki worldwide. In 1993, after we reorganised the company, Michael moved to Bermuda as the CFO of our whole travel operation. There then followed a period during which he travelled between Bermuda and New York, concentrating on our acquisitions.

This brief required Michael to travel all over the world, something which he took to like a duck to water. It was a job at which he excelled. However, in 2000, after many years of near-constant travelling, he came to see me to say he felt the need to settle. He wanted to put down some roots.

Michael did not really see himself living in either New York or London and, given the amount of travelling he needed to do, it was almost immaterial whereabouts in the world he was based. He asked me whether it might be possible for him to operate from South Africa. I recognised the importance to Michael of establishing some geographical roots, and also of the logic behind basing himself in South Africa. I happily agreed, and Michael has operated out of South Africa ever since.

Michael is Chairman of Cullinan Holdings, the old diamond company. Cullinan is still listed on the Johannesburg stock exchange, and the family holds in excess of 80% of its shares. Sadly, it is no longer in diamonds, but it is one of the largest travel-related companies in Africa. Michael is also on the board of Africa's largest safari company, Wilderness Safaris, as is Gavin. Wilderness is a highly successful business, a 70-lodge enterprise which we in large part helped to build.

In many ways, Michael has been a third son to Bea and me – in reality, becoming part of the family. And he has been hugely supportive through both good times and bad. During my court attendances as part of the extradition proceedings, he was always at my side. And when I was recovering from the botched hernia operation, Michael would sit alongside me in court during the various hearings, helping me to stand when necessary. Upon his return from Canada, Gavin would sit on my other side.

This brings me back to the extradition, and to the judicial review for which the US Government sought permission in February 2006. Bear in mind it was now 18 months since the start of the second extradition attempt, and there had been no fewer that 12 hearings before the Senior District Judge, two of which had taken two days. In addition, there had been three short hearings at which decisions had been handed down.

What little had been achieved during the whole of that period was an order for disclosure of documents. Beyond that, consideration had been given as to whether the Magistrates' Court had the power to order disclosure, as to public interest immunity and legal professional privilege. But no other progress of any kind had been made. Bea and I were now 18 months older, as were the alleged offences of which I stood charged. And in the meantime a number of people had died, including Arnold.

Alun Jones QC and John Hardy had applied to seek permission for a judicial review of almost everything which had taken place at the initial hearings at Bow Street and, later, at Horseferry Road Magistrates' Court (Horseferry Road having replaced Bow Street for five years before it, too, was closed in 2011).

On 15 June 2006, the Divisional Court, in the shape of Lord Justice Thomas and Mr Justice Silber, granted permission in respect of the entirety of the application for judicial review, even though some parts of the application were out of time. The view was taken by the Divisional Court that the application raised issues of general public importance, hence the more 'flexible' approach to deciding which matters which would be subject to the review. In granting permission, Lord Justice Thomas made the comment:

> *"It is clear that it was the purpose of the 2003 Act to try and remedy many of the delays inherent in the extradition process under the 1989 Act. The course taken in this case has been defended by none of the parties before us.... the way in which this case has proceeded gives rise to concern as to the way in which such cases should be dealt with so that the extradition process can be determined within a time that is infinitely more expeditious than what has so far happened with this case. In this case, as Mr and Mrs Tollman are in their 70s, it is particularly unjust that so little has been achieved over such a protracted period of time."*

It was difficult to disagree with what Lord Justice Thomas said. It had all taken a very long time, and little real progress had been made. At the very first court hearing on 17 August 2004, my legal team had challenged the basis on which the extradition was now being attempted under the new Act, when the extradition had already been initiated under the old Act. At that same hearing, counsel acting for the United States replied, "I understand that the Government of the United States was advised that there was insufficient evidence to proceed with the request, and the request was withdrawn."

That succinct explanation was perhaps the closest I ever got to hearing the truth. Things went downhill from that point, with differing, and increasingly less credible, explanations being provided by the US Government as to why the original requests had been withdrawn. Two years later, we had been comprehensively prevented from getting to the bottom of things.

In connection with my lawyers' application for disclosure, in May 2005 an affidavit from Stanley Okula had been placed into court. The affidavit was submitted, it explained, "with respect to the circumstances surrounding the withdrawal of the original extradition requests (which were filed in or about March 2003) and the re-submission of those requests in 2004". Okula provided the following four-point explanation for the withdrawal of the original requests.

First, he said that additional evidence had been received by the United States throughout 2003 and 2004 and that the receipt of evidence was continuing.

Second, he said that in April 2003, the Grand Jury had returned a 'Third Superseding Indictment' against me which included an additional money laundering charge. He added, "Our withdrawal of the initial request was predicated in significant part on our desire to have this charge serve as a basis for prosecution."

Third, that the original request had been made close to the commencement of the trial of Monty Hundley and the others and that because the preparation for the trial "required the complete attention of all the prosecutors and investigators, we simply did not have the time and resources necessary to revise or supplement the initial papers – which papers we had in any event decided not to proceed upon".

"Finally," he concluded, "and most significantly, I believed that the withdrawal of the initial papers and the re-submission (with the additional charge, and supported by the significant additional proof) was irrelevant from an evidentiary standpoint because I fully believed – and believe to this day – that we possessed more than sufficient proof under both the old Act and the new Act to sustain a *prima facie* case."

Okula's affidavit was complete tosh from start to finish. For instance, when a state requesting extradition finds that it has additional evidence which it would like to add, the normal practice is to file a supplementary affidavit. It was unprecedented for the United States to withdraw an extradition request simply because they had received additional evidence. To suggest otherwise is madness, a view which I later discovered was shared by the Magistrate who had to read this twaddle.

The money laundering charge 'reason' was a complete red herring from the beginning. Not only was this in any case a complete irrelevance so far as Bea was concerned – she was, after all, never indicted – but the United States shortly thereafter withdrew reliance of any kind in relation to alleged money laundering.

The next excuse had concerned Monty Hundley's trial. But Monty's trial ended in February 2004, and the extradition requests were not withdrawn until two months later. Besides, the prosecution of Monty and the others was carried out not by Okula, but by others in the Office of the US Attorney. Shortage of time was never the issue insofar as the extradition request was concerned. Okula's real problem was lack of evidence.

Okula also professed ignorance of the rules of procedure in United Kingdom extradition proceedings. But Okula had been working closely with the CPS and with two experienced UK extradition barristers. Not only that, in late January 2004, the Home Office had made the US authorities aware of the new extradition regime. The Home Office guidance made crystal-clear that the determining factor as to whether the 1989 Act or the 2003 Act applied was simply whether a request had been made before 31 December 2003. In our cases, such a request had undeniably been made.

The only logical explanation for the withdrawal and resubmission of our extradition requests was that it had been done to secure a more favourable reception under the new, rather than the old, Act. But Okula did not admit that this was his reason. His affidavit was fiction from beginning to end.

The judicial review was heard on 17 July 2006 in the High Court, and before no less a figure than the Lord Chief Justice himself, Lord Phillips of Worth Matravers, assisted by Mr Justice Cresswell. But it was not until early September that the judgment was handed down. This was not a happy day. I knew that it was bad news when I heard that Clive Nicholls and James Lewis wanted to come to debrief me on the judgment. This was not the way things normally happened. But this offer was made even more exceptional because I was not at home in London, but was staying in Dorset, at Summer Lodge – a three-hour drive away. I expected the worst. When Clive and James eventually negotiated their way through the late holiday traffic, that is exactly what I got.

The United States had in essence succeeded on every count. On the matter of disclosure of documents, Lord Phillips said (my emphasis):

> *Both our civil and our criminal procedures have complex rules in relation to disclosure of documents.* **In each of the cases before us the persons whose extradition is being sought have persuaded the judge that he should make an order for disclosure. We do not consider that this was the appropriate course to take.** *Neither the rules governing disclosure in a civil action, nor those governing disclosure in a criminal trial can be applied to an extradition hearing. Furthermore, those rules form part of an adversarial process which differs from extradition proceedings. Where an order for disclosure is made, it requires one party to disclose documents to the other, not to the court. But where extradition is sought, the court is under a duty to satisfy itself that all the requirements for making the order are satisfied and that none of the bars to making the order exists.*

And in relation to the allegations of abuse of process:

> *The judge should be alert to the possibility of allegations of abuse of process being made by way of delaying tactics. No steps should be taken to investigate an alleged abuse of process unless the judge is satisfied that there is reason to believe that an abuse may have taken place. Where an allegation of abuse of process is made, the first step must be to insist on the conduct alleged to constitute the abuse being identified with particularity. The judge must then consider whether the conduct, if established, is capable of amounting to an abuse of process. If it is, he must next consider whether there are reasonable grounds for believing that such conduct may have occurred. If there are, then the judge should not accede to the request for extradition unless he has satisfied himself that such abuse has not occurred. The common issue in the two sets of appeals before the court relates to how he should do this.*

The judgment then went on to make what I continue to consider an extraordinary statement, bearing in mind the clarity with which Parliament had spoken on the matter of application of the old and new Extradition Acts (once again, my emphasis):

> **We think that it is clear from all of this that the United States Government decided to withdraw the first requests, not because it had decided not to proceed with their attempts to extradite Mr and Mrs Tollman under the 1989 Act, but because they had concluded that this could be more satisfactorily achieved under the 2003 Act.**
>
> *We do not consider that these facts, of themselves, constitute an abuse of process. If Mr and Mrs Tollman are to demonstrate an arguable case of abuse of process they need to demonstrate that there are grounds for suspecting that the present proceedings are being pursued for some improper motive, or are otherwise abusive.*

In other words, the High Court believed that everything we had been alleging for the last two years, and about which we had been fighting tooth and claw, was indeed *true*. Hoorah! But even though it accepted that the United States had switched in order to gain a tactical advantage, the High Court was nevertheless prepared to allow the extradition to continue as though nothing at all had happened. This was absolutely breathtaking!

In finding for the United States, Lord Phillips also agreed, amongst other things, to quash the disclosure order which had been made by the Senior District Judge. Disclosure was now, of course, an irrelevance. Forget 'smoking gun'. There could have been the equivalent of an arsenal of Weapons of Mass Destruction within those documents. And in the eyes of the High Court, this would have made not a ha'porth of difference. The Americans had been given *carte blanche* to proceed under the 2003 Act, even though the world agreed that they had started under the 1989 Act and were simply trying (and succeeding) to make life a whole lot easier for themselves by switching.

Lord Phillips also agreed to an order requiring the Senior District Judge to fix a date for the start of the extradition hearing without delay. Believe it or not, two years and 20 hearings later, the extradition proceedings had not yet actually commenced. A combination of adjournments on the part of the United States, and an unwillingness by them to own up to the real reason for the switch, had meant that months and months had drifted by. But we were all now being told to get on with it. The new, so-called fast-track extradition procedures were about to be applied to us – and in short order. And the 2003 Act, it seemed, provided very little about which we had grounds to argue. Worse, there was no facility to guarantee oversight of the process. It would have been wrong to describe the new approach as a 'rubber stamp', but it did not seem very far short of it.

The High Court's decision that day in September 2006 plunged the family into deep depression. Arnold was dead. Brett had been to jail. Gavin had been exiled away from his children, his home and his job in Canada. Bea was ill and her health was deteriorating fast. And our hopes of being able to fight the extradition on a reasonably level playing field had just been dashed. Until now, maintaining the morale of the family had been a near impossible task. Now it had become positively Herculean. I dug very deep indeed, trying to summon up the courage which I knew was necessary. Maintaining a brave face and calming and encouraging the others was very, very difficult. At times like these, and with considerable humility, I thought of the words of Theodore Roosevelt, and asked myself whether I could live up to them:

> *It is not the critic who counts; not the man who points out how the strong man stumbles, or where the doer of deeds could have done them better.*
> *The credit belongs to the man who is actually in the arena; whose face is marred by dust and sweat and blood; who strives valiantly; who errs and comes short again and again;*
> *because there is not effort without error and shortcomings;*
> *but who does actually strive to do the deed; who knows the great enthusiasms, the great devotion; who spends himself in a worthy cause;*

who at the best knows in the end the triumph of high achievement;

and who at the worst, if he fails, at least he fails while daring greatly.

So that his place shall never be with those cold and timid souls who know neither victory nor defeat.

My face was certainly marred with dust, sweat and blood, and there were plenty of shortcomings, but as to whether or not I displayed daring, I will let others judge. In the meantime though, the gloves were most decidedly off. We were about to square up for Round One. But this was not going to be a fair contest. In proceeding under the 2003 Act, my legal team had very little scope within which to operate. We were going to have to pull a rabbit out of the hat if Bea and I were going to survive. Gloom descended on the whole team.

FIGHTING BACK
AGAINST GOLIATH

In preparing ourselves for the fight which we now knew was ahead of us in London, we augmented the legal team with the addition of two very important new members.

The first was an additional QC who would become my lead advocate in Court, and who would allow Clive Nicholls to concentrate on a supervisory role in relation to our team of barristers. The man we chose for this role was yet another exceptionally bright lawyer, as well as being a wonderful human being. Edward Fitzgerald, unlike the rest of the team, was based at Doughty Street Chambers rather than 3 Raymond Buildings. He came to us with an exceptional record of achievement, especially in the field of human rights. In addition to his professional skills, Edward brought to the team his larger-than-life character, erudition and his inexhaustible consumption of Post-it® notes. His files and documents were peppered with so many crumpled yellow tags, it is amazing that he ever found anything. Perhaps he never did.

The other important addition to the legal team was not a lawyer at all. Upon his return from Canada, my nephew Gavin Tollman, who had been forced to spend the best part of the last two years being forced up a very steep learning curve of the law, took over the co-ordination of the various international legal teams. His experiences in Canada had shown him the importance of detail and of organisation, and he had learned and grown in stature a very great deal. He brought both new energy to the task, and a unique perspective from which to co-ordinate the work of the teams. This had now become an almost industrial exercise, and included the London-based team of Simmons & Simmons and the five barristers from Gray's Inn; the lawyers from Canada, Michael Code and David Martin; the New York-based lawyers who had been assisting Gavin and who were now providing crucial ongoing assistance and Chris Todd and Jim Webster at Kellogg Huber Hansen in Washington. Gavin's recently-appointed New York lawyers were Bob Cleary and Mark Harris of Proskauer Rose. Gavin became a veritable demon in the marshalling of everything that had to be done if we were to stand any chance at all of defeating the extradition requests. The odds were clearly stacked hugely against us.

I mentioned earlier that Bea only ever attended one court hearing in relation to our extradition proceedings – the first hearing of all, at Bow Street Magistrates' Court in August 2004. Although Bea was treated with kindness and politeness by all concerned that day, she understandably found the experience of arrest and her subsequent appearance in court deeply unsettling. This had triggered anxiety within her which I observed had been building for some time. Ever since the time of my indictment, her fears had been growing steadily.

I think the first time that I felt that Bea had a more deep-seated problem was when we were warned to expect a possible early-morning knock on the door from the police. On the face of it, a sensible warning – but, as it transpired, ungrounded. Yet it was nevertheless very, very disturbing. Bea began to develop an almost irrational fear, almost bordering on paranoia. If Okula had wanted to get to me through the family, he was certainly doing a good job. Brett had been arrested and indicted. And Bea was going through mental agonies of a kind I had never seen in her in 50 years of marriage. And we had certainly shared some terrible times together. But this was different, and I began to get seriously worried about her, and about other members of the family too.

We sought medical advice, and each of the doctors Bea saw confirmed that the stress of the whole dreadful business had got to her. One of the strongest women I had ever been privileged to meet was being driven to despair, and to ill health, by the pressure which Okula was being allowed to place on the family. Bea was steadily becoming unwell. But at that stage I did not know just how unwell.

I spoke to James Lewis and explained the problem. No-one was trying to do anything other than face up to what Okula was attempting, but Bea's health had to be taken into consideration. James approached the Senior District Judge, who thankfully agreed to dispense with the necessity for Bea to attend hearings. At the time that this was agreed, all that was envisaged was a temporary moratorium until her health improved. But her health did not improve. In fact, it got a whole lot worse.

Bea's health was to become a major factor in the whole extradition process, as you will soon see. In the meantime, though, and with the consent of the Judge, her absence from court continued. She never became well enough again to return. Alun Jones QC would repeatedly whine on that he had forgotten what Mrs Tollman looked like, but there was nothing that could be done. Bea was just too unwell to be there. And she never was.

The team knuckled down to the task. And if we did not already know how difficult it was going to be, we were soon in no doubt at all. The Administrative Court had ruled that the switch from one Act to the other was perfectly acceptable, and they also effectively prevented an appeal of their decision to the Lords. But they did make one very positive – and potentially crucial – point clear. At least, we thought it was clear. Sadly, the Senior District Judge did not see things the same way as us.

The Lord Chief Justice had agreed to a declaration that the Senior District Judge "should hear any evidence and argument that the claimant's request for the extradition of Mr and Mrs Tollman is an abuse of process in the context of sections 79-87 of the Extradition Act 2003". We took the view that the door had clearly been opened for Tim Workman to hear our abuse arguments in full.

Sadly, the man himself did not agree with that interpretation. I had a sense that he felt that he could have succumbed to too much persuasion by our team in relation to the matter of disclosure, and that the High Court had 'rapped his knuckles' just a little as a result. Suitably chastened, he was determined now to behave. And I think he had simply taken the principle of good behaviour a little too far. Thus it was that in early December, and despite the order of the High Court, Tim Workman ruled that he would not hear the abuse arguments in full. He said that he was "of course bound by the decision of the High Court". We did not agree with his interpretation but, rightly or wrongly, he ruled that he would not consider reasons for staying the extradition on grounds of abuse alone.

But that did stop him from making his feelings otherwise about the case perfectly clear. He even went as far as to say, "I am satisfied that the conduct which is alleged to constitute the abuse has been identified. ...(that) the extradition proceedings against the defendants are being made in bad faith by the Prosecutor personally."

He acknowledged that there were "allegations that the Court is being deliberately misled by the Prosecutor Mr Okula". He went on:

> *In respect of the allegation of bad faith by the Prosecutor Mr Okula, the allegations include inappropriate and abusive conduct towards Mr and Mrs Tollman. In particular comments that are said to have been made by Mr Okula are that he 'intends to make life for them as miserable as possible' and that he intends that Mrs Tollman should be seen publicly in handcuffs in demeaning circumstances. Mr Okula has been criticised by both American and Canadian courts. If the allegations were proved it would establish that Mr Okula was displaying animosity towards Mr and Mrs Tollman which went far beyond the responsibilities of a thorough prosecutor.*

He continued by noting that Gavin's extradition from Canada had been refused on what the court had found to be an unequivocal abuse of the process of the court. And that Okula came to his court with a "somewhat tarnished reputation":

> *It is alleged by the defence that Mr Okula, on behalf of the United States Government, deliberately delayed the extradition process under the 1989 Act until it had been superseded by the 2003 Act. I find that the delay in issuing the authority to proceed under the 1989 Act was exceptional. Mr Okula in his affidavit assures the court that he had a prima facie case. That is in contrast to the advocate for the Government before this court on the 17 August 2004, when it was said that the order to proceed was not issued because there was insufficient evidence. The issue as to whether the*

case should have proceeded under the 1989 Act is therefore not merely an academic point.

Given these comments, it was difficult to believe that it was I who had lost this ruling, rather than the United States. But there it was, abuse of process was off the table. We would have to revert to Plan B, whatever that might entail. In the meantime, this is the way *The Lawyer* reported matters:[99]

Extradition protestors frustrated as Simmons appeal is dismissed

Another blow was dealt to those campaigning against the extradition regime between the US and UK last week after Simmons & Simmons failed in its attempts to have an extradition case thrown out for abuse of process.

Simmons litigation head Colin Passmore is acting for retired hoteliers Stanley and Beatrice Tollman, who are wanted in the US on fraud charges.

Their case has been through several preliminary hearings, including an Administrative Court hearing in September this year when the Lord Chief Justice Lord Phillips of Worth Matravers ordered a fast-track extradition hearing within 60 days.

Passmore, instructing Three Raymond Buildings' Clive Nicholls QC and James Lewis QC for Stanley and Beatrice Tollman respectively, filed a witness statement alleging abuse of process against the couple.

The defendants alleged that the extradition proceedings were being made in bad faith by the US prosecutor Stanley Okula; that Okula had deliberately delayed proceedings so that the extradition was governed by the 2003 extradition treaty, which has not yet been ratified by the US; and that Okula was deliberately misleading the court.

On Monday 4 December senior district judge Timothy Workman, sitting in the City of Westminster Magistrates' Court, found that, while Okula had been found responsible for abuse of process in a Canadian court against Stanley Tollman's son Brett and nephew Gavin, that did not mean that the same was true in the UK. Workman therefore dismissed the claim.

---

99 *The Lawyer*, 18 December 2006.

Meanwhile, Alun Jones QC continued to bleat about the behaviour of our team, and especially about the comments of James Lewis. It became clear that there was little love lost between the two of them, despite the fact that they had worked together closely in the past. Jones had made various references in hearings to "serious allegations made by those representing the defendants", including "that the US prosecuting attorney, Mr Stanley Okula, has lied to the United Kingdom authorities and courts, perjured himself, is obsessive and vindictive towards the defendants, and has deliberately misled the courts in Canada".

Referring to our team, he had gone on to point out that "at the heart of their arguments is a sustained attack upon the integrity of the prosecution attorney, and his allegedly obsessive and vindictive attitude towards them". He then threw down the gauntlet, "it is a clear principle of English professional practice that such allegations are not to be made without an evidential basis".

This was a gauntlet which any member of our team would dearly have liked to have been able to pick up. However, having been deprived of an opportunity to argue the question of abuse head-on, it was not at that point clear how we would achieve this objective. But time would soon prove that there is indeed more than one way to skin the proverbial cat.

As part of the proceedings which were about to start, I made a witness statement. I will not bore you with too much detail of that statement, but it contained the following sentiments:

These proceedings have come to dominate my life on a daily basis for five years now and have taken their toll on both myself and my wife, as well as on the rest of our family. Both my wife and I have increasingly come to feel the pressure of the legal proceedings brought against us

"My wife is in very poor health as a result of the stress and pressure she is under, compounded by our belief that Mr Okula has engaged in a personal vendetta against me, my business interests and most importantly my family. In recent years I too have suffered increased ill health on account of the stress, resulting in significantly increased medication.

I pointed out that I was taking no fewer than 14 different medications each day, a feat of both memory and organisation. I continued:

> There have been many unhappy events in the course of these proceedings which have placed an enormous strain on me as I have watched and suffered the consequences of Mr Okula's vendetta, particularly as it has been targeted against my close family members. It has been an indescribably awful experience to know that Mr Okula has come good in many respects on the threat that he made to my lawyers, Kellogg, Huber, Hansen, Todd and Evans in 2002, that he would make my life as miserable as possible and pressurise me through attacking my family if I did not return voluntarily to the United States.

It was now 2007, and two-and-a-half years had passed since the extradition process had begun. It was now clear that my extradition request would hinge on delay: on the question of passage of time. In Bea's case, sadly, the question of her poor health became the determining factor. So, whilst Edward Fitzgerald and Hugo Keith prepared to go into battle on passage of time, James Lewis and James Hines, together with Bea's doctors, began to consider what was to be done about the question of Bea's health.

Edward and Hugo pieced together the arguments which would allow me to request the Court to discharge me (i.e. to refuse the extradition request) by reason of the passage of time. These arguments were to hinge on what they described in Court as the "unconscionable and culpable delay by the United States".

As the arguments developed, the team began to recognise the importance of calling witnesses to provide evidence, and a list of potential names was put forward. This grew almost by the day. And as it grew, so too did the realisation that much of the evidence could only be properly examined by the physical presence in court of some of those who were providing it. The difficulty was that the individuals were almost entirely based in North America, rather than in the UK. It was clear that we would have to try to get some of them, at least, to come to London.

As our legal team produced evidence from a number of very credible witnesses, each of whom called into question the way in which the prosecution of our case was being handled, Okula and his advisers became increasingly concerned. Alun Jones was called to New York, to spend a day with Okula. Upon his return, a witness statement was handed in to Westminster Magistrates' Court as part of the proceedings in the name of none other than Stanley J Okula Jr.

The affidavit was a long and rambling document, and I will touch on a little of its contents only. Central to most of what he had to say was the assertion that I must have known what was going on at all times, and that if time had indeed passed, I was the one responsible for any delay.

Okula's statement referred to me accusing him of engaging in a vendetta and explained that "very serious allegations" had been made in the London courts about his conduct as prosecuting attorney in New York, and about the conduct of the prosecuting extradition lawyers in London. He followed this up by suggesting that I had personally accused him, through my lawyers, of lying and perjury, and of acting maliciously. He had been told, he suggested, that on three occasions at a two-day hearing in November 2006 James Lewis had accused him of "blackmail". From what you have read earlier in the book, you will not be surprised to learn that I had little reason to challenge these assertions.

He complained that he had no expectation that a personal attack upon me would be renewed at the passage of time hearing, and was surprised that I was once again accusing him of serious misconduct.

Amongst the many dubious suggestions which his affidavit contained was that a New York lawyer called Charles (Chuck) Clayman would have kept me fully informed of developments at all times. He pointed out that Chuck Clayman had represented a number of people who had been caught up in some way in the investigation, and that Chuck had been "enlisted" by my former lawyer, Jack Tigue. Clayman and Tigue had, he suggested, a "close professional and personal relationship".

Chuck Clayman's clients included a number of companies, clerical assistants and accountants who had worked either for the family or for Tollman-Hundley. Okula's hypothesis was that because Clayman was able to keep copies of the documents supplied by the US Attorney to the grand jury, he could then pass these on, 'no questions asked', to my own lawyers. This, Okula suggested, meant that I was at all times abreast of what was being investigated, and the nature of the allegations against me. This was, of course, merely an hypothesis and, as it happened, entirely untrue.

Chuck Clayman is a veteran criminal lawyer. A larger-than-life character with a huge walrus moustache, he was educated at Harvard and at the University of Pennsylvania Law School. He served as an Assistant District Attorney in Manhattan under the legendary New York County District Attorney Frank Hogan, otherwise known as 'Mr Integrity', later becoming an Assistant United States Attorney in the Eastern District of New York. For the last 25 years, he had been in private practice, representing clients in federal and state investigations and prosecutions throughout the United States. Chuck Clayman is very much his own man. He most certainly does not behave in the manner which Okula was suggesting.

When he heard what Okula had said, Chuck Clayman was, as he later told Westminster Magistrates, "… personally outraged. At all times I represented my clients ethically, honestly and effectively, and based upon my professional duty to them."

"The investigation spanned several years," he continued. "It involved scores of lawyers, many of whom I have known professionally for decades. To suggest that I would act in a manner that was in any way not in my clients' best interests because of these relationships is both false and malicious, and without any basis in fact."

Okula's affidavit had also gone on to mention the interview which he had conducted with Arnold in London in March 2002, although quite what point he was trying to make escaped me. He said that the grand jury had originally taken testimony from Arnold in May 2001, at which time Arnold had been given immunity from prosecution.

And in 2002, Arnold had agreed to give further evidence at the offices of Kingsley Napley in London, which Okula had attended. I knew from those who had been involved that the whole process had been a fiasco, rendered utterly pointless because Arnold was by then completely deaf, unable to hear a word Okula or anybody else had said to him.

Okula then laid out what he claimed to have been the basis of a possible plea bargain, which had been delivered to Morvillo Abramowitz and subsequently discussed with me. I, of course, dealt with this point earlier in the book. You may remember that the 'deal', if Okula and I are talking of the same thing, had been communicated to me by Bob Morvillo thus: "This is the deal. $100 million. Wife walks. Brett serves one year. You serve two. Best deal I can do." As you know, I had not even been asked to express a view about Morvillo's extraordinary communication, nor had I offered one. I knew nothing of the meeting which had preceded that sketchy early evening conversation.

The last time anyone from Morvillo Abramowitz had spoken to me about all this – just a few weeks earlier – I had been told that I was considered to be not "at the forefront" of the "alleged fraudulent activities". I had also been told it was OK to sign a voluntary extension of time in respect of tax liabilities. Then, out of the blue, came Morvillo's shocking staccato. I had not even known what to think, let alone to convey any thoughts by way of response.

Okula was then foolish enough to suggest that our team had lied when accusing him of making a reference to looking forward to a perp walk with Bea. "I note also that none of the witnesses to be called on Stanley Tollman's behalf refers to the false 'perp walk' allegation, which Mr Tollman says is 'detailed elsewhere' I respectfully request that Mr Tollman's lawyers be required to substantiate this comment (which they cannot, because it was never said) or withdraw it." Okula would soon learn to rue the day when he made this rash and untruthful challenge.

Okula's affidavit then referred to various members of my family, and the manner in which each of them had reacted to events. Once again, he was less than truthful. But the affidavit was supposed to have been a statement of fact. In places, demonstrably it was not. Talking of me, for instance, he said that I had "decided to run rather than fight the United States charges, thus becoming, under United States law, a fugitive." At the risk of sounding like a stuck record, I had, of course, run nowhere. In fact, I had hardly moved for five years.

Okula then went on to refer to Brett and Bea, and I will at this point simply repeat the two relevant paragraphs:

> *"Unbeknownst to us, Brett Tollman had been in London with Stanley Tollman when the charges against Stanley Tollman were voted by the grand jury, but he returned (again, without our knowledge) to New York in or about late April or May 2002. When we learned that Brett Tollman had been seen in or around his apartment at 485 Park Avenue, IRS agents effectuated his arrest near his home on Park Avenue. Again, the point that requires emphasis is that Brett Tollman's New York attorney never informed us that he returned to the United States, nor did the New York attorney contact us after Stanley Tollman fled and indicate that Brett was prepared to surrender on any charges.*
>
> *"Brett Tollman was arrested, quite simply, because we feared he might leave the country, or simply follow the course taken by Beatrice Tollman – who, although in the United States when Stanley Tollman was charged in April 2002, fled the United States and all of her properties here in May 2002 and joined her husband in London."*

As you can see from Okula's own admission, Brett was arrested on the sidewalk, close to his home, and in the heart of his neighbourhood – a neighbourhood within which he was extremely well-known. A public arrest was of course entirely unnecessary, and was carried out by some very unpleasant people in order to create maximum embarrassment. It is simply not true that the US Attorney's Office had not been informed that Brett had returned to New York. The Office not only knew that he was back, but had been told that he was willing to answer any questions they might have. And once again, the fiction is repeated that Bea had 'fled' in May, a month after I had left

New York. Bea and I went to London on the same flight in April, as Okula knew only too well.

Okula then went on to answer criticisms of his treatment of Gavin, saying simply that he "disagreed" with many of the factual comments and findings made by Judge Molloy in Canada. He continued by stating something which, if true, was profoundly disturbing, given the devastating comments which had been made about him by the Toronto court. He said, "Suffice it to say that there has been no criticism of me by any of my seniors with respect to this matter."

As to the underlying facts of the matter, Okula's final sign-off was in fact positive, and in large part agreed with my own account of events. "The prosecution accepts that Mr Tollman was less involved in the detailed discussions with the bank than other defendants, though he did attend a number of critical meetings, as the documents disclose. He did indeed spend a portion of his time travelling between his various homes in the United States, in entertaining, and regular international travel."

Why then, given these admissions, had I not been viewed simply as a minor player in the Tollman-Hundley debacle? Why, given my subsidiary role and my remoteness from what was happening, had I been treated as the central figure and the man who was expected to put up ten times more in bail than even Monty Hundley? And why had I never been given credit for paying millions and millions of dollars in taxes to the IRS?

The first hearing of 2007 took place at the end of February in the unglamorous setting of Court 3 of the City of Westminster Magistrates' Court. The Magistrates' Court was at that time situated in Horseferry Road, close to London's Millbank, a stone's throw from the Palace of Westminster. Since then, Westminster Magistrates' Court has relocated once again, this time to a purpose-built home on the Marylebone Road. The February 2007 hearing lasted three days, and was followed by further hearings in April and May. For the purposes of reporting what happened I am going to concertina the proceedings as though they had all occurred at one time. The reality was that the hearings took place sporadically over a period of several months.

Arrangements had been made for a number of key people to visit London to give evidence, and what thus began was the kind of extradition trial which many said was not possible under the new Act. What the legal team were about to achieve was a thorough examination of the extradition requests, and not the superficial rubber-stamping which was considered to be inevitable. We were about to demonstrate that the impossible could in fact happen.

Edward Fitzgerald began by explaining what it was we were about to show. In essence, this was the nature of my defences to the bank fraud allegations, and the extent to which my ability to defend myself had been prejudiced by the passage of time.

He pointed out that the initial extradition request, which dated from March 2003, related to ten counts (charges) only, but that the US Government was now seeking my return in relation to no fewer than 23 counts. The very considerable widening of the request was unexplained. It was not, for instance, justified by the second superseding indictment of November 2002 having been itself 'overtaken' by the third superseding indictment of April 2003. The third superseding indictment had, after all, differed from the second only by the addition of a single money-laundering charge. There had been no obvious changes which would have explained the reason for the change. But whatever the reasoning behind it, and irrespective of difficulties resulting from the passage of time, defending myself would now be a much more complex challenge.

Edward reminded the court that if I were to be extradited, it was unlikely that any trial would take place until 2008 at the earliest. This would be some 15 years after the events in question and approximately five years after the Hundley trial. And by that time I would be aged 79. He said that we would show that there was a serious risk of injustice, and that my "forensic ability" to make good my defences has been "irreparably prejudiced". Vital witnesses had died, witness recollections would inevitably have faded, and key documents would no longer be available.

Our first witnesses included Bernie Patrusky, a partner of WeiserMazars, New York, and George Boronkay, a New-York based banking expert, who had for many years been a Managing Director of Deutsche Bank, prior to which he had been the Bank's Senior Credit Officer. Bernie brought both accountancy and legal skills to a forensic examination of Tollman-Hundley's relationship with its banks and George, an expert on asset-based lending, was able to assess the Creditor Repayment Agreement.

George also examined whether the banks would have been aware of the HFS Earnout Agreement, and expressed an informed view about the likelihood of being able to access historic records. He made clear that, given the passage of time, there would have been an inevitable loss of documentation. He told the court that bank records were usually kept for only six to seven years. Most of the transactions which were at issue were much older than that.

No fewer than ten lawyers appeared as witnesses in Court – three from Washington, DC, three from New York, one each from London, Monaco and Durham, North Carolina and, finally, one who worked between Toronto and Ottawa. Two of the Washington lawyers were Chris Todd and Jim Webster, the partners of Kellogg Huber Hansen who had taken over from Morvillo Abramowitz.

Jim's evidence was a tour d'horizon of the charges against me, and of my ability satisfactorily to defend myself. Alun Jones attempted unsuccessfully to unseat Jim at various times along the way. One of the points on which Jim was pressed was the suggestion he had made that the death of Arnold had had a seriously damaging effect on my defence. As far as Jim was concerned, Arnold's death meant that I had lost a very important defence witness. Okula had challenged this in his witness statement, claiming that it was "utterly absurd" to suggest that, had he still been alive, I would have called Arnold as a witness. Alun Jones repeated this comment during Jim's cross-examination. But Jim came back at him swiftly. "I disagree strongly. Arnold Tollman was never indicted, let alone convicted. On the other hand, the US Government's 'star' witness, James Cohen. was a man convicted of multiple felonies, a fact well known to Okula."

James Cohen, the key government witness to whom Jim was referring, was a man whom I never knew, but who I believe had been involved in the exercise which led up to the Paternoster and Chelsea Acquisitions transactions. Cohen, in a conscious effort to curry favour with the US Attorney's Office, had begun 'co-operating' with Okula as early as 1997. He had been used as a witness at the trial of Hundley and the others, even though it emerged at trial that Cohen had lied to the prosecutors numerous times during the period when he was supposed to be co-operating. Cohen had even continued lying to the prosecution after entering into a signed agreement with them which expressly obliged him to tell the truth. Despite this, and despite the fact that he had been convicted of multiple felonies in both State and Federal Courts, Cohen was still considered by Okula to be a credible witness.

Jim Webster pointed out to the London court that Cohen was the only person prepared to testify that I had personal knowledge of the alleged bank fraud, and went on to comment,

> "I think the use of Mr Cohen by the Government is much more outrageous than any effort we would make to use Arnold Tollman as a witness. Moreover, Arnold Tollman would have had very helpful testimony to our defences of knowledge and intent. He would have testified that Stanley Tollman did not recruit him to participate in Paternoster; that Stanley Tollman did not have prior knowledge of his involvement in Paternoster; that Stanley Tollman never had any detailed discussions with him about the activities of Paternoster; that at most they discussed it in passing, that Arnold Tollman never had any intent to cancel debt; that Arnold Tollman relied on the professionals that were guiding him in the use of Paternoster; that Arnold Tollman viewed Paternoster as a potential investment and not as a sham entity.
>
> "Arnold Tollman's death has irreparably undermined Mr Tollman's ability to demonstrate that there was no conspiracy to conceal cancellation of debt income from the IRS because Arnold Tollman would have testified that, as the sole shareholder of Paternoster and the 90% shareholder of

Chelsea Acquisitions, he always viewed the purchase of the deficiency notes as an investment opportunity and never agreed to cancel or forgive those notes."

Jim continued by reminding the Court that the allegations against me were, as Okula's affidavit had agreed, "complex", "wide-ranging" and "massive", involving, as they did, a vast number of companies, individuals and financial transactions. The allegations had been formulated within the context of a programme of re-negotiation of hundreds of millions of dollars of debt. The re-negotiation itself reflected complex transactions, effected over a number of years, involving a large number of financial institutions and individuals, and also involving numerous financial and legal advisors. In addition, there was the alleged use of sham or puppet corporations both in the United States and Guernsey, and the involvement of relatives and business partners as nominees. Furthermore, it was alleged that I was party to false statements which had been submitted to financial institutions, and that I had in some way conspired to defraud federally-insured United States banks. This was an enormous challenge. And as if this frightening catalogue of allegations were not it itself enough, Jim informed the Court that Okula had refused to supply us with the evidence which allegedly supported the charges. His justification for the refusal? The Fugitive Disentitlement Doctrine of course.

Jim then reminded the court that it was not just Arnold who had died, but that several other key witnesses had also passed away, notably Lionel Lipkin, Derek Evans and Robert (Bob) Hausman. He summed up his evidence thus, "It is my opinion that the passage of time has materially harmed Stanley Tollman's ability to receive a fair trial in the United States." Finally, he was kind enough to remind all those present of my "advanced age", and of the state of my health.

Chris Todd had a very different role to that which Jim had performed. Like Jim, Chris is a partner in Kellogg, Huber, Hansen, Todd, Evans & Figel. Also like Jim, he had previously been an Assistant United States Attorney, a role he had performed at SDNY for nine years, in time becoming Chief of the General Crimes Unit.

But Chris was perhaps best known for serving between 1987 and 1989 as Associate Independent Counsel in the Iran-Contra Investigation.

The Iran-Contra Affair was a clandestine action which had not been approved of by Congress. It began in 1985, when the Reagan administration supplied weapons to Iran — a sworn enemy even then — in hopes of securing the release of American hostages held in Lebanon by Hezbollah terrorists loyal to the Ayatollah Khomeini, Iran's leader at the time.

To complicate matters further, the United States had taken millions of dollars from the Iranian weapons sale and routed monies and guns to the entirely unrelated right-wing Contra guerrillas in Nicaragua.[100] This was the clandestine equivalent of killing two birds with one stone.

In 1986, the Lebanese magazine *Ash-Shiraa* published a series of articles in which it exposed the weapons-for-hostages deal. This created a wave of interest, of which Washington took note. In November 1987, Congress published a report on the affair, and this stated that the President of the United States bore "ultimate responsibility".

The report from Congress prompted further investigation, as a result of which Attorney General Edwin Meese verified the concerns, and an independent Special Prosecutor, Lawrence E. Walsh, was assigned to investigate the deals involving the arms sale and the Contra support. Lawrence Walsh appointed five deputies, one of whom was Chris Todd:

WASHINGTON TALK:
THE IRAN-CONTRA AFFAIR; 5 YOUNG
LAWYERS WHO WOULD BE HEROES...[101]

For talented young prosecutors, it is the best assignment since the fall of Richard M. Nixon.

The five deputies to Lawrence E. Walsh, the special prosecutor in the Iran-Contra affair, have the chance to make legal history, and to make legal celebrities of themselves as well.

---

[100] The Contras were the armed opponents of Nicaragua's Sandinista Junta of National Reconstruction.

[101] *New York Times*, 7 July 1987.

Watergate, as they well know, offered legal stardom to a group of elite but largely unknown prosecutors. Archibald Cox, the first Watergate prosecutor, became a household name, and his deputies, including Richard Ben-Veniste and Philip A. Lacovara, found themselves described as national heroes.

"My theory of modern history is that things run in 15-year cycles," said John W. Keker of San Francisco, one of the deputies in the Iran-Contra investigation. "And it's been close to 15 years since Watergate."

Since his appointment last December, Mr. Walsh, whose formal title is independent counsel, has hired 25 lawyers. Known as associate counsel, many were chosen from the nation's most prominent law firms; others were veteran Federal prosecutors in New York and Washington.

Mr. Walsh, a New York lawyer, quickly divided the lawyers into teams focusing on different aspects of the arms affair. To run the day-to-day investigation, he named these five key lieutenants: (Other four names omitted.)

Chris Todd, 40, former chief of the General Crimes Unit at the United States Attorney's office in Manhattan, heads a team reviewing activities at the White House and the National Security Council.

Collectively the five are slightly older and more experienced than the rest of the staff. Defense lawyers say that the deputies are bright and, according to one, "frighteningly tenacious.".

"They go a bit overboard in their thoroughness," the lawyer said. "But I don't think you'll find a brighter group of attorneys. These guys are all quiet but crafty. They're honorable sharks, if there is such a thing."

The hearings over the controversial dealings were televised, featuring the public examination of such people as Lt Colonel Oliver North, a former marine who had been acting as a military aide, John Poindexter, who was National Security Advisor, and Casper Weinberger, a former Defence Secretary. In time convictions – and subsequently pardons – ensued.

Chris Todd is a highly-principled individual, and Okula would have been wise to look at Chris's record in relation to Iran-Contra before, in effect, accusing him of lying. It is a matter of public record that Lawrence Walsh admitted that one of his assistants, Christopher Todd, had stepped down early from his position because he had become "privy to tainted information". Walsh said he never heard specifics of what had worried Chris because "he didn't want to taint me". In other words, Chris had resigned from a plum position in order to maintain the integrity of the investigation. He had taken one for the team.

In a witness statement, Chris had referred to the conversation at White Plains when Okula had said that if I did not return to the United States, he intended to make my life as miserable as he possibly could. In his affidavit, Okula denied ever having said that, not a smart move when the allegation was corroborated by another former Assistant US Attorney. Even so, Chris was asked about this in the witness box, "Are you sure in your own mind that that statement was made?"

Chris confirmed that it was and that, what was more, he had referred to the comment in a letter to Okula written shortly afterwards. Okula had replied at the time, and had not challenged that he made the remark. But now, it seems, Okula was keen to rewrite history. This was as unattractive as it was unpersuasive.

Chris was also asked by Edward Fitzgerald about Okula's reference to looking forward to doing a perp walk with Bea. Tongue in cheek, and speaking as though he were himself a federal prosecutor, Edward said, "I am looking forward to doing a perp walk down Fifth Avenue with a 70-year-old defendant? Is this appropriate or not?"

The answer from former federal prosecutor Chris Todd was both swift and unambiguous, "It is not appropriate. In my view it is beyond being inappropriate. It is simply wrongful. A perp walk is an event where someone notifies the media that a person will be arrested, so that the media can be present as the person arrested is brought in handcuffs to the flash of cameras. It impacts the greatest humiliation on a person."

"I came to the conclusion," Chris continued, "based upon this statement and other things, that Mr Okula had lost his way. It was clear to me that the message to Stanley Tollman was that I, Stanley Okula, am going to make your life as miserable as I possibly can by going after your family, first your wife, then your son and then your nephew."

Colin Passmore's role as a witness was perhaps the least glamorous, but was no less important for that. Alun Jones, who until that time had displayed little respect for the man, was, as a result of Colin's robust withstanding of his aggressive cross-examination, to reassess the mettle, and the nickname, of the man of whom he had until then been somewhat dismissive. Colin was rock solid.

Bob Fink appeared in his capacity as Brett's New York attorney, a man who had been in private practice for nearly 40 years. Bob had been told by Okula in 2002 that, where the Tollmans were concerned, he would "not stop until that family is penniless and destitute." Bob's view of Okula was clear: the whole case of Brett Tollman and the Tollman family had become very personal to him and he had lost his objectivity as a prosecutor. This was a view shared by Bob's partner, Caroline Rule, who had written, "Any assurances you rely on from Okula *must* be in writing, as Okula is simply not to be trusted."

Bob was the man to whom Okula had made the reference about the perp walk, and Alun Jones, keen to undermine this part of the damaging evidence against Okula, pressed Bob firmly on the matter. Although Bob had recounted the perp walk reference to a number of people at the time that the words were said, it emerged that he had not recorded this in writing at the time. As Alun Jones sensed that there was a possible point to be scored here, he pressed Bob mercilessly. Indeed, he accused him of having invented the whole thing. Finally, Jones asked Bob expectantly whether he was aware of anyone else having recorded the perp walk allegation in writing. It was clear that Mr Jones was expecting to hear the answer, "No".

I was always told that one of the golden rules for a barrister is never to ask a question unless you already know the answer. Upon being asked whether he knew of anyone who had ever recorded the perp walk allegation in writing, much to Alun Jones' surprise Bob answered, "My partner, Caroline Rule." "Has she recorded it?" Alun Jones asked. "Yes," was Bob's reply.

A few days earlier, Bob had told Caroline Rule that he was coming to London. He had told her that he was giving evidence, and that one of the matters in relation to which he would be questioned was the perp walk allegation. Her recollection of the event, it seems, was even sharper than Bob's own memory.

"She reminded me that she was present when this happened, which I had not remembered. She had recorded it. She gave me an affidavit, which I brought with me." With that, Bob handed over a document. Alun Jones looked as though someone had just given him a bomb, and both it and he were about to explode, although not necessarily in that order. "This is just done deliberately as a last-minute stunt, is it not, Mr Fink? This has not been disclosed to me in advance for obvious reasons."

The truth was that no-one had realised that Caroline had also been privy to the incident. Bob had shown the UK legal team her affidavit when he had arrived in London, but it had been concluded, with regret, that it was too late for the document to be admitted into Court. But now Jones had himself in effect introduced the document into Court by his rash line of questioning.

A petulant Jones continued to accuse us of trickery. "It is a stunt to produce evidence like this." At this point, Edward Fitzgerald stood up. "My learned friend did not have to make the accusation that the perp walk story had been invented. He has made the accusation and the witness has come up with his response. It is perfectly and entirely proper." And so it was that the record of these hearings includes the entry, "A further statement of an American lawyer, Caroline Rule, made on behalf of Mr Tollman, was introduced into evidence by Counsel for the United States of America."

The Court should have heard evidence from Arnold's doctor, who had looked after Arnold in Monaco up until the time he died. But Dr Sharara had been so intimidated by Okula that he was not prepared himself to appear in a London court. Instead, Arnold's Monaco-based lawyer, Donald Manasse, appeared, and he incorporated the evidence of Dr. Sharara.

Donald Manasse was one of our more cosmopolitan witnesses. Born and raised in Italy, Manasse is the son of a German father and American mother, and has joint American and German citizenship. Educated in the United States, he originally obtained a master's degree in journalism before studying at New York Law School. With offices in Monaco and Nice, he has represented some very high-profile clients, including cycling champion Lance Armstrong.

Dr Sharara is the official registered doctor for the French Embassy in Monaco, and is a highly respected practioner. His evidence was to the effect that he was contacted by Okula concerning the medical certificate which he had provided stating that Arnold could not possibly even travel to New York, let alone appear before a Grand Jury. He told Okula that he had issued the certificate, and that he stood by it.

Okula, who had somehow got hold of Dr Sharara's telephone number, then began calling him in Monaco when it was the middle of the night in New York. Okula pressurised Dr Sharara, suggesting as an alternative that Arnold be interviewed at his care home. Dr Sharara had said that even this was not possible, amd that the certificate was not subject to appeal.

Dr Sharara was then subjected to personal threats by Okula and accused of obstruction of justice. He was threatened with being blacklisted, and generally insulted. On Dr Sharara's behalf, Donald Manasse referred to these "unacceptable remarks impugning Dr Sharara's dignity and honesty". Dr Sharara had then asked Okula to stop contacting him, and told Okula that he would refuse any call from him or his office.

I have of course already provided a blow-by-blow account of the manner in which Arnold was then treated by the New York court, and of Okula's ridiculous insistence upon a second medical opinion in relation to a man who was so unwell he could no longer even see or hear, and who died shortly thereafter. Donald Manasse recounted from his own experience, and from the experience of Dr Sharara, his recollection of their client's dealings with Okula. As I listened to his testimony I became very angry that my brother should have been made to suffer in that way.

A charming lady called Sara Sun Beale, Lowndes Professor of Law at Duke University in Durham, North Carolina, provided the Court with expert academic evidence on the United States legal proceedings which I was facing. Her expertise included the federal government's role in the criminal justice system, the laws defining federal crimes, and various issues of criminal procedure, including prosecutorial discretion. A highly respected legal academic, she had been appointed Reporter for the Advisory Committee on Criminal Rules by no less a figure than the legendary Chief Justice of the United States Supreme Court, William Rehnquist. This Committee drafts the Federal Rules of Criminal Procedure. Rehnquist had called Beale a "superb choice" for the position, referring to her extensive writing on criminal law and procedure, as well as her public and private experience as an attorney.

She gave evidence from a uniquely relevant US perspective on the treatment of delay within the federal criminal justice system, pointing out that protections within the process such as the Statute of Limitations and limitations on pre-and post-indictment delays do not always protect. "It is extremely difficult for a defendant to prevail on a due process claim of pre-indictment delay."

Gavin's Canadian attorney, Michael Code, also gave evidence. You will remember Michael is himself today a Judge of the Superior Court of Justice in and for the Province of Ontario. But when Gavin had met him for the first time in 2005, Michael was in private practice with the firm of Sack Goldblatt Mitchell. Prior to that, he had been Ontario's Assistant Deputy Attorney General (Criminal Law) – the equivalent of the Director of Public Prosecutions in other jurisdictions.

As Michael gave evidence, he was examined by Edward Fitzgerald, who was particularly interested in a paragraph in Okula's witness statement where Okula had said the following:

"... the approach taken with respect to Gavin Tollman in Canada was discussed with appropriate officials at the Office of International Affairs in Washington DC, who must be consulted on matters like this. They suggested, and assisted in implementing, the approach that we took, which is an approach taken in other extradition matters and, more to the point, does not violate any United States law or practice."

Edward asked Michael whether the involvement of the Office of International Affairs (OIA) had been claimed during the course of Gavin's proceedings in Canada. Michael replied that the involvement of the OIA had never been claimed by counsel for the USA, and went on to say that this was something in which they had been very interested. "It is an issue that we squarely raised, and the position taken there (in Okula's witness statement) is not the position taken in the Canadian proceedings by counsel for the USA."

Michael went on to say that they were particularly interested in finding out whether what Mr Okula had done in his dealings with Gavin was carried out with the approval of his superiors in the OIA or not. He added that it was a matter which had been raised in two separate sets of correspondence.

Edward pressed Michael a little further. "So you were asking expressly, 'Was Mr Okula behaving towards Gavin Tollman with the approval of the OIA?' And, if Mr Okula had been saying, 'The OIA approved all this', would they have had to disclose that fact to you?"

Referrring in his answer to Thomas Lemmon, the counsel who had acted for the United States in Gavin's proceedings, Michael said, "Had Mr Lemmon been told that Mr Okula had obtained prior authorisation and approval from the OIA, he would not have been allowed to stand by and allow the court to be misled. According to the documents disclosed to us, the submission had been put squarely to the effect that the OIA had not been involved. At no time did the USA intimate or acknowledge during the course of the abuse of process proceedings, that the OIA had suggested or assisted."

Edward continued, "So the Canadian court was left with the impression that Mr Okula had acted on his own without approval? What conclusions can be drawn from that?"

Michael gave Edward a very steely reply. "It is obviously very serious whenever a court is misled. It happens very, very rarely and, when it does happen, it is extremely serious. The thought that counsel for the USA would knowingly have misled the court is completely aberrant to me. I cannot for a moment believe that Mr Lemmon would have stood by and knowingly allowed the court to have been misled."

"Let us assume," Edward said by way of follow-up, "that, when Mr Okula says, in his affidavit, 'I acted throughout with the approval etc' that he is now telling the truth, and that he was acting throughout with the approval of the OIA. What inference does that lead to as to his conduct in relation to the Canadian proceedings?"

Michael answered, "One can only assume that Mr Okula misled Mr Lemmon knowing that Mr Lemmon would in turn be misleading the court on this point, or allowing the court to be misled on this point."

Edward Fitzgerald summed up what had been said: "So, If he is telling the truth, the Canadian court was misled. If he is not telling the truth – that is to say that in fact the OIA did not approve his actions – then I think perhaps the conclusion is obvious." Edward stopped short of articulating something which everyone was thinking – including, as we would later discover, the District Judge. And that thought was that Mr Okula was a bare-faced liar.

It was around this time that Alun Jones QC, representing the US Government, appeared to sense that things were slipping away from him, and he decided to complain about what he saw as the disparity of resources in the courtroom. This provoked a sharp retort from Edward who, with all the indignation he could muster, said, "It is inappropriate for a representative of the world's biggest megapower to give us a lecture on the inadequacy of resources! This is a complex matter, and the defendant's witnesses should be allowed to be heard."

At the end of the various hearings Edward summed up what the Court had heard from the witnesses, many of whom had appeared in person to give evidence. But before I allow Edward's words to close this chapter, I must mention James Lewis and the defence which had been offered for Bea. I said earlier in the chapter that James, together with James Hines and Bea's doctors, was considering what was to be done about the question of Bea's health. Whilst those representing me were arguing that I should not be extradited by virtue of the passage of time, James Lewis and the rest of Bea's team had been arguing that Bea should not be extradited because of her health.

For a number of reasons, but principally for reasons of privacy, it would not be appropriate to go into any detail as regards Bea's health, and what was said about that subject in Court. The outcome of Court findings in relation to Bea would however prove extremely important, if not decisive in the weeks ahead, and I will return to that subject in the next chapter. For the time being, it is enough to say that the whole dreadful business had made Bea a very unwell lady.

Edward's closing of the arguments was swift yet persuasive. From the evidence of the expert witnesses, he said that it was plain "that the forensic prejudice that they detail is both extensive and causatively linked to the passage of time. Accordingly, the defence submits that such prejudice unequivocally renders Mr Tollman's return unjust. His return would be inordinately oppressive. Never before have the English courts contemplated the return of a man of his age to face such complex allegations after the passage of so much time, particularly when set against the background of unique prosecutorial abuse."

We had given it our best shot. Given the very limited scope which was available as a result of the Americans' successful shift from the 1989 Act to the 2003 Act, our team had done a remarkable job. They had succeeded in having a proper trial of many of the key aspects of the request, including the abusive manner in which it was being prosecuted. They had managed to get 17 live witnesses in front of the District Judge, and our case had been made as thoroughly as anyone could have hoped. We were now in the hands of God and the Senior District Judge. We had thrown ourselves at their mercy.

DAYS OF RECKONING

When I was younger, I used to say that if someone were foolish enough to allow life to terrify them, their life was unlikely to be worth living. As I have grown older, I have had cause to rethink those words. I realise that throughout my life I have awoken every morning with a tight feeling in my gut. I now admit that I have always been, for want of a better word, anxious. I have come to learn that a healthy feeling of fear, as distinct from terror, actually helps one to be more successful. Someone who considers that they are always the smartest guy in town, and have little to worry about, will always fail. We need self-doubt. It improves our judgement.

Fear was certainly an emotion which featured prominently in my life during 2007, as we edged towards the outcome of the extradition proceedings. There was no middle way in the possible outcomes. Either we would succeed, or we would lose. And losing was quite simply unthinkable.

I was in my late 70s. If the United States were to be successful in their extradition request, the choices available to me at that point would have been limited to say the least. Irrespective of guilt or innocence, I would have been offered a choice between negotiating a guilty plea or going to trial. A guilty plea was not an option. It would unquestionably have sent me to prison for what was left of my life, so a trial would have been the only possible route. And defending myself against allegations concerning events which were so old that few could remember them was difficult to contemplate. To make matters worse, many of those who would have been key witnesses in my defence had died. And any trial would inevitably have been heard before a New York jury, which would have been most unlikely even to listen, let alone be persuaded by the arguments of a wealthy man accused of tax evasion. Irrespective of my innocence, or lack of it, the smart money was most definitely on conviction.

The choice was therefore between death in jail and death in jail. Rocks and hard places do not get much more uncomfortable. I was fighting for my life, and I knew I had to win. The alternative was unthinkable. So it was that we awaited District Judge Workman's decisions, the first of which came in May 2007. To say that these were anxious days is a monumental understatement.

The first decision concerned Bea, and the Senior District Judge handed down his judgment in relation to her possible extradition on 29 May 2007. James Lewis had asked the Court to invoke Section 91 of the Extradition Act 2003 and discharge Bea. In other words, to refuse her extradition.

Section 91 applies in situations where the physical or mental condition of the individual is considered such that it would be "unjust or oppressive" to extradite them. James had sought reports on Bea's health from three highly qualified doctors, each of whom produced a detailed report and appeared before the Court.

As you might imagine, given the privacy surrounding medical reports, there had been a good deal of discussion concerning the protection of the confidentiality of Bea's medical condition. When it came to delivering his judgment, Tim Workman said that he had hoped that agreement might be reached between those representing the US Government and Bea's legal team as to how medical reports could be disclosed whilst still preserving a degree of confidentiality. Counsel for the US Government had taken the view that they were unable to give any undertakings as to confidentiality. I will pick up Tim Workman's judgment from this point:

> *Eventually, in an attempt to avoid any delay, I made an order on 24 April requiring that the redacted medical reports and certificates should be served upon the Crown Prosecution Service identifying the areas over which confidentiality was claimed. Those reports were to be treated as confidential by English counsel, the Crown Prosecution Service* (in other words, those representing the US Government) *and any doctor appointed by the Crown Prosecution Service to review the medical reports.*

I am told that those redacted reports were provided but were not accepted by those acting for the Government.

The three doctors gave evidence before me on 14 and 15 May. A doctor instructed by the Government did not attend the hearing and I gave leave to the Government, if so advised, to call rebuttal evidence at the adjourned hearing on 29 May. Mr Jones on behalf of the Government has told me that it has not been possible to instruct a doctor for today's hearing and that he is content that I should make my decision upon the evidence available at present. He urges me to approach the evidence that I have heard with caution.

All three doctors gave me their expert evidence, all have the highest qualifications and extensive experience and I have no reason to doubt the evidence that they gave me. In her present state of health, all doctors agree that Mrs Tollman is unable to instruct lawyers in these extradition proceedings and all three doctors were emphatic that she was not in a fit state to give evidence. As she is unable to effectively participate in these extradition proceedings, in the procedures of a trial in the United States of America, or to give evidence, I conclude that it would be unjust to extradite her at this stage.

I therefore conclude under s 91 of the Extradition Act 2003, that I should order Mrs Tollman's discharge. As the section enables me to order the discharge at any time, I do so now.

And there it was, Britain would not extradite Bea to the United States. She, at least, was safe – for the time being anyway. It would soon be my turn to discover my fate. On 28 June, the District Judge was set to deliver his decision in relation to my own challenge. But before that day arrived, the United States lodged an application to seek leave to appeal Bea's discharge, something which we of course suspected would happen.

I have said before that Westminster Magistrates' Court was not the most comfortable of surroundings. As I sat there, I often used to feel sorry for those whose daily employment required them to suffer the shortcomings of a building which was far too cold in the winter, and correspondingly too hot during the summer months. Fans were often deployed, but to little effect. I am convinced that the effectiveness of all concerned was seriously affected by the dire working conditions.

It was also an incredibly difficult place within which to hear what was being said, especially if one was sitting at the back. My customary 'bookends' for those hearings, especially when I was not fully fit, were Gavin and Michael, but Toni and Vicki were often there too to provide me with moral support. The sound problem in the courtroom was especially difficult for Vicki because of her tinnitus. She got around this by sitting in the area set aside for the Press, which meant that she could be right next to the witness, in line with the barristers, and only a few feet from the judge. In my mind, I have that picture of Vicki sitting in court almost alongside the judge in order to be able to hear what everyone had to say.

Vicki had been joined in the Press box one day by a distinctive-looking figure in his late fifties. The other journalists who visited the box from time to time were of a much younger vintage, and tended to flit in and out of the courtroom. But this man, who wore a floppy and greying moustache of the kind popularised in the 1960s by The Beatles and Tariq Ali, appeared to be taking his visit much more seriously.

He, I was told, was none other than the legendary Michael Gillard, arguably the most well-known business journalist in London. But Michael Gillard's byline has appeared far less frequently than has his alias. Although he writes in his own name for many other newspapers, Gillard is best known for his *'In the City'* column in the fortnightly satirical magazine *Private Eye*, written under the pseudonym Slicker.

Adam MacQueen, who was commissioned to write a history of *Private Eye* to mark the magazine's 50th anniversary, said of Gillard[102]:

> *It was a decade before I realised that the locked room on the top floor wasn't a stationery cupboard, but the domain of one of Britain's most feared financial journalists – Michael Gillard, writer of the Slicker*

---

[102] An Eye inside the vaults: Making sense of Private Eye's messy archives, *The Independent*, 15 September 2011.

column since 1969. He only appears at night, when deputy editor Francis Wheen claims to have caught him watching boxing on the telly downstairs.

Little is known or has been written about Gillard. One of the other very rare references to him explained[103] :

There is an anonymous and somewhat sinister character in this symbiotic scene who is writing his own script. Michael Gillard is a native of Nuneaton, Warwickshire, and a graduate of the London School of Economics. Gillard has worked at Private Eye for more than 30 years and is a man of great secrecy – Private Eye doesn't even have a home address or home telephone number for him. The Gillard armoury is a phalanx of peerless contacts. People in high places who have a sense of justice will talk to Slicker because they know he is dogged in pursuit and believe him to be incorruptible.

What, I wondered, was the much-feared Michael Gillard doing at my extradition hearing? And who invited him? I suspected that I did not have too far to look to get an answer to those questions. Even though there were no greetings between the two, it was no secret that Mr Gillard was well-known to one of the barristers in the courtroom. And when I read the piece which Mr Gillard wrote following his visit, he appeared to be surprisingly well-briefed. But I will come to that a little later on.

In the meantime, let me return you to Tim Workman's judgment on my extradition request. As you know, I was asking the Court to resist my extradition, and to discharge me on the grounds of the passage of time. The District Judge made a point of noting that the fraud charges which I was facing referred to events which had taken place between 11 and 16 years earlier, and that those concerning alleged tax evasion had taken place between eight and 13 years earlier.

Alun Jones QC had submitted that I had been declared by the American courts to be a fugitive, and that any delay in the

---

[103] Who is 'Slicker'? Dominic Prince, *Management Today*, 1 April 2000.

proceedings was therefore my own fault, it having been brought about by my 'flight' from the United States. For this reason, he had argued, I was not entitled to raise passage of time as an argument to avoid extradition. But the District Judge took a different view. "I accept that Mr Tollman is described under United States law as a fugitive. I do, however, consider that description to be a term of art in United States law. I do not regard it as evidence that the accused fled the country or that he is therefore responsible for the delay. I am, therefore, satisfied that Mr Tollman is entitled to raise the issue of passage of time." So far, so good.

The Senior District Judge was required under Section 82 of the Extradition Act to bar extradition, he pointed out, "if (and only if) it appears that it would be unjust or oppressive to extradite the defendant by reason of the passage of time since he is alleged to have committed the extradition offence". He noted that, even though the investigation of fraud and the preparation of cases for prosecution is often time-consuming, it was not until six years after the investigation had begun that the Grand Jury handed down the first indictment. And it had been a further two-and-a-half years before the extradition request had been made.

Professor Beale had told him that under American law, submissions in relation to delay have to meet a very high threshold, and that in any case no such remedy would be available to those alleged to be 'fugitives'. Tim Workman said that he was satisfied that the American courts had deemed me to be a fugitive, and that I would therefore be unable to ask the court for protection from injustice due to the passage of time.

He also accepted that Arnold's death had had a material effect, the importance of his evidence being apparent from the fact that Arnold had been given immunity from prosecution. And although his evidence may have assisted the prosecution, it was clear that it might well have assisted me too.

He placed corresponding importance on the loss of Derek Evans, especially in relation to the tax allegations, and he referred to the evidence which he had received concerning the likely destruction of records retained by the banks. And he recognised the difficulty in tracking down witnesses in relation to the bank fraud allegations, and of the general deterioration in recollection over events so long ago.

Perhaps the most telling parts of his judgment were those which related to Okula, and to the evidence of oppression. He said:

> *This complaint turns upon the behaviour of the United States Prosecuting Attorney, Mr Stanley Okula. It is alleged that Mr Okula has displayed personal animosity towards Mr Stanley Tollman and his family which went far beyond the responsibilities of a thorough prosecutor. He is said to have declared that he intends to make Mr Tollman's life 'as miserable as possible' which is a comment he has not denied. He is also said to have commented that he was looking forward to have a 'perp walk' with Beatrice Tollman. I understand this to mean that he intended to walk publicly with Mrs Tollman through the streets of New York from the processing centre to the courthouse with her handcuffed and chained for the benefit of the press. In his affidavit, Mr Okula denies this allegation.*
>
> *I have heard evidence from Mr Robert Fink to whom this statement was made. Mr Fink represented Mr Tollman's son, Brett Tollman. His evidence was corroborated by Caroline Rule who made a contemporaneous note of the conversation when it was repeated to her by Mr Fink shortly afterwards. I found Mr Fink to be an entirely honest and trustworthy witness. I believe his account to be true and I find Mr Okula's affidavit on this point to be untruthful.*
>
> *Gavin Tollman is Stanley Tollman's nephew and whilst Gavin Tollman was in Canada, Mr Okula attempted to secure Mr Gavin Tollman into United States custody without proceeding through the extradition process. In September 2006, the Canadian court found that there had been an unequivocal abuse of the process of the court and that Mr Okula had misled the Canadian court. In these proceedings, Mr Okula claims that his actions had the support and approval of his superiors. I find that evidence unlikely to be true.*

With the conclusion of each of these two paragraphs, Tim Workman had made extremely important findings. In each case, he had found that Okula had been untruthful in the affidavit which he had sworn for these proceedings. Although these findings came as little surprise to me or to the legal team, it was nevertheless shocking that a judge should consider it necessary to make findings of this kind in relation to a prosecutor. But those conclusions momentarily gave us hope.

But hope was very swiftly dashed, for the District Judge went on to say:

> *Mr Okula's actions, although reprehensible, when taken alone, do not, in my view, amount to sufficient evidence to make a finding of 'oppression' which would bar extradition.*

Once again though, the pendulum appeared to swing back – and my mood with it – as the judgment continued:

> *However, they are factors to be considered when assessing the overall fairness in reaching the decision as to whether it would be unjust or oppressive for Mr Tollman to be returned.*

Finally, after pointing out that the medical evidence concerning Bea led to the overwhelming conclusion that my extradition would also undoubtedly endanger Bea's health still further, he reached his conclusion:

> *Taking all these factors into account, I am satisfied that by virtue of the passage of time, it would now be unjust and oppressive for the defendant to be extradited. The defendant is discharged in relation to each offence pursuant to Section 79 (3) of the Extradition Act 2003.*

We had done it. Not only had Bea been discharged but now, so too had I. A ripple of relief went through the courtroom. But we all knew that this was not in itself the end. The United States had already begun the process of seeking leave to appeal Bea's discharge.

And they were certain to appeal my own discharge too. We had won a couple of battles. But, make no mistake, we still had a war to fight.

For the time being, though, our spirits were a lot higher, and we left the courtroom that day in good heart. The District Judge's decision was widely reported. The Times, for instance, said[104]:

Hoteliers turn the tables on 'reprehensible' prosecutor

Two elderly hoteliers won their battle against extradition to the US yesterday as a British judge suggested a prosecutor had lied to get his hands on them.

Stanley and Beatrice Tollman spent four years trying to escape the clutches of Stanley Okula, an assistant US attorney, who once threatened to make their life "as miserable as possible". Their nemesis was found by District Judge Timothy Workman to have given untruthful evidence, even under oath. The judge condemned his behaviour as "reprehensible".

The judgment turns the tables dramatically on Mr Okula, who faces the risk of an action for perjury and the possibility that he would have to fight extradition to Britain.

However, his office last night rejected the accuracy of the judgment and gave warning that the US was planning to appeal for the Tollman extradition to go ahead.

The Tollmans were the most prominent remaining alleged white-collar criminals sought by the US under fast-track extradition. Their lives became a misery after Mr Tollman failed to attend an early court hearing in New York for alleged bank fraud. Mr Okula, a local prosecutor, is said to have decided to pressurise Mr Tollman's relatives to make him give himself up. "It is alleged that Mr Okula has displayed personal animosity towards Mr Tollman and his family, which went far beyond the responsibilities of a thorough prosecutor," the judge said at City of Westminster Magistrates' Court yesterday.

He is said to have declared that he intends to make Mr Tollman's life 'as miserable as possible', which is a comment he has not denied. He is also said to have commented that he was looking forward to having a 'perp walk' with Beatrice Tollman. I understand this to mean that he

intended to walk publicly through the streets of New York from the
processing centre to the courthouse with her handcuffed and chained for the
benefit of the press. In his affidavit, Mr Okula denies this allegation."
But the judge said that a lawyer to whom the "perp walk" threat had been
made, gave entirely honest and trustworthy evidence. "I find Mr Okula's
affidavit on this point to be untruthful," Judge Workman said.

Judge Workman decided it would be oppressive to extradite the
Tollmans owing to the time since the alleged offences, dating back to the
early 1990s, and Mrs Tollman's poor health

A spokeswoman for the US Attorney's Office for the Southern
District of New York, where Mr Okula works, said: "We respectfully
disagree with the court's factual and legal findings and expect to appeal."

The *New York Times* also reported the story, but could not
bring itself to repeat the Judge's criticisms of one of the United
States' own prosecutors[105]:

Britain Won't Extradite New York Hotelier in Fraud and Tax Evasion Case

After three years of hearings and recriminations, a British judge yesterday
refused to extradite the multimillionaire hotelier Stanley S. Tollman to
New York, a major setback for prosecutors seeking to bring him to trial on
charges relating to a $100 million bank fraud and tax evasion scheme.
The United States attorney's office in Manhattan, which first opened the
case against Mr. Tollman and other executives in 1996, said it was
not giving up. "We respectfully disagree with the court's factual and
legal findings and expect to appeal," said Rebecca Carmichael, a
spokeswoman for Michael J. Garcia, the United States attorney.

And finally, the *Financial Times* said[106]:

Businessman wins battle against US extradition

A wealthy businessman sought by US authorities on charges of bank
fraud and tax evasion on Thursday won an extradition battle at the City
of Westminster Magistrates' Court.

---

[105] *New York Times*, 29 June 2007.
[106] *Financial Times*, 28 June 2007, Nikki Tait, Law Courts Correspondent.

The legal victory by Stanley Tollman is the most significant success to date by an individual accused of white collar crimes in the US but contesting extradition under the controversial new US-UK arrangements, which have so worried the business community.

District judge Tim Workman ruled yesterday that it would be "unjust and oppressive" for the 76-year-old businessman to be sent to the US to face trial because of the "passage of time". His decision, however, can be appealed to the High Court, and US government lawyers indicated this would be done.

To complete my review of the press coverage, I include a piece from *Private Eye* which resulted from Michael Gillard's presence in the courtroom. You will remember the reference in the earlier press cutting, "The Gillard armoury is a phalanx of peerless contacts. People in high places who have a sense of justice will talk to Slicker because they know he is dogged in pursuit."

His article, whilst not inaccurate as to what happened in court, was augmented with additional material which the author either acquired by telepathy or osmosis, or with a little help from a representative of his phalanx of peerless contacts. I noted for instance, the references to "the unique 'long lunches' defence", "signed what was put in front of him without reading", and "spent most of the time lunching at '21'". Such phrases were reminiscent of the earlier musings of Senior Counsel for the United States, who is on record as saying, for instance, "the deployment of what any criminal lawyer recognises as the last defence of the scoundrel: the 'long lunches' defence". Well, whomsoever Mr Gillard's peerless contact happened to be, it was particularly interesting to learn their assessment of Mr Okula's contribution to proceedings. (I have emboldened the relevant section):

'In the City'[107]

Last week, Senior District Judge Tim Workman at the City of Westminster Magistrates' Court rejected the US extradition request for Stanley Tollman on the grounds that it would be "unjust and oppressive".

---

[107] *Private Eye, 6-19 July 2007.*

He had already rejected the request for Mrs Tollman on medical grounds. In March 2003, US prosecutors requested the extradition of both Tollmans but did nothing to push the case until August 2004, when they were arrested and legal proceedings began.

By then, the controversial new Extradition Act had come into force, allowing the US to fast track the extradition of anyone without the boring necessity required under the previous law of having to prove that there was a case to answer. Since then there has been much furore about the unfairness of a system designed for terrorism but increasingly used for white collar crime and for which a supine Labour government obtained no reciprocity.

The failure of the US to push for extradition certainly caused the delay until August 2004. But since then, defence tactics of contesting, however legitimately, a variety of collateral legal issues bear much responsibility for exactly the type of delay which was supposed to be prevented by the new act. Issues such as disclosure and abuse of process, plus whether the US was able to withdraw its 2003 request under the old act and resubmit a 2004 request under the new one, took until September 2006 to resolve.

As Lord Justice Thomas pointed out in a High Court ruling in June last year in favour of the US: "The conduct of extradition proceedings is expected to be expeditious." The aim was to resolve the issue "within a matter of a few months". Twenty-two months after the first hearing, there had been 12 hearings and all that had been achieved was "an order for disclosure of documents… No other progress has been made… The course taken in this case has been defended by none of the parties."

Perhaps not surprisingly, Lord Justice Thomas commented: "The way in which this case has proceeded gives rise to concern… It is particularly unjust that so little has been achieved over such a protracted period of time."

Well, there were hearings in November – and February, March, April and May. These were mainly concerned with the injustice caused to the Tollmans by the "passage of time" since the alleged offences in the 1990s. At one of the final hearings an exasperated Alun Jones QC for the US Government declared: "After 33 months enough is enough." It was *not until 29 May that there was a decision on Beatrice Tollman and a month later on her husband.*

Arnold Tollman, Stanley's brother, died in 2004. However, he may have been of limited help seeing that he allegedly confessed to "a massive scheme to evade taxes" and "extensive tax crimes" by using bank accounts in Guernsey. Another missing witness, Tollman's British accountant Derek Evans, who handled the Guernsey paperwork, died in 2002 before any trial could begin. London lawyer Lionel Lipkin, who set up offshore trusts for Tollman, died even earlier.

The US case has not been helped by the crudely aggressive tactics and comments of prosecutor Stanley Okula. These did not play well in London – where remarkably he was twice called a liar by Workman in his judgment – or in Canada where his bid to extradite Gavin Tollman, Arnold's son was rejected and denounced as "egregious" by a judge.

His unique "long lunches" defence is that he was rarely in New York and when he was in the office there he rarely looked at documents, signed what was put in front of him without reading, and spent most of the time lunching at "21" and other expensive Manhattan tables.

Slicker

As predicted, leave was also sought by the United States to appeal my discharge too. And on 30 July, as expected, Lord Justice Leveson and Justice Stanley Burton ordered that appeals be heard by the Divisional Court in the autumn.

So it was that in late November we were due back in the Divisional Court for a second time. These were the kind of proceedings which I did not need to attend, and that was just as well, for the reports of what was said there made my blood boil. Had I been present, I suspect that I might have had trouble controlling myself.

Just over a week before the hearing, Alison Riley of the CPS Extradition Unit sent Simmons & Simmons an email. Attached to this, and out of the blue, came a witness statement from none other than Howard Zukerman, one of the defendants in Monty Hundley's trial. Alison Riley said that the United States intended to rely upon the statement as additional evidence in the forthcoming hearing. This was clearly designed to prejudice the Court against me. And if I am honest, it worked.

Zukerman's statement said, "Rather than becoming a fugitive like Stanley Tollman, I stood trial... which trial resulted in the February 2003 convictions... I was previously convicted of certain tax offenses in the United States District Court for the Eastern District of New York. Those tax charges stemmed from my employment at the Tollman-Hundley companies where I and other Tollman-Hundley employees were paid significant amounts of income that was knowingly not reported to the Internal Revenue Service."

A brief word of explanation. Zukerman is referring here to his personal delinquency in reporting his own income to the IRS, and thus evading tax. His conviction in relation to that offence was unconnected to the subsequent trial. The inclusion of these comments was little more than a calculated attempt to smear me.

He claimed in his witness statement that through his "review of various newspaper articles and other databases" he had been "monitoring" the proceedings – out of his own interest of course. He had become "outraged" that I was taking the position that I had far less information than others as to what was going on at Tollman-Hundley. He then claimed that "Stanley Tollman was intimately and significantly involved in the negotiations" with the banks, and that he personally reported to me no less.

He then went on to say that the foregoing was "just some of the evidence I am prepared to provide in any future proceeding" against me. "I have come forward at this point because of my outrage at the factual assertions being made by Stanley Tollman." I suspect the real reason for his 'coming forward' was to be found in the paragraph where he expressed the hope that the judge in Manhattan might be prepared to reduce his prison sentence as a result of his co-operation.

What could one say about a document which was pure artifice from start to finish? Zukerman was even 12 months out as to the year when he and Monty had been convicted. It was ludicrous to imagine that he had been able to find out from newspapers or 'databases' what

I had been saying, because 'what I had been saying' had never been reported. And surely only the mentally deranged or the pathologically untruthful could imagine that a full-time middle-ranking executive could report personally to a non-executive director who was rarely even in the country, much less in the office?

We were soon to discover, however, that serious damage had been done by Zukerman's statement. This had dropped onto fertile ground when it came to at least one of the two judges who were to decide the United States' appeals. Sadly, this man was very obviously in charge of proceedings, which began on 20 November.

Lord Justice Moses, so I am told, was a man who gave the appearance of being irritated with life. Even his own wig appeared to be the cause of intense annoyance. His colleague, Justice Ouseley, displaying good sense, tucked into his colleague's slipstream from the outset, and stayed there throughout.

Moses was keen to get on with things. Alun Jones QC, for the United States, endeavoured to introduce the proceedings. "As your Lordships know, these are appeals brought…" But Lord Justice Moses cut him off immediately. "You needn't introduce it. We understand the bit about the background, and with the confetti that's been flying around we've got some grasp of the basic details. So you can go straight into the argument."

Alun Jones thanked the Court, and tried to start once more. "My Lord, the position that we wish to…" But again he was interrupted, this time by James Lewis, who was attempting to say something before the hearing got going. But this attempted intervention was far from welcome. Lord Justice Moses was having none of this. "Can we just get on with it. One gentleman is opening; let's hear him uninterrupted." Moses was clearly a man on a mission.

Jones then introduced the appeals in relation to both Bea and me, submitting that they should be dealt with together, and for reasons with which we might in places have taken exception. But on the whole, we were content that they should be heard together, and this later proved to be very helpful indeed.

Jones' introduction was full of the snide comments and bile with which we had all become familiar, liberally seasoned with prejudicial remarks aimed at the legal team almost as often as at Bea and me.

"The Government," said Mr Jones (as the United States was always referred to in the proceedings) "argues that the judge held wrongly that the 'passage of time' bar was available to the First Respondent on the facts of the case." The First Respondent was of course me. He then explained the chronology of events, pointing out that the High Court had power either to allow the appeals, direct the District Judge to 'decide the relevant question again', or to dismiss the appeals.

He then accused us of being the ones responsible for the delay. "Both Respondents have, through their lawyers, deliberately set out to delay and frustrate the proceedings by a variety of tactical and procedural devices; thus bringing about the delay which has led, for different reasons, to their discharge." Then, rather helpfully, he set out what he said was the accusation at the heart of our abuse of process allegation. That the United States authorities – or more specifically Okula – had pursued extradition proceedings against us in bad faith, and in a deliberately disproportionate and vindictive manners. Specifically:

- *Okula had known that he could not make out a prima facie case and so deliberately delayed the extradition process until the 1989 Act had been safely superseded by the 2003 Act.*

- *Okula had blackmailed me, and prosecuted Bea, Brett and Gavin vindictively, because I had declined to travel voluntarily to the United States. Okula had placed improper pressure on us to waive our rights to defend ourselves, and had subjected the family to a sustained campaign of personal attack.*

- *Okula had vindictively and falsely characterised me as a 'fugitive', and had set out to mislead the Court by giving false and misleading evidence in his affidavit.*

Jones then went on to deal with matters which he saw as a weakness in our arguments, and to endeavour to repair the damage to Okula's reputation by the findings of the District Judge. He was especially dismissive of Bob Fink's evidence regarding the 'perp walk'. "As a forensic stunt, Mr Fink, probably a jury advocate, produced with a flourish in cross-examination a recently signed statement, happily complying with section 102 of the Magistrates' Courts Act 1980... This was not only time-wasting and irrelevant; it demeaned the entire proceedings."

He then went on to point out the challenge which Okula had raised to Bob's testimony in April at the Magistrates' Court, where Bob had referred to the court hearing where Brett's bail conditions had been set. Mistakenly, Bob had referred to Okula's oppressive behaviour during the bail hearing. Okula had reacted to this, properly, by pointing out that he had not actually been present at the hearing, a fact which was verified by a transcript of the proceedings. Bob had made a simple mistake. A human error for which he apologised. But Alun Jones portrayed this as a heinous crime: "Mr Fink has seriously misled the court."

The relevant section of Bob's evidence to the Magistrates' Court had been:

> *I had trouble dealing with him as a prosecutor from the very beginning. The first difficulty was when Brett Tollman had returned to the United States. He was arrested, Mr Okula realised that he had returned to the United States voluntarily from England, but he insisted that there would be no bail whatsoever. The magistrate found this difficult to understand and said to Mr Okula: there must be bail. There must be some figure that could keep this man in the United States. My goodness, he returned to the United States.*

Colin Passmore had been called upon to explain and to set the record straight. In a witness statement, he had pointed out that Brett's bail hearing had in fact been handled by Peter Neiman, another prosecutor who had on a number of occasions stood in for Okula. Referring to a transcript of the hearing, he pointed out that Neiman had said that if the Court were to be prepared to consider bail it should be set at $50-$100 million, secured by assets within the United States. If that were to be the case, Neiman had said, "we would have something that was realistic". Neiman's rationale was as follows:

> So we have a circumstance where there is a strong incentive to flee; that is, very serious charges. There is an enormous ability to flee; there is access to a tremendous amount of wealth offshore. And there is, you know, a family history of using that wealth to facilitate flight. And we're not suggesting that Brett Tollman can be punished for the sins of his father. That's not at all the submission of the Government. But I think looking at this realistically, we have here a defendant who has, you know, seen the example of what to this point has been a successful flight from justice by his father…

Bob Fink had replied:

> Your Honor, the prosecutor very carefully and skilfully chose his words. Notice he said he has access to wealth, his family has access to wealth, his family has moved money. He never said my client had wealth. The fact of the matter is last night when we had this conversation, he phrased it a little less carefully. He said the father is a fugitive, and I want to bring back the father's money. I think that that is close to ransom.

Neiman later reduced his demand, Bob had repeated his assertion that this was 'ransom' and a means to put pressure on Brett to attempt to get me to return to the United States. Bob had then likened the Government's approach to "dealing with a terrorist". In the event, bail had been set at $25 million. On the basis that it was in practical terms impossible for Brett to post the whole of the bail that day, Bob had requested that Brett be given 72 hours within which to complete the exercise. In the meantime, he had said that Brett would post bail of $8 million and relinquish his passports. But that had not been good enough for Peter Neiman, who resisted the proposal vigorously. Much to Neiman's chagrin, the Judge had nevertheless granted Brett bail on those terms.

So there it was, the coercive behaviour may not have come directly from Okula himself, but it had come from somewhere else within the US Attorney's Office. Did Bob seriously mislead the Court? I think not.

Jones also took a few completely unjustified swipes at me personally. He accused me of what he described as "self-serving attempts to ingratiate" myself with the court. He mentioned, for instance, that I had wanted the Court to know that I was opposed to apartheid but that my "aversion" had not deterred me from building Tollman Towers in Johannesburg in 1969, the "first 5-star hotel in South Africa, where apartheid presumably applied". Had Mr Jones bothered to find out the truth, he would not of course have been able to drip such untruthful, but highly prejudicial poison into the ears of the judges. Perhaps it was simply more convenient to imagine the lie, and then to avoid the inconvenience of the truth.

We also learned through this hearing that the Government of the United States was concerned about the "damaging publicity in both the USA and the UK" which had been attracted by Tim Workman's findings that Okula had deliberately given false evidence. This was a bit rich, to say the least. The Government of the United States would have been far better advised to save their concern for Okula's behaviour, rather than any publicity which may have resulted from it.

As the hearing progressed, it became more and more apparent that Lord Justice Moses did not view me sympathetically. On the contrary, Jones' attempts to prejudice the Court against me were clearly working. Lord Justice Moses clearly did not like the way in which our legal team had handled the proceedings thus far, and he had a curiously imprecise and unfavourable grasp of what had happened in the United States.

Referring to the history of the UK proceedings over the last three years, Moses said, "What's the judicial word? Faffing around. Overblown litigation, which in the end came to nothing." Then, in relation to the trial of Monty Hundley, "Now, the co-defendants were… one of his sons, was it?" Alun Jones corrected him, "The others were not his family." Lord Justice Moses continued, "Were they employees? I mean Zukerman was one of them?" Jones confirmed that Zukerman was indeed one of them, to which Moses remarked, "They're pretty fed up with the chap who was head of all of this, but manages to escape even a trial while they all take the rap."

A little later in the hearing, in the context of the fight to ensure that the United States continued under the 1989 Act, he said, "Anyway, it was all beating the wind, because later on it was accepted that there was a prima facie case." Once again, Jones corrected him, "Oh no, my Lord, it's never been accepted." To which Moses said, "But it's hopeless, isn't it, after the trial in 2003?"

It was clear that Lord Justice Moses had made his mind up about me. He viewed me as a crook who had compounded his wrong-doing by running away and allowing others to take the blame. This, and the prospects for the outcome of the appeal, were eventually brought into the sharpest focus when Moses said that, unlike other members of my family, I "had not had the courage to face the same music that they had faced." He then went on to say disparagingly that he had, "known people like Stanley Tollman" all his life. This from a man who has never even met me. Open mind? I don't think so.

After three uncomfortable days, it was over. Those who had sat through the proceedings were gloomy – more gloomy, I suspect, than they shared with me. They knew the importance of keeping hope alive, even if they had privately concluded that everything was lost. There then began an agonising period of waiting. This lasted for ten weeks, before Lord Justice Moses and Justice Ouseley delivered their judgment, which they did on on 7 February 2008.

Lord Justice Moses began by pointing out that the appeal was the second occasion on which the extradition of Mr and Mrs Tollman to the United States had occupied the Divisional Court for three days. Since that earlier decision of of the Divisional Court there had been five further hearings before the Senior District Judge, making a total of no fewer than 18 hearings.

Moses then pointed out that on the previous occasion, the Lord Chief Justice had emphasised that one of the objects of the 2003 Act was to ensure expedition. He added that "the obligation of the parties and those acting for them is to co-operate to ensure that objective is achieved. The observations of the Lord Chief Justice have had no effect."

He carried on by saying that it was "unnerving" to recall what Lord Justice Thomas had said 18 months earlier:

> *The course taken in this case has been defended by none of the parties before us. Why it has come about is not a matter for this court on this application to determine, but plainly the way in which this case has proceeded gives rise to concerns in the way in which cases should be dealt with, so that the extradition process can be determined within a time that is infinitely more expeditious that what has so far happened with this case. In this case, as Mr and Mrs Tollman are in their seventies, it is particularly unjust that so little has been achieved over such a protracted period of time.*

Moses underlined this by saying, "The stance taken by the parties since those observations is one of studied intransigence. Neither side has proved other than obdurate in fighting its corner. This uncompromising approach to the litigation is conducive neither to an expeditious, still less a rational, disposal of the issues."

I was shocked when I read those words for the first time, and I am no less shocked now. This was a matter of life and death for us, and to criticise us for fighting as hard as we were able is outrageous. He says 'obdurate'. I would say 'determined'. What did he expect is to do? Go quietly? In whose interest was it merely to seek an 'expeditious disposal'? Certainly not ours.

And revealing more than a little of his personal assessment of the case against me, Moses made a point of adding the following to the chronology of events something which he described as a 'significant omission'. "Between 2003-2004, four of Mr Tollman's co-accused were tried for and convicted of the conspiracy for which Mr Tollman was indicted and due to be arraigned in April 2002."

Another matter which appeared to underpin his thinking was the belief that I had chosen not to return to the United States because I was fearful that I would not get bail: "…it demonstrates that the reason he did not return to face justice in the United States was his fear that he would be denied bail". I can honestly say that such a thought never, ever crossed my mind. I was always certain that I would be granted bail and, in all practical terms, this could have been negotiated in advance of my return at any stage in the proceedings. No. If I had a fear, it would have been whether I could ever get a fair trial.

The judgment said that I was entitled to leave the United States, but the fact that I had "not returned to face the indictment with his co-accused is in our judgment a significant factor in assessing the justice of requiring him to return now. Mr Tollman chose not to attend his trial because of fears that he would not get bail. He left others to face the trial, which his own lawyers expected him to attend."

"To expect a man of 77 to face trial in relation to offences alleged to have been committed when he was already over 60, does not lead us to the conclusion that it would be unjust to do so. He had the opportunity to participate in the trial but chose not to do so and left others to face the consequences. In those circumstances, we do not conclude that the passage of time has caused him an injustice."

In saying this, Moses and Ouseley recognised that their thinking was at odds with Tim Workman. "In reaching a conclusion that it would not be unjust to extradite the defendant we are conscious that we are differing from the conclusion reached by the Senior District Judge. His value judgment as to injustice must be treated with the very greatest respect." Polite words perhaps, but however respectful they may have been in their language, they continued to hold a different view. In fairness though, they did agree with the District Judge in relation to the tax charges where, because of the passage of time, they agreed that I could no longer receive a fair trial in the United States. In relation to the tax charges, therefore, they agreed that extradition should be barred. But in relation to the other key element – the bank fraud charges – they took an opposing view. There, they considered that the passage of time had not caused me an injustice, and did not prevent my extradition.

I may have won half the battle, but the defeat in relation to the other half meant of course that I had lost. The United States had won in its appeal against the District Judge's refusal to extradite me. Short of being able to appeal now to the House of Lords, all appeared lost.

In relation to Bea, the outcome of the appeal was happier. Moses and Ouseley concurred with the District Judge's decision, and the United States' appeal was dismissed. This meant that the United States would also be looking to the House of Lords, otherwise Bea was completely safe from the threat of extradition.

Consent to appeal to the House of Lords was also an ambition of the United States in relation to the District Judge's findings about Okula's conduct, because Moses and Ouseley did not disturb those findings in any way.

But we all needed consent from the Divisional Court to be able to appeal the various decisions to the House of Lords, and this was not determined on the spot. We went away and waited nervously for that decision. And a decision did not come quickly. There were three anxious weeks before we heard the answer, which arrived on 29 February 2008, and which was a comprehensive refusal for all concerned. That avenue was not available.

Bea was now completely safe. And the findings against Okula would stand for ever. But I had not been allowed to appeal to the House of Lords. In relation to the decisions which had been taken by Moses and Ouseley, the die was considered cast.

But I have moved on a little too far, for the Moses and Ouseley judgment, although on the face of it disastrous, did contain a section which represented a glimmer of hope in the darkness, and to which I now return.

Moses and Ouseley pointed out that Tim Workman had concluded in his judgment that my extradition would endanger not only Bea's health, but possibly her life. They said that if the appeal in relation to Bea was to be rejected (which of course it was) it was difficult for them to see how the same factual conclusions could then be appealed in relation to me. Their conclusion was that there would be "no sufficient basis for challenging" if I were to rely upon the risk of exacerbation of Bea's medical condition. Their reasoning was that the risk was a cause of oppression, not just to Bea, but to me as well.

But this argument, and any judgment which resulted from that argument, was not the matter which had been appealed, and they were not being asked to rule on it. Therefore, even though they could see the logic clearly, that did not mean that the appeal before them could be detemined in my favour. The Senior District Judge had not considered that question, and it was by no means clear what his view would have been if this had been the only ground for resisting extradition:

> We cannot say that the judge ought to have decided the relevant question differently and thus would not have been required to order the person's discharge. But we can and will direct the judge to decide the relevant question again in the light of our conclusions as to injustice. He should consider whether the oppression to Mr Tollman, through endangering Mrs Tollman's health, would of itself be sufficient to maintain his decision to discharge, in the light of our observations as to injustice generally and the risk of prejudice.
>
> The prospect of yet a further hearing in relation to this extradition is dispiriting. The Senior District Judge will no doubt be concerned to ensure that there is only a short further oral hearing at which any further evidence is produced well in advance and arguments are reduced to writing.

So, my extradition request was sent back to the Senior District Judge to reconsider just one point: to decide whether endangering Bea's health by extraditing me would be oppressive to me. If it did, then this could be sufficient to justify refusal of extradition, and such a decision could not be appealed. All was not yet lost. I still had a chance.

Acting on the directions of the Divisional Court, the Senior District Judge moved swiftly. A hearing was set for 27 March 2008, and Tim Workman gave directions that we should put in all our relevant evidence by 14 March, with the United States being required to serve by 20 March all the evidence upon which it intended to rely. As required, we served all our evidence – in full, and on time. The prosecution, on the other hand, served no evidence at all by 20 March. The lawyers set about preparing for the hearing, knowing that there would now be nothing new – or so they thought.

As the hearing drew closer, the team's collective view was that matters were well in hand, and the lawyers gathered for one last session at Edward Fitzgerald's chambers on 26 March, the day before the hearing. This gathering was intended simply to finalise matters. But things did not go as planned. No sooner had the meeting started than a letter from the Department of Justice arrived, courtesy of the CPS. This was signed by Guy Petrillo and Stanley J Okula Jr, on behalf of the Southern District of New York, and had been sent to Alison Riley of the Extradition Unit. The team was informed that the letter had been placed into court and, notwithstanding the Judge's instructions as to deadlines for submission of material, was expected to be considered as part of the hearing the following day.

The letter had been designed to explain a possible means by which Bea might be able to travel safely with me, should I be extradited. And it had been constructed with the intention of undermining all of my remaining arguments. The submission of such a letter would have been unsettling at the best of times. With the hearing so close, its receipt had an immensely sobering effect on the team's morale. Confidence had been dashed in a matter of moments, and gloom descended over the meeting.

But it was then that something remarkable happened. It was almost as though eight people silently and independently reached the same conclusion simultaneously. We are not going to take this lying down. These people cannot be allowed to get away with it. We can do something about this. And we absolutely intend to do something about it. Eight disheartened individuals suddenly became four teams of two, each having a specific task, and each of which had to be concluded successfully, and in no time at all. There was a very great deal to be achieved before the next morning's hearing.

The United States' letter was intended to respond to a comment Lord Justice Moses had made in November. He had asked whether it might be possible for Bea to have been protected in some way if she were to choose to come with me to New York, if I were to be extradited. Alun Jones had responded at the time to that suggestion by referring to the Fugitive Disentitlement Doctrine, meaning that the US could not, and therefore would not, deal with Bea.

Notwithstanding the Fugitive Disentitlement Doctrine, at the conclusion of the appeal the High Court had made the following observation:

> *Were the United States Government to agree not to prosecute Mrs Tollman, particularly in light of her ill health and the fact that we have not disturbed the Senior District Judge's refusal to extradite Mr Tollman in relation to those matters with which his wife is charged* (by this, they were referring to the tax charges), *she could return to the United States and be cared for there during the period of Mr Tollman's return and during his trial.*

The letter from the Department of Justice began by addressing my situation, predominantly the conditions which they considered appropriate for my bail. Starting with the confiscation of my passports, these included a bond of $50 million secured against the properties in Park Avenue, Connecticut and Palm Beach, the wearing of an electronic tag at all times, and the imposition of a home detention curfew, which I think is more usually known around the world as 'house arrest'. But the most important part of the letter was the suggested basis upon which Bea might be able safely to accompany me. It was this section of the letter and its implications which were now preoccupying the four sub-teams.

One team set to work on addressing the true significance of the contents of the letter in the United States, and a second on the attitude of Bea's doctors as to what was planned. The third team applied itself to the implications as to what was being countenanced for the evidence which would be provided by Toni and Vicki. And the fourth urgently reviewed the authorities and documentation which would be needed in the morning. It was a deeply impressive piece of legal team work, at the heart of which was a young lady whose name I have yet to mention, but who played a vital role. Claire McLeod was Colin Passmore's very able Cambridge-educated assistant, who joined the team whilst still young and who grew enormously in her experience and capability in large part as a result of the part she played for us.

When the time came for the hearing on the following day, Tim Workman began by expressing unhappiness with the United States' behaviour. "In the light of these observations, it is surprising that this issue was left until the day before this hearing, thereby requiring the Defence to bring expert evidence from New York on a few hours' notice."

And he was right to be unhappy. For we had had to jump through hoops when that letter had arrived so late in the day. We had asked Bea's US lawyer, Gerry Feffer of Williams & Connolly, to examine the letter and to express an opinion as to the value of its contents. And we had also arranged to get one of Gerry's partners to drop everything he was doing and get on a plane in order to appear in court in London the following day.

Gerry Feffer's assessment of the letter was instructive:

The letter purports to give comfort that Mrs Tollman could accompany her husband Stanley Tollman to the United States, in the event he was extradited, without fear of arrest, prosecution or separation from Mr Tollman during the proceedings against him in the United States.

It is obvious to me, however, that the letter does not ensure that Mrs Tollman would avoid arrest, prosecution or separation from her husband if she were to travel to the United States. The letter does not confer immunity on Mrs Tollman, either with respect to the charges that might be brought by the United States or with respect to charges that might be brought by New York State or another state.

Based on the letter, I could not advise Mrs Tollman that she could travel to the United States secure in the belief that she would not face arrest, prosecution or separation from her husband.

The man whom we had flown in overnight from Washington was James Bruton, a man who had become a partner of Williams & Connolly 20 years earlier. James, another American lawyer with an expansive moustache, had later stepped away from the firm for five years to become Principal Deputy Assistant Attorney General in the Tax Division of the US Department of Justice. And he had then returned to Williams & Connolly.

James could not have been better qualified to give evidence about the the value of the Department of Justice's letter which had been served on the Court the day before. He is one of the many people to whom I have reason to be grateful. Getting a call on Wednesday in Washington asking you to be in a courtroom giving evidence in London the morning after is no small request. James came straight from the airport to the Court, barely breaking his stride before appearing in the witness box. He had little hesitation in pointing out that the letter from the Southern District really wasn't worth the paper on which it was written.

He pointed out that the letter had said that the Southern District "does not intend". James pointed out that 'an intention' can always be changed, and that the letter could not be considered to take the form of a binding, enforceable agreement. He also informed the Court that whatever the Southern District 'intended', ultimately it would be the District Court's decision and that a Prosecutor could not bind the Court. Moreover, no US Attorney can bind another US Attorney. The assurances offered within the letter would not be binding even in the neighbouring Districts of New York itself, let alone the rest of the country.

In short, the letter did not provide any form of immunity. Any alleged immunity would be meaningless unless it came from a considerably higher official, probably from the Attorney General himself.

Our evidence had included submissions from both Vicki and Toni, who then both gave evidence before the Court on 27 March. I remember clearly each of them, tears in their eyes, giving evidence in court about their father. They explained how things worked in the home, and how important Bea and I were to each other, and the support we had given and received through some 55 years of marriage.

Finally, the Court also heard from one of Bea's doctors, who gave advice to the Court on the likely effect on Bea's well-being of the arrangements which had been described within the letter. He was in no doubt that the offer within the letter contained suggested arrangements which would be highly prejudicial to Bea's health. For this reason, he could not advise Bea to travel.

At the end of the one-day hearing, we all felt, once again, that we had done the best we could. The matter was now, for the final time, in the hands of the Senior District Judge. We returned in strength to court to hear his verdict on 7 April 2008 for what proved to be a very short, but extremely decisive hearing.

The Senior District Judge said that he had found the evidence of James Bruton and Bea's doctor to be "entirely reliable and convincing". In hearing the evidence from Vicki and Toni, he was equally persuaded. He said, "I found their evidence to be truthful and persuasive." He then went on to the meat of his judgment:

The High Court have concluded that there will be no injustice in returning Mr Tollman to the United States of America and the sole issue, which has been returned to me, is whether there will be oppression to Mr Tollman if Mrs Tollman's health was endangered were he to be extradited to the United States of America.

I have concluded that the arrangements proposed by the Prosecuting Attorney for New York are not open to Mrs Tollman by virtue of the

*gravity of her illness and because of the legal advice she has been offered
as to the risk of future prosecution.*

*I therefore conclude that the bar to extradition contained in Section
82 of the Extradition Act 2003 applies in this case in that it would now
be oppressive to return Mr Tollman to the United States of America, and
the Defendant is therefore discharged.*

With those few short, but crucial words, Tim Workman had
brought proceedings to a close. There could be no appeal. It was over.

My legal team, expertly marshalled by Gavin and by Colin
Passmore, had achieved what many had thought, and still think,
impossible. We had won, we had beaten the United States against
all odds.

Pehaps surprisingly, I will close this chapter with the words of one
of the two Counsel who had spent the last three years trying to ruin
my life. I said earlier in the book that I found it impossible to dislike
John Hardy, whom I knew to be a thoroughly decent man. As our case
drew to a close, he became a Queen's Counsel. In looking him up
recently for this book, I observed that the matter of *United States
of America – v – Stanley Stephen Tollman* appears, curiously, to be missing
from his CV.

Speaking on Radio 4 at about the time of my discharge, Hardy was
asked about extradition by Clive Anderson[108]. This is what he said:

*"There has been a move over the years in Western countries to make more
easy the extradition of those suspected of committing serious crimes. And
there has been steady progression in terms of legislation and treaties
aimed at making the process of extradition swifter, more expedient and
more effective, whilst retaining certain basic protections.*

*"The real issue seems to me to be whether the protections have
virtually been done away with or are too weak and flimsy to afford
individual citizens the possibility of contesting extradition proceedings.
The legislative thrust of the Extradition Act 2003 overbalances the odds
in favour of the requesting state, and removes protections from the citizen
previously thought to have been necessary."*

---

[108] *Unreliable Evidence*, BBC Radio 4, 12 December 2007.

TIME TO TALK

The extradition process may have been over. But I was now 78 years old, and my health and the health of others had suffered badly as a result of the stress under which we had all been placed. Nevertheless, we *had* fought the United States, and we were still around to talk about it. Together, we had successfully ensured that the family business was in one piece, and that the eye-watering legal and other bills had got paid. Throughout, I had needed to offer emotional support to the entire family, every member of which, in their own very personal way, was suffering. Most disturbing of all was the steady decline in Bea's health. We may have driven off the United States as far as Britain was concerned, but this did not mean that life was back to normal. Far from it.

There was no guarantee that, should we attempt to travel again, the Americans would not try again – this time somewhere else in the world. Although there was a thought that I might be safe to return to South Africa, even destinations as close as Europe could not be relied upon as being safe. Theoretically, Bea and I could have lived out the rest of our days within set limits, but it was unreasonable for the rest of the family to live in fear every time they travelled. This was especially unacceptable, given that the family's business was travel. There appeared to be no alternative. We absolutely had to talk to the other side. The time was long overdue to sort out this whole thing properly.

The irony was that, since all of this had kicked off, we had been trying to talk to the US Attorney's Office. But each and every time there had been a blanket refusal to speak. We were told that the Department of Justice does not talk to fugitives, the only exception being a conversation about a return to the United States to face trial.

In 2002, Chris Todd and Jim Webster had endeavoured to talk to Okula at White Plains, without success. In October 2003, James

Lewis, who had been observing the trial of Monty Hundley, approached Peter Neiman, the Assistant US Attorney who was in charge of the trial, in the hope of establishing a channel of communication to the Southern District. James too was sent packing. Finally, in 2004, Ben Brafman had attempted to approach Okula, receiving a similar response. It takes two to tango, and these guys, it seemed, had no interest in dancing at all.

At this point in the story, I need to reintroduce someone about whom I wrote earlier. This gentleman brought about an important introduction which, although in itself not decisive, led itself to a further introduction which, in time, would prove crucial. You may recall the reference to the time I had spent in the mid-1990s in Greenville, Mississippi, with a man called Clarke Reed. Clarke was the highly influential Southern Republican who had been closely connected with Presidents Nixon, Ford, Reagan and George H.W. Bush. It was Clarke who had watched his protégé Haley Barbour rise first to National Party Chairman and then to Governor of Mississippi.

In 2004, Clarke encouraged me to talk to the Washington lobbyists, Barbour Griffith and Rogers (BGR), a firm founded by Haley Barbour before he became Governor of Mississippi. Although Haley was very much Clarke's man, I too had met him on numerous occasions. But it needed Clarke's prompt for me to approach BGR myself. By this time, of course, Haley[109] had stepped away from BGR, and I dealt instead with the 'G' in BGR – a gentleman called Lanny Griffith.

Lanny is a great guy and, like Haley and Clarke, also a Mississippi man – from Corinth. Lanny had worked for the Republican National Committee, and had managed Haley Barbour's U.S. Senate race in 1982. Before joining BGR, which he did in 1993, Lanny had filled various roles in President George HW Bush's administration. In 1989, he had been named Special Assistant to the President for Intergovernmental Affairs, acting as the White House's liaison to governors and other statewide-elected officials.

---

[109] At the time of writing, Haley Barbour has just completed his term as Governor of Mississippi, and has rejoined BGR. Although at one stage tipped as a potential Presidential candidate, lobbying was really what made Haley Barbour tick.

I do not think I have ever met another man who is as comfortable in his own skin as Lanny Griffith. Lanny flew over to London from Washington one day to join the tail-end of a multinational meeting, which had been extended until the following morning simply in order to accommodate his personal schedule. However, instead of an early night to adjust to the time difference, Lanny was more keen on extending his knowledge of the extensive range of malt whiskies in the Milestone bar.

Thus it was that 12 of us waited in vain the following morning as Lanny, still operating on Washington time, slumbered. Not even the physical shaking administered by two of his colleagues made any difference. Lanny was in the deepest sleep possible. Nothing could wake him. The meeting with Lanny never happened, and those present dispersed.

Had I been Lanny's latter-day Rip van Winkle, when eventually I awoke little short of *Hara-kiri* would have assuaged my guilt. I am obsessed with punctuality and would have been overcome with embarrassment and shame if I had kept 12 people waiting in vain for a meeting, the timing of which had been fixed for me. But when I bumped into Lanny at the Milestone that evening, he hardly even mentioned it. He smiled wryly, and mumbled a home-spun Southern anecdote. He told me that his recent brain scan, conducted following a pattern of headaches, had terrified the operator of the scanning equipment, who could find no evidence of brain activity when Lanny fell asleep. Boy, when Lanny sleeps, he really sleeps. I learned one thing that day. Never arrange to meet this man before noon.

Lanny came to see me in London on a number of occasions, and we had several very interesting conversations. None of these really translated into any serious work. But in 2006, BGR had the foresight to introduce me to someone who was to prove highly significant in the ultimate resolution of our problem. This was not a member of the firm, but a young Vietnamese-born lawyer, now a US citizen, who was practising in Washington, DC.

Viet Dinh had been born in Saigon in 1968 of Vietnamese parents. When I first met him, he was only 38 years old. He had already been Assistant Attorney General of the United States and, amongst others things, was currently Professor of Law at Georgetown University and a member of the Board of Directors of News Corporation.

Viet's story is a remarkable testament to opportunity, the American dream, and everything for which the United States should stand, and in some things still does. I will allow the *Financial Times* to start the story:[110]

> *In 1978, as a ten-year-old boy in Vietnam, he and his mother fled the communist government on an overcrowded boat. As they approached a harbour in Malaysia a patrol boat fired warning shots and they were forced to retreat. Finding shelter on a deserted beach, Mr Dinh watched his mother break holes in their boat's hull to ensure they could not be forced to return to international waters in the morning.*
>
> *The family immigrated to the US that year, and Mr Dinh's family began picking strawberries in Oregon. They moved again when Mount St Helens erupted, destroying the crops. As a teenager in Fullerton, California, Mr Dinh made money by flipping hamburgers while he mastered English and excelled at school.*
>
> *He was accepted to Harvard and was known on campus as an energetic and gregarious up-and-comer. He then went straight into Harvard Law School. "It's almost as if he was plopped down at Harvard," said Laurence Silberman, senior judge on the US Court of Appeals for the District of Columbia Circuit, who Mr Dinh clerked for. "Despite having an accent, he was totally at home."*
>
> *Soon after graduating from Harvard Law, Mr Dinh found himself in the national spotlight, working as associate special counsel to the US Senate Whitewater Committee, which investigated then president Bill Clinton's real estate holdings. He went on to become special counsel to Senator Pete Domenici during the impeachment trial of President Clinton.*

Viet served as Assistant Attorney General of the United States from 2001 to 2003, under the presidency of George W Bush. He was confirmed in the Senate by a vote of 96 to 1, with the single 'No' vote

---

[110] *Financial Times*, 27 July 2011.

coming from none other than Hillary Clinton. I wonder why? After 9/11, Viet conducted a comprehensive review of Department of Justice priorities, policies and practices, and played a key role in developing the USA Patriot Act. As I write, Viet, together with fellow News Corporation board member (and also a former Assistant Attorney General) Joel Klein, is responsible for the internal investigation of the *News of the World* phone hacking affair.

When Viet left the US Department of Justice and went back into civvy street, he was one of the best-connected lawyers in private practice. Many of those in 'Main Justice', as the Department of Justice in DC is known, as well as a number of US Attorneys, had grown up through the ranks alongside Viet, and were well known to him. These were relationships which Viet understandably maintained and cultivated.

Our first idea was that we would put Viet together with Ben Brafman in order to open up a proper conversation with the Southern District. As a former Assistant Attorney General, Viet would have been able to call the US Attorney direct, even if the individual were not known to him. When I was indicted, the US Attorney was a man called James Comey, but he had been replaced in December 2003 by an acting US Attorney, David Kelley. Fortunately, just after we started working with Viet, David Kelley was replaced in September 2005 by a person whom Viet knew really well: a man called Michael Garcia.

Like Viet himself, Michael Garcia had been a political appointee of the Bush administration, and the two of them were close friends. Each, it became clear, was scrupulously professional in relation to any contact other than their social relationship. There would be no sweetheart deal here. But the fact that Viet and Michael Garcia knew each other had the potential to alter the dynamics of the situation. We hoped we might just get the ear of someone who could make a difference. Okula wanted one thing only – my head on a plate. The head of Stanley Tollman was most definitely off the menu. I had to find a way of changing the rhythm of all of this.

In deploying the unlikely double act of Ben Brafman and Viet Dinh, we hoped to cover all the corners. Viet would try to open the door – even just a little – and Ben would have all the appropriate local knowledge and credibility, given his outstanding reputation as a New York criminal defence attorney. Only after we had decided on this course did we discover, remarkably, that the two had worked closely together only recently, and had developed a mutual admiration.

After some tough overtures, Viet and Ben finally managed to get their combined foot in the door of the US Attorney's Office. As a result, a series of decreasingly less awkward meetings took place between the autumn of 2006 and the summer of 2007. These meetings took place against the backdrop of events in London, which were changing almost by the day. They were initial conversations only, building towards what was perceived as the main event. Initially, they were with junior figures, but in time the meetings involved line managers higher up in the organisation. One such meeting had been attended by Okula. Ben Brafman, superb trial attorney that he is, eloquently demolished every single one of the Tollman-Hundley charges as they applied to me. "Your case is rubbish, and I would beat you in court," he concluded. The only response from a flustered, and clearly unsettled, Okula was, "That's as may be. But what about Guernsey?" This was an important moment, for it revealed that not even Okula himself believed in the Tollman-Hundley charges. Guernsey, and tax, had instead become the justification for his pursuit of me.

Whilst the lower level conversations continued, throughout it had been our hope that they would culminate in a meeting with the US Attorney himself, who we presumed was being kept abreast of what was happening. However, even though Viet and Ben's initial approach had taken place in the Autumn of 2006, a private conversation with Garcia a full 12 months later revealed that the US Attorney was aware of the case in only the broadest sense. And he was viewing the matter with little concern at all. Not only did he not have a detailed understanding, he was not even aware of the possible ramifications of what was happening. He knew nothing, for instance, of the Okula witness statement, nor of its impending consequences. "It's just litigation, Viet. Isn't it?" he had asked, uncertainly.

His lack of knowledge was hardly surprising. On criminal matters alone, Michael Garcia oversaw the investigative, trial and appellate work of 150 Assistant United States Attorneys, of which Okula was just one. The AUSAs and their support staff were based in two separate offices, and were handling issues ranging from terrorism and national security to organised crime; corruption to narcotics; and fraud to asset forfeiture. Bea and I hardly registered as a blip on the radar.

Viet and Ben's last meeting prior to the final one, at which Garcia would be present, took place in early June 2007. By that stage, everyone knew that Tim Workman would announce his decision about the extradition on 28 June, when the pendulum of advantage would swing decisively one way or another. We did not press too aggressively for a date for the follow-up meeting, even though we knew it could prove decisive, for fear that we might look too concerned as to the outcome of the Workman judgment. Eventually, we were told that the meeting with Garcia could not be until 12 July – two weeks after the judgment. But when I received and read the contents of the judgment, and in particular the comments about Okula's behaviour, my confidence about the meeting with the US Attorney grew. Surely, this provided a backdrop for a sensible negotiated conclusion?

Both Michael Garcia and the Chief of the Criminal Division, Lev Dassin, attended the 12 July meeting. As the meeting kicked off, Viet and Ben were hopeful, but those hopes were very quickly dashed. Garcia's knowledge of our case had altered significantly. Having known almost nothing about the matter a few weeks earlier, he had clearly asked for some detailed briefing. Sadly, this briefing had not been delivered by Viet and Ben. Garcia not only came to the meeting fully prepared, but with his mind already made up. He was not prepared even to consider a negotiated settlement, and for three reasons. He was adamant.

First. The Southern District did not negotiate with fugitives. Although Garcia recognised that there was dispute as to whether I was a fugitive, Fugitive Disentitlement was a hard and fast rule.

Second. Very serious charges had been levelled against me, and for that reason he was not prepared to agree to the kind of settlement which I might consider acceptable.

Finally, he wanted to 'correct' some of Tim Workman's findings about Okula.

It was clear that Garcia was not prepared to allow the music to stop at that point – with all the accusations of abuse and resulting criticism of his Office standing unanswered. I also suspected that Okula and the UK barristers had together concluded that they would get Tim Workman's discharge overturned on appeal. But what was undeniable was that the door had been shut firmly behind Viet and Ben as they left the building. We were back out in the cold.

It would be more than a year before it was possible for talking to start again. Matters in London had to be resolved beyond doubt. But in April 2008, they were, when the extradition requests were finally defeated. We were now beyond the reach of Southern District.

I became aware that there were moves to get talks started again but, personally, I was largely indifferent. As far as I was concerned, I really didn't want to speak to the United States ever again. But others took the view that we would be foolish not to explore the possibility, calculating that talking was the only possible way by which the Americans could save a little face, and through which we might recover a little of our freedom.

Ben Brafman, as always, had done an outstanding job with the earlier discussions, and his advocacy had drawn great praise from Viet. However, Ben had not been involved with any of the detail of the tax allegations, and we knew that these would be central to any conversation. Neither had Viet, of course, but we needed Viet to try to find a way to re-open the door. But we thought that pairing Viet this time with a key member of the UK legal team would facilitate the only type of conversation which was now likely to succeed.

In the meantime, resolution of the extradition requests in London was not the only development which had taken place. At the beginning of 2008, Michael Garcia had announced a number of important staff changes within Southern District. Lev Dassin had been promoted to Deputy US Attorney, and in his place as Chief of the Criminal Division had been appointed a man called Guy Petrillo, who joined from Dechert LLP, where he was a partner. But Petrillo was no stranger to Southern District, having himself been Assistant United States Attorney in the Criminal Division in the 1990s. And he would now play an important part in the resolution of our case.

Before I explain what happened when we at last talked to Southern District, I would like to provide a background as to what was about to take place. First, throughout the whole of the period during which the United States was attempting to extradite me from Britain, I had continued to pay US taxes. Second, in the nearly 30 years since I first filed tax returns in the US, I had been called upon endlessly to find monies to pump into various businesses, to pay millions of dollars in taxes, and to bail Monty Hundley out of various scrapes. Finally, I can honestly say that I had never taken as much as a nickel out of the United States. All of the money that I had put into the United States had been earned elsewhere in the world. Nothing had come back in return. This had been a one-way street throughout.

I knew from the start that peace would have its price tag. After all, what was there other than money? But there was little alternative. If I were to be honest, I admitted to myself early on that there was no alternative other than to settle. For the benefit of the entire family, now and into the future, there was a price which had to be paid. The only question was, how digestible was I going to find all this? Could I actually stomach it?

In the autumn of 2008, Viet, accompanied by James Lewis QC, began a new series of meetings with the Office of the US Attorney for the Southern District of New York. The first meeting involved both Guy Petrillo, the new Chief of the Criminal Division, and Shirah Neiman, the unpleasant woman known to all and sundry as 'the US Attorney's attack dog'.

The meeting began with James Lewis making two things clear. First, he told those present to make no mistake, Bea and I were safe in London from the clutches of the US Department of Justice. Second, Okula had lied to a British Court in a sworn statement, and he had been found by a judge to have lied. Steps were now being taken which, if followed through, could lead to Okula being required to stand trial for perjury in London. "No-one in this room," he said, "wants to see an Assistant US Attorney tried in a London court for perjury. That would have implications for every future US extradition request from Britain."

Fortunately, the customary intransigence for which Shirah Neiman was well-known was not allowed to cloud the tentative spirit of exploration, which had enabled Viet to set up the meeting. Instead, James' dark hints coupled with Guy Petrillo's workmanlike pragmatism set the tone for both the meeting and a possible way forward. Neither party was terribly keen to start talking, but both sides recognised that there was no other way. This was going to be tough, but there was a glimmer of hope that something just might be possible.

The negotiations lasted four months. A book could be written on the minutiae of those negotiations alone. But I have no intention of adding still further to the length of this book by spending too much time explaining precisely what happened. There were many hiccoughs along the way, but there was, in truth, only one matter which became a potential showstopper, and that was a matter which was still on the table at the 59th minute of the 11th hour. And this was the position of Gavin.

As the weeks had progressed, the team on our side had expanded to include Bob Cleary and Mark Harris of Proskauer Rose. They had started out as Gavin's New York lawyers but, as it became clear that Gavin's position and mine were in some ways inseparably connected, they acted for me too.

As Viet and James edged towards a possible financial settlement, I made clear that it was essential that the whole family was safe and that every member of the family would be properly protected. One by one, the question of Bea, Brett, Vicki and Toni had been raised and resolved satisfactorily. However, I was told the day before we were due to settle that, given what had happened in Canada, and the number and complexity of loose ends in relation to Gavin, his position was too complex to resolve in time. I was advised to press on and and settle on behalf of myself and the other members of the family. Gavin's position would, I was told, resolve itself swiftly thereafter.

I was having absolutely none of this. Remember, Justice Molloy stayed the extradition proceedings against Gavin because of abusive conduct by American and Canadian authorities. The court had found that Canadian immigration processes had been manipulated by Okula in an attempt to get a UK resident, temporarily present in Canada, into US custody to face charges without the safeguards of an extradition proceeding. This conduct has been referred to as 'disguised extradition' or 'rendition'. I prefer 'kidnap'. Only after those attempts failed, had the US finally commenced extradition proceedings, and in Toronto rather than London.

I remembered vividly Okula's misleading of the Canadian authorities, as well as the Canadian courts and tribunals. Even though Judge Molloy had also found that the Canadian Border Services Agency were not without culpability as well[111], my distrust of Okula was absolute. Gavin's position had to be agreed at the same time as the rest of the family. This was not a negotiable point, and it took us to the wire. I knew that the chances of a swift and acceptable resolution of Gavin's position would diminish hugely once the ink was dry on any settlement agreement from which he was excluded.

I held my ground and, for a moment, it looked as though all bets were off. Eventually, though, the other side applied extra energy to the loose ends of Gavin's position, and the deal which was now on the table was one with which all parties were prepared to live. (At a push, and only after a very deep breath.)

It was a fine achievement following much hard work, and all credit was due to Viet and James, to Colin Passmore and, of course, to Gavin. Together, they had delivered a comprehensive agreement which – although financially painful, and fraught with emotional torment for yours truly – would enable the family to sleep easy and to get on with life.

---

[111] Mrs Justice Molloy found that officials of the CBSA were willing to take actions they would not otherwise have taken if not for the United States request, "and are therefore complicit, at least to that extent, in the scheme".

Gavin flew to New York for the closing stages of the deal, safe in the knowledge that Okula had been muzzled. This could now be wrapped up without fear of further monkey business. Gavin's personal, and public, role in this part of the saga was played out in Courtroom 12A, 500 Pearl Street, New York on 20 November 2008.

Remember, when the Canadian Border Service Agency had introduced Gavin to the judge in Toronto when he was abducted, he had been described as the mastermind behind a $450 million fraud, whose release on bail should be resisted at all costs. "No amount of money could hold him. He is an indescribable flight risk." Those comments had been instrumental in Gavin being exiled from his family, his home and his job for two painful years. But when the allegations against him were examined properly, all that Gavin was asked to do was to plead guilty to a misdemeanor involving just $18,000 of allegedly unpaid tax – a figure which was in fact disputed. Gavin was sentenced to just one day's unsupervised probation.

Gavin had lost two years of his life over just $18,000. In that time, every aspect of his personal and professional life had been pored over, even to the extent of being asked to account for a bag of six bagels which he had bought ten years earlier and which had appeared on his expenses claims. Matters such as this were the 'justification' for imprisoning a man for two years in a foreign country away from his children, his home and his career.

Gavin has recovered from that dreadful period, but no-one can give him back two years during an irreplaceable period of his children's lives. This episode will not easily be forgotten – nor forgiven.

GETTING OUR LIVES BACK
PART V

Finally, the time had come.

Colin summoned me to join him within range of the camera. Along with James Lewis and Jim Webster, Colin and I took our places ready for the hearing. As we did so, we stepped, in effect, into the Daniel Patrick Moynihan United States Courthouse at 500 Pearl Street, Foley Square, Manhattan. Ironically, this was a building which had been officially opened in 1996 by none other than my old 'friend' Senator Al D'Amato. Here we were, the four of us, in a building in the City of London, participating in a court hearing which was actually taking place in a building in New York, 3,000 miles away.

The District Judge herself, the Hon. Loretta A. Preska, arrived to take charge of the proceedings. I could see that the US Attorney's Office was represented by no less a person than Michael Garcia himself, whom I recognised from photographs I had seen. I knew that Okula would be with him, and imagined him to be the angular man sitting next to Garcia. This, then, was my first sight of the man who had been the cause of so much grief for my family over so many years. This though was an experience which I had no wish to repeat. Once was most definitely going to be enough. Beyond Okula were a lady and a man whom I did not know. Apart from Garcia and Okula, I was able to recognise Viet Dinh, the bearded figure of Bob Cleary, Bob's colleague Mark Harris, and a fourth man whom I did not know.

Okula began the proceedings by introducing the two people sitting alongside him. We learned that the woman was none other than Christine Mazzella, the woman from the IRS who had arrested Brett. And that the man next to Mazzella was James O'Connor from the FBI. Viet introduced our team in New York and I learned that the fourth gentleman was Mark Davidson who, like Bob Cleary and Mark Harris, was also from Proskauer Rose. Viet then looked up to the video screen in New York and from it he introduced first of all me, then Jim Webster, Colin Passmore and, finally, James Lewis.

At this point I was asked to raise my right hand and be sworn. I confirmed my age and where I was born. I was then asked by the judge whether I read, wrote, spoke and understood English. This question was immediately clarified by Judge Preska by the addition of the words, "or at least the British form of English". I smiled to myself, and confirmed that I did. Having then answered to the satisfaction of the court that I was not under the influence of alcohol or narcotics, we got down to business.

I had agreed to plead guilty to a single count, and the court needed to satisfy itself that everything had been done properly. Had I, for instance, genuinely decided that it was in my best interest to waive indictment on that count? Okula was required to explain to the Court the elements of proof that the United States would have had to provide if it were to proceed to trial. He spelled out the need to prove a tax deficiency, and then to prove that I had committed an act of evasion, and that I had done so wilfully.

The judge then referred to the agreement which we had concluded the day before and which had been signed that very morning. Okula explained that the agreement had been the result of "extensive investigation" and had "myriad provisions". I, he said, had promised to plead guilty to tax evasion charges for a five-year period from 1994. The tax deficiency for the period in question, as calculated, and including interest and a "75% penalty for fraud", was "approximately" $60,381,691. I remember thinking that this seemed far too precise a number to qualify for the description "approximately".

In addition to the tax figure, Okula told the court that I had also agreed to pay $44,711,947 in order to "settle the civil forfeiture action". (This was an important and, taken in the round, substantially positive point, to which I will return later.) I had also agreed to make an immediate payment of $25 million, and to deal with the agreed balance over five years. Finally, I had accepted that my heirs and successors would be responsible for any outstanding payments after my death.

It was galling to listen to these vast sums of money being referred to as though they were merely numbers, and to the fact that I had agreed to hand all this money to the US Government. But the future peace and security of the family which this agreement would secure meant that I could see advantage in what I was about to do. But that did not make it right. As I have told you, Gavin's position had been resolved the day before, and Okula now stated openly in court that the United States Government would no longer pursue Bea, Brett, Vicki or Toni either.

Now came the difficult bit.

Having been satisfied with the preamble, Judge Preska then addressed me once more, "Am I correct that your offer to plead guilty is due in part to this agreement between you and the Government?" I confirmed that it was. She then asked me the tough question. "Do I correctly understand that you are offering to plead guilty because you are in fact guilty, Sir?"

At this point, there was a pause. A long and, so I was later told, very uncomfortable pause. The conflicting emotions inside my head had rendered me speechless. I was in mental turmoil. I could hear my father's words about honesty, yet I also knew that the family could suffer no longer. A line had to be drawn. But I just could not bring myself to do it.

The transcript of the proceedings of that day reflects accurately the series of exchanges which took place between Judge Preska and me. She politely puts various questions to me, to which I equally politely provide answers. But what the transcript does not reflect is the agonising silence between the key question and the key answer. And I was not the only one who was suffering. My legal team afterwards admitted that they had each been worried that, when it came to it, I would not say those words. That I would not admit guilt.

Eventually, I managed to get the words out. Lest you have forgotten by now, those words were in reponse to the question from Judge Preska, "Do I correctly understand that you are offering to plead guilty because you are in fact guilty, Sir?" I swallowed deeply, and gathered my composure. "Yes, your Honor," I said.

I thought of Brett in particular at this point for, like Brett, I too was required to read out an allocution, an admission of what it was that I had done which was wrong. My words ran as follows:

In the 1990s, I had a number of bank accounts in Guernsey, Channel Islands. I received, reported and paid tax on millions of dollars income from those accounts. During the period 1994 to 1999, I wilfully failed to report on my income tax returns approximately 18 million in income that I received from two of the Guernsey accounts, Buffalo Holdings and New York Investments.

"And you knew that was unlawful? Correct, Sir?"

"Yes, your Honor."

At this point the collective relief was almost tangible. If the judge herself had said, "Phew" it would have surprised no-one. Swiftly, she got on with the sentencing. Given all the build-up, and the fact that we had got the monetary penalties out of the way already, this was remarkably simple. I was sentenced to one day of unsupervised probation, and ordered to pay a 100 dollar special assessment.

Judge Preska wrapped up proceedings, "Very well, gentlemen. I do congratulate you all on working out a most lawyer-like solution. Good morning, Mr Tollman. Good morning, counsel. Good morning gentlemen, ladies."

With that, it was all over. Every single one of the long-standing charges against me were dismissed. I was not guilty of the bank fraud, nor of any of the various and extensive charges of tax fraud of which the defendants in Monty Hundley's trial had been convicted. In relation to Tollman-Hundley I had been exonerated.

As I waited for my coat, I reflected on what had just happened. As a result of the hearing, there was little doubt in my mind that Judge Preska was a thoroughly decent woman. And 'thoroughly decent' are words which, unhesitatingly, I would also use to describe Tim Workman.

In the immensely difficult journey over the last seven years, I had seen examples of the worst type of human behaviour. But I had also seen the best – sometimes in the most unlikely or challenging places and often in the face of adversity. Ultimately, when it really mattered, things had worked out. And for that I will be eternally grateful to those who played a part in making it happen. I will retain for ever some happy memories and many friendships which were born out of the darkness.

But there are also some deeply unhappy memories which will never be forgotten. The malevolent behaviour of Stanley Okula throughout was matched only by his lack of supervision. The consistent absence of oversight leads to only one conclusion. His behaviour is, at a minimum, tolerated by those who have responsibility for his actions. It is perhaps even encouraged.

In 2006, Judge Lewis A. Kaplan dismissed charges against 13 defendants in a tax evasion case brought in the Southern District against the accounting firm KPMG. Judge Kaplan did so after finding that the Department of Justice had interfered with KPMG's payment of the defendants' legal fees.

Southern District had extracted fines of $456 million from KPMG over the matter of tax shelter arrangements which KPMG had put in place for clients. As part of that deal, the partnership escaped indictment, but 19 partners of the firm were not so fortunate.[112] Assistant US Attorney Stanley Okula was one of those prosecuting, and he stood charged with pressurising KPMG into withdrawing legal support from the accused partners.

In his ruling dated 26 June 2006, Judge Kaplan found that the US Government's actions had violated the due process rights of the defendants. Okula was one of those singled out by the judge as having provided "information that was inconsistent with the facts before the Court". Shirah Neiman, Chief Counsel to the US Attorney, was also singled out for criticism.

On 16 July 2007, Judge Kaplan handed down his final judgment on the KPMG matter, which Okula had been prosecuting. In discharging every single one of the defendants, he said:

---

[112]United States of America v Jeffrey Stein et al S1 05 Crim 0888 (LAK)

The Department of Justice and the Office of the US Attorney deliberately and callously prevented many of these defendants from obtaining funds for their defense that they lawfully would have had, absent the government's interference. They thereby foreclosed these defendants from presenting the defenses they wished to present and, in some case, even deprived them of the counsel of their choice. This is intolerable in a society that holds itself out as a paragon of justice. The responsibility for the dismissal of this indictment as to 13 defendants lies with the government.

The Court well understands, moreover, that prosecutors can and should be aggressive in the pursuit of the public interest. It respects the distinguished record of the United States Attorney's office for the Southern District of New York, which long has been, and continues to be, a model for the nation. But there are limits on the permissible actions of even the best prosecutors.

Judge Kaplan then quoted from a US Supreme Court judgment. At the time of writing, the US Department of Justice is today offering advice to Federal Prosecutors as to the correct way to pursue a prosecution. Central to that advice is the very same statement made in the US Supreme Court which Judge Kaplan used, and which dated from not long after I was born. As the Department of Justice now clearly recognises, those words, which were penned by Justice Sutherland[113], are every bit as telling today as when they were written 70-odd years ago:

The United States Attorney is the representative not of an ordinary party to a controversy, but of a sovereignty whose obligation to govern impartially is as compelling as its obligation to govern at all; and whose interest, therefore, in a criminal prosecution is not that it shall win a case, but that justice shall be done. As such, he is in a peculiar and very definite sense the servant of the law, the twofold aim of which is that guilt shall not escape or innocence suffer. He may prosecute with earnestness and vigor – indeed, he should do so. But, while he may strike hard blows, he is not at liberty to strike foul ones. It is as much his duty to refrain from

[113]George Sutherland was an English-born jurist, and was one of four appointments to the Supreme Court by President Warren Harding.

improper methods calculated to produce a wrongful conviction as it is to use every legitimate means to bring about a just one.

Every time I read those words, I think of all the things Okula did, and the criticisms which were levelled in his direction. Apart from the KPMG matter, we knew from our own experience that Okula had been accused of egregious behaviour by a senior Canadian judge, and of lying to the court by a senior English judge. Any one of these three elements should have been considered a disciplinary matter in any country which valued its system of justice. But Okula has been neither criticised, nor punished. The continued acceptance and approval of prosecutorial abuse by Okula, and indeed by other prosecutors, remains a lasting stain on the character of a fine nation and its people.

In recent years, I have had cause to re-assess my attitude to the United States. I have loved that country since I was a young man, and have thought that it represented much of what truly matters. Its people are not the philistines that many Europeans would have us believe. I have met many well-read, intelligent and cultured Americans, although I confess, too, to having met a few who might not meet this definition. But it is the American spirit of adventure and enterprise which I have always found most stimulating, and where I have felt most at home.

I have always considered the United States to be a fair country, with a justice system which works. But that was before I had anything to do with the US system of justice. I appreciate that much that has been written in this book is critical of the actions of just one man. But I was forced long ago to abandon the thought that Okula was simply a lone maverick, operating with neither the knowledge nor the approval of his superiors. Why for instance does he remain to this day in his job, despite the devastating criticism of him which has emerged from so many quarters?

Throughout this whole dreadful period of my life, I had often been advised against doing things which it was felt would upset the US Attorney's Office. "It could be a mistake to do that. You don't want Okula to get pissed-off, do you?" My answer to that was simple. "He is pissed-off! How much more pissed-off can he get?" The sister conversation related to the US Attorney's office protecting their own. The analogy which was always used was from the Wild West. "They'll circle the wagons", I heard endlessly, summoning up an image of the hero being protected from the outlaws or the Red Indians. But what they should have said is that they will always protect their own, however inappropriate. They will always cover up. How else could Okula have survived Justice Molloy's withering condemnation of his behaviour? Or District Judge Tim Workman's accusation of untruthfulness to the Court?

The answer, I was told recently, is as simple as it is shocking. And I was told this by a former colleague of Okula. The assessment is frightening, but I am forced to admit that it is also believable. In response to the question as to why Okula was still in office, having been so devastatingly criticised by Mrs Justice Molloy and District Judge Workman, this was the answer: "You need to understand something. We are the United States. We just don't care. Those were foreign judges. We just don't care what they say." And there it is. So much for the American approach to international relations.

Even though everything had been settled, and all the charges relating to Tollman-Hundley dropped completely, the US Attorney's Office issued the customarily mean-minded and pejorative press release[114] following the transatlantic court hearing. I assume it was the last chance Okula had to smear me, and once again the press release contained the entirely untruthful allegation that I had fled the United States. Thankfully, however, it was not widely-circulated, nor was it accompanied by much effort to ensure that it was extensively reported. For the record, its essential elements were as follows (having omitted Okula's smears):

[114]United States Department of Justice Press Release – 21 November 2008.

HOTEL EXECUTIVE PLEADS GUILTY AND AGREES TO PAY RESTITUTION AND FORFEITURE IN CONNECTION WITH TAX EVASION SCHEME

Michael J. Garcia, the United States Attorney for the Southern District of New York, announced that Stanley S. Tollman pleaded guilty today to tax fraud charges relating to his participation in a multimillion-dollar tax evasion scheme utilizing foreign bank accounts.

Tollman, 78, agreed as part of his plea to pay $60,381,691 in restitution to the IRS in the form of back taxes, interest, and fraud penalties. Tollman also agreed to pay $44.7 million to settle a separate civil forfeiture action brought by the United States relating to the allegations in a 2002 Indictment charging Tollman and six others with various fraud offenses.

Tollman, who entered his plea from London, England, via video-link, was sentenced at the time of his plea to a one-day term of probation. Consistent with the plea agreement between Tollman and the Government, the Court dismissed the open bank fraud and other remaining counts in the 2002 Indictment.

In addition, earlier this week, Gavin Tollman pleaded guilty to failing to supply information to the IRS on tax returns that he filed, specifically, the authority he had with respect to two foreign bank accounts. Gavin Tollman, who pleaded to this misdemeanor tax offense before Judge Preska in Manhattan federal court, agreed to file certain amended tax returns and was similarly sentenced to a one-day term of probation.

The battle was over, we had drawn a line in the sand, and the family could once again sleep more easily. We drank a little champagne, and we set about rebuilding our lives.

PICKING UP THE PIECES

During the period of the settlement talks with the US Attorney, it became obvious to all concerned that I was very uncomfortable with what was going on. Given what had happened to the family, the very idea of negotiating a compromise with Southern District was almost unthinkable. My poorly-concealed distaste for the process prompted David Martin, Gavin's lawyer, to take me aside one day.

He told me of another client for whom he had concluded a multi-million dollar tax settlement, negotiated under threat of prosecution. At the time, it had proved very painful for his client, who resented bitterly what he was being forced to do. As far as he was concerned, the whole thing was completely unjustified. (I knew exactly how he felt.) But when the client had bumped into David in the street a couple of years later, he said that settling had been the best decision he had ever taken. As far as he was concerned, the deal had been forgotten, and he was rebuilding his life. David assured me that a settlement was the right thing for me too. I would soon forget and be able to get on with my life. Any plea agreement would quickly fade from my memory.

But David was wrong. More than a thousand days have passed since I agreed to settle. True, I have been able to get on with my life. But there has not been a single one of those thousand-odd days when I have not thought about what I did, and when I have not asked myself whether I took the right decision. It's as though I am carrying a sack of grain on my back – a sack every bit as big and as heavy as the sacks my father used to carry at my grandfather's mill in Riteve. Like Atlas, I am doomed to carry that burden for the rest of my days. And I know I will go to my grave with that question unanswered.

But this does not mean that I have lost interest in living. Quite the reverse. With the passage of the years, I have learned the truth of the saying, 'The older you get, the older you want to get'. There remains a great deal that I still want to do and, besides, I would never permit negative thoughts to rule my life. I am far too positive to allow that happen.

Indeed, they say that a man does not become old until regrets take the place of his dreams. I may *feel* a little ancient sometimes, but I am quite sure that regrets will never take the place of my dreams, which have always been a vital part of my life. Sometimes, dreams have quite simply been the thing that has kept me going. Even at the darkest moments of my struggle against the United States, I continued to dream of better things, always confident that determination and luck would see me through. My worst nightmares may have been realised but, in the past, so had all my dreams. I was convinced that the music was not going to stop for me at that point, and in that dark place. A dance or two was most certainly left in me yet.

I would often say to the lawyers, "When we get out of this, I am going to invite the whole of the team to join us on safari." (Please note the '*when* we get out', rather than '*if...*') I have no idea whether anyone believed what I said, but I was giving my word. And I keep my promises. So it was that, one night in September 2010, I found myself sitting by a camp-fire in the African bush with almost every member of the legal team – lawyers from Britain, from the United States, and from Canada. We were all enjoying a few days at some of our lodges in Botswana, witnessing the majesty of life and death against the backdrop of one of the world's finest settings. Bea and I were saying thank you.

Having enjoyed supper, we began exchanging anecdotes in the glow of the embers. One-by-one, the lawyers felt the need to stand and say a few words. The cynical will no doubt be unmoved to hear of lawyers wanting to stand up and talk. Indeed, a story about attorneys being struck dumb would be more worthy of note. Cynicism aside, though, Bea and I were genuinely moved that evening by what each of these hard-bitten professionals said.

The words may have differed but, speaker-by-speaker, there was a common and unmistakeable theme. The lawyers said that the journey upon which we had travelled together had been unlike any professional assignment which they had experienced. Each had found it impossible to remain detached. One-by-one, they admitted that they had become emotionally involved in the fight – something which had not happened to them before.

They were kind enough to suggest that this was in part because they liked us. More importantly, though, each considered that they were helping to prevent an injustice. It had become personal, and they were determined to be on the winning side. And win is exactly what they did. The family – and especially myself – are forever in their debt. I raised several glasses of wine to them that evening, and I raise a glass of wine to them now.

A very big thank-you to the London barristers Clive Nicholls, James Lewis, Edward Fitzgerald, Hugo Keith and James Hines, and to the solicitors instructing them – Colin Passmore and Claire McLeod. And a big thank-you too to Chris Todd, Jim Webster and Viet Dinh from Washington, and to Michael Code and David Martin from Canada. There are many others whom I could also name and thank, but space of course prevents me. I must say a word of thanks, though, to New York attorney Bob Fink. Bob and I did not see eye-to-eye at first but, in light of his coming to London and giving evidence in our support, I re-assessed my view of him completely. Bob has to deal with the US Attorney every week of the year, and giving evidence in London against Okula required real courage.

At the time of writing, I believe that Bea and I are the only people to have successfully defended an extradition request from the United States under the new Act. That we were successful is remarkable, given that the odds are so heavily stacked against the individual, and given the tactics which the Office of the US Attorney was prepared to adopt in order to win. As you would expect, I have spoken to Gavin about those tactics on a number of occasions, and he has a very interesting take on the approach of the US authorities.

Gavin has spent a good deal of time thinking about all of this, and points out that it is not perhaps insignificant that the rules of the three 'all-American' sports – baseball, American football and basketball –

do not provide for a game to finish with a draw or a tie. Such an outcome would be considered unthinkable in the United States. In America, sport, like life, is all about winning. And that mentality extends to the American system of justice. It is not about an equitable outcome, it is about winning – whatever the cost. Contrast the American approach with the way sport operates in civilised countries. The Laws of Cricket, for instance, begin with the following preamble:

> *Cricket is a game that owes much of its unique appeal to the fact that it should be played not only within its Laws but also within the Spirit of the Game.*
>
> *Any action which is seen to abuse this spirit causes injury to the game itself. The major responsibility for ensuring the spirit of fair play rests with the captains.*

I think that Gavin's analysis of the American state of mind is very interesting. And I also think that the words above, penned by the great English captains, Colin Cowdrey and Ted Dexter, have a curiously striking relevance for those who oversee the work of Assistant US Attorneys – *"The major responsibility for ensuring the spirit of fair play rests with the captains."*

In the matter of *United States of America – v – Stanley Stephen Tollman*, fair play was in very short supply indeed. Thankfully, though, it was we who won. But, although a great deal was said around that campfire in the bush back in 2010, no-one thought to ask how it was that we had succeeded. Had I been asked, I would have answered, "Careful team selection, hard work, and a generous helping of good luck." I remember being asked a very similar question once before – not in the aftermath of an extradition battle but on a much more pleasant occasion. Bea and I were attending a ceremony at Schiller International University in London, where I was being awarded an Honorary Doctorate for the "outstanding contribution" which the University considered that I had made to "the advancement of world tourism". I was receiving my degree as part of the graduation ceremony for that year's crop of students – a very proud moment, as you might imagine. I was asked to speak, and then to answer questions.

One of the first was from a serious young man who asked whether I could let him in on the secret. How had I succeeded? I probably disappointed him when I confessed that I didn't have a secret formula. All I could tell him was what Bea and I had done to get where we were. We had applied ourselves with dedication, kept our heads down, and kept going. In other words, our 'secret' had been sustained hard work. "If you do the same," I told him, "I have no doubt that you could be successful yourself." I could have added that I might not have known the magic formula for success, but I did know how to guarantee failure. "If you want to fail", I might have told him, "try to please everyone."

Attempting to please everyone was not the way I would have described the settlement which I reached with the United States Department of Justice, even though it had a number of obvious benefits. Having concluded an agreement, I was able to take advantage of the peace which ensued in order to survey the damage which had been done to many aspects of my life. Almost every member of the family had been affected in one way or another by what had happened, and many of our businesses had suffered because we had been unable to provide the focus which at times they had needed. Because of the financial elements of the settlement, the family's fortunes had also taken a big knock – although not as large as appeared likely at first sight, for reasons I will explain.

Part of the settlement had included a payment of almost $45 million to the United States in respect of the civil forfeiture which had arisen from the Hundley trial verdicts four years earlier. This order had enabled the US Government to seize Monty Hundley's assets. What we negotiated meant that I, in effect, stepped into Monty's position – in other words, becoming the liable party, even though, unlike him, I had filed countless tax returns over the years. In return, though, the Government had to hand us assets which they had seized. This meant that we received the 50% interest in Bryanston which had previously belonged to Monty.

As a result of the 2004 forfeiture, for the last four years we had been in partnership at Bryanston with Stanley Okula. Unsurprisingly, this had not been good for business. In negotiating into our ownership the element of Bryanston which the family did not already possess, we succeeded in getting rid of Okula. This enabled us, unfettered, to begin to claw back some serious money, and thus reduce the impact of the settlement in terms of net cost.

Now undistracted, every member of the Tollman family got back to work, re-applying ourselves anew. We had three important challenges – repairing the family, rebuilding the businesses, and recovering investments where others, imagining that our eye had been taken off the ball, had taken advantage. I can only suppose that they thought we wouldn't notice or, more likely, that we would not be in a position to do anything about it. They were quite wrong.

Picking up the reins of the businesses once more was perhaps the least troublesome of the three. Although we had been under something of a siege, the businesses had adapted well, responding with flexibility and determination. Various members of the family had covered for others – Michael, Vicki and Toni in particular filling many of the gaps. And in some areas the stimulus provided by the troubles meant that we were actually more resilient as a business. But, although we were more robust overall, certain parts of the empire were in need of attention.

At this point, I would like to talk a little about the Travel Corporation. Not because that business was in serious need of attention – far from it – but because my earlier references to the Travel Corporation have not given a sense of the scale and importance of that enterprise. In fact, the history of the Travel Corporation is perhaps deserving of its own book. For the purposes of my own story, though, the following highlights are intended merely as a snapshot, and a snapshot taken from 30,000 feet at that.

The Travel Corporation is a truly international enterprise. I often struggle to think of another which is as genuinely international. Not only are our products and services created independently and discretely right across the globe, and are therefore very different from each other, but each of those businesses has its own largely multinational customer base. But, unlike most multinational businesses, which are built upon the offer of the same homogenous goods or services to everybody, largely irrespective of where in the world they happen to be, the Travel Corporation embraces and celebrates individuality in both the services we offer and the customers we serve.

It has taken a long time to build this unique enterprise, and its story is complex. Given the individual history of the Corporation's many component parts, identifying the actual beginnings of the Travel Corporation would appear to be like trying to establish the source of the Nile. Thankfully, though, it is much more straightforward. The Corporation's origin was the formation, in 1947, of Industrial Recreational Services by de-mobbed soldier Bill Nunn, an enterprise which was later to become Trafalgar Tours. And Trafalgar, of course, became the cornerstone for the creation of the Travel Corporation. The comparison between today's Travel Corporation and Bill's organised visits to Ramsgate and Brighton after the war, which involved a handful of coaches and a few hundred people, is nothing less than extraordinary.

Sixty-five years after those seaside outings, the Travel Corporation is a very large business indeed, delivering well over a million holidays a year. It comprises hundreds of international travel and tourism companies under the umbrella of 22 global brands, including Trafalgar itself, Insight, Contiki, Red Carnation, AAT Kings, Brendan and Evan Evans. It operates in more than 60 countries, with 35 offices worldwide.

We cater to all travel styles and budgets, and we operate from the United States to New Zealand, from Switzerland to South Africa, from Canada to China, and from Russia to Brazil. I am immensely proud of what we have achieved with the original investment in Trafalgar, and I have to restrain myself from writing too much about it now. But I would like to make mention of a few names from a remarkable team of people, some of whom have been part of the business for 20, or even 30, years. At the top of this list is of course

Mike Ness, who has been a very important figure for longer than I care to admit, and to whom I owe a great deal. Other key and long-standing members of the team are David Hosking, John Weeks and Fenella Bishop, but there any many others who are not named here but whose contribution is no less valued. But there is one other name which I must mention, and that is Richard Masefield. He too was a long-standing member of the team, and deserves particular note because of his own problems with Okula.

Richard was pursued by Okula in relation to a personal tax matter and was repeatedly offered leniency if he was prepared to lie about me. There is little doubt that his compliance as demanded would have made his life a lot easier and that, conversely, his refusal to do what Okula wanted made it much more difficult. In the face of intense and sustained pressure from Okula, he stuck to his guns and refused to lie, and he suffered terribly as a result. Yet another transgression for which Okula will have to account on Judgement Day.

In addition to the travel business team, and in relation to recent initiatives, I would also like to give particular credit to members of the family. The first is a not-for-profit affiliate of Travel Corporation called the Conservation Foundation. This is the brainchild of my son Brett, who is today President & CEO of Travel Corporation. The Foundation has the dual objectives of supporting sustainable tourism and of protecting and preserving popular tourist destinations for future generations.

Brett is exceptionally well-placed to lead an initiative of this kind, given his passionate commitment to the Foundation's objectives, and given his ability to deploy influence within the travel industry. He has been a member of the World Travel & Tourism Council since 1998, a position which I held myself for some years. Today, Brett is also one of the Council's Vice Chairmen.

He has also been the Foundation's inspiration within our own travel companies, and it is no exaggeration to say that the Travel Corporation is very much at the spearhead of the worldwide move towards responsible and sustainable tourism. Like much of what Brett is engaged in, I am immensely proud of this work.

The other initiative I want to mention is our investment in river boat cruising. This sector is expanding rapidly, a trend we anticipated and where we have been making serious investments. Long over-shadowed by bigger, ocean-going vessels, river cruise ships are becoming increasingly popular. Many of the world's most beautiful cities sit alongside major rivers rather than on the coast, and river boats not only offer non-stop scenery from destination to destination, they dock right in the heart of the cities which they visit.

In 2004, Travel Corporation bought the Uniworld Boutique River Cruise Collection, a business established in 1976 and based in Los Angeles, California. Uniworld operates in more than 20 countries, and recently became the first major operator to cruise Italy's Po river and the Venetian Lagoon. The scope of its operations, as well as its fleet of vessels, is growing like Topsy and much of this is due to the energy and endeavour of my daughter Toni.

Toni is a remarkable lady. She has the most wonderful sense of humour: one which always makes me smile. And she has inherited Bea's loyalty to those for whom she cares. At the same time, she has an ability to get right to the core of any issue with which she is dealing, and heaven preserve those who don't come up to the mark. Her warmth is matched only by her toughness.

When Gavin was stranded in Canada, not only did she give him her complete support in Toronto, but at the same time she cared for her children in England and helped to look after the family's business interests in various parts of the world, notably in South Africa. Vicki had thrown herself into this too, as you will soon discover, but Toni was a trained hotelier, whilst Vicki had a great deal to learn. Between the two of them they did an extraordinary job.

Toni's two children have since became adults and both now work for the family businesses. Toni's daughter, Alexandra, works for Red Carnation in London, and Andrew works for the Travel Corporation in Canada. Together, they represent the fourth generation of the family within the business. Alexandra is in fact the eldest of our grandchildren, and I want to thank her and also the other grandchildren for their extraordinary support during our time of troubles. Those who were old enough to understand what was going on were amongst our staunchest supporters, something I will never forget.

Returning, though, to Uniworld, we are currently in the middle of a massive programme of investment. As I write, no fewer than five new boats are under construction. They will join our existing fleet, which already contains two new ships. These are the *River Beatrice*, a 410ft vessel which was inaugurated in 2009 and which plies the Rhine and the Danube, and the *SS Antoinette*, which was inaugurated in 2011. The *Antoinette* is a larger vessel at 443ft, which is not only named after Toni but was designed by her. Under Bea's ever-watchful guidance, Toni is the driving force behind the design of all the latest additions to the Uniworld fleet. Unsurprisingly, she took a special interest in the *Antoinette*, which was built and fitted out in Holland. Toni is on record as saying that she must have bought every mirror in that country in order to complete the fitting, and yet she still needed more. If the bills are anything to go by, she was right.

Her approach to river cruiser design is to inject a little of the boutique hotel luxury for which the family is well-known into what was seen as a somewhat staid sector of the market. Consistent with this approach, the *Antoinette* has a fabulous two-storey marble lobby featuring a ten-foot Baccarat crystal chandelier with a very interesting history.

One of the New York restaurants which I used to frequent was the Tavern on the Green in Central Park. It is no longer open as a restaurant, and is perhaps best known these days as the finish line for the New York Marathon. But it was once very famous, its regular diners including film stars and politicians. In 2009, though, the Tavern on the Green closed its doors forever after filing for bankruptcy, and the restaurant's fixtures were auctioned off. Toni stepped in and bought the chandelier, which now has pride of place in the *Antoinette*.

The *Antoinette* also boasts both a heated swimming pool and the world's first cinema on a river cruise ship. It cruises the Rhine between Amsterdam and Basel. A further ship is currently being built in the Netherlands, and this will be christened the *River Victoria* – named after Vicki of course. This will operate within Russia. Beyond that, the next SS's (Super Ships) will be the *Alexandra* and the *Katherine*, and the two smaller ships – *The Orchid*, which will operate within Vietnam, and *The Spirit*, which will cruise the Douro in Spain and Portugal.

As a contrast to the excitement and rewarding nature of the more positive aspects of business, I also find myself having to resolve problems linked to family investments which have been exploited by others. This is as tedious as it is galling, but I am determined to see these things through to a successful conclusion. Like most people, we hate to be taken advantage of.

On a more positive note, I mentioned earlier – several hundred pages and many years earlier – that one of my life's great interests is wine. For most of my life, that interest has been restricted to drinking it. However, as I reached the age of 70, I was given the opportunity to invest in the making of wine and, even better, to do so in South Africa. Wine in South Africa has an interesting history, one which I am delighted to say is founded upon the pursuit of good health – a thought which reassures me when I partake myself.

By the mid-17th Century, dietary ailments such as scurvy had become a major problem on long sea voyages around the Cape, a problem which had to be addressed. The Dutch East India Company sent surgeon Johann van Riebeeck to Cape Town with the task of establishing a market garden for the production of fresh fruit and vegetables. This was the foundation of a food-and-watering station in the Cape of Good Hope, becoming central to the improvement of the diet of seafarers in that part of the world. But Van Riebeeck had also taken grape vines to plant within his market garden. These flourished, producing wine within their very first year. Such were the beginnings of South African wine production.

But it is only in recent times that the country has become viewed as being a serious producer of fine wine. And one of the key figures in the tremendous growth in that reputation has been a man called Peter Finlayson, named South African winemaker of the year in 1989. His prize was a trip to Burgundy, as a guest of Paul Bouchard, of Bouchard Aîné et Fils. As a result of that trip, Peter Finlayson and Paul Bouchard became great friends, and together they created a winery in the Cape, in the Hemel-en-Aarde[115] valley at Walker Bay, near Hermanus.

That winery, Bouchard Finlayson, was bought by my family at the turn of the century, with Peter Finlayson carrying on as the winemaker. Since then, this investment has become one of the most interesting parts of my life. The 300-acre estate contains just under 50 acres of wines, the balance being left to nature. And in that part of the world, the natural shrubland, known as Cape Fynbos, is something to behold. Difficult to describe, the Cape Fynbos is a remarkable and highly diverse mix of flowering plants and provides nature's magnificent backdrop to our winery.

Bea and I have built a home within the estate, where the two of us – and the dogs, of course – spend February each year. This is the time of the annual grape harvest, a wonderful time to be around. We are very proud of that house, designed and built as it is in the traditional Cape vernacular. It is a tremendously satisfying place to spend time.

Peter Finlayson is recognized as being one of the world's greatest experts in the cultivation of pinot noir, known to be one of the hardest varieties of grape with which to succeed as a winemaker. But succeed Peter has, as demonstrated by the numerous accolades which we have won in recent years. The vines are planted to emulate Burgundian principles: high-density planting with low, but high-quality, yields. Pinot noir is by no means our only variety, but it does dominate, especially where the soil is thinner, as it is ideally suited to the clay shale *terroir* of the valley. From these vines we produce a wine each year called Galpin Peak. Exceptional vintages also enable the selection of outstanding barrels for our award-winning Tête de Cuvée.

---

[115]Hemel-en-Aarde is Dutch for Heaven and Earth.

We also grow chardonnay and sauvignon blanc, which are planted in the deeper soils, and from which we produce a number of white wines. Amongst these is Kaaimansgat (Afrikaans for crocodile's lair), which is made from chardonnay grapes. This exceptional wine generates excellent reviews in the international media. Jancis Robinson wrote about the Kaaimansgat 2001 vintage, "Very fine, lean, delicate – burgundian in fact. And a very unburgundian price."[116]

But Bouchard Finlayson also has some very interesting Italian varietals, including that great Tuscan grape, the sangiovese. This is the backbone of a very interesting red wine called Hannibal, which also contains pinot noir, nebbiolo, barbera, and either mourvedre or shiraz, each of which is fermented separately, then blended.

Writing about Bouchard Finlayson provides me with an opportunity to pay credit to another member of the family – this time, my younger daughter, Vicki. Amongst the many things she does for the family businesses, Vicki oversees the winery, working closely with Peter Finlayson, and with our distributors in other parts of the world. In this, as in everything else to which she turns her hand, Vicki does an outstanding job, and I cannot speak highly enough about her. After living for some years in Morocco, and then in Paris, Vicki and her husband sadly became divorced. She came with her three young daughters to live in Palm Beach for a while, but returned to Europe – first to Paris and then to Geneva, which is now her home.

I really admire her. Despite the ups and downs of her life, Vicki has managed to bring up three wonderfully well-balanced girls, two of whom have now graduated from university. But, until seven or eight years ago, although for some time a major shareholder in the family enterprises, Vicki had not been involved day-to-day. In fact, she had little business experience to speak of at all. With Toni stranded in Canada for well over a year whilst she supported Gavin, and with Bea and I stuck in London and Brett serving his sentence in Alabama, Vicki realised that her family was both out of commission and, worse, under threat. She rose to the challenge, knowing that she had to learn, and quickly, and also travel a great deal. She applied herself to the business and grew into this new role remarkably, becoming an essential part of the team.

Vicki has many qualities but, for me, one stands out from the rest. When she enters a room, it is almost as though she has brought the sunshine with her. Always laughing and smiling, she makes people naturally at ease. Vicki is a wonderful person to have around.

I am very proud of the work that Vicki is doing with Bouchard Finlayson, and it is always pleasing to be able to do something within South Africa. I mentioned earlier how delighted we had been to create the Solomon Tollman Community Centre in Paternoster. And for many years we have been making the award of the Tollman Art Prize to a South African artist, an annual award which is worth 100,000 rand to the recipient. But our commitments to South Africa are not restricted to philanthropy and wine-making. As I made clear with my earlier comments about Cullinan Holdings and Wilderness Safaris, these days our involvement is mostly about business. In fact, the family's investments within the country have been growing steadily in recent years. Today, amongst other things, we are once again important hoteliers in our own homeland. And, with this in mind, I am aware that I have written a good deal about our travel businesses, but have said very little about Red Carnation Hotels, of which Bea is the Founder and President.

Bea is a serious business person, something which should not be overlooked. Ten years ago, she was recognised by the Star Foundation in the United States as being amongst the world's 100 leading women in business. And rightly so. From the beginning, Bea took to business like to a duck to water. This began with food, working with the chefs in our hotels and restaurants and then standing behind each of the hotel managers – much as she does today – with advice and encouragement. Her ventures into decorating also gave her the confidence to realise that she had an ability to apply herself equally in other areas too.

Red Carnation, very much Bea's baby, now includes no fewer than 14 award-winning luxury boutique hotels situated in the UK, the Channel Islands, South Africa, Switzerland and the United States. Red Carnation hotels are predominantly 5-star, providing a level of service which many recognise to be unparalleled, as is reflected by the countless industry and media awards which the hotels win with astonishing frequency. But these awards pale into comparative insignificance when measured against the overwhelming recognition which Red Carnation receives from regular guests whose repeat business, reviews and recommendations to others are a source of enormous pride for everyone involved.

Within Red Carnation, there are far too many people deserving of a mention, and singling just a couple of names out for mention is in some ways unfair to those whom I appear to overlook. But it is a remarkable team, every member of which knows how much Bea and I value the contribution which they make. But I must make mention of Jonathan Raggett, Red Carnation's Managing Director, and of Brian Brennan, Project Director. In 2009, Jonathan was deservedly named Hotelier of the Year, an outstanding achievement. He is a man with great ability and with a tremendous 'can do' attitude. During the period of our difficulties with the United States, Jonathan was hugely supportive of the family. Brian Brennan is a long-standing member of the Red Carnation team, and is currently assisting Bea and Toni with the work which is being done to extend the Uniworld fleet.

In London, Red Carnation has the Milestone, 41, Egerton House, the Chesterfield, the Montague and the Rubens. In Evershot, in Dorset, it has Summer Lodge, an outstanding country house hotel. In St. Peter Port, Guernsey, Red Carnation has two hotels – the Old Government House and the Duke of Richmond. In Geneva, Red Carnation has the Hotel d'Angleterre, situated on the shores of Lake Geneva. And in Palm Beach, Red Carnation has the Chesterfield. Finally, in South Africa, Red Carnation has three hotels – the Twelve Apostles, just outside Cape Town; Bushmans Kloof, a Relais & Château hotel situated in the heart of the bush, nearly 200 miles from Cape Town; and the Oyster Box at Umhlanga.

Mention of the Oyster Box provides a convenient link to a close friend who has supported us through some of our most difficult times.

I mentioned him much earlier, although anonymously. I wrote of the South African friend who loaned us 10,000 rand when we were down on our uppers in 1976, and when nobody else was prepared to help. His name is Maurice Shawzin. Having left South Africa, our paths crossed once again with Maurice in Florida, where he was Monty Koppel's partner in Lion Country Safari at Loxahatchee. Maurice lived for many years in Palm Beach. Today, he is back in South Africa once more, and he was one of our guests at the official re-opening of the Oyster Box.

As I also mentioned earlier, Prince Buthelezi spoke at the re-opening of the hotel. As part of his speech, he had some words for Maurice himself:

> *It is a pleasure to see Maurice Shawzin. Many years have passed since I last had the opportunity to see Mr Shawzin, who was one of the producers of a movie in which I starred as a much younger man. It was very touching for me to receive pictures from him which were shot for that movie – Zulu. In those pictures, Mr Shawzin looked a very young man indeed. Albeit that his appearance has now changed, I am pleased to see that he has not lost his enthusiasm for life and his boundless optimism. I am also pleased to learn that he is one of those who believed enough in the future of South Africa to come back from the United States where he succeeded in business, to invest again in the future of his homeland.*

Earlier in the book I thanked a number of friends from the United States and from Canada who were extraordinary in their support during our troubled times. Notably, these included Max Fisher, Kate Ford and Frank Chopin, Brian and Mila Mulroney, and Isadore and Camilla Rosenfeld.

But there are others whom I must thank too, such as Dixon Boardman, from both Palm Beach and New York, and also from New York, George Kaufman. There is my old polo-playing pal Derek Goodman and the now sadly-departed David Metcalfe. And of course Nicky Kerman, Gordon Jones, Hugh and Evelyn McNeil, Joan Penn, Philip Harari, Patrick Mavros and Ronnie Hersov.

Finally, my old school chum Raymond Eskapa and his late wife, Shirley. They were all brilliant. Sadly, though, it is not possible to name everyone who stood by us throughout our troubles. Those who did know who they are. And to all of you I say, "A million thanks!"

The most important person in my life is of course Bea, and I will be forever grateful to her for everything she has done for me. Her loyalty to her family and to her close friends is breathtaking. One has to know Bea to appreciate just how powerful that loyalty is. When, thanks to the US Attorney, the world was told that Bea was involved in something dreadful, loyalty was put to the test, with friends behaving in one of two ways. Some offered support, and became closer. Others disappeared so quickly they were not seen for dust. This test of friendship quickly sorted the wheat from the chaff, and I witnessed Bea's pain and the ill health which followed those departures. Ten years on, she still regularly quotes Martin Luther King: "In the end, we will remember not the slurs of our enemies, but the silence of our friends."

Perhaps because she herself is so loyal, when Bea discovered that some of her closest friends had no hesitation in abandoning her, she suffered terribly. It was deeply shocking and extremely hurtful that they would believe the worst, even though some of them had known us for many years. All of this is now behind us, of course but, even now, it is worth making it absolutely clear that at no time was Bea ever indicted – despite press reports to the contrary. And in 2008, the complaint which had been made against Bea was dropped completely, without any charge ever being made against her, and she was never required to make any payment to the IRS. It was accepted by all parties that, throughout, Bea had been completely innocent.

Great trauma in a family is often destructive of even the closest husband-and-wife relationship. But even in our darkest days, Bea has always stood by me and been there – not just for me but for every member of the family. Her extraordinary loyalty to me has meant that I have developed a devotion to her of a strength and depth of which I never knew that I was capable.

Through my eyes, Bea remains exactly the same as she has been throughout the 60 years I have known her. Impeccably and beautifully dressed, and always there with a smile and a word of encouragement, she looks after and tends to family and friends in the way in which she has done since I first met her. I was certainly lucky when I married this remarkable woman.

Any description of Bea would be incomplete without reference to her cooking, and to her dogs. Dogs have been a permanent feature of Bea's life from the day I first met her. I knew even then that if I was going to live with Bea, I would also have to live with her dogs. As a young man, I remember vividly calling at Bea's home to collect her to go out on a date, only to be told by Bea's father that she would be late. No. It was not on this occasion a result of last-minute alterations to her dress, but the fact that she was suffering with a bad back. "Baby's going to be a little late because she slept on the floor all night, and her back is hurting," he told me. "Her dog Rex," he went on, "has hurt his back. So, Bea let him sleep on her bed, and now Bea's back is bad too!" And if I ever doubted that story, the next 50-plus years would provide me with ample evidence that it must have been true. Our dogs go everywhere with us, and I often think that they are better looked after than we are. Day or night, rarely a moment passes when Bea is not thinking of the dogs or actively caring for them.

The other aspect of Bea's character which must be mentioned is her cooking, which started as a passion and which became a profession. But she never lost her passion for food, and her recipes and her cooking are amongst the most important reasons for many of the repeat visits to Red Carnation hotels. Indeed, Bea's cooking has now been immortalised in her book, *A Life in Food*, which is now in its third edition, with all proceeds going to Great Ormond Street Children's Hospital in London.

I want to make clear, should there remain any doubt, that Bea – and indeed Brett and Gavin – were merely pawns in a game which was never remotely about them at all. The fight with the United States was always about me, and only me. Yet the three of them suffered terribly at the hands of supposedly public servants, and one man in particular. There is little doubt in my mind that if there was any crime here, it was committed by those who are charged with investigating and prosecuting crime. They themselves were the perpetrators. What happened to my family was little short of institutionalised coercion. In any another situation, that behaviour would have been described, with justification, as racketeering.

The stress of the fight undoubtedly affected my health. My high blood pressure, which had been controlled successfully for thirty years, became erratic and increasingly difficult to treat. I developed prostate problems and I even had a cancer scare. Thankfully, and I am touching wood as I write this, since we successfully defeated the extradition requests in 2007 my health is somewhat improved. During the last three years or so, I have unashamedly been enjoying myself, and thoughts of retirement have long since been forgotten. Indeed, I now have absolutely no intention of retiring – ever.

Although my son and my two nephews, Brett, Gavin and Michael represent the triumvirate which today runs our businesses, I work every day with each of them, giving assistance whenever I am able. They are doing a great job, but they know I am always there if they need me. Brett, Gavin and I recently went on a tour of our Asian offices which finished in Hong Kong. A tradition which has been established over 50 years demands that on such occasions the trip ends with a celebratory dinner in the Man Wah, the exquisite Cantonese restaurant on the 25th floor of the Mandarin Oriental hotel. The Man Wah is a wonderful restaurant, with spectacular panoramic views across Victoria Harbour and the cityscape that is Hong Kong.

By chance, the dinner happened to be on the occasion of my 81st birthday, and I was away from home for a birthday for the first time in many years. I felt especially proud that evening, and for two unrelated reasons, neither of which were connected with the fact that it was my birthday. The Travel Corporation had just announced the opening of a new sales office in São Paulo, Brazil, representing the final piece in the expansion of our travel businesses. The establishment of an office in Brazil meant that we would now be operating, rather than just trading, in every continent of the world. This was cause for celebration alone, but when I looked at the restaurant's wine list, I found that one of Man Wah's offerings was Finlayson's Blanc de Mer, one of our very own wines. That evening was a truly wonderful occasion, and one of which I have the happiest memories.

As this, my final chapter draws to a close, I am prompted to consider a crude audit of my life thus far. Had I, ten years ago, made a mental checklist of all those things I would have wished for, I would have been able to tick most of the boxes. There would have been exceptions, of course, notably my failure with Wynn, but to be honest my failures would have been few in number. But if I were to complete the same checklist today, there would have to be one additional box into which I would not be able to place a tick. That box is the one which concerns my reputation.

My good name suffered a fatal blow on the day on which I was indicted. From that day onwards, every time there was an opportunity to issue a press release, however irrelevant the subject may have been, the Office of the US Attorney went out of its way to discredit me, and to discredit other members of the family too. Untruths were piled up as though they were facts, and further monstrous assertions were then built upon this edifice of lies.

Every single one of the allegations contained within that original indictment ultimately fell away. I should have been pleased when they did, but that made very little difference to my reputation. Mud undoubtedly sticks. And it was of course not helpful when I decided to plead guilty of failing to declare income to the United States taxman, a charge with which I was not originally indicted.

The negotiations which preceded that guilty plea led of course to agreement on a substantial financial reparation, but I was sentenced only to a fine of $100 and 24 hours unsupervised probation. And, as everyone knew then, and knows now, this was little more than a slap on the wrist. Imagine my surprise, therefore, to realise only after the dust had settled that I had pleaded guilty to a felony! I cannot explain how or why but I had been under the impression that I was pleading guilty to a misdemeanour; a very important difference.

My lack of comprehension of what was going on is extremely difficult to explain, and even more difficult to justify. I would be the first to admit that the words which disprove my understanding are all spelled out in the transcript. But quite where my brain was for that part of the proceedings, goodness only knows. Judge Preska had asked me the question, "Do you understand, Mr Tollman, that the offense to which you are pleading guilty is a felony?" Her question could not have been clearer or less ambiguous. Nor could my answer, which was, "Yes, your Honor." Admittedly, this exchange formed a small part only of the preamble to the admission of guilt itself, and was one of a series of questions to which defendants are expected merely to nod acceptance – mere formalities. Additionally, though, in my defence, I was preoccupied with the big question that was yet to come in those proceedings, and which I knew would give me difficulty. I appreciate, though, that this is no excuse. I should have concentrated equally on the whole of the proceedings, and not just thought about my response to that big question. This very serious oversight cost me dearly, and I regret profoundly that I ever allowed it to happen.

I made the point many pages (and the lion's share of a lifetime) ago that, as a young man, the thing I valued most in life was my reputation. The Court Hotels debacle meant that my reputation suffered a severe knock, one from which it took many years to recover. But, in time, recover it did.

Today, however, if I am referred to in the press – which I am delighted to say is a rare event indeed – I may now, it appears, be referred to legitimately as a 'convicted felon'. This is uncomfortable to say the least. I certainly do not feel like a 'convicted felon'. Not only are those words inconsistent with a sentence of 24 hours unsupervised probation, but being saddled with that description represents a far, far higher price to have paid than any number of noughts on the cash which was handed over in respect of the tax calculation and the forfeiture.

I know only too painfully that, in the eyes of many, my reputation has been destroyed. If I am honest, I share their view. There is no coming back from this. Believe me, this is no easy admission, and the writing of these words is not cathartic. It is merely painful. I have tried to live my life as honestly as possible, and to discover, late in life, that one's actions and one's words are doubted, is difficult to stomach.

I am still here though. I may be slightly bruised but I am hardly battered. If you have, thank you for reading this book.

The dogs bark. But the caravan moves on.

INDEX